CLASSICAL MEMORIES/MODERN IDENTITIES
Paul Allen Miller and Richard H. Armstrong, Series Editors

Tragic Effects

Ethics and Tragedy in the Age of Translation

Therese Augst

 The Ohio State University Press · *Columbus*

Copyright © 2012 by The Ohio State University.
All rights reserved.

Library of Congress Cataloging-in-Publication Data
Augst, Therese, 1967–
  Tragic effects : ethics and tragedy in the age of translation / Therese Augst.
    p. cm. — (Classical memories/modern identities)
  Includes bibliographical references and index.
  ISBN-13: 978-0-8142-1183-0 (cloth : alk. paper)
  ISBN-10: 0-8142-1183-6 (cloth : alk. paper)
  ISBN-13: 978-0-8142-9284-6 (cd)
  1. German drama (Tragedy)—History and criticism. 2. German drama (Tragedy)—Greek influences. 3. Greek drama (Tragedy)—Translations into German—History and criticism. 4. Greek drama (Tragedy)—Appreciation—Germany. I. Title. II. Series: Classical memories/modern identities.
  PT671.A94 2012
  438'.042081—dc23
                                        2011043812
This book is available in the following editions:
Cloth (ISBN 978-0-8142-1183-0)
CD-ROM (ISBN 978-0-8142-9284-6)

Cover design by Jerry Dorris, authorsupport.com
Type set in Adobe Garamond Pro

∞ The paper used in this publication meets the minimum requirements of the American National Standard for Information Sciences—Permanence of Paper for Printed Library Materials. ANSI Z.39–1992.

CONTENTS

Acknowledgments   vii
Abbreviations   ix

Introduction	Thinking in Translation	1
Chapter One	Contexts: Why Translate? Why Study the Greeks?	25
Chapter Two	Distancing: Oedipal Solitude	47
Chapter Three	Difference Becomes Antigone	86
Chapter Four	The Translator's Courage	122
Chapter Five	Out of Tune? Heidegger on Translation	146
Chapter Six	Ruined Theater: Adaptation and Responsibility in Brecht's *Antigonemodell*	192
Conclusion	Re-writing	228

Bibliography   253
Index   265

ACKNOWLEDGMENTS

Reflecting on how friends and colleagues have helped me with this book affords me the very happy opportunity to revisit many unexpected and often serendipitous moments along the way.

For her constructive advice and tireless feedback on the earliest drafts of the Hölderlin chapters, I am grateful to my superb adviser at the University of California, Santa Barbara, Elisabeth Weber.

For their careful reading of the project in development as well as their unfailing encouragement, I thank my first professional colleagues at Princeton: Mike Jennings, Barbara Hahn, Stanley Corngold, and Brigid Doherty. The graduate students in my seminars there, especially Florian Becker, Nicola Gess, Günter Schmidt, May Mergenthaler, and Kata Gellen offered fresh ideas and helped me to curb my use of Heideggerian and Hölderlinian formulations, and the star undergraduates in my capstone seminar at Lewis & Clark College renewed my enthusiasm for the study of translation. Jennifer Ballengee heroically provided help with Greek passages during a very busy time in her life. My new colleagues at Lewis & Clark have offered me a warm and welcoming intellectual home.

I am grateful to Princeton University, the Mellon Foundation, and Lewis & Clark College for providing financial support and above all time to complete the project. For invaluable advice on revisions, I thank my series editors, Paul Allen Miller and Richard Armstrong, and Eugene O'Connor at The Ohio State University Press, as well as the anonymous reviewers who took the time to read the manuscript so carefully.

Writing is a solitary process, to be sure, but I would find it impossible to write successfully without the support of loved ones. Karen Barkemeyer and Sally Poor have both provided a sounding board and a sympathetic ear for more years than I feel like counting. My "writing partners" at Lewis & Clark, Isabelle DeMarte and Katja Altpeter-Jones, have inspired me with their warmth and dedication. Most of all, I am grateful to Thomas and Eva Augst, who have accompanied me on this journey with much love and seemingly endless reserves of empathy and good cheer.

ABBREVIATIONS

FA: Friedrich Hölderlin. *Sämtliche Werke ('Frankfurter Ausgabe')*. Ed. D. E. Sattler. Frankfurt: Roter Stern, 1975-.

StA: Friedrich Hölderlin. *Sämtliche Werke (Große Stuttgarter Ausgabe)*. Ed. Friedrich Beissner. Stuttgart: Cotta, 1946.

GS: Walter Benjamin. *Gesammelte Schriften*. Ed. Rolf Tiedemann and Hermann Schweppenhäuser. Frankfurt: Suhrkamp, 1974.

SW: Walter Benjamin. *Selected Writings*. Ed. Marcus Bullock and Michael W. Jennings. Cambridge: Harvard University Press, 1996-.

GA: Martin Heidegger. *Gesamtausgabe*. Frankfurt: Klostermann, 1944.

I: Martin Heidegger. *Hölderlin's Hymn "The Ister."* Trans. William McNeil and Julia Davis. Bloomington: Indiana University Press, 1996.

BFA: Bertolt Brecht, *Werke: Große kommentierte Berliner und Frankfurter Ausgabe*. Ed. Werner Hecht et al. Berlin and Weimar: Aufbau, and Frankfurt: Suhrkamp, 1992.

AJ: Bertolt Brecht, *Arbeitsjournal 1938–1955*. Berlin and Weimar: Aufbau, 1977.

INTRODUCTION

Thinking in Translation

> Ich kenne mich zwar nicht selbst genug, um zu wissen, ob ich eine wahre Tragödie schreiben könnte; ich erschrecke aber bloß vor dem Unternehmen und bin beinahe überzeugt, daß ich mich durch den bloßen Versuch zerstören könnte.
>
> I do not know myself well enough to know if I could write a true tragedy; however, I am terrified of the very undertaking and am nearly convinced that I could destroy myself in the mere attempt. (Goethe to Schiller, 9 December 1797).[1]

GOETHE KNEW. Perhaps it is not surprising to discover that he knew, but in the shadows cast over the generations that followed him, his words possess an especially marked poignancy. While Goethe does arrive at his own version of classical tragedy in *Iphigenie auf Tauris*, he ultimately criticizes that attempt as too "damned humane" (*verteufelt human*); meanwhile, there is little doubt that the peril he describes in confronting the tragic continued to haunt those who bore his legacy: Hölderlin, Kleist, Hegel, Nietzsche, Freud.[2] To produce "true tragedy" in a modern age implies nothing less than the pursuit of a phantom. Anyone who attempts it must reconstruct a world out of elements that are not only of another language but also of another time, another place, an entirely other system of thought. It demands, in other words, a constant engagement with a past that in

---

1. *Der Briefwechsel zwischen Schiller und Goethe, Erster Band: Briefe der Jahre 1794–1797*, ed. S. Seigel (Munich: C. H. Beck, 1984), 451f. Translations are my own unless otherwise indicated.

2. Speaking of the development of German drama after Goethe and Schiller, George Steiner describes Kleist and Hölderlin, as well as Georg Büchner and J. M. R. Lenz, as a "family of hectic genius" for whom "drama is the embodiment of crisis." Steiner, *The Death of Tragedy* (New York: Knopf, 1961), 216, 218.

many ways has come to define us, but nevertheless remains just beyond our reach; and whoever does not heed this imperative risks losing contact altogether with his distant source. The project of modern tragedy departs from a nucleus that is at once magnetic and inaccessible.

Nonetheless, this inaccessibility has hardly proven a barrier to tragedy's longevity as a model and point of departure in the post-Enlightenment age. Greek tragedy treats themes that remain universally familiar and provocative for modern readers, and nowhere is this more true than in the intellectual history of modern Germany. Since the birth of what Peter Szondi has called the "philosophy of the tragic"[3] in the late eighteenth century, tragedy has served as a paradigm in aesthetic and intellectual efforts to define, illuminate, and stabilize modern subjective experience. Essential to the development of both Weimar classicism and German idealism, tragedy's presentation of a society and a central figure in crisis has inspired confrontations with fundamental questions of social justice, ethical action, and individual responsibility. Why have so many poets and thinkers chosen to return again and again to a small set of dramatic texts written for a specific occasion, the Athenian Dionysia festivals, over two thousand years ago?[4] And perhaps even more importantly, what does it mean to appropriate the themes and structures of ancient tragedy in the service of defining modernity? What is lost in such a transmission from ancient text to modern context? What is gained?

This study will place such questions into sharper relief by focusing on a progression of thought inspired by the often controversial practice of translating the Greeks. In 1804 Friedrich Hölderlin published translations of Sophocles' *Oedipus Tyrannus* and *Antigone* that were widely ridiculed by his contemporaries as incomprehensible products of a disturbed mind.[5] "Is the man insane, or is he only pretending to be," wrote Heinrich Voss, the son of the great translator of the *Odyssey*, "and is his Sophocles secretly a satire

---

3. "Since Aristotle there has been a poetics of tragedy, but only since Schelling a philosophy of the tragic" (*Seit Aristoteles gibt es eine Poetik der Tragödie, seit Schelling erst eine Philosophie des Tragischen*). Peter Szondi, *Versuch über das Tragische* (Frankfurt: Insel, 1961), 7.

4. Classical scholars admit that our knowledge of what went on at those festivals is limited by our considerable historical distance from the events and the small proportion of remaining artifacts at our disposal; as Christian Meier asserts, Aeschylus, Sophocles, and Euripides each likely composed about one hundred plays, of which only about a dozen now remain, and they were not the only tragedians to participate in the festival's competitions (*The Political Art of Greek Tragedy*, trans. Andrew Webber [Cambridge: Polity Press, 1993], 54). For a concise explanation of the festival setting, see also John J. Winkler and Froma Zeitlin's introduction to *Nothing to do with Dionysos? Athenian Drama in its Social Context* (Princeton: Princeton University Press, 1990), 4–5.

5. In the Frankfurt edition of Hölderlin's works, D. E. Sattler includes extensive notes on the reception of these translations in the nineteenth century. Friedrich Schelling, for example, claimed in a letter to Hegel that the translations "express fully his ruined mental condition" (*Seinen verkommenen geistigen Zustand drückt die Übersetzung des Sophocles ganz aus*). In FA 16: 20.

of bad translators? . . . You should have seen how Schiller laughed" (FA 16: 20). In an age of celebrated and masterful translations, from Voss's Homer to Humboldt's Aeschylus and Schlegel's Shakespeare—an age in which translation, in fact, was regarded as a tactical necessity in the development of German cultural identity[6]—Hölderlin's Sophocles project could perhaps only have appeared hermetic, tortured, mad. Although philosophers of language such as Herder and Schleiermacher soon argued for a translation practice in which the receiving language gains from being "bent toward an alien likeness," the most celebrated translations of the time were still clearly characterized by their accessibility and stylistic beauty.[7] The best sort of translation, as Wilhelm von Humboldt stipulated in his introduction to his translation of *Agamemnon*, benefits from the encounter with the source language while avoiding the loss of identifiable cultural markers: the translator must approach "the foreign" (*das Fremde*) without crossing over into "foreignness" (*Fremdheit*) (Schulte 58). No wonder, then, that Hölderlin's Sophocles, with its jarring hybrid syntax and often disorienting word choice, seemed to have fallen to earth from a distant star.

While Hölderlin's engagement with Greek tragedy may have begun as a somewhat bizarre digression within the culture of translation around 1800, however, it has maintained a relevance far beyond the reach of its more conventionally readable cohort. In a general sense, as poet Hölderlin has gained nearly all of his renown since the start of the twentieth century, but it is his Sophocles that has captured a particularly large share of scholarly and creative interest.[8] Both between and since the two world wars, no other

---

6. See, for example, the now-classic discussions by George Steiner (*After Babel: Aspects of Language and Translation* [Oxford: Oxford University Press, 1998], 257f.) and Antoine Berman (*The Experience of the Foreign: Culture and Translation in Romantic Germany*, trans. S. Heyvaert (Albany: SUNY Press, 1992). For a thorough treatment of the mania for translation, see *Weltliteratur: Die Lust am Übersetzen im Jahrhundert Goethes. Eine Ausstellung des Deutschen Literaturarchivs im Schiller-Nationalmuseum Marbach am Neckar*, ed. Reinhard Tgahrt (Marbach: Deutsche Schiller-Gesellschaft, 1982).

7. Friedrich Schleiermacher, "On the Different Methods of Translating," trans. Waltraud Bartscht, reprinted in *Theories of Translation: An Anthology of Essays from Dryden to Derrida*, ed. Rainer Schulte and John Biguenet (Chicago: University of Chicago Press, 1992), 47. This tension between translation theory and practice around 1800 might perhaps inhere precisely in the cultural agenda that sought to define German national identity in relation to an abstract and mutable concept of the "foreign." As Lawrence Venuti has argued, Schleiermacher's advocacy of the "foreignizing" translation was perhaps based on an agenda of bourgeois nationalism: "Since the category 'foreign' here is determined by the educated, Schleiermacher is using translation to mark out a dominant space for a bourgeois minority." *The Translator's Invisibilty: A History of Translation* (Routledge, 1995), 103.

8. M. B. Benn already noted this retroactive interest in 1967; see "Hölderlin and the Greek Tradition," *Arion* 6:4 (Winter 1967): 495. In the subsequent 40 years the degree of creative and intellectual fascination has more likely intensified than subsided.

rendition of Sophocles' *Antigone* has had a more profound impact on the German stage, and perhaps only Hegel's reading of the same tragedy has proven a more influential intellectual confrontation with the modern experience of the tragic. Cited and adapted by prominent artists and intellectuals such as Walter Benjamin, Martin Heidegger, Bertolt Brecht, Heiner Müller, Martin Walser, and Philippe Lacoue-Labarthe, Hölderlin's translations and accompanying remarks have become something of a specimen piece in the attempt to actualize ancient tragedy.

Discussions of how tragedy continues to raise ethical questions of relevance to modernity have become almost commonplace in literary and cultural criticism, as notable thinkers from Jacques Lacan and Luce Irigaray to Judith Butler and Carol Jacobs have offered valuable insight into the genre's continuing relevance. Most of these discussions focus on thematic issues, taking up in particular the conflict between state decree and individual will in Sophocles' *Antigone*. At least since Hegel placed tragic art at the center of the ethical universe in the *Phenomenology of Spirit* (1808), the figure of Antigone has maintained an exemplary status within a modern ethical debate encompassing the tensions between civic and religious laws, public and private spheres, the state and the individual, man and woman. Meanwhile, the more contemporary recasting of the ethical sphere sheds new light on the fundamental questions that arise when we are confronted with the tangle of relationships and motivations at the heart of this tragedy—questions that address the claims of justice and the legitimacy of crime; the nature of love and the effects of hatred; the status of siblings, of lovers, of family duties; the articulations of community, of responsibility, of resistance, of violence.

By placing emphasis on the problems inherent in translation, however, my study approaches the question of ethics from another angle. Contemporary discussions of translation address ethics extensively, in the wake of postcolonial and postmodern critiques of the power structures inherent in the relation between a source text (and culture) and its rendering in another form and context. In examining the ever-changing status of Greek tragedy in German translation, however, my focus turns not toward the interchange between radically different yet contemporary cultural discourses, but rather toward the historical implications of translation as palimpsest, over what Samuel Weber has called "instances" of translation.[9] Insofar as translation

---

9. " . . . translation always involves not merely the movement from one *language* to another, but from one *instance*—a text already existing in another language—to another instance, that does not previously exist, but that is brought into being in the other language." Translation thus designates "both a *general process*, involving a change of place, and *a singular result* of that process." Samuel Weber, "A Touch of Translation: On Walter Benjamin's 'Task of the Translator,'" in S. Bermann and M.

is always an act of close reading, requiring its practitioner to maintain an interpretive position with respect to her source text, it also forces a confrontation with the unfamiliar, the inconceivable, the untranslatable—those elements that, in the case of Greek tragedy, lie amid the ruins of the distant past. At the same time, this practice of reading—defined by distance from its interlocutor and hence a certain hermeneutic urgency—is fluid and profoundly mutable, marked irrevocably by the particular cultural, linguistic and historical context (the "instance") in which it occurs. In appropriating the themes of tragedy in the service of constructing the modern subject, some readers have failed to account for this stubborn distance and allowed their work to glide seamlessly over the problems it poses, rendering them invisible to the reader; tragedy essentially becomes the property of modern Western intellectual discourse, often functioning—as in Hölderlin's time—in the service of "nation-building."[10] The works of translation and adaptation I discuss in the following pages, however, attempt to confront those problems of undecidability head-on: the persistent unfulfillment that the transfer between linguistic and semiotic systems underscores; the experience of the radical limits of one's own language and the vulnerability that those limits reveal for a subject constituted by his relation to language; the difficult tension between the task of making the past understandable and the responsibility to preserve its radical singularity.

Hölderlin's attempt to translate the Greeks in a new way offers a fascinating case study for any reader interested in the history of efforts to make sense of modernity through the confrontation with an ancient past that is both foundational and inscrutable. Rather than adapting the themes and language of tragedy unproblematically to modern modes of thought, Hölderlin's project affirms their difference in the very obscurity of his translation. His Sophocles reflects a profound commitment to exposing the relation between the structure of Greek tragedy—with its stark separation of chorus from characters, the isolation of the tragic hero, and the unsettling effects of poetic language—and the problem of translation as a mode of transfer from ancient to modern registers. Foreignizing word choices, through which Hölderlin aims to reconstruct the distinctiveness of the ancient source text, continually let translation speak its name, intensifying the precarious expe-

---

Wood, *Nation, Language, and the Ethics of Translation* (Princeton: Princeton University Press, 2005), 66.

10. See the brief but pointed discussion of the tradition of German Romanticism for translation theory and practice in Buden and Nowotny, "Translation Studies Forum: Cultural Translation," *Translation Studies* 2.2 (2009): 199–200.

rience of tragedy's effects by lingering at the fraying margins of language.[11] This affirmation of disjunction as a mode of representation, both on the tragic stage and in the process of transmission, redefines the ethical impulse of tragedy not in the founding of the self in a modern sense but in the responsibility to a differentiating movement to which the self is continually subject. By tracing the striking influence of these translations within a discourse on tragedy, ethics, and subjectivity extending to Benjamin, Heidegger, Brecht, Müller, Walser, and Lacoue-Labarthe, I aim to unravel the complex dynamics through which the perception of ethical responsibility, having long taken its cues from the themes of classical tragedy, might find resonance with a particular relationship implicit in the theory and practice of translation.

I. Tragedy

While the transmission of ancient text into modern forms models an intersubjective exchange that is fundamentally ethical, discussions of ethics and violence in the context of Greek tragedy have generally taken place on a thematic level. Although in the following chapters I will be more concerned with the translation and adaptation of tragic form and language into the context of modernity, a brief summary of these thematic discussions will nevertheless help to illuminate the fundamental questions at stake in that process of transmission.

By staging a historical moment of transition from the age of myth to that of the Athenian polis, as Jean-Pierre Vernant has discussed, tragic drama has always presented a forum through which to confront political and ethical conflict against the backdrop of violence.[12] With the phenomenon of tragedy coinciding with the formative years of the polis, Vernant and others claim that the plays typically portray a clash of the new burdens of citizenship with the traditional mythic world that precedes them. While the Chorus corresponds more closely to the contemporary point of view of the civic community, the hero represents a figure "more or less alien to the ordinary condition of a citizen" (Vernant 1988, 24). Within this framework the hero's

---

11. In *After Babel*, Steiner eloquently expresses the disorienting effects of Hölderlin's translation style: Hölderlin "compels us to experience, as in fact only a great poet can, the limits of linguistic expression and the barriers between languages which impede human understanding" (323).

12. See Jean-Pierre Vernant, "The Historical Moment of Tragedy in Ancient Greece: Some of the Social and Psychological Conditions" and "Tensions and Ambiguities in Greek Tragedy," in *Myth and Tragedy in Ancient Greece*, ed. Vernant and Pierre Vidal-Naquet, trans. Janet Lloyd (New York: Zone Books, 1988).

virtues and exploits are no longer glorified by an admiring public, as was the case with epic; rather, "the hero has ceased to be a model. He is, both for himself and for others, a problem" (25). Insofar as it presents the conflicts and discrepancies contained within a moment of historical transition, then, tragedy does not merely reflect the social reality of its time but calls it into question: " . . . tragedy is born when myth starts to be considered from the point of view of a citizen" (33).[13] That point of view is rent by a fundamental distance, a gap which has developed at the heart of social experience between a mythic past and a political present—a gap "wide enough for the oppositions . . . to stand out quite clearly . . . [yet] narrow enough for the conflict in values to be a painful one and for the clash to continue to take place" (27).[14]

Nor is this gap, reconstituted on the tragic stage, destined to find resolution there. As Charles Segal notes, the "systems of linked polarity" that determine the tragic universe—conflicts between "mortal and divine, male and female, man and beast, city and wild" (Segal 1986, 57)—operate as a critical instrument that reveals "not the orderly process of transition from one stage of life to another, but the inbetweenness, the marginality, the ambiguity in the juxtaposition of the two sides . . . " (60). By thinking through this lack of a solution, through the detached discovery on manifold levels "that words, values, men themselves are ambiguous, that the universe is one of conflict," the spectator "acquires a tragic consciousness" (Vernant and Vidal-Naquet 43). From its very start, then, the viewing of tragedy is linked to a critical perspective that extends beyond the identificatory dynamics that have since become associated with Aristotle's notion of catharsis.

Such polarities extend deeply into the heart of tragedy, such that the dramatic scene does not merely reflect its social context in all of its ambiguity but also presents marginalized outliers, "others" that do not fit neatly into that context but are able to use their difference as a source of power. For example, by elevating female figures to the atypical status of autonomous

---

13. On this point see also Charles Segal's comments in "Greek Tragedy and Society: A Structuralist Perspective": "As part of a public festival, a ritual in honor of the god Dionysus, tragedy validates the social order. . . . At the same time the violence of its action, its radical questioning of justice, both human and divine, its searching explorations of the failure or the betrayal of public and private morality take us outside of that order." In *Greek Tragedy and Political Theory*, ed. J. P. Euben (Berkeley, Los Angeles: University of California Press, 1986), 47.

14. In an important article, Froma Zeitlin asserts that Thebes, setting of many tragic plays, takes shape as the essential scene of such conflict; it functions in the context of tragedy as the "Anti-Athens" (116), allowing problems to be displaced onto a city imagined as the "negative model to Athens's manifest image of itself" (102). Insofar as Thebes comes to contain the tragic space, it becomes possible to conceive of Athens by contrast as a space where reconciliation and transformation are possible. "Thebes: Theater of Self and Society in Athenian Drama," in Euben 101–41.

decision-makers, as Helene Foley argues, tragedians were able to present the possibility of other modes of ethical reasoning that involved "the unknowable and the uncontrollable both within and outside the self."[15] Indeed, Dionysus himself was frequently identified with a femininity that, as Froma Zeitlin has shown, lends power to both him and the theatrical spectacle created in his name.[16]

With its focus on historical moments of painful flux, then, tragedy was designed to leave its spectators both attuned to contradiction and yearning for its resolution. And in its appetite for the paradoxical pleasures of tragic pathos, modern Western culture has readily identified with both the oppositional structure and the will to dialectical resolution that this transitional dynamic inspires. Indeed, interpreters of tragedy in the post-Enlightenment era commonly relate their return to the Greeks to the perception of a crisis not unlike that which brought tragic art to light in the first place; the present day is perceived as a time in need of radical transformation, as Dennis Schmidt states in his book on tragedy and German philosophy, a time in which "those who argue most powerfully for a revitalization of the question of tragedy are united by the assumption that the present era is a time of crisis, of exhaustion, of historical limits reached."[17] Much of that crisis thinking is reflective of the sense that contradiction, the essence of tragedy, lies at the heart of experience and must be confronted. In her study of ethics and luck in ancient tragedy, Martha Nussbaum asserts that modern interpreters of tragedy often view its conflict as a kind of adversity that one should be able to avoid through the application of practical reason, by structuring life and commitments to avoid serious conflict (Nussbaum 51). This is an intellectual movement somewhat separate from the debates surrounding Aristotle's conception of tragic effect, the awakening of fear and pity in the spectator, that Lessing initiated in the eighteenth century and Schiller transformed into a means of moral education. The German Idealists were also concerned with the problem of how tragic experience can bring resolution despite its

---

15. Helene Foley, *Female Acts in Greek Tragedy* (Princeton: Princeton University Press, 2001), 15. On this point, see in particular her comprehensive reading of *Antigone*, 172–200. See also Martha Nussbaum's comments on moral luck and ethical ambiguity in *The Fragility of Goodness: Luck and Ethics in Greek Tragedy and Philosophy*, rev. ed. (Cambridge, 1986), also in particular with respect to *Antigone*, which she introduces as "a play about teaching and learning, about changing one's vision of the world, about losing one's grip on what looked like secure truth and learning a more elusive kind of wisdom" (52).

16. "Playing the Other: Theater, Theatricality, and the Feminine in Greek Drama," in Winkler and Zeitlin 66.

17. Dennis Schmidt, *On Germans and Other Greeks: Tragedy and Ethical Life* (Bloomington: Indiana University Press, 2001), 5. Schmidt's excellent and comprehensive book also contains new translations of many key texts on tragedy, to which I will refer in the following chapters.

unbearable contradiction, but their field of inquiry was that of dialectics: for Schelling (and in a different sense for Hegel), the affirmative moment of tragedy comes with the reinscription of the possibility of human freedom, despite the downfall of the individual subject. Although Hegel submits that both Antigone and Creon suffer the consequences of their actions in the name of divine or human laws—for within Hegel's tragic universe both are unquestionably guilty—the restoration of equilibrium brought about by "justice" (*Gerechtigkeit*) ensures that universal Spirit shall continue its forward trajectory. For Nussbaum, then, Hegel regards tragedy as representative of a "primitive or benighted stage of ethical life and thought," which suggests that his incorporation of the tragic into his dialectical system is at its heart no less a model for *Bildung* than the poetic efforts of Lessing and Schiller (Nussbaum 51).

For many others who follow in Hegel's wake, however, Greek tragedy offers an ethical legitimacy outside the conventions of modern concepts of law and crime, innocence and guilt. While Nussbaum maintains that the Greek tragic universe is uniquely complex insofar as it presents the incommensurability of conflicting value systems (such as those of Antigone and Creon) as a permanent condition, untouchable by reconciliation,[18] others such as George Steiner and Susan Sontag echo this idea to argue that "true" tragedy in Goethe's sense is unsustainable within the modern Judeo-Christian framework of "moral adequacy":[19]

> Tragedy says there are disasters which are not fully merited, that there is ultimate injustice in the world. So one might say that the final optimism of the prevailing religious traditions of the West, their will to see meaning in the world, prevented a rebirth of tragedy under Christian auspices—as, in Nietzsche's argument, reason, the fundamentally optimistic spirit of Socrates, killed tragedy in ancient Greece. (Sontag 137)

Central to these readings is a sense of historical distinction; Greek tragedy participates in a historical movement that presents it as capable of

---

18. This frames Nussbaum's central criticism of Hegel; what she sees as his tendency to eliminate conflict represents a "dangerous reform" of the tragic universe which neglects the possibility of separateness or difference in the world of value: " . . . to do justice to the nature or identity of two distinct values requires doing justice to their difference; and doing justice to their difference . . . requires seeing that there are, at least potentially, circumstances in which the two will collide"[68].

19. Thus it is certainly fitting that Steiner and Sontag wrote pieces with the same title. See Steiner, *The Death of Tragedy*, 4–8 and Sontag, "The Death of Tragedy," in *Against Interpretation and Other Essays* (New York: Picador, 1966), 132–39. With respect to the demise of Goethe's "true" tragedy, Steiner offers some intriguing if schematic comments about Goethe's "avoidance of the tragic," 166–68.

speaking to modernity and at the same time maintaining its secrets. (To be sure, Hegel himself also addressed this issue of historical development as it pertains to tragedy, but not in the interest of preserving any trace of secrecy within that movement of history.) However, Hegel's reading of *Antigone* has become such a mainstay of modern ethical discourse that its version of tragic events, even more so than Sophocles' play itself, often assumes center stage. Many such critics take issue with Hegel's account of sexual difference in his reading of tragedy, arguing that the tragedy of *Antigone* in particular, far from codifying gender roles in relation to the "laws" of family and state, calls established categories of sexuality and kinship radically into question.[20] Judith Butler's essay on *Antigone* is a case in point: the tragic heroine "upsets the vocabulary of kinship that is a precondition of the human, implicitly raising the question for us of what those preconditions really must be."[21] However, not unlike the models it criticizes, Butler's reading of "kinship trouble" in the *Antigone* finally runs aground in its claim to an essential universality—the universality of multiplicity, as it were—in its presentation of the Greek tragedy as a work that conveys truths into a modern context with minimal disruption.

While the philosophy of the tragic, born in the long eighteenth century, has thus given rise to much important debate, in some ways the *text* of tragedy tends to remain isolated from this. (It is perhaps no coincidence that Schelling and Hegel refer only obliquely to tragic situations; Schelling never even names Oedipus, though he is evidently the subject of his discussion, and Hegel's only citation of Sophocles' *Antigone*, as we will see later, is taken badly out of context.) Thus a new question arises where the Idealists leave off: where must the ethical stance of tragedy be situated, if it is not to become a mere reflection of modern systems of philosophy? And how does its performativity—the particularity of its language and rhetorical sway—come into play in the recognition of that stance? While Hegel and Schelling engage with the enduring legacy of tragedy, the perception that it expresses certain universal truths, it is their friend Hölderlin who considers

---

20. See, for example, the essays by Luce Irigaray ("The Eternal Irony of the Community") and Patricia J. Mills ("Hegel's Antigone"), in Mills, ed., *Feminist Interpretations of G. W. F. Hegel* (University Park, PA: Penn State University Press, 1996).

21. Judith Butler, *Antigone's Claim* (New York: Columbia University Press, 2000), 82. As Butler emphasizes, the family headed by Oedipus and Jocasta hardly remains within a recognizable kinship structure, as Oedipus is both father and brother to Antigone and her siblings; and Antigone herself, as Butler and other readers have pointed out, is described in Sophocles' language not only as a sister and daughter but also as a man (the Greek *aner*), a son (see Butler 62), and a mother (Jacobs, "Dusting Antigone," *MLN* 111 [1996]: 910).

above all the differences that tragedy also expresses, both in structure and in language. And who allows his writings on tragedy—the translations, but also his weirdly hermetic essays—to reflect those differences in a manner that makes their existence, if not always their explicit content, intelligible.

II. Translation

Even when the material of a "true" tragedy such as Goethe describes above aims to be wholly original, any modern attempt to approximate tragedy approaches the transformative dynamics of a translation. The modern tragic poet must strive to illuminate the obscurities of the original form, to connect, however imperfectly, to the inscrutable quality that within the context of modernity would still lend tragedy its "truth." As Goethe's dread at the very thought implies, taking on the ancient forms of the tragic involves the acknowledgment of a distance both within the work and from it, a recognition and suspension of the work's foreignness that may be destructive.

Matters become even more complicated when that confrontation also involves the mechanics of translation itself, as it so frequently has in the two centuries since Goethe's remarks. Inspired to a "most comprehensive predilection for all things Greek" by the classical aesthetics of Johann Jakob Winckelmann, Goethe's own age featured a rash of classical material in translation, from Voss's celebrated Homer (1781) to Humboldt's translation of *Agamemnon* (1816) and Hölderlin's and Solger's translations of Sophocles (1804 and 1824).[22] Under these circumstances, the undertaking redoubles the risk to which Goethe referred. If any act of translation is inherently violent insofar as its need for comprehensibility is also a call to assimilate the distinctive elements of the other (text) to the familiar cadence of native language and thought, that violence may exact a toll not only upon the translated object but the translating subject as well. Particularly in the extensive discourse concerning translation in and around Goethe's age, these two forms of violence frequently stand in direct tension with one another; the translator who aims to mitigate the violence of transmission also exposes himself to the limits of his own language and process of thought, that which had been most radically his "own."

---

22. Of these, Voss's Homer was the most influential and held in the highest regard; Goethe, for example, described Voss's translations as the most perfect of their kind, achieving a "perfect identity" with the original in which "one does not exist instead of the other but in the other's place" (Schulte and Biguenet 61). For a concise but nevertheless engaging summary, see Charlie Louth, *Hölderlin and the Dynamics of Translation* (Legenda: European Humanities Research Center, 1998), 5–53.

This consideration only renders more curious—and perhaps, at the same time, more understandable—the most intriguing aspect of the long tradition of translating the Greeks, particularly in Germany: the prevalence of translators who are also, or even primarily, poets. To be sure, one of the most prolific and enduring of all modern translators, A. W. Schlegel, was also involved in the Romantic aesthetic project presented in the *Athenäum* and other literary documents, but he was not a poet in the same vein as Hölderlin, Goethe, Hofmannsthal, Brecht, Pound, Müller, or Heaney.[23] Nor did he attempt, as they did, to translate Greek tragedy. Does the encounter with the outermost limits of expression inherent in the task of translation—which Enlightenment theorists of translation such as Bodmer and Herder already regarded as essential to the development of thought itself[24]—demand, in the extreme case of tragedy, a poet's sensitivity to the openness of one language to another, to the elasticity of representation and the conveyance of image? And what happens—to the poet, to the text, to the reader—if that encounter fails?

Indeed, one might ask what "failure" means at all in this context. In one sense, Hölderlin's translations have continued to be an object of interest precisely because they violate an essential pact at the heart of translational practice: in their foreignizing tone they allow language, and therefore that which produces language—the voice of the translator—to be heard between the lines of text. Yet as we know from the writings of Lawrence Venuti, the translator has long been expected to strive for the opposite pole: to remain invisible. The translator is meant to be a mere intermediary, not to have a voice of her own but to reproduce, seamlessly, the voice of another (Venuti 1995, 2). But this is a false transparency, as Venuti has shown: while maintaining the *appearance* of unmediated access to a source text and author, the smooth transition from one language to another by an "invisible" translator

---

23. Josephine Balmer discusses the "close, symbiotic relationship" between creative writing and classical translation, claiming that the "translator of a classic text can be seen more as an innovator, making their own mark on an already well-known work, reimagining it for a new generation, a new audience. . . . [I]n certain circumstances, a translation can supersede the original and become iconic in its own right." "What comes next? Reconstructing the classics," in Susan Bassnett and Peter R. Bush, *The Translator as Writer* (London: Continuum, 2006), 184.

24. Bodmer and Herder were early proponents of the idea, further developed by the Romantics, that translation offers a means of confronting one's own language that is essential to the edification of the self. Bodmer advocated the expansion of language, and by extension the expansion of the possibilities of thought, via the translation of "substantial instances of special beauty," figurative expressions that exhaust a particular thought through descriptive images. Such "instances" differ from language to language, yet each is intuitively comprehensible in any language because the images are recognizable. See Bodmer, *Der Mahler der Sitten*, reprinted in *Translating Literature: The German Tradition from Luther to Rosenzweig*, ed. and trans. André Lefevere (Assen/Amsterdam: Van Gorcum, 1977), 18–20.

in fact requires a particularly violent degree of intervention (16f.). A common thread among newer theories of translation, then, involves advocating a more activist and ethical mode of translation, regarded not as a seamless transfer but as a creative practice that remains receptive to the distances—cultural, linguistic, temporal—traveled between languages and modes of expression.[25] This represents a different sort of transparency than the illusion of the "invisible" translator: translation acts as a layer of "translucence" over the source text, not concealing it with the appearance of transparency but rather engaging with it in a manner that allows new connections to emerge in the context of the receiving culture.[26] Gayatri Chakravorty Spivak describes this level of engagement as "the most intimate act of reading," a "surrender" to the source text that attends to its specificity.[27] The translator's invisibility is displaced by her readiness to disturb her own language, to let it reflect the otherness of the foreign text rather than offer it to the reader in familiar forms.

Yet this truer form of translation may exact no less a price than the "true" tragedy in Goethe's estimation. As we must realize from Hölderlin's example, this approach to the source text carries with it a potentially dangerous imperative for the "true translator," who, as Friedrich Schleiermacher had already suggested in 1813, subjects himself to "the most extraordinary form of humiliation that a writer . . . could inflict upon himself."[28] More than merely receding into invisibility, the translator in Schleiermacher's model must deliberately expose himself to danger, must be willing to bear the stain of failure and sacrifice the quality of his own expression, all for the sake of a voice that would otherwise be effaced in the transmission from one language to another.

> Who would not like to have his native tongue appear everywhere in its most enticing beauty, of which every literary genre is capable? Who would not rather beget children who are in their parents' image rather than bastards? Who would like to show himself in less attractive and less graceful move-

---

25. The recent work of Susan Bassnett, a translator, poet, and scholar, is particularly interesting in this respect. See her discussion in "Writing and Translating" (Bassnett and Bush, *The Translator as Writer* [London: Continuum, 2006], 173–83), as well as her creative dialogue with the Argentinian poet Alejandra Pizarnik in *Exchanging Lives: Poems and Translations* (Leeds: Peepal Tree, 2002).

26. For a discussion of this idea of "translucence" in translation, see Sherry Simon's response in Buden and Novotny 211.

27. Spivak, "The Politics of Translation," in Spivak, *Outside in the Teaching Machine* (New York: Routledge, 1993), 180.

28. Friedrich Schleiermacher, "On the Different Methods of Translating," trans. Waltraud Bartscht, reprinted in Schulte and Biguenet 47.

ments than he is capable of, and at least sometimes appear harsh and stiff, and shock the reader as much as is necessary to keep him aware of what he is doing? . . . These are the sacrifices that every translator must make; these are the dangers to which he exposes himself. . . . (Schulte and Biguenet 46f.)[29]

Along with Johann Jakob Bodmer, who sixty years previously had likewise prevailed upon translators to have the courage to make use of the "natural freedom" of language ("so that the freedom of words matches the freedom of things" [Lefevere 31]), Schleiermacher equates a translator's fidelity to the foreign text with the possibility of ridicule on the home front. However, this does not by any means lessen the significance of the exercise. If, as Schleiermacher advocates, the proper method of translation is indeed to move the reader to the author rather than the author to the reader ("leaving the author alone as much as possible" [Schulte and Biguenet 42]), then the translator's fidelity to his text may have an even more disconcerting result than invisibility; it may imply vulnerability of a most fundamental sort. To translate in these terms is to assume responsibility for communicating the foreign text while renouncing regard for one's own voice, to enact a relation that refuses to reduce the difference of another voice to the discourse of the same. It represents, in other words, testing ground for a relation between self and other that evokes the ethical as such.[30]

This call to ethical responsibility remains a vital aspect of the current field of translation studies, which approaches the history of such appropriations of the "foreign" (such as Schleiermacher's here) far more critically.[31] Schleiermacher composed his theoretical remarks in a period in which the practice of translation was regarded as essential to the construction of a national culture, and his advocacy of the foreign as a vehicle for establishing identity, while

---

29. "Wer möchte nicht seine Muttersprache überall in der volksgemäßesten Schönheit auftreten lassen, deren jede Gattung nur fähig ist? Wer möchte nicht lieber Kinder erzeugen, die das väterliche Geschlecht rein darstellen, als Blendlinge? Wer wird sich gern auflegen, in minder leichten und anmuthigen Bewegungen sich zu zeigen als er wol könnte, und bisweilen wenigstens schroff und steif zu erscheinen, um dem Leser so anstößig wie möglich zu werden als nöthig ist damit er das Bewußtsein der Sache nicht verliere? [. . .] Dies sind die Entsagungen die jener Übersetzer nothwendig übernehmen muß, dies die Gefahren denen er sich aussetzt . . ." (Störig 55).

30. This tone of responsibility to an other that the subject does not negate or appropriate but rather recognizes as primary and ineffaceable recalls the ethical thought of Emmanuel Levinas, for whom the relation to the Other constitutes "first philosophy," the primary dimension of experience. For a perspective on the relevance of Levinas's ethics for translation theory, see Robert Eaglestone, "Levinas, Translation, and Ethics," in Bermann and Wood 127–37.

31. See Lawrence Venuti, *The Scandals of Translation: Towards an Ethics of Difference* (London: Routledge, 1998). In his discussion of "the power of translation to form identities and to qualify agents" [6], Venuti attempts to outline an ethical stance through which both the practice and the reading of translation take place with a more nuanced view towards linguistic and cultural difference.

common among theories of translation in his time, also betrays a reliance on essentialist categories such as "nation," "culture," "equivalence" and even "the foreign" that contemporary critics call radically into question.[32] Rather than an interaction between two static poles of identity (what Michael Cronin calls a "zero-sum of binary opposition" between "source and target language, source and target culture, author and translator, translator and reader"[33]), translation today exemplifies flux; and the translator must once again muster her courage for the path that lies ahead, for she is charged with maintaining the productive tensions and discontinuities between a text and its translation. Susan Bassnett describes the practice of translation as "a process of negotiation between texts and between cultures, a process during which all kinds of transactions take place mediated by the figure of the translator."[34] Both source and product of translation cannot remain unaffected by this process: while the text in translation introduces discontinuity and conflict into the perception of uniformity, the "original" obtains meaning in a new and different context. This transaction lies at the heart of Walter Benjamin's notion that translation represents the "living on" (*Fortleben*) of a given text.

The responsibility of the translator in such models is no trifling matter. The basis for the translator's more ethical stance—the imperative of "keep[ing] the reader aware of what he is doing," in Schleiermacher's terms—is risk: risk of exposure, of ridicule, and ultimately of failure. Indeed, the specter of failure looms large in any attempt at translation, and reflections on the ultimate impossibility of translation are as common in the theoretical discourse as discussions of its significance.[35] Benjamin—who famously praised Hölderlin's translations as "prototypes (*Urbilder*, originary images) of their form" that confirm "every important aspect" of his own thoughts on translation—alludes to this limit in his concept of the translator's "Aufgabe," a term which contains within it not only the idea of a task but also, as Paul De Man first pointed out, of giving up (*aufgeben*): "It is in that sense also the defeat, the giving up, of the translator. The translator has to give up in relation to the task of refinding what was there in the original.[36]

To be sure, in light of the contemporary discourse on translation, De Man's remarks about "*refinding* what was *there* in the *original*" sound posi-

---

32. For a good summary, see Doris Bachmann-Medick, "Introduction: The Translational Turn," trans. Kate Sturge, in *Translation Studies* 2:1 (2009): 2–16.
33. See Cronin's contribution to the forum in Buden and Nowotny 218.
34. Susan Bassnett, *Translation Studies* (Routledge 2002), 6.
35. Paul De Man, *The Resistance to Theory* (Minneapolis: University of Minnesota Press, 1986), 80. For another perspective on translation's impossibility, see Robert Eaglestone, "Levinas, Translation, and Ethics," in Bermann and Wood 127–37.
36. De Man, *The Resistance to Theory*, 80.

tively antiquated. In an interview on his concept of the "third space" in translation, Homi Bhabha argues that the "original," precisely insofar as it is open to translation, does not constitute an *a priori* totality.

> . . . translation is a way of imitating, but in a mischievous, displacing sense—imitating an original in such a way that the priority of the original is not reinforced but by the very fact that it *can* be simulated, copied, transferred, transformed, made into a simulacrum and so on: the 'original' is never finished or complete in itself.[37]

Likewise, the familiar allusion to the translator's inevitable "failure" reflects an attitude that newer translation theory aims to transcend, not least since translators succeed in completing translations all the time. Where Benjamin's interest in Hölderlin becomes most instructive for contemporary translation theory, then, is with respect to more fundamental questions about the nature of translation as "Aufgabe": what if the task of translation, for Hölderlin in particular but also in a more general sense, were not to "refind what was there" at all? Not to reconstitute an "original" but rather simply to produce a relation between texts and contexts that reflects the differential and variable use of language as such?[38] The relevance of that relation would then persist and evolve over time, offering a key means by which to address the ethical implications of translation practice within literary and cultural histories. Jorge Luis Borges claimed that Homer in translation represented not merely the Greek classic itself but also "different perspectives of a mutable fact, . . . a long experimental lottery of omissions and emphases," and examining a translation's evolution within a given language sheds much light on the stakes inherent in that process.[39] The critical study of a text's "living on" in other forms and contexts shifts the central question of translation away from a binary of success or failure: from a yes or no to a why and how.[40]

---

37. Jonathan Rutherford, "The Third Space: Interview with Homi Bhabha," in Rutherford, ed. *Identity: Commnunity, Culture, Difference* (London: Lawrence and Wishart), 210.

38. See Weber on Benjamin's notion of "origin" in "A Touch of Translation," Bermann and Wood 65–78.

39. Jorge Luis Borges, "Some Versions of Homer" (1932), trans. Suzanne Jill Levine, *PMLA* 107.5 (Oct. 1992): 1136.

40. An outstanding example of this type of study is Antoine Berman's *Experience of the Foreign*, in which he outlines the process by which degrees of receptivity to difference as well as pockets of resistance become legible in the ambivalent manner in which a translating culture approaches its object: "We may formulate the issue as follows: Every culture resists translation, even if it has an essential need for it. The very aim of translation—to open up in writing a certain relation with the Other, to fertilize what is one's Own through the mediation of what is Foreign—is diametrically opposed to the

As that progression aims to cross ever broader temporal and spatial chasms, moreover, as the orientation of the original grows more distant from what is familiar, the potential violence of translation cuts deeper still, necessitating not only the negotiation between languages but also the conceptual transmission of an alterity that cannot be entirely recovered. Winckelmann's double imperative of imitating the Greeks and surpassing them ("the imitation of the ancients is the only way for us to become great—yes, if it is possible, inimitable"[41]) left poets and would-be translators around 1800 acutely aware of this dilemma. Friedrich Schiller may have best described its implications in his essay *On the Use of the Chorus in Tragedy* (*Über den Gebrauch des Chors in der Tragödie*)—an essay that accompanied his only attempt to reproduce classical Greek forms in a modern drama, *The Bride of Messina*:

> The palace of the kings is locked up now, the courts have withdrawn from the gates of the cities into the interiors of houses, writing has suppressed the living word, the people have therefore become an abstract concept, the gods have retreated into the hearts of men. The poet must open up the palaces again, must lead the courts back out into the open air, he must prop up the gods again, he must reproduce everything immediate that has been annulled through the artificial institution of real life and cast off, as the sculptor does with modern garments, all of the artificial constructions on and around the human that hinder the appearance of his inner nature and his original character; he must take up, from all of his external surroundings, nothing except that which makes visible the highest of forms, the human.[42]

---

ethnocentric structure of every culture, that species of narcissism by which every society wants to be a pure and unadulterated Whole" (4).

41. "Die Nachahmung der Alten ist der einzige Weg für uns, groß, ja wenn es möglich ist, unnachahmlich zu werden" (*The imitation of the ancients is the only way for us to become great, yes, if it is possible, to become inimitable*). J. J. Winckelmann, *Sämtliche Werke*, ed. J. Eiselein (Osnabrück: Otto Zeller, 1965), 8.

42. "Der Palast der Könige ist jetzt geschlossen, die Gerichte haben sich von den Toren der Städte in das Innere der Häuser zurückgezogen, die Schrift hat das lebendige Wort verdrängt, das Volk ... ist ... folglich zu einem abgezogenen Begriff geworden, die Götter sind in die Brust der Menschen zurückgekehrt. Der Dichter muß die Paläste wieder auftun, er muß die Gerichte unter freien Himmel herausführen, er muß die Götter wieder aufstellen, er muß alles Unmittelbare, das durch die künstliche Einrichtung des wirklichen Lebens aufgehoben ist, wieder herstellen, und alles künstliche Machwerk an dem Menschen und um denselben, das die Erscheinung seiner innern Natur und seines ursprünglichen Charakters hindert, wie der Bildhauer die modernen Gewänder, abwerfen, und von allen äußern Umgebungen desselben nichts aufnehmen, als was die Höchste der Formen, die menschliche, sichtbar macht" (Friedrich Schiller, *Werke und Briefe, Band V,* ed. M. Luserke [Frankfurt: Klassiker, 1996], 286f.).

Schiller's lines here evoke an arduous and solitary process of reconstruction that captures both the exertion and the artistry of confronting the ancients, highlighting the special task of anyone who aims to become their translator. The long tradition of translating Greek tragedy, insofar as it demands a degree of transformation perhaps unmatched by the exchange between modern works, may subject both text and author to a particularly ruthless form of violence. Perhaps this is what Goethe knew.

III. Other Ethics

In her introduction to the recent anthology *Nation, Language and the Ethics of Translation,* Sandra Bermann proposes that translation as an object of study "might be effectively re-thought in historical and temporal terms rather than only in ontological and spatial ones." In this sense, translation gains relevance not only as a means of intercultural exchange but "in terms of a history of 'instances' or of linguistic negotiations occurring over time, each a poeisis, each establishing a new inscription and, with it, the possibility of new interpretation" (6). Bermann's model provides a compelling framework for examining the impulse to translate the Greeks since the Enlightenment, with each new version a different manifestation of the exchange between modernity and its nearly imperceptible shadows.

In seeking to frame this exchange as it develops diachronically, I examine a constellation of texts that reflect upon the ethics of translation as a way of thinking—an epistemological category that proposes to call a dialectical-mimetic progression of thought (what Heidegger will call "metaphysics") into question. Hölderlin's translation project, emerging out of a discourse in which both translation and tragedy operate in the service of *establishing* identity (in conversation with and in opposition to the "foreign"), allows language to slip its moorings in a manner that effectively *undermines* a fixed concept of identity. The intersection of tragedy and translation thus opens up the possibility of thinking otherwise, of experiencing the foreign not only as it relates to the perception of identity or the process of *Bildung* but rather also as that which cannot be reconciled, that cannot offer any greater lesson than its own fundamental, permanent dissonance. In the sense that it aims to reveal tragic experience as both radically foreign and curiously foundational, Hölderlin's translation project prefigures, as Heidegger recognized, a concept of "das Unheimliche."

Nowhere does this intersection of tragedy and translation have more lasting effects than in the German intellectual tradition. Chapter 1 thus makes the case for considering the significance of translation for the modern understanding of tragedy by situating Hölderlin's project within the intellectual climate of the late eighteenth and early nineteenth centuries, a time in which translation was regarded as a crucial means toward national and individual *Bildung* and most German intellectuals had something to say about the relationship between ancient Greece and modern subjectivity. While many of the models that emerged were essentially ahistorical in approach, treating the themes of tragedy as universal truths to be mined for their modern relevance, the texts of Greek tragedy themselves were regarded by translators and educated readers as immutable ideals to be rivaled, perhaps, but never changed. Hölderlin, who grappled with the issue of the tragic for most of his productive life, finally manages in his translations to hollow out a space between these two poles, neither appropriating ancient tragic concepts in the service of a modern intellectual agenda nor pledging unquestioned fidelity to the original text. Neither a relic nor a modern transformation, Hölderlin's translations represent a space in which transition itself can come to light.

It is this concern for marking the space between texts that defines Hölderlin's project as a valuable counterpoint to a conception of ethics more commonly shaped by the thematics of Greek tragedy. Most voices in this debate address the identity of tragic figures more than the structure of tragedy itself. However, Hölderlin's illumination of the process of transmission represents something else in its rapt attention to the otherness of tragic language and structure; as a result, the writers that follow in his footsteps inevitably reflect on problems that his translations both confront and produce. What questions, if any, can we answer by reading Greek tragedy today? How do we represent a past that eludes our comprehension? What can we understand of tragedy at all, and what can we glean from that which we do not understand?

The following two chapters focus on Hölderlin's translation project, the uniqueness of which lies in his attempt to make the experience of translation an integral part of the tragedy's effect on a modern audience. That modern experience rests upon the sheer foreignness of the material and is intensified by a strange and hauntingly beautiful syntax that is neither German nor Greek. Thus not only the plight of Oedipus and Antigone but the language of the plays themselves is unsettling, unfamiliar—and nevertheless captivating. In this synthesis of form and content, translation and tragedy, Hölderlin's texts suggest that the modern subject is brought to a place that the tragic figures already inhabit: a place in which, as Antigone's Chorus testifies, "Much is monstrous, yet / Nothing more monstrous than the human." While other readers of Antigone's tragedy, most notably Hegel, understand her decision to bury her brother as representative of divine law in conflict with the law of the state, in Hölderlin's translation she not only resists that gesture of assimilation into the structure of legitimacy but also brings those around her "outside of the law." The modern subject's apprehension of Antigone's solitary entry into the tomb, and of a language that constantly slips its moorings, forms the basis for the recognition of an essential difference—a "monstrosity"—that exceeds that subject's presupposition of his own immanence. What others in his time see as the ethical context of tragedy—the conflict of divine and human realms, the dialectical advancement of subject, community and finally history—is thus complicated by a model of tragic experience inseparable from the dynamics of translation. For Hölderlin the ethics of tragedy is grounded in nothing more than the imperative to preserve the dignity of an unfathomable and ultimately untranslatable difference; by calling into question the reflected immanence of the subject, it brings into focus that subject's responsibility for engaging with a form of alterity that both disrupts and defines it.

In the following chapters, I extend my discussion to Hölderlin's most influential twentieth-century readers, all of whom problematize the ethical stance that these translations illuminate. Common to these engagements with the same set of texts is an emphasis on the particular timeliness of tragedy, and particularly of Hölderlin's translations, in the political and cultural milieu of the present day. Consequently, the relationship between the ethical and the political becomes central, particularly with respect to the question of identity (both national and individual). Insofar as all these writers attempt to engage their thinking about tragedy with the horrors of recent events and with efforts to come to terms with the violence of the past, the question of responsibility gains even greater urgency.

Walter Benjamin's engagement with Hölderlin's Sophocles, which opens this second section, is a thread, an accumulation of reflections over two decades rather than a single essay or text. At no point does Benjamin offer a sustained reading of the translations and remarks in the manner of his writings on Goethe's *Elective Affinities* or even Hölderlin's twinned poems "Dichtermut" ("The Poet's Courage") and "Blödigkeit" ("Timidity"). There is no question, however, that Hölderlin's Sophocles represents a crucial foundation not only for Benjamin's concept of translation but for his theory of criticism in a more general sense. From his early essay "Two Poems by Friedrich Hölderlin" through the celebrated "Task of the Translator" and his monumental habilitation, *The Origin of German Tragic Drama*, it is apparent that Benjamin regards Hölderlin not only as a poet but also always as a translator—as a translator, in fact, of the very highest order. If Benjamin was not the first reader to acknowledge this, he was certainly the most impassioned.

For Benjamin, Hölderlin's renditions of Sophoclean tragedy underscore the ethical implications of translation as a mode of reading and engaging with the continued "life" of a text; and in this sense, they inch closer to a relation to an abstract notion of "truth" to which all poetry, and essentially all cultural artifacts, refer. By examining the individual moments in which Benjamin turns to this text, either directly or obliquely, as an example of his own thinking, I consider the extent to which a concept of translation informs not only his notion of *Aufgabe* or "task" in that celebrated essay but also, in a much larger sense, the idea of criticism itself as integrally related to the expression of a higher truth. Although his earliest reading of Hölderlin emphasizes the idea of the *poet's* courage ("Dichtermut"), I attempt to trace the less-trodden path by which the translator comes to express a particularly Benjaminian (and thus profoundly ethical) fortitude.

In his remarks on translation and tragedy in his lecture "Hölderlins Hymn 'The Ister,'" Martin Heidegger also develops his own concept of courage, particularly with respect to the poet or thinker, but that courage is ultimately expressed in a political rather than an ethical realm, and its ramifications are considerably more controversial. Delivered in 1942–43, the lecture has drawn much criticism for its violent and transformative readings of Hölderlin's poetry and Sophoclean tragedy, which many critics view as indicative of the totalitarian streak still legible within Heidegger's philosophy. To be sure, Heidegger's usual reading practice is in evidence in the lecture; the texts he examines are ultimately brought in line with a disturbing conception of "the Germans" that renders the past a mere reflection of the destiny about to be fulfilled. However, I argue that the lecture also presents a fascinating tension between this totalizing violence that silences reading in any genuine sense and a more fluid reading practice, thematized in the concept of dialogue or "Zwiesprache," that both describes Hölderlin's relationship to the Greeks and frames Heidegger's own reading on a rhetorical level.

This is not an attempt to "rescue" Heidegger, whose methods of interpretation remain problematic on many levels, but rather to engage with his text in a way that goes beyond the often knee-jerk tendency to expose Nazi sympathies in his writings of the 1930s and 40s. Heidegger's concept of "Zwiesprache" represents a movement away from the totalizing violence that characterizes his earlier texts on Hölderlin, offering a mode of reading posited on a semiotics of *in*comprehension, on the possibility that the failure of reading can also convey a certain kind of knowledge. That failure is highlighted in the clash of differences that ancient tragedy represents in a modern context. In the negotiation between foreign and familiar that informs both Sophoclean tragedy and Hölderlin's writings, Heidegger argues, the unsettling experience of being "not-at-home" (*Unheimischsein*) constantly underlies the process of "coming to be at home" (*Heimischwerden*)—is, in fact, integral to that very process. By allowing this instability to permeate the practice of interpretation itself, Heidegger performs the same exchange with Hölderlin that Hölderlin, as he argues, undertakes with Sophocles: a "dialogue" that allows for the possibility of being moved by the past and its echoes—even those still to be heard—in the present.

In Chapter 6, the 1948 adaptation of Hölderlin's *Antigone* by the notorious anti-Aristotelian Bertolt Brecht highlights this issue of violence as expressed within the various media that form history. With his *Antigonemodell*, a collection of script, notes, photographs, and sketches that creates a record of the play's performative genesis and development, Brecht attempts to lay bare the process by which recorded history marks and shapes dramatic forms and possibilities. His presentation of the modern ruins of Greek tragedy offers a model and an ethical argument for what he calls the "ruination" of German theater in the immediate post-war period. By basing his adaptation on Hölderlin's alienating translation, he underscores the sheer foreignness of the Greek original and thereby rejects the violence of transformation that would leave the past as a mere version of the present. Meanwhile, his construction of the *Modell* serves both as an example and as open-ended stimulus for continued adaptation. The "Modell" introduces another dimension of historical transformation by assuring at its very foundation its own infinite variability, thus the impossibility of ever being "finished" with the past.

The concluding chapter deals briefly with more recent appropriations of the translations by Heiner Müller (*Ödipus, Tyrann*, 1967), Philippe Lacoue-Labarthe (*L'Antigone des Sophocle*, 1977), and Martin Walser (*Antigone*, 1989). All three authors emphasize the special timeliness of tragedy for the historical moment in which they write their adaptations; all consequently grapple more or less openly with the ethics of mining the past for the sake of its affinities with the present, in particular with respect to the particularly German task of coming to terms with the past (*Vergangenheitsbewältigung*). Composed in three different milieus—the GDR, France, and the Federal Republic—the texts express vastly different comfort levels in setting parameters for this process of appropriation. As each adaptation is intriguingly mirrored upon Hölderlin's own structure—a text accompanied by detailed remarks—I show how each author takes a particular conception of "rewriting" as a point of departure in the attempt to situate tragedy within modernity. Rewriting the past as text thus gains a metaphorical significance that underscores the responsibility inherent in any process of remembrance:

a responsibility to preserve the traces of singularity, even eccentricity, that resist the sway of ideology, of tradition, of historical transformation.

As a side note, I am painfully aware of the considerable ironies of presenting a text of and about translation, *in* translation. As a compromise I have provided the German texts of most primary sources, particularly where the use of language is consequential or intentional, either in the body of text or in footnotes. Where an author's particular mode of expression in German must be foregrounded – in poetic passages, as well as in much of Hölderlin's, Benjamin's and Heidegger's theoretical language—I have placed the German source text ahead of the English translation; for passages in which content is more important than expression, I have placed the German text in footnotes. Moreover, while many translated passages are based on published material, I have often modified those existing translations to correspond more precisely to the arguments I wish to make. This is not in any way meant to suggest that the published translations of Hölderlin, Heidegger, or Benjamin are deficient—on the contrary, in general they are admirably precise—but rather to underscore the extent to which translations are always individual inscriptions within a multitude of possible readings.

IV. The Task of the Reader

Each of the texts I will examine in this study undertakes the challenge of engaging with difference through a particular mode of performance that I would describe as rhetorical—taking shape through the effects of discursive form rather than through the transmission of content alone[43]—and that ultimately concentrates its effects on the practice of reading rather than spectatorship. Hölderlin's performative expression rests in his concept of translation, Heidegger's in *Zwiesprache;* Brecht's in the *Modell,* which is presented as a kind of "image-text" that is meant to represent the text's infinite malleability and yet also carry the same weight as Sophocles' and Hölderlin's written "originals." That practice of reading takes place in the unmistakable presence of difference, of distances both temporal and conceptual that lead the reader in each case to limits that remain uncrossable: to the untranslatable in Hölderlin; the unreadability of "poetic knowledge" in Heidegger; the gaps between word and image, between text and performance in Brecht.

---

43. See Spivak on the distinction between the focus on rhetoric and the reliance on logic in translation: "Logic allows us to jump from word to word by means of clearly indicated connections. Rhetoric must work in the silence between and around in order to see what works and how much" ("Politics of Translation" 181).

All these texts, in other words, demand from the reader a receptivity to the singularity of the past and a preservation of the distance that separates past, present and future.

In this regard, the translation of tragedy takes on precisely the characteristics that its German synonyms suggest: it is at once a crossing from one "instance" to another (*Über-setzung*), a carrying-over (*Über-tragung*) and a passing-on, the reception of a history (*Über-lieferung*). For the reader, this trifold context involves an engagement with the material of that translation that goes beyond the traditional sense of "tragic effect." Reading in this manner implies not an active, identificatory suffering for the sake of a tragic hero but a suffering more closely related to receptivity, to the effort involved in finding one's way through a text that is transparent, in the sense that Martin Buber claimed all translation should be transparent: not clarifying the "true" meaning of the "original" but on the contrary, as in Buber's Bible translation, allowing the obscurities of the source text to shine through its language so that "its otherness in comparison with much that is familiar will become clear, but so will the importance of our receiving this otherness into the structure of our own life."[44] It is an experience of reading that implies a suffering of distance itself, a relentless attentiveness to singularity, an ethical challenge to modernity.

---

44. Martin Buber, "On Word Choice in Translating the Bible," in Martin Buber and Franz Rosenzweig, *Scripture and Translation*, trans. Lawrence Rosenwald and Everett Fox (Bloomington: Indiana University Press, 1994), 76f., Buber, in making the case for his and Rosenzweig's new Bible translation in 1930, argues forcefully that the reader *should* have to work his or her way into a foreign text, rather than receiving it in familiarized form—that in fact such a mode of reading bears all the more fruit: "Readers openmindedly looking for the way to the Bible will find words of the new version at odds with what they are used to; but then they will seek to pass from those words to the realities that are expressed in them, will consider whether the usual rendering does justice to the special character of these realities, will measure the distance between the two, and will consider how the new rendering holds up in comparison. For such readers the biblical world will in their reading be revealed, sector by sector; its otherness in comparison with much that is familiar will become clear, but so will the importance of our receiving this otherness into the structure of our own life."

ONE

Contexts
Why Translate? Why Study the Greeks?

TWO RELATED intellectual projects frame the context in which Hölderlin would translate Greek tragedy in the long eighteenth century: on one hand the ongoing discussion of how classical Greek models—including, but not limited to tragedy—might provide the aesthetic ideal to which German culture should aspire, on the other the discourse surrounding the importance of translation for the development of German language and identity. These developments were multifaceted, to say the least, and expressed the underlying principles of the Enlightenment on several fronts. Winckelmann inspired a pan-European frenzy for ancient Greece in 1755 with his treatise on the imitation of classical art, which he considered the only possible path to cultural greatness;[1] meanwhile, Lessing spearheaded efforts to reinvent German drama in the spirit of classical and Shakespearean tragedy (and Schiller aimed for its culmination in Weimar). At the same time, the language philosophers Bodmer, Breitinger, and Herder promoted the expansion of German language and thought through the confrontation with foreign texts and authors, and pioneering translators such as Wieland and Voss paved the way for the Romantic-era achievements of A. W. Schlegel and Goethe. Literary language, confronted with difference and consolidated

---

1. See Winckelmann, "Gedanken über die Nachahmung der griechischen Werke in der Malerei und Bildhauerkunst," *Sämtliche Werke I* [1825] (Osnabrück: Otto Zeller, 1965), 1–58. Winckelmann formulates here what will become the motto for Weimar classicism, the notion of "noble simplicity and quiet grandeur" (*edle Einfalt und stille Grösse*). See the discussion of the trend towards classical models in Reinhardt, "Goethe and Antiquity," *Tradition und Geist: Gesammelte Essays zur Dichtung*, ed. Carl Becker (Göttingen: Vandenhoeck & Ruprecht, 1960), 276ff.

by its contact with foreign models, offered a unifying means by which, as George Steiner writes, "the hitherto divided provinces and principalities of the German-speaking lands could test a new common identity."[2]

It is no coincidence that the German national character stands as the uncertain, unformed center of these developments, given the ambivalent cycling between the aspiration to models and their overturning that characterized the age of Enlightenment. A generation later, that ambivalence would be inscribed in most artistic and intellectual production. Hölderlin's was, after all, the generation that had absorbed Winckelmann's remarks on imitating the ideal abundance inherent in Greek beauty and yet also struggled mightily with new questions of subjectivity posed by Kant's critical philosophy, had responded to the revolutionary fervor of the French revolution only to revert to a safer stance in support of enlightened absolutism,[3] and had arrived at the notion of *Bildung* as a compromise between the compulsion to emulate ancient ideals and the creation of new knowledge.[4]

This general awareness of a sea change in and following the age of Enlightenment suggests an intriguing affinity with the "historical moment of tragedy" in ancient Greece as Vernant describes it. Whereas Vernant introduces this concept to describe the clash of the Athenian *polis* with the traditional values it continually challenged on the tragic stage, the term could be used with nearly equal relevance to describe the political, social, and aesthetic upheavals that characterized the "Kunstepoche."[5] If the painful contradictions at the heart of tragedy, the "linked polarities" (Segal 1986, 57) that perpetuate its conflicts reflect the messy ambiguity of historical flux, then

---

2. Steiner, *After Babel*, 80.

3. See Harold Mah, *Enlightenment Phantasies: Cultural Identity in France and Germant, 1765–1914* (Ithaca: Cornell University Press, 2003), 157–63. Mah claims that German intellectuals initially regarded the revolution as a culmination of the Enlightenment conception of linear progress through the exercise of reason (159f.), later struggling with the conflict between that ideal and the reality of extreme violence.

4. For a discussion of the status of "revolutions" in German culture, see Susanne Marchand's excellent study of the institutional effects of philhellenism in Germany: "That this was a cultural, rather than a political revolution . . . owes both to the more limited aims of reform-minded German intellectuals, and to the more repressive states in which they lived. Over the years, historians have often lamented the unwillingness of this generation of Germans to confront political issues head-on, without recognizing that by avoiding political confrontations, the poets and thinkers of the Golden Age were able to accomplish something more feasible given their small numbers, and something they wanted more passionately than political change: the remaking of German culture and cultural institutions" (*Down from Olympus*, 4).

5. Moving away from the traditional designation "Goethezeit," which cannot help but evoke (in some ways appropriately, to be sure) a crushing anxiety of influence, the Metzler German literary history introduces this more general term to describe the period between 1789 and 1830—the age of revolution, classicism, and Romanticism. *Deutsche Literaturgeschichte von den Anfängen bis zur Gegenwart*, 5th ed. (Stuttgart: Metzler, 1994), 154.

a similar set of contradictions may also serve to concretize the dissonances inherent in an age of revolutions. Greek tragedy's modern reception, its continued translation into the language of modern thought, bears at least as rich and conflicted a history as its initial production. The study of tragedy *in* translation thus requires a certain duplicity of approach, a consideration not only of its ancient historicity but also of its resonance in the development of a modern cultural consciousness.

Hölderlin was no stranger to the vacillating mood of his age, and his approach to the Greeks will reflect both poles of influence, the reactionary and the revolutionary. In his early novel *Hyperion*, for example, Hölderlin echoes Winckelmann's principles by letting Greek landscapes and scenarios evoke the permanence of the classical ideal within modernity, while his tragedy *The Death of Empedocles* represents the attempt to heal the division placed by Kant's critical philosophy within the subject's potential for self-recognition.[6] Yet his Sophocles could not have taken its particular shape without the simultaneous development of a discourse on translation that valorized the encounter with the foreign in a more general sense extending beyond ancient Greece. While for Winckelmann the Greeks represented the only model worth imitating, Hölderlin's contemporaries a generation later were more polymorphous in their choices of foreign objects of interest. Within this context, translation did not merely imply reverent imitation but suggested the creation of new life within existing things, the step forward rather than the backward gaze. The experience of the foreign was the means, at once identificatory and contrastive, by which the modern subject might come to recognize himself.[7] This determination led to a virtual explosion in the appearance of foreign works in Germany in the early nineteenth century. When Hölderlin began his project of translating, the German intelligentsia had had its first tastes of Shakespeare and Homer, in new translations by Wieland and Voss; by the time he was finished, Goethe and A. W. Schlegel alone had translated Dante, Petrarch, Boccaccio, Diderot, Voltaire, Corneille, Calderòn, and, of course, Shakespeare once again (in Schlegel's brilliant rendition, which is often still used today).[8]

Interestingly enough, however, this German fascination with the foreign did not typically include extensive travel to far-flung locations. As David

---

6. See David Constantine, *Early Greek Travellers and the Hellenic Ideal* (Cambridge: Cambridge University Press, 1984), 41.

7. For an extensive treatment of translation as both concept and practice in the Romantic period, see Berman.

8. Both Goethe and Schlegel continued to translate well into the nineteenth century; Schlegel eventually turned his attention to the *Bhagavad Gita* and lesser-known poets of Spain, Portugal, and Italy, while Goethe tackled Lord Byron's *Manfred*. See Berman 54 and 129.

Constantine has observed, no noted German artists or thinkers of the age traveled to Greece—not even Winckelmann, who had settled in Rome but ventured no further east—and German Hellenists relied instead for their conceptions of Greece on various mediating devices, such as descriptive accounts written by English and French travelers, sketches, and plaster reproductions of statuary.[9] This marks what Suzanne Marchand calls Germany's "peculiar asceticism and aestheticism," in which a distance from the desired ideal is stubbornly upheld; like Faust's love for the inaccessible Greek beauty Helen, the German fascination with Greece was "a marriage in spirit alone, an unsatisfied and unsatisfiable longing."[10] Far from seeking to alleviate this longing, however, intellectuals and artists preferred to let it define their relationship to Greece, proudly transforming a concrete limitation into a noble abstinence.[11] Wilhelm von Humboldt, the educational reformer and learned translator of Aeschylus, summed up this philosophical stance as an obligation: "Only from a distance . . . only as separate from all that is common, only as a thing of the past should antiquity appear to us" (cited in Constantine 1984, 2: *Nur aus der Ferne . . . nur von allem Gemeinen getrennt, nur als vergangen muss das Altertum uns erscheinen*). For the thinker or scholar focused on the ideal, this view offered a degree of safety: divided from both the quotidian and the mutable, Greece could remain a static entity contained within the past and effectively defined within the limits of existing tradition.

In this light—with ancient Greece a statue cast in stone and immortalized as the embodiment of "noble simplicity and quiet grandeur"—Hölderlin perceived the twin burdens of Winckelmann's Greek models and the new classical *Bildungsideal* taking shape in Weimar. With not only the entire array of classical Greek works but also a generation's worth of imitations and adaptations to consult, it is no wonder that Hölderlin first regarded the Greeks as at once a model for perfection and a burden that had stifled his own nation's potential for artistic originality. "We dream of originality and independence, we believe we are saying nothing but new things, and yet all of this is just reaction and at the same time a mild revenge against the servitude with which we have behaved with respect to antiquity," he writes in the 1799 essay "The Perspective from which we must regard Antiquity" (*Der Gesichtspunct aus dem wir das Altertum anzusehen haben*).[12] His antidote to

---

9. See Constantine 1984, 2f.

10. Marchand, *Down from Olympus*, 16.

11. Herder describes the Germans in similar terms: "Since we are not very used to this kind of travelling, since we are vaguely repelled by it. . . . " the translator should expose us to the "awesome secrets of state which abound in Greek literature." Cited in Lefevere 33.

12. "Wir träumen von Originalität und Selbstständigkeit, wir glauben, lauter Neues zu sagen, und alles dies ist doch Reaktion, gleichsam eine milde Rache gegen die Knechtschaft, womit [wir] uns verhalten haben gegen das Altertum" (FA 14: 95).

this condition of servitude is awareness—of the roads already traveled, of the paths that lie as yet unexplored—and forward motion, propelled not by the constant reflection on past ideals but rather by the measure of distance from those ideals: "For there is a difference in whether this *Bildungstrieb* affects us blindly or with our awareness, whether or not it knows from whence it came and in what direction it strives."[13]

This marking of distance will ultimately become the hallmark of his approach to translating the Greeks. Although a certain attitude of distancing was already common in the reluctance of German artists and scholars to visit Greece, for Hölderlin that distance from the source is accompanied less by that sense of unsatisfiable (yet paradoxically satisfying) longing for the ideal than by the questioning of ideals as such. Only by considering the fluidity of the relationship to models, by reflecting on the part those models play in the development of one's own language and literature, can one gain a sense of cultural history that is "alive" rather than (as Herder put it) "vague or dead." In suggesting that the modern distance from classical models marks the work's contextual life in the present, Hölderlin prefigures an idea of textual "history" that Benjamin will later posit, as always in conversation with both Romantic philosophy and Hölderlin's translation practice. In effect, Hölderlin's translations will express a subtler version of Novalis's provocative claim that "the German Shakespeare [i.e., Schlegel's translation] today is better than the English."

I. The New Day: *Translation is good for the Germans*

> Where there is a translator who is at the same time a philosopher, a poet, and a philologist: he is to be the morning star of a new era in our literature. (Johann Gottfried Herder, *Fragmente* 1766–67 [Lefevere 32])

As dawn breaks, a literature, a language, and a culture emerge; and the translator—tasked, it appears, with the probably impossible feat of being all things to all people—guides the nation into the new day. Herder's challenge places the translator at the center of a movement that would help to shape the social and intellectual contours of the second half of the eighteenth century. In the course of several decades the general view of translation in Germany would shift dramatically, from a concrete exercise to a universal category of thought, from a practical means of developing the artist to a

---

13. "Es ist nämlich ein Unterschied, ob jener Bildungstrieb blind wirkt, oder mit Bewußtsein, ob er weiß, woraus er hervorging und wohin er strebt" (FA 14: 96).

crucial mode of conceiving both national culture and subjective identity.[14] Likewise, the discourse on Greek tragedy and the concept of the tragic would migrate from the stage to the writing-desk and from the optimistic quest to establish identities, both national and individual, to the questioning of the contours of identity as such. For Hölderlin, the convergence of these two ideas would prove essential, as translation became the vehicle for engendering and intensifying tragedy's effect in a modern context.

Herder was certainly not alone in his sentiment that the German nation stood before a new dawn;[15] that same rhetoric of potentiality found ample public expression in other intellectual arenas at the same time, from Lessing's refutation of French classical models on the German stage to Kant's self-proclaimed "Copernican" revolution in thought. Their mutual call for an intellectual and cultural shift in the age of reason (which is also, of course, the age of revolution) lends credence to that rhetoric; taken together they represent two prongs of what Lacoue-Labarthe and Nancy have called the "triple crisis" of the eighteenth century: the social and moral crisis of the bourgeois subject, the political crisis of the French Revolution, and the Kantian critique.[16] And indeed, Herder's depiction of a newly creative and intellectual approach to translation highlights its crucial role in the drive toward cultural autonomy. In this sense it carries clear echoes of Lessing's famously scathing critique of the neoclassical traditionalist Johann Christoph Gottsched; both Lessing and Herder reject the traditional acceptance of French artistic superiority in favor of the development of more intrinsically German modes of expression. However, there are also important differences between Lessing's and Herder's models of German nationhood, chiefly with respect to their views on the ways in which the Germans might learn or profit from the exposure to foreign models.[17]

---

14. Louth describes Germany's particular openness to a historical moment of translation, whereas British intellectuals were less receptive to the "potential lying in translation" (31).

15. Schmidt submits, in fact, that every thinker concerned with Greek tragedy in the post-Enlightenment era, from Schelling to Nietzsche to Heidegger, departs likewise from the assumption that "the present age is a time in need of radical transformation." *On Germans and Other Greeks,* 5.

16. See *The Literary Absolute: The Theory of Literature in German Romanticism,* trans. Philip Barnard and Cheryl Lester (Albany: SUNY Press, 1988), 5. Their designation alludes to Friedrich Schlegel's Athenäum fragment from 1798: "The French Revolution, Fichte's *Science of Knowledge,* and Goethe's *Meister* are the greatest movements of our age. Whoever takes exception to this combination, to whom a revolution cannot seem important if it is not noisy and physical, this man has not yet raised himself to the high, wide standpoint of the history of humankind." (*Die Französische Revolution, Fichtes* Wissenschaftslehre *und Goethes* Meister *sind die grössten Tendenzen des Zeitalters. Wer an dieser Zusammenstellung Anstoß nimmt, wem keine Revolution wichtig scheinen kann, die nicht laut und materiell ist, der hat sich noch nicht auf den hohen weiten Standpunkt der Geschichte der Menschheit erhoben*). F. Schlegel, *Kritische Schriften,* ed. Wolfdietrich Rasch (Munich: Hanser, 1964).

17. For an illuminating discussion of their respective views on translation, see Katherine Arens,

In the seventeenth installment of his immensely popular journal *Letters Concerning the Latest Literature* (*Briefe, die neueste Literatur betreffend*), published with Mendelssohn and Nicolai in 1759, Lessing had argued passionately for a turn from French ornamentation to a more Shakespearean approach to tragic theater, while his *Hamburgische Dramaturgie* (1767) offers a reading of Aristotle's *Poetics* that reframes the conventions established by the likes of Corneille and Racine.[18] His campaign is clearly intended to incite rebellion in German theatrical circles, as is immediately evident in the seventeenth letter:

> "No one," say the authors of the library, "will deny that the German stage has Professor Gottsched to thank for much of its initial improvement." I am this no one; I deny it point-blank.[19]

The final lines of the text are equally audacious in their call for a more specifically German mode of expression. After presenting a scene from a Faust drama purportedly written by one of his "friends" (who turns out to be Lessing himself), he challenges the reader directly: "You wish to see a German play full of such scenes? So do I!" (Lessing 60).[20]

Herder composed his *Fragments* as a direct response to Lessing's *Briefe*, and he takes aim at the same target as his compatriot, submitting that the "French" mode of translation (which Gottsched had also come to represent) is just as imperfect a model for the Germans as their theater was for Lessing:[21]

"Translators who are not Traitors: Herder's and Lessing's Enlightenments," *Herder Yearbook* 5 (2000): 91–109.

18. This pairing of Shakespeare and Aristotle is itself a risky gesture, since in fact Shakespeare was likely unfamiliar with Aristotle's *Poetics*. Still, as Steiner points out, Lessing's assertion continues to color our view of modern tragedy (*The Death of Tragedy*, 188).

19. "'Niemand, sagen die Verfasser der Bibliothek, wird leugnen, dass die deutsche Schaubühne einen großen Teil ihrer ersten Verbesserung dem Herrn Professor Gottsched zu danken habe.' Ich bin dieser Niemand; ich leugne es geradezu" (Gotthold Ephraim Lessing, *Werke und Briefe* IV, ed. Wilfried Barner [Frankfurt: Deutscher Klassiker Verlag, 1985]: 56).

20. "Sie wünschen ein deutsches Stück, das lauter solche Szenen hätte? Ich auch!" Arens indicates that the *Letters* generally represented a new, satirical style of criticism not previously seen in German (Arens 91).

21. Gottsched regarded translation primarily as a useful exercise for aspiring authors, just as copying the works of great painters would train beginning art students. Although he does not directly reference the "French" manner of translation in the way that many of his contemporaries do, he advocates a form of translation that leans toward the transformative description others give: " . . . express everything by means of locutions that do not sound strange in your own language, but have a familiar ring to them" (Lefevere 16).

> The French, who are overproud of their national taste, adapt all things to it, rather than to try to adapt themselves to the taste of another time. Homer must enter France a captive, and dress according to fashion, so as not [to] offend their eye. But we poor Germans, who still are almost an audience without a fatherland, who are still without tyrants in the field of national taste, we want to see him the way he is. (Lefevere 33)

The tone of the passage, just as that of Lessing's letter, implies a rivalry of cultural values: although the Germans may be "poor" in their lack of "national taste," they already surpass the French in recognizing that foreign models must be allowed to exert particular influence on cultural life.[22] Translation in Gottsched's view functioned as a useful exercise for the aspiring author, just as copying the works of great painters would train beginning art students (Lefevere 15). For Herder, however, translation has a higher potential as an instrument of cultural enrichment and identity formation. As an audience "almost . . . without a fatherland," the Germans are more capable than the French of accepting the patronage of Shakespeare, or Homer, or Sophocles; and as a result, German language and culture profit by exposure to the previously unknown, unheard, and unseen.[23] For Herder, who regarded thought as directly conditioned by its relation to language, a translation of the properly expansive sort sheds light on other ways of thinking and perceiving the world, unique to particular linguistic, cultural, and historical contexts. A proper translation does not attempt to transform these unique structures but rather makes it "incumbent on each writer, critic, scholar, and translator to perceive and preserve the perspectival alterity of the products of each foreign nation."[24] What Berman identifies as the two key concepts for translation in the Enlightenment period, *Erweiterung* (expansion) and *Treue* (fidelity), collaborate in Herder's view, not as a slavish literalness but as the "ability to capture the uniqueness of the original in its form, expression, characters, 'genius,' and 'nature'" (Berman 40). Referring to the *Bildung* of language itself, Herder elaborates in another context: "Thus we edify [*bilden*] our language through translation and reflection" (*Man bilde also unsre Sprache durch Übersetzung und Reflexion*).[25] Translation plays a significant role, therefore,

---

22. Berman identifies the German cultural problematic as "the *reverse* of the French" (36).

23. This idea of "profiting" through the study of foreign models is common in the theoretical discourse of translation during the Enlightenment: Bodmer, for example, describes the "*enrichment* of [one's] stock of words and images," and Herder encourages German readers to "make use of the *treasures* of one of the most excellent nations" (Lefevere 20 and 32; my emphasis).

24. *Übersetzung, Translation, Traduction: An International Encyclopedia of Translation Studies*, ed. Harald Kittel, Juliane House, and Brigitte Schultze (Berlin, New York: W. de Gruyter, 2007), 1587.

25. Herder, *Werke: Band I* (Munich: Hanser, 1984): 195.

in the development of a free subject who is, as Kant will posit in 1784, "mündig" (a word which denotes a subject's maturity but which the Grimms' dictionary also relates to the mouth [*der Mund*]). As Johann Jakob Bodmer, one of Gottsched's contemporaries, writes already in 1746, "we are living in a country in which we would like the freedom of words to match the freedom of things" (Lefevre 21).

While Herder insists here that the Germans must meet Homer "the way he is" rather than forcing him to conform to familiar patterns—a dislocating experience in which Homer remains essentially inimitable ("unnachahmlich")—Lessing regards the encounter with foreign models as a meeting on more common ground. An important distinction between Lessing's dramaturgy and the view of translation advanced by Herder emerges, therefore, with respect to the question of identification. Lessing's theoretical framework for a new German theater in the *Hamburgische Dramaturgie*—anchored by his influential rereading of Aristotle's *Poetics*—depends on a more self-centered idea of recognition. Only through identification with tragic heroes (and heroines, as was the case for much German bourgeois tragedy of the eighteenth century) "of like kind" (*vom gleichen Schrot und Korn*) can the audience experience dramatic effect as both sympathy (*Mitleid*) and fear (*Furcht*), which Lessing identifies as a self-reflexive form of sympathy (*das auf uns bezogene Mitleid*).[26] The recognition of my likeness on the stage, along with the accompanying fear that the same fate could befall me, has a didactic aim in the awakening of a moral capacity for sympathy (*Mitleidsbereitschaft*).[27] Whereas Aristotle regarded recognition (*anagnorisis*) as an essential plot element of tragedy, Lessing displaces that gesture upon the spectator, who recognizes his similarity to the tragic figure on the stage—specifically, with a figure who faces misfortune as a result of his or her all too human imperfections.[28]

---

26. Max Kommerell captures the main thrust of Lessing's conception of the tragic stage in describing it as a "school of compassion" (*Schule des Mitgefühls*). *Lessing und Aristoteles: Untersuchung über die Theorie der Tragödie* (Frankfurt: Klostermann, 1941 [1957]), 72 and 91.

27. Kommerell 1957, 82. As he notes, the formality of classical tragedy is thereby replaced by a psychological intimacy that is, in fact, a far cry from Aristotle's *Poetics* (121). This also renders problematic the issue of guilt and innocence, insofar as pity, through its proximity to identification, becomes situated "jenseits von schuldig und unschuldig" (120).

28. See *The Complete Works of Aristotle*, vol. 2, ed. Jonathan Barnes (Princeton: Princeton University Press, 1984): 2324f. Terence Cave offers an interesting analysis of the term *anagnorisis*, suggesting that the prefix ana- represents a double negative, thus that *anagnorisis* would be "the shift from 'not-knowing' to 'not not-knowing.'" The truth has been present from the start in veiled form, and the hero was only unaware of it until the crucial moment. Lessing's version of recognition on the part of the spectator corresponds well with this analysis; even if it is not exactly Aristotelian in style; the spectator, too, is implicated in a relationship that he suddenly recognizes as true. Cave, "Recognition and the

Although Lessing claims, therefore, that his dramaturgy represents a radical departure from established models—a true statement, to be sure, with respect to its break with the French tradition—that upheaval does not lead the Germans beyond themselves but rather ensures that they remain within a recognizable comfort zone. As von Wiese explains, the discovery of a character's imperfection allows the spectator to feel sympathy rather than awe (*Bewunderung*), and thus to retain an experience pertinent to the human as such: "In tragedy man discovers who he is, a being between perfection and error."[29] If the viewer is disturbed by the fear that emerges from this universal sense of likeness, he is more than compensated by the greater understanding of "who he is." The encounter with another on the stage only counts if it is, in the end, an encounter with a version of the self.[30] Herder's journey towards Homer also assumes identification, and even empathy (*Einfühlung*), as the reader must attempt to imagine the sensations that underlie another's words in order to understand the meaning of those words.[31] That identification occurs, however, on the rather more unsettling terms of the other rather than those of the self: a translation must present Homer "the way he is," and it is the task of the receiving culture not only to "see" him, but to attempt to see *like* him.

As uncomplicated as it sounds, however, the translator's task of bringing Homer to the Germans "the way he is" is deceptively arduous. Herder himself writes in the *Fragmente* that a translator must be a "creative genius" (*schöpferisches Genie*) in order to carry out his craft successfully, must not just imitate a text but recreate its language in every nuance of its relation to culture and history. For Herder, then, a good or "authentic" translation has no chance of being a perfect one; even as translation remains a necessary task, every foreign text remains "fundamentally untranslatable" (Arens 103).

Reader," in *Comparative Criticism: A Yearbook, Vol. 2,* ed. E. S. Shaffer (Cambridge University Press, 1980): 51.

29. Benno von Wiese, *Die Deutsche Tragödie von Lessing bis Hebbel* (Hamburg: Hoffmann und Kampe, 1948), 30.

30. For a comprehensive discussion of the birth and development of bourgeois tragedy in relation to the emergence of the autonomous subject of the Enlightenment, see Szondi, *Theorie des bürgerlichen Trauerspiels im 18. Jahrhundert: der Kaufmann, der Hausvater, und der Hofmeister* (Frankfurt: Suhrkamp, 1973). Rainer Nägele offers a helpful gloss of Szondi's theory in *Theater, Theory, Speculation: Walter Benjamin and the Scenes of Modernity* (Baltimore: Johns Hopkins University Press, 1991), 10–13.

31. See Michael N. Forster's detailed treatment of Herder's concept here: "in order to understand another person's concepts an interpreter must not only master the person's word-usage in an external way but must also in some manner recapture the person's relevant sensations. . . . [I]n order really to understand the Greeks, we must learn to see like them. . . . " "Herder's Philosophy of Language, Interpretation, and Translation: Three Fundamental Principles," *The Review of Metaphysics* 56:2 (Dec. 2002): 353–54.

Still, there are degrees of success among translations, chiefly with respect to a translator's ability to render the specific tone of a foreign work in the target language. In this vein Herder describes a particularly good translation of Sophocles:

> For the geniuses that read "ethereally," it [the translation] leads them securely by the hand to a clear source. They see the tragic spirit of the Greeks, learn of that which is most particular to their manner of thinking and their feeling: can follow their simplicity and their composition, their talents and development through to the construction of a purpose.[32]

If a translation can never perfectly capture the particularity of an age and its language, that does not imply that the translator is exempt from responsibility for its success. An "authentic" (Arens 98) translation must, at best, replicate a text's "primary tone" (*Hauptton*), must reveal the "spirit" of the source text rather than copying its form.[33]

Yet even if Herder's notion only functions as an ideal—and he indicates himself that his model of translation is more aspirational than achievable[34]—the concept he advances of bringing the reader to the foreign text persists throughout the period as a central aspect of translation theory and practice, echoed in the writings of A. W. Schlegel, Goethe, Schleiermacher, and Humboldt. Little wonder, then, that the translator who transports readers across great distances is frequently characterized as needing "courage" for the journey. Translation in Herder's form calls to mind at once the ubiquity of translation as a concept and its persistent practical inadequacy.[35]

---

32. Cited in Arens 104: "Den Genies, die bloß ätherisch lesen, ist sie eine sichere Handleiterin zu einer klaren Quelle. Sie sehen den tragischen Geist der Griechen, lernen das Eigentümlichste ihrer Denkart und ihrer Rührung: können ihre Einfalt und ihre Zusammensetzung, ihre Anlage und Fortleitung bis zur Errichtung des Zwecks verfolgen."

33. Sauder discusses what Ulrich Gaier has called Herder's concept of "restorative translation" (*restaurative Übersetzung*), in which the translator "attempts to reach 'behind' the original texts—for example, when he tries to discover behind Macpherson's *Ossian* the 'palimpsest' of ancient and undocumented folk poetry" ("Herder's Poetic Works, His Translations, and His Views on Poetry," in Koepke 2009, 320). This idea suggests an intriguing link to Hölderlin's later formulations about bringing out the "Oriental" behind the Greek source text.

34. Herder jokingly suggests that the "best translator" who is also the "best explicator" would be able to produce a book with the title, "A Poetic Translation of Hebrew Poems, Explained in the Context of the Country, the History, the Opinions, the Religion, the Situation, the Customs, and the Language of their Nation and Transplanted into the Genius of Our Time, Our Thinking, and Our Language" (Lefevere 31).

35. Arens claims that Herder's argument ultimately renders any foreign text "fundamentally untranslatable," since the best translator must be able to explain and form ideas (*bilden*) rather than merely recreate them (103).

As a young philosopher-poet deeply engaged with both the intellectual icons and the volatile politics of his time, Hölderlin was well aware that the path to *Bildung* demanded the study of foreign models, and he also recognized the potential of translation as a mode of communication and linguistic expansion. (An avid reader of Herder, moreover, he would likely have had some knowledge of his views on translation as outlined in the *Fragmente*.) At an early stage, however, he also identified the translator's particular vulnerability in that process. In February 1794 Hölderlin writes a letter to Ludwig Neuffer, who was working on translations of Virgil as well as the Roman historian Sallust. Hölderlin first praises his friend's efforts to remain "loyal" (*treu*) to Virgil, since that struggle will pay off in the strengthening of both language and spirit: "The spirit of the great Roman will surely strengthen yours wonderfully. Your language will gain more and more agility and strength in the struggle with his" (StA 6, 1: 109f.).[36] A few months later he writes to Neuffer again, extolling the "healing gymnastics" (*heilsame Gymnastik*) of translation practice, in which one's own language becomes more "supple" (*geschmeidig*) through striving for "foreign beauty and magnitude" (*nach fremder Schönheit und Größe*).[37] Despite its beneficial effects, however, the practice also carries risks for the translator: in what Charlie Louth describes as "an uncanny proleptic evocation of the whole of his development as a translator" (58), Hölderlin proposes that spending too much time in "foreign service" might cause a dangerous loss of contact with one's own language.

> Language is the organ of our heads, our hearts, the sign of our fantasies, our ideas; it must obey us. If it has lived too long in foreign service, I think it is nearly to be feared that it will never again become entirely the free, pure expression of our spirit, formed out of nothing but our interiority, thus and not otherwise.[38]

"Translation is good for you," then, to cite the title of a recent lecture

---

36. "Der Geist des hohen Römers muß den Deinen wunderbar stärken. Deine Sprache muß im Kampfe mit der seinigen immer mer an Gewandheit und Stärke gewinnen."
37. In this letter he also describes the pitfall of remaining so long in "foreign service" that one cannot safely return to one's own language, an uncannily prescient observation that both Louth and Constantine have discussed in some detail, see Louth 58f. and Constantine, "Translation Is Good for You," lecture at Swansea University, 30 June 2010.
38. "Die Sprache ist Organ unseres Kopfs, unseres Herzens, Zeichen unserer Phantasien, unserer Ideen; uns muss sie gehorchen. Hat sie nun zu lange in fremdem Dienste gelebt, so denk' ich, ist fast zu fürchten, daß sie nie mehr ganz der freie reine, durch gar nichts, als durch das Innre, so und nicht anders gestaltete Ausdruk unseres Geistes werde" (StA 6, 1: 125).

by David Constantine, but not always.[39] To be more precise, it is surely good for the Germans but not necessarily good for the translator. Friedrich Schleiermacher would later recognize the extent of the translator's exposure, describing the "extraordinary form of humiliation" to which he must subject himself for the sake of his source text; Hölderlin—at least in the eyes of many readers, from his contemporaries to the present day—has come to embody its consequences. Within the specific context of the nascent German nation, however, the sacrifice *makes sense;* translation, which is at once a look backward and a step forward, a negotiation with difference and a gesture that constitutes new identity, grants the source text a renewed hermeneutic urgency. This was especially true for Greek tragedy, given the distances the form had traveled and the passionate responses it nevertheless continued to inspire. An ancient text has the potential to *mean* something different in a modern context, Hölderlin and his cohort imply, and by that other relevance to lend shape to the intellectual and aesthetic activity of the day.

II. The Step Forward: Romantic Translation

> When I read Homer I have no choice but to become a Greek. . . . The reader's soul secretly translates him for itself, wherever it can do so . . . (Herder, cited in Lefevere 34)

The secret of reading, at least for Herder and the early Romantics who studied his work, is that it is always a process of translation. (Novalis will eventually agree with and radicalize this notion, suggesting that "not just books, everything can be translated" in the differentiated ways in which he imagines the process [Störig 33]). In the moment that Homer speaks to the reader, that reader becomes a Greek, identifies with that position and occupies it in absentia. The idea that we have "no choice" in the matter, that reading transports and transforms us secretly and regardless of our will, does not invalidate this process as a crucial step on the path of *Bildung*. Translation thus exceeds the boundaries of literary practice and becomes a metaphor, a "category of thought" (Lefevere 30) that describes and validates a particular mode of aesthetic experience.[40] Such an experience goes beyond

---

39. David Constantine, "Translation is Good for You," keynote address, The Author-Translator in the European Literary, Context, Swansea University 30 June 2010.

40. Indeed, as Louth points out, translation as a theoretical construct in the long eighteenth century closely resembles the process of *Bildung* in microcosm, sending the self on a journey into the unknown that ends with the return to a more complete self (24). At least for Herder, then, the

the mere study of models, engaging the soul, rather than the intellect alone, in following the "flight" of Homer's Greek.

> To understand Homer is one thing, says Winckelmann, to be able to explain him to yourself another; and this happens in my soul only by means of a secret translation, a rapid change in thought and language. (Lefevere 34)

Herder invokes a contrast here that will continue to resonate in the coming decades as the study of the Greeks gains momentum alongside the will to translate. On one side is Winckelmann, with his idealizing, even paganistic passion for the beauty of ancient Greece, and those readers who would seek to follow, by "secret translation," the paths laid along those distant shores; on the other, "a commentator, an annotator, a schoolmaster, or a learner of languages"—the reader who studies the Greeks, who understands their language and traditions in a concrete sense, but does not surrender to the transporting experience of "secret translation" (see Constantine 1984, 101f.) Herder describes this reader's approach to classical Greece—or any such encounter with foreign shores, for that matter—as "vague or dead." Hölderlin will likewise equate this latter approach with "dead" reading, with the collector of artifacts and his excessive concern for "everything positive" (*alles Positive*); as Constantine explains, "'positives Beleben des Todten' [*the positive reanimation of the dead*] was the way of the antiquarians rummaging in the ruins of Athens, and by extension it is the illusion, under many forms, that a living work can be made by assembling enough material" (Constantine 1984, 102f.). Meanwhile, as we will see, one of Hölderlin's primary concerns in translating the Greeks was to render their texts "more alive" to a modern audience. Far from a static artifact, the "living" text is one that engenders an effect, not just passive admiration but surrender to its "flight."[41]

Herder's comments on the practice of translation uphold this distinction between antiquarian and aesthete, as he pegs the ideal translator as "creative genius": "A German Homer, Aeschylus, Sophocles . . . builds a monument unnoticed by pedants and schoolmasters, but it holds the eye of the wise by virtue of its silent grandeur and simple splendour" (Lefevere 31). At the

---

practice of translation turns this secret self-transformation into a conscious exercise in individual and universal betterment. The one who translates, however, bears a heavy burden: as the transmitter of the foreign, he is responsible to both text and reader. Little wonder, then, that such a translator must be, in Herder's estimation, a "creative genius" (Lefevere 31).

41. Spivak 1993, 180: "Translation is the most intimate act of reading. I surrender to the text when I translate."

same time, however, he complicates Winckelmann's notion of *Nachahmung*, since the emphasis on the translator as "creative" force suggests an engagement with the text that shifts away from reverent imitation. In this light he imagines the preface to the ideal translation as a challenge both to aspiring translators and to the reader as such:

> And should you want to make use of the treasures of one of the most excellent nations: look, they are here. I want to teach you their art of transforming history and religion into poetry; do not steal what they have invented; steal their art of inventing, of creation, of expression. (Lefevere 32)

Steal the *art* of inventing, not its substance: the primary task of translating is not to copy foreign material (what Herder calls "wretched imitation" [Lefevere 31]) but to learn from foreign methods in the creation of new material, "an imitation which manages to remain original." As Gerhard Sauder discusses, Herder's formulation clearly echoes the aesthetic ideology of the *Sturm und Drang*, with its emphasis on the essential role of genius for achieving great art, and we also see most clearly his influence on the Jena Romantics' thinking on translation as expansion and improvement over the original (Sauder 319). His comments find an echo in Novalis's provocative claim, in a 1797 letter to A. W. Schlegel, that "the German Shakespeare (i.e., Schlegel's translation) today is better than the English." This process of improvement does not suggest, as it would have for Gottsched or even for Lessing, that the translation must compensate for a source text's poetic weaknesses.[42] Rather, as Berman discusses, Novalis refers here to the Romantic idea that "the original has an *a priori* scope that never quite *is*" (106); translation, in the sense that it implies continued aesthetic and intellectual reflection, represents a potentiating process that moves the work of art toward its culmination. The look backward is always a step forward—and for Novalis, a step upward.[43]

---

42. Lessing: "the hand of a master [. . .] has compensated, with countless little improvements and corrections, for that which in the original text is often a bit cross-eyed, a bit affected" (eine Meisterhand [. . .] mit unzählig kleinen Verbesserungen und Berichtigungen desjenigen, was in der Urschrift oft ein wenig schielend, ein wenig affektiert ist, kompensiert hat" [cited in Arens 96]). Gottsched: " . . . you should leave each writer his own nature, which identifies him, in the translation. Yet I would not therefore advise to leave together in one piece all the long-winded sentences. . . . No, in this case a translator is rightfully entitled to the liberty of splitting up a convoluted sentence into two, three, or more parts" (Lefevere 16).

43. Louth calls Novalis's formulation an example of "Bildung . . . von außen hinein" (from the outside in, quoting Friedrich Schlegel), in which the translation of Shakespeare has "taken him up and transmuted him into a continuum, extended his reach, introduced that self-reflexivity which unsettles the finished work . . . and exposes it" (Louth 35).

For the celebrated translator and language philosopher Wilhelm von Humboldt, translation was certainly a "potentiation," as Berman describes it (77), though not as much for the text itself as for the subject who reads it; insofar as it has the capacity to illuminate—or, even better, to provide readers with the tools to illuminate for themselves—the dark contours of ancient text, classical translation provides the basis for the subject's dialectical progress toward enlightened citizenship. A comparison between Humboldt's approach to translating Aeschylus's *Agamemnon* with Hölderlin's work on Sophocles is instructive, not only because the two projects are nearly contemporary but also because of their starkly divergent perspectives on what a translation can and ought to achieve. If Humboldt retains in his approach a touch of the "antiquarian," in stark contrast to Hölderlin, he also provides precisely the kind of critical reflection on the text that Herder and the Romantics regarded as essential to its "improvement."[44]

III. Divergent Methods: Humboldt and Hölderlin

Humboldt embarked on his translation of *Agamemnon* at approximately the same time as Hölderlin began translating Sophocles (although Humboldt devoted another decade and a half to the project before publishing it in 1816). Yet although the two projects emerge from similar contexts, their respective approaches—as well as the finished products—are quite different. While Hölderlin used a source widely regarded as corrupt, the Frankfurt Juntina edition of 1555, Humboldt consulted closely with Greek philologists to achieve the "historical rigor and conscientiousness" that the source text merited (*historische Strenge und Gewissenhaftigkeit*, Störig 85). While Hölderlin's remarks are cryptic and offer little explanation of the texts they introduce, Humboldt's introduction evinces a careful engagement not only with the material of Aeschylus's text but with the "monstrous background" (Störig 77) of the Trojan war. Situating the plot of the *Agamemnon* within the broader context of the Greek world, he repeatedly invokes metaphors of darkness and light to argue that the text represents a bridge to greater understanding of myth and history, for Greek and modern audiences alike: " . . . a line of torches binds Asia and Europe in one shining night" (*eine Fackelreihe verbindet in einer glanzvollen Nacht Asien und Europa*, Störig 78).

---

44. Steiner has particularly high praise for Humboldt in *After Babel*, describing him somewhat quaintly as "among the last Europeans of whom it may be said with fair confidence that they had direct professional or imaginative notions of very nearly the whole of extant knowledge" (*After Babel* 80).

Where darkness once obscured the potential for connection, a row of flickering flames lights the crossing; a description of the mythic-historical impact of the play thus also stands as a metaphor for its translation in Humboldt's able hands.

In general, Humboldt advances the argument that a critical and learned approach to ancient text enhances its aesthetic impact. This applies not only to the translator's work but also to that of the reader. Aeschylus's text does contain obscurities (*Dunkelheiten*), Humboldt suggests, particularly in the Choral passages, but it is not the translator's duty alone to illuminate them; the reader is primarily responsible for negotiating his own understanding of the text's dark contours.

> As one thinks oneself into the mood of the poet, into his time, into the characters he puts on the stage, the obscurity gradually fades and is replaced by a high clarity. A part of this careful attention must also be given to the translation: never expect that what is sublime, immense, and extraordinary in the original language will be easily and immediately comprehensible in the translation. (Schulte and Biguenet 59, trans. modified).[45]

The basis of reading here is attention, "*thinking* oneself into" another age and mode of expression; darkness fades and is replaced by "high clarity" (*hohe Klarheit*), implying the elevation of the viewing subject to an elevated level of understanding (indeed, his word choice recalls the German Enlightenment [*Aufklärung*] itself). This is somewhat reminiscent of Herder's "secret translation," in the sense that the reader is swept away, by the power of his own reading, to another time, place, and "mood," but Humboldt's model insists on activity, the *work* of thinking, rather than surrender to the effects of foreign expression. Indeed, the reader must be challenged to think through a text's obscurities, left conspicuously in place by the translator, while avoiding the interference of "feeling" at all costs: "Least of all should one allow the influence of so-called aesthetic feeling, to which translators may feel themselves called, if one wants to avoid encroaching on the text in a manner that sooner or later will make space for other encroachments (the worst thing that can happen to an interpreter of the ancients)."[46]

---

45. "Sowie man sich in die Stimmung des Dichters, seines Zeitalters, der von ihm aufgeführten Personen hineindenkt, verschwindet sie [die Dunkelheit] nach und nach, und eine hohe Klarheit tritt an die Stelle. Einen Theil dieser Aufmerksamkeit muss man auch der Uebersetzung schenken; nicht verlangen, dass das, was in der Ursprache erhaben, riesenhaft und ungewöhnlich ist, in der Uebertragung leicht und augenblicklich fasslich seyn solle" (Störig 84).

46. Störig 85: "Am wenigsten darf man dem sogenannten ästhetischen Gefühl, wozu gerade die Uebersetzer sich berufen glauben könnten, darauf Einfluss gestatten, wenn man (das Schlimmste was

The idea that translation from the Greek involves and fosters intellectual *work*, not only for the translator but for the reader as well, strongly reflects Humboldt's vision for the reform of educational institutions in the early decades of the nineteenth century. As a model of *Bildung*, the philological study of the ancients would instill in the individual the drive toward "self-willed citizenship" (Marchand 28). (Again—as with the translation that leaves some obscurity in place for the reader's "attention"—the subject's momentum toward clarity emerges as an act of volition rather than in the form of Herder's surrender to "secret translation.") As Marchand discusses, Humboldt's model of *Bildung* identified "appreciation of the Greeks with the ideal of individual self-cultivation, thereby drawing him away from, rather than into, the public sphere" (26); the individual subject, turning inward in the interest of developing intellectual skill, places himself (and for Humboldt it can only be *him*self[47]) on the path to active citizenship.

Only one "feeling" proves productive for both translator and reader in Humboldt's estimation, namely, a form of aesthetic judgment concerning the extent of a translation's effect of "foreignness." Some foreign feeling is essential if a translation is to remain "loyal" to its source: a "certain shade of foreignness" (Störig 83: *eine gewisse Farbe der Fremdheit*) must coexist with a "love for the original." However, that touch of the foreign (*das Fremde*) may not cross over into outright foreignness (*die Fremdheit*), or the translation will merely reveal its translator's lack of skill:

> The line . . . can easily be drawn. As long as one does not feel the foreignness (*Fremdheit*) yet does feel the foreign (*Fremde*), a translation has reached its highest goal; but where foreignness appears as such, and more than likely even obscures the foreign, the translator betrays his inadequacy to the original. (Schulte and Biguenet 58; trans. modified)[48]

Humboldt goes on to say that "the feeling of the unbiased reader (*das Gefühl des unvoreingenommen Lesers*) is not likely to miss this true line of separation:" the reader will simply know when a line has been crossed.

It is at this juncture, where impressions of the foreign are governed by

---

einem Bearbeiter der Alten begegnen kann) nicht dem Text Einfälle aufdringen will, die über kurz, oder lang andren Einfällen Platz machen."

47. See Marchand 28: with his educational reforms Humboldt sought to promote "civic harmony and loyalty to the state" by curing "one-sidedness" in learned men. However, he did not consider this "one-sidedness" to be a bad trait at all for women.

48. "Die Gränze . . . ist hier sehr leicht zu ziehen. Solange nicht die Fremdheit, sondern das Fremde gefühlt wird, hat die Uebersetzung ihre höchsten Zwecke erreicht; wo aber die Fremdheit an sich erscheint, und vielleicht gar das Fremde verdunkelt, da verräth der Uebersetzer, dass er seinem Original nicht gewachsen ist" (Störig 83).

the reader's "feeling," that Humboldt's and Hölderlin's projects contrast most productively. In granting the reader authority to place a limit on a translation's degree of foreignness, Humboldt implies that the translator must not only be sufficiently learned to command both source and target languages but eloquent enough to make that command accessible to a reading public. And it is undeniable that Hölderlin as translator would stumble under both of these conditions. Not only were his contemporaries bewildered by the tone and language of his Sophocles, but, as Beissner has thoroughly shown, the combination of his limited knowledge of Greek and his imperfect source text led to numerous errors and nonsequiturs that undermined his scholarly credibility.[49] Yet Humboldt's "true line of separation," easily recognized by the unbiased reader, has its limits: it cannot account for the gradual *expansion* of cultural tastes and preferences (in an age, moreover, in which those values were most definitely in flux). Goethe would later (1819, in *Noten und Abhandlungen zu bessern Verständnis des west-östlichen Divans*) suggest a more dynamic model, arguing that an audience becomes accustomed to and prepared for new forms through the development of translation as medium, that with time and experience an audience comes to tolerate more and more "foreignness." His distinction among three different "epochs" of translation posits a final phase, the "highest and last," in which "the goal of the translation is to achieve perfect identity with the original, so that the one does not exist instead of the other but in the other's place" (Schulte and Biguenet 61).[50] Of the three phases of translation, this last one elicits the most resistance from its audience and yet offers the greatest potential reward, as Goethe argues with the example of Voss's Homer:

> At first the public was not at all satisfied with Voss ... until gradually [*nach und nach*] the public's ear accustomed itself to this new kind of translation, became comfortable with it. Now anyone who assesses the extent of what has happened, what versatility has come to the Germans, what rhetorical, rhythmical, metrical advantages are available to the spirited, talented beginner ... may hope that literary history will openly acknowledge who was the first to choose this path in spite of so many and varied obstacles. (Schulte and Biguenet 61)[51]

---

49. Friedrich Beissner, *Hölderlins Übersetzungen aus dem Griechischen* (Stuttgart: Metzler, 1961), 65f.

50. Steiner justifiably points out that Goethe's model is in general "unsatisfactory," leaving too much open to conjecture, but that it does fit in well with Goethe's central philosophical beliefs: "Translation is an exemplary case of metamorphosis" (*After Babel*, 259).

51. "... Voß konnte das Publikum zuerst nicht befriedigen, bis man sich nach und nach in die neue Art hinein hörte, hinein bequemte. Wer nun aber jetzt übersieht, was geschehen ist, welche

The gradual (*nach und nach*) education of a modern audience is accomplished for Goethe through the process of "sich hineinhören" (literally, *hearing oneself into* the foreign work); by exposing the senses to new and unfamiliar forms, the public makes *itself* comfortable with those forms (Goethe's formulation is "sich hineinbequemen," an echo of "hineinhören;" interestingly enough, Humboldt had insisted on the importance of "sich hinein*denken*," emphasizing once again the work of the intellect rather than the senses). Voss's translations may never be duly appreciated in his own age, Goethe suggests here, but their time will come. Humboldt's easily recognizable distinction between the desirable "foreign" and undesirable "foreignness" is perhaps only temporary, then, and the question of its limit must continually be posed anew as the senses expand to meet more challenging material. Goethe's notion of an audience in flux points to a dynamic and historical dimension of *Fremdheit,* thus of translation itself: if translators such as Voss or Hölderlin push the boundaries of their readers' tolerance for the foreign, it does not mean that their works are failed or "ruined" translations. Indeed, to follow Goethe's point, perhaps a translation *must* be situated at this limit, must risk foreignness in order to sustain that experience of the foreign that even Humboldt regards as essential. The continued life of the text in translation (its "living on," in Benjamin's terms) depends on the translator's maintaining that precarious balance.

This is where Hölderlin enters the picture as translator: he holds the text in a suspended position between foreignness and familiarity, refusing ever to cross completely over into the safe zone of the "familiarly" foreign. Indeed, perhaps it is because his translations are situated on this precipice that they have remained an object of interest to literary history. By challenging Humboldt's limit of *Fremdheit,* he effectively ensured that his project would not become a relic of a particular historical period but rather would continue to resonate as a set of questions that would engage audiences over time. The very difficulty of the text, its suspension between sense and nonsense, guarantees its "living on."

IV. Suspension

> Der scheinet aber fast
> Rückwärts zu gehen und

Versatilität unter die Deutschen gekommen, welche rhetorischen, rhythmischen, metrischen Vorteile dem geistreich-talentvollen Jüngling zur Hand sind . . . der darf hoffen, dass die Literaturgeschichte unbewunden aussprechen werde, wer diesen Weg unter mancherlei Hindernissen zuerst einschlug" (Störig 37).

Ich mein, er müsse kommen
Von Osten. Vieles wäre
Zu sagen davon. Und warum hängt er
An den Bergen gerad? ("Der Ister")

That one seems, however, almost
To go backwards and
I think it must come
From the East. Much could
Be said of this. And why does it cling
To the mountains, just there? ("*The Ister*")

As is so typical for Hölderlin, the poetic depiction of the Danube's flow evokes the depth of his relation to the ancient past (here "the East"): the look back, the reflective contact with the source, the fleeting effect of suspension as the river, seemingly moving forward and backward at once, clings momentarily to the mountainside.[52] In a similar way, his translation practice will enact a suspension between two languages where the reader must hold each one in brief abeyance, dislocating herself from the steady flow of her own language in order to measure the distance traveled by the text. In a recent article, Stanley Corngold eloquently describes a similar "delay" in the process of translation that implies a fundamental ethics:

> How should we begin to know such a person—and we must—otherwise than by becoming acquainted with dislocation, our own dislocation, outside language, outside competence? What room is there for this difficult strangeness, if we have not learned to stand firm in the midst of it, abiding a moment of inexpressibility, an incommunicable sense of otherness, of intimacy with a common human grain.[53]

Although Corngold's comments here do not refer directly to Hölderlin, they nevertheless evoke this scholar-translator's long engagement with the poet-translator. His image of "holding together in the mind" two disparate ways of meaning—of affirming, at once, not only likeness but unlikeness—sketches out Hölderlin's mode of translation quite precisely and highlights its key distinction from the theory and practice of translation as the path to

---

52. See Constantine's discussion of the poem and its depiction of a river that "puzzles him" with its west-east current, *The Significance of Locality in the Poetry of Friedrich Hölderlin* (Modern Humanities Research Association, 1979), 61f.
53. Stanley Corngold, "Comparative Literature: The Delay in Translation." In Bermann and Wood 144.

Bildung. For Hölderlin, translation is not "good for you" because it expands subjective horizons outward but because its effects unsettle identity at its very core. This leaves his translation practice at some distance not only from the "antiquarian" mode of imitating the ancients but also from the idea of "surrender" to the text that Herder proposes (and that contemporary translation theorists like Spivak have continued to refine). Hölderlin's investment lies rather in the possibility of rendering tragedy "more alive" by allowing the translation to speak, always imperfectly, of the complexity of relation between contexts and languages. The resonance of such "tragic effects" is evident, as we will see, in the extent to which Hölderlin's Sophocles has sent (and continues to send) ripples through modern concepts of translation, reading, and interpretation.

TWO

Distancing
Oedipal Solitude

> (it should be said from the start that Hölderlin will repeatedly prove to be an exception and so needs to be singled out as offering something unique) (Schmidt 2001: 19)

> But you, you must not put yourself at risk; your noble nature, the mirror of all that is beautiful must not shatter in you; you also owe to the world what appears to you transfigured in a higher form. . . . Few are like you![1]

Few are like him, as his muse Susette Gontard insists; and already, with the mirror placed both before him and in him, we begin to reflect on what has set him so very far apart. To be sure, the dominant image of Hölderlin in the German cultural imagination remains that of the *Einzelgänger*: the sensitive loner, the conflicted revolutionary, the tragically silent madman. His translations, moreover, were widely regarded as the unfortunate product of precisely that habit of risk-taking against which Susette warns here. "The translation of Sophocles fully expresses his ruined mental condition," a concerned Schelling wrote to Hegel in July 1804 (FA 16: 20), introducing a bias in reading these translations that would extend well into the twentieth century.[2] Yet starting from this point of departure, however

---

1. "Dich selbst darfst Du auf's Spiel nicht setzen, Deine edle Natur, der Spiegel alles Schönen darf nicht zerbrechen in Dir, Du bist der Welt auch schuldig zu geben, was Dir verklärt in höherer Gestalt erscheint . . . Wenige sind wie Du!" Letter from Susette Gontard to Friedrich Hölderlin (June 1799), StA VII: 80. There are several highly usable editions of Hölderlin's collected works, the Stuttgarter edition (StA) and the other, more recent and arguably more definitive edition, the "Frankfurter Ausgabe" (FA). Although I refer primarily to the FA in my discussion of the Sophocles translations, at certain points the StA is more clearly organized, in which case I have elected to refer to the StA..

2. Many commentators do strive to locate Hölderlin's tragedy project within its Idealist context,

tempting it may be, shifts our attention from the possibility that strangeness can itself mark out a path, even if the one less traveled by. If Hegel's and Schelling's attempts to define the tragic have come to represent the beginnings of a philosophical debate concerned with ethics and modern subjectivity—a debate that spans centuries and continents and still has not ended—then Hölderlin's engagement with Greek tragedy may have begun as a somewhat bizarre digression within that debate. Yet it proves to be a digression of almost uncanny fortitude, one that does not exhaust itself in its own incongruity but maintains a voice of its own. That likewise spans centuries and continents, and likewise has not ended.

While Hölderlin's confrontation with the tragic may appear as an anomaly in the tradition of reading and translating the Greeks, it also initiates a progression that has had a significant impact on concepts of tragedy and translation in the twentieth century. For readers at several different stages in the twentieth century, this translation project is not an isolated instance but the reflection of another way of thinking about the tragic within modernity. This other way raises questions that confront above all the problem of the work's place in history and thus make possible a more nuanced relationship to the past. How do we represent a past that eludes our comprehension? What is the responsibility of the translator or reader of ancient text vis-à-vis her "original"? Can the fundamental distinctiveness of an ancient source text be preserved in any meaningful way in the transition to a modern frame of reference?

Hölderlin began to reflect on such questions at a time when "the tragic" represented something else, namely, a retrieval of ancient themes in the service of modern aesthetics and epistemology. If this debate considered at all the gap between ancient and modern tragic experience, it was in the form of a question—how are we to understand the relevance of ancient tragedy for us today?—that had always already been answered, in the very intentionality of posing the question. However, such logic forecloses the possibility of preserving that which is not understood, that which cannot be made relevant—of allowing comprehension to slip its moorings in a manner that unsettles the solid ground on which the modern subject aims to stand. If Hölderlin's theoretical reflections on the tragic stand alone in any sense, it is here: while his contemporaries in Romantic and Idealist circles were largely

---

if only to demonstrate how it unsettles that context from within; see, for example, the seminal essays by Szondi ("Überwindung des Klassizismus," in *Hölderlin-Studien* [Frankfurt: Insel, 1967], 85–104) and Lacoue-Labarthe ("The Caesura of the Speculative") . See also Nägele, "Ancient Sports and Modern Transports," in *The Solid Letter: Readings of Friedrich Hölderlin,* ed. Aris Fioretos (Stanford: Stanford University Press, 1999): 250–51.

concerned with grounding experience in a self-recognition that would eradicate the epistemological gap embodied by the Kantian subject, Hölderlin's most salient contribution to the thinking of the tragic lies in his exposure of the instability at the heart of speculative thought, the ruptures underlying the conciliatory aims of both Romantic and Idealist philosophies in the wake of Kantian critique.[3] Ultimately, it is this naked instability that allows Hölderlin's Sophocles to appear so profoundly anomalous in its time—to appear, in fact, touched by madness—and yet also compel such passionate response in its wake.[4]

In the larger context of Hölderlin's work on tragedy and the idea of the tragic, which spans most of his productive life, these translations represent both culmination and resignation.[5] After failing three times between 1797 and 1800 to complete an original tragedy, *The Death of Empedocles*, Hölderlin turned to the translation project in earnest around 1801 with the probable intention of eventually translating all of Sophocles's works (Beissner 107f.). Idealist in initial conception if not in execution, the translations of *Oedipus* and *Antigone* with their accompanying remarks achieve a marriage of philosophy and poetic performance that eluded him in the *Empedocles* drafts. As his last published works, they represent his final accounting of the Idealist program and reveal, in place of that program's presumption of totality in the concept of intellectual intuition, the impossibility of conceiving totality. Nevertheless, they do not represent mere failure. While his three incomplete versions of *Empedocles* may anticipate the collapse of speculative thought into irreducible difference (both thematically and in practice), his Sophocles project introduces another trajectory of mediation, an "askew perspective" (*linkischer Gesichtspunkt*) through which the process of translation itself becomes the vehicle for a different conception of what tragedy can effect within modernity.

---

3. See Lacoue-Labarthe, "The Caesura of the Speculative," 61f.: "If . . . the culmination of philosophy is the stop-gap measure attempting to close the wound (re)opened, in extremis, by Kant in the thinking of the Same . . . —if, in short, it is this patching-over of the Kantian crisis . . . then Hölderlin . . . will have represented . . . the impossibility of overlaying this crisis, this wound still open in the tissue of philosophy, where the hand which attempts to close the wound only succeeds in reopening it."

4. Silke-Maria Weineck offers a rich discussion of Hölderlin's theory of tragedy in relation to (his) madness: she argues that the madness of the tragic hero, in contrast to the fantasy of poetic inspiration or "mania" that surrounded Hölderlin in his lifetime, is primarily an anti-poetic, philosophical construct "that must be contained by the counterforce of poetry." *The Abyss Above: Philosophy and Poetic Madness in Plato, Hölderlin and Nietzsche* (Albany: SUNY Press, 2002), 50f.

5. His publisher Friedrich Wilmans claimed that the translations were the result of ten years' work, an accurate representation if one goes back to Hölderlin's earliest attempts to translate Antigone in 1794. See D. E. Sattler's timeline in FA 16: 13–18.

As we have already seen, readings of the ethical dilemma played out in Greek tragedy have long shaped the construction of the modern subject in a profound sense; but Hölderlin's writings suggest another ethics, in which not only thematic details but also the dynamics of translation itself engender a specific effect. As the translations and notoriously difficult remarks will show, it is precisely as figures *in translation* that Oedipus and Antigone both mark and efface their own mythic status. Unlike the tragic heroes of classicism and Idealism, they present to modern culture neither an unattainable ideal, nor a mimetic challenge, nor a mere ethical prototype.[6] Instead, their particularity produces an effect that is more alienating and yet resonates more powerfully than these more conventional frameworks. While, as Karl Reinhardt has argued, a pattern of isolation is already set into motion in Sophoclean tragedy by a hero who stands alone,[7] for whom "the race is run,"[8] Hölderlin's logic expands this definition to encompass modern tragic experience as such, striving to make palpable an alienation that affects the hero but also implicates the subject who encounters him in another age and another mode of representation (what Hölderlin calls *Vorstellungsart*). Not only do Oedipus and Antigone stand defiantly apart from the *mise en scène*, but poetic language itself undergoes a process of insistent distancing from and disruption of the subject who aims to comprehend its message.[9]

This hinge between ancient text and modern experience is made most evident through Hölderlin's often disorienting practice of translation. Wedded to a syntax neither German nor Greek, his rendering of Sophocles evokes, as the translator and critic Susan Bernofsky has noted, "a space between

---

6. With respect to this question of Hölderlin's image of Greece and his view of mimesis, see Lacoue-Labarthe, "Hölderlin and the Greeks," trans. Judi Olson, rpt. in *Typography: Mimesis, Philosophy, Politics,* ed. Christopher Fynsk (Stanford: Stanford University Press, 1998), 236–47.

7. For Reinhardt, the "Sophoclean situation" involves above all the hero's recognition of his own radical solitude: "so erfaßt er sich als Mensch doch erst in seinem Preisgegeben- und Verlassen-Sein." Reinhardt, *Sophokles* (Frankfurt: Klostermann, 1947), 10.

8. Jacques Lacan invokes this phrase with reference to Sophoclean heroes in general, appropriating an observation by the Reinhardt. According to Lacan, Reinhardt is alone in pointing out the "special solitude" of Sophoclean heroes " . . . for in the end tragic heroes are always isolated, they are always beyond established limits, always in an exposed position and, as a result, separated in one way or another from the structure." This point has bearing on the solitude of Hölderlin's Oedipus as well. Jacques Lacan, *Seminar Book VII: The Ethics of Psychoanalysis,* trans. Dennis Porter (New York: Norton, 1992): 271.

9. Schmidt discusses this modern dilemma of the alienated subject in relation to Plato's claims about the dangers of tragic art for political life: "tragic art fosters a sense of the apartness of people thereby weakening, if not destroying, the sense of the common that is needed for a community to thrive" (Schmidt 2001, 43). This concern for the "anarchic potential" of language to isolate the individual at the expense of the community will certainly haunt Hegel's reading of the ethical conundrum of the *Antigone*. For Hölderlin, however, the isolation of the tragic hero—which is also always a confinement within language—is essential for tragedy to engender its most powerful effect.

languages" that can leave the reader at some distance from comprehension in any conventional sense.[10] Rather than attempting to adapt the tragic model to a modern setting or modify classical characters to make them recognizable to their new audience, his project disavows the prevailing perception in his time of tragic experience as a process of identification that evokes fear and pity for the hero onstage, offering the pleasurable relief of catharsis. If we can speak of catharsis at all in Hölderlin's reading of *Oedipus*, we will see it defined not as a mode of identificatory reconciliation between spectator and hero but as a gesture of severance, of a paradoxically purifying disruption of identification. Moreover, that disruption finally comes to inhabit a figure—that of Antigone—in a manner that magnifies a strangeness inherent to the modern subject itself.

Along with his general theory of tragedy, Hölderlin's model of translation in the Sophocles project diverges in significant ways from his contemporaries' views on the subject. Novalis, A. W. Schlegel, and Friedrich Schleiermacher all delineate the Romantic conception of translation as a fundamental element of apprehension itself, maintaining that translation should enact the expansion or *Bildung* of the self via the experience of the foreign, a "positing oneself beyond oneself" that is literally an *Über-setzung*, a crossing-over.[11] Hölderlin's model appears similar, at least at first glance; even if much of what constitutes the foreign text is necessarily "lost in translation," both theories aim to reveal what is gained at the same time. However, while both Hölderlin and the Romantics wish to potentiate the original by enabling it to say something other than what it had said in the source language, Hölderlin's project and the figure at its center do not replicate the Romantic dynamics of expansion into the unknown and reappropriation into a more perfect self. Indeed, as evidenced in a letter to his publisher Wilmans in April 1804, his efforts aim in quite another direction:

> Ich hoffe, die griechische Kunst, die uns fremd ist, durch Nationalkonvenienz und Fehler, mit denen sie sich immer herum beholfen hat, dadurch lebendiger, als gewöhnlich dem Publikum darzustellen, dass ich das Ori-

---

10. Susan Bernofsky, "Hölderlin as Translator: The Perils of Interpretation," *Germanic Review* 76:3 (Summer 2001): 231.

11. See Berman's discussion of the Romantics' view of translation as critical movement: "Its scope is not merely the original in its crude being. . . . The original itself, in what the Romantics call its 'tendency,' possesses an *a priori* scope: the Idea of the Work which the work tends towards . . . but empirically never is. In this respect, the original is only the copy—the translation, if you want—of this a priori figure which presides over its being and gives it its necessity." Translation, by contrast, distances the work from this initial empirical layer that separated it from the Idea, hence bringing it closer to its truth" (Berman 107).

entalische, das sie verläugnet hat, mehr heraushebe, und ihren Kunstfehler, wo er vorkommt, verbessere.

> I hope to represent Greek art, which is foreign to us through the conformity to the national and the flaws to which it has always resorted, as more alive than usual to the public by bringing out the Oriental element that it has disavowed and by correcting its artistic flaw where it occurs. (FA 16: 19)

Hölderlin's desire to render the Greek text "more alive than usual" does not reflect the Romantic subject's attempt to come to individual terms with the foreign, since for Hölderlin it is the conformity to "national" forms of expression that has siphoned the life out of Greek art. Rather, he aims to bring to light a secondary alterity, the "Oriental," that not only mobilizes the experience of the foreign in modern translation but undermines the stability of the original as well, by highlighting an element of Greek identity (the "Oriental") that remains inaccessible to itself. What previous modern renderings of Greek tragedy lack is thus a subversive facet of the text that is silent in the language of the original but makes itself heard in another register, namely, in the manner in which the tragedy, through its disclosure of that previously imperceptible alterity, becomes "alive" to its audience: in simpler words, in its dramatic effect. If tragedy has always implicitly borne the impression of that source of "life," Hölderlin aims to grant it a voice through his translation. Neither reinforcing the Romantics' expansionist logic nor attempting to recover a unified, idealized identity of Greek art, for Hölderlin the dynamics of translation retrace and even intensify the *dis*-appropriating process by which tragedy produces its most unsettling effects. And it is precisely within this logic of (tragedy in) translation that the defiant solitude of his principal characters will eventually come to represent an ethical stance like no other.

The translation project is the central pillar of Hölderlin's confrontation with Greek tragedy, but the roots of this project extend deeply and broadly within his poetic and philosophical writings. As Charlie Louth has shown, structures of translation infiltrate his poetry to a considerable extent,[12] and even a cursory examination of Hölderlin's writings both previous to and contemporary with his translation work indicates that classical tragic figures are central to his theoretical reflections.[13] An understanding of the context

---

12. See in particular Louth's Chapters 5 and 6, which examine Hölderlin's later writings, including the Sophocles translations.

13. For a detailed discussion of Hölderlin's use of mythic figures in the service of messianic thought, see Robert Charlier, *Heros und Messias: Hölderlins messianische Mythogenese und das jüdische*

in which Hölderlin undertook these translations can not only help to illuminate their more obscure elements but also underscore their crucial status within his overall body of work.

IN THE EXCERPT from Susette Gontard's letter at the start of this chapter, the mirror maintains a corrective role, not just reflecting the world as it appears to the poet but also altering what it means to reflect by presenting it in a higher form. By contrast, Hölderlin's own representation of the mirror image, composed some years later, assumes a less familiar, even monstrous cast. In the disputed text "In lieblicher Bläue . . . " (*In lovely blueness*), a late but undated piece whose origins remain murky, we find a mirror image that both resonates with the stabilizing gesture of Gontard's description and alludes to its potential disruption:[14]

> Wenn einer in den Spiegel siehet, ein Mann, und siehet darin sein Bild, wie abgemalt; es gleicht dem Manne, Augen hat des Menschen Bild, hingegen Licht der Mond. Der König Ödipus hat ein Auge zu viel vielleicht. Diese Leiden dieses Mannes, sie scheinen unbeschreiblich, unaussprechlich, unausdrücklich. (StA II: 1, 372)

> When someone looks into a mirror, a man, and sees in it his image, as if painted; it resembles the man, the human image has eyes, whereas the moon has light. King Oedipus has one eye too many, perhaps. The sufferings of this man, they seem indescribable, unspeakable, inexpressible. (Schmidt 2001, 170; trans. modified)

Denken (Würzburg: Königshausen & Neumann, 1999). However, Charlier focuses not on Oedipus and Antigone but on the recurrence in Hölderlin's thought of other Greek heroes who are, strictly speaking, not "tragic"—Icarus, Heracles, and Proteus—as well as the tragic figure of Dionysus.

14. The poem was first published in prose form by Hölderlin's biographer F. W. Waiblinger in his 1823 novel *Phaëton;* however, Waiblinger contended that the original text was written by Hölderlin in a Pindaric style of verse ("nach Pindarischer Weise"). Norbert von Hellingrath, editor of an early version of Hölderlin's collected works, was the first to attempt reconstruction of that poetic structure (*Hölderlins Sämtliche Werke, Sechster Band,* eds. Hellingrath, Friedrich Seebass and Ludwig Pigenot [Berlin: Propyläen, 1923]: 26 [*Lesarten* 490ff.]). Heidegger also employs the version in verse in his body of work on this text ("Hölderlin und das Wesen der Dichtung," " . . . dichterisch wohnet der Mensch . . . "), while Beissner reproduces the text as prose (StA II:1, 372). Though Beissner maintained that the text may have been written by Waiblinger himself in a somewhat "Hölderlinian" style, the image of Oedipus in particular resonates so strikingly with Hölderlin's other writings that Waiblinger's claims about the text's authenticity seem convincing. More recently scholars have attempted to make a case for the poem's authenticity. See A. den Besten, "Ein Auge zuviel vielleicht: Bemerkungen zu einem als apokryph geltenden Hölderlin-Gedicht," in *Poesie und Philosophie in einer tragischen Kultur,* ed. Heinz Kimmerle (Würzburg: Königshausen & Neumann, 1995), 87–122.

Compared with the "mirror of all that is beautiful" in Gontard's letter, this passage represents both an echo and a distancing, a reinforcement and a disruption. The image of the mirror does approximate a man closely enough that he may recognize it as "*his* image," but without apprehending the particular beauty that this image reflected for Gontard; eyes see the image that both resembles and equals (*gleicht*). But what on earth does it equal? If for Susette the gleam of the mirror reflects all of the beauty that the poet's soul has to offer, here that light projects something far less remarkable—something even marked by a reduction, "as if painted" (*wie abgemalt*)—with eyes lacking luminescence when compared with the moon. If the reflected image does equal something here, that something remains remote from the intuition of plenitude that the "mirror of all that is beautiful" initially calls to mind.

Moreover, any semblance of complementarity between subject and image is overturned in the very next moment with the emergence of a figure that, as the text suggests, cannot possibly become "equal." In an abrupt turn of phrase that fractures the elongated prosaic flow of the sentence before it, a tragic figure interrupts. "King Oedipus has one eye too many, perhaps": the familiar image in the mirror shatters and comes tumbling down. Far from being an exemplary figure, Oedipus is is the jarring exception to the universality of the mirror scene. But what does it mean to say that he has "one eye too many"? What does having "too many" eyes have to do with the ability to see, and what does that have to do with the suffering of the tragic hero, not to mention its troubled representation in poetic language? For after all, if the mythic Oedipus has a figurative excess in eyes, that factor does little more for him in the end than to force him to see too much—and then quite literally not to see at all, only to suffer. It is this "one eye too many" that marks Oedipus with an excess of suffering; it introduces a difference that is marred by deformity, that shatters the glass and the *Gleichnis* of the mirror with its resistance to the dialectical equation that generated the human image.

This resistance is timely, emerging just as German intellectuals seek to come to terms with a rift in the possibility of grounding knowledge in self-consciousness. Indeed, it begins to expose Fichte's statement "Ich bin ich," his fundamental conception of a subject's potential for absolute self-intuition, as riven by a difference that exceeds that equation.[15] In the *Critique of Pure Reason*, Kant had introduced a division not only characteristic

---

15. Thomas Pfau locates the backdrop for the Idealist project in precisely this dilemma, introduced by the thought of Kant and Fichte. Pfau, *Idealism and the Endgame of Theory* (Albany: SUNY Press, 1994), 26.

but constitutive of the subject. Proclaiming in the preface the equivalent of a Copernican revolution in philosophy, he reversed the conventional view that knowledge must conform to objects, proposing instead the principle of objects' necessary submission to the subject.[16] Yet this "revolution" bears other consequences, for insofar as it distinguishes the subject's apprehension and understanding of phenomena from the *Ding an sich*, which cannot be known, it also sets limits for the subject *an sich;* the Kantian subject is unable to present itself to itself, absolutely. By asserting, in the section on the Transcendental Aesthetic, that the "I" cannot assume its own unity or autonomy beyond internal intuition, Kant revealed that the subject can only ever presuppose its own identity.

> If the faculty of coming to consciousness of oneself is to seek out (to apprehend) that which lies in the mind, it must affect the mind, and only in this way can it give rise to an intuition of itself. But the form of this intuition, which exists antecedently in the mind, determines, in the representation of time, the mode in which the manifold is together in the mind, since it then intuits itself *not as it would represent itself if immediately self-active,* but as it is affected by itself, and therefore *as it appears to itself, not as it is.* (my emphasis)[17]

With this axiom Kant constructs the subject's potential for self-recognition in the inescapable terms of reflexivity rather than immediacy; the "I," just like the objects it apprehends and which affect it, can only ever appear as representation.[18] The imposition of this limit on knowledge was devastating to the notion of an enlightened autonomous and self-present subject—

---

16. See Deleuze's discussion of Kant's reversal here, its consequences, and its difference from the subjective idealism that follows it in *Kant's Critical Philosophy: The Doctrine of the Faculties,* trans Hugh Tomlinson and Barbara Habberjam (London: Athlone Press, 1984), 13f.

17. Immanuel Kant, *Critique of Pure Reason,* 2nd ed., trans. Norman Kemp Smith (Houndmills: Palgrave MacMillan, 2003), 88. "Wenn das Vermögen, sich bewusst zu werden, das, was in Gemüte liegt, aufsuchen (apprehendieren) soll, so muss es dasselbe affizieren, und kann allein auf solche Art eine Anschauung seiner selbst hervorbringen . . . da es dann sich selbst anschauet, *nicht wie es sich unmittelbar selbsttätig vorstellen würde,* sondern nach der Art, wie es von innen affiziert wird, folglich *wie es sich erscheint, nicht wie es ist*" (*Kritik der reinen Vernunft,* in *Werke:* Band III, ed. Wilhelm Weischedel ([Frankfurt: Suhrkamp, 1974] 93 [B69]). My emphasis.

18. Deleuze illustrates Kant's position with a citation from Rimbaud, "I is another." The form of the inner sense as time is one that is only thought in spatial (thus distant, mediated) terms, while the receptive experience of changes in time (Ego, *moi*) remains separated from an active synthesis of time (I, *je*): "The I and the Ego are thus separated by the line of time which relates them to each other, but under the condition of a fundamental difference. [. . .] 'Form of interiority' means not only that time is internal to us, but that our interiority constantly divides us from ourselves, splits us in two: a splitting in two which never runs its course, since time has no end." *Kant's Critical Philosophy,* ix.

such as the subject Lessing hoped to condition through a new approach to theater—and the turmoil that ensued would continue to ripple through discourses of philosophy and literature for decades to come. While Idealists endeavored, through the labor of the concept, to reclaim the subject's self-presence in the face of division, Romanticism aimed for the subject's auto-production in the work of art, within the experience of beauty.[19] What both these attempts present above all is the desire that triggered their movement, what Lacoue-Labarthe and Nancy have called the will to System (*la volonté du Système*). The aims of both speculative Idealism and Romanticism form an exigency announced in the future, an overcoming of dissonance, not yet there but "to do;"[20] as Schelling writes in a letter to Hegel, "We must continue with philosophy!—Kant has swept *everything* away" (*Wir müssen noch weiter it der Philosophie!—Kant hat alles weggeräumt*).[21]

Given the convergence of this crisis in philosophy with the attempt, after Lessing and Winckelmann, to reinvent tragedy in the spirit of enlightened humanism, it is perhaps no surprise that the Greeks are very soon placed into the service of this "to do" as the exemplary text of post-Kantian philosophy. A philosophical inquiry into the essence of the tragic is initiated in the same moment that German Idealism gives birth to itself in the throes of a crisis; thus while Lessing remained within the sphere of poetics, Friedrich Schelling represents for Szondi the first philosopher of the tragic.[22] The dif-

---

19. See also Walter Benjamin's *Concept of Criticism in German Romanticism* (*Begriff der Kunstkritik in der deutschen Romantik*), in which he discusses the Romantic conception of reflection as capable of bearing the absolute; despite its infinite character, thought (including the concept of the "Ich") is "substantial and fulfilled in itself,"(*in sich selbst substanziell und erfüllt*). *Gesammelte Schriften*, Band 1:1, ed. Tiedemann and Schweppenhäuser (Frankfurt: Suhrkamp, 1974): 31.

20. Lacoue-Labarthe and Nancy 33. To be sure, their heavy privileging of philosophy as the precursor to Romanticism has not gone unchallenged; Jean-Pierre Mileur argues that their "philosocentrism" neglects the equivocity of Romantic literary practice, reducing it to a mere effect of theory ("The Return of the Romantic," in Rajan and Clark, *Intersections: 19th-Century Philosophy and Theory* [Albany: SUNY Press, 1995], 325–48). While Lacoue-Labarthe and Nancy, according to Mileur, suggest that literature "lacks propriety" and thus requires a "properly philosophical" orientation, he invokes the "possibility that literature's impropriety, even if or even because it encourages a proliferation of approaches to criticism, might be a positive advantage, its main advantage in contrast to philosophy . . . " (337)

21. Letter from Friedrich Schelling to G. W. F. Hegel, 6 January 1795. In *Briefe von und an Hegel, Band I: 1785–1812,* ed. Johannes Hoffmeister (Hamburg: Felix Meiner, 1952), 14. As the youthful triumvirate of Schelling, Hölderlin, and Hegel posited in their collaborative fragment *Das älteste Systemprogramm des deutschen Idealismus* (1796), that aspiration also marks the culmination of humankind: "A higher spirit, sent from heaven, will found this new religion among us; it will be the last great work of humankind" (*Ein höherer Geist, vom Himmel gesandt, muss diese neue Religion unter uns stiften, sie wird das letzte große Werk der Menschheit sein*). In FA 14: 17 (trans. Schmidt 85). The *Systemprogramm* is included in the collected works of all three of its purported authors.

22. Peter Szondi, *Versuch über das Tragische*, 7 (*An Essay on the Tragic*, trans. Paul Fleming [Stanford: Stanford University Press, 2002], 1). Szondi begins by distinguishing poetics from philosophy

ference emerges in their disparate accounts of what tragedy can and must represent in their day and age; while Lessing, following tradition as well as attempting to establish his own, regards tragic art as a means to edify the self, for Schelling tragedy, as the highest form of art, has the potential to take over where philosophy reaches its conceptual limits (Schmidt 74). Where speculative reason can no longer account for contradiction, the tragic aesthetic both highlights that contradiction and makes it bearable to the viewing subject.

The contrast between Hölderlin's monstrous image of Oedipus and that of his close collaborator Schelling is intriguing enough to warrant a brief elaboration. Schelling's discussion of the tragic in the tenth of the *Philosophische Briefe über Dogmatismus und Kritizismus* (1795–96) is framed by his efforts to differentiate between two poles of philosophical inquiry with respect to (as Peter Fenves writes) "the nature of the unconditioned, the absolute, or to use a misleading term, God."[23] Dogmatism, represented by Spinoza and Leibniz, and criticism, represented by Fichte and Kant, were for Schelling the only valid ways to conceive of the absolute and thereby found a philosophical system.[24] The former is based on a conception of the absolute object or Not-I, the latter on the absolute subject or I, and the task that remains of philosophy is to determine by which path the unconditioned might be reached.[25] For Schelling, this task can only be addressed

---

insofar as poetics, ancient and modern, offer a strictly empirical approach to the tragedy, not its "idea"; its concern is specific dramatic effect, whereas Idealist philosophy placed emphasis on determining what, it fact, *is* tragic. Historically speaking, Szondi, citing Hegel, finds it logical that tragic theory can only ever follow its praxis with considerable delay: "To understand the historical relation prevailing between nineteenth-century theory and seventeenth-century and eighteenth-century practice, one must assume that the flight of Minerva's owl over this landscape also begins only with the onset of dusk" (Szondi 2002, 2) (*Vielmehr wäre zum Verständnis des historischen Bezugs, der zwischen der Theories des neunzehnten und der Praxis des siebzehnten und achtzehnten Jahrhunderts waltet, anzunehmen, dass die Eule der Minerva ihren Flug auch über dieser Landschaft erst mit der einbrechenden Dämmerung beginnt* [Szondi 1961, 8]).

23. Peter Fenves, "The Scale of Enthusiasm," in *Enthusiasm and Enlightenment in Europe 1650–1850*, ed. Lawrence E. Klein and Anthony J. LaVopa (San Marino, CA: Huntington Library, 1998), 136.

24. To a certain extent, however, Kant does not ideally represent the standpoint of criticism for Schelling, because his *Critique of Pure Reason* is not just a philosophical system among others but the point of departure for all philosophical systems, whether informed by criticism or dogmatism. See the "Editorischer Bericht" written by Annemarie Pieper in Schelling, *Werke 3*, ed. Hartmut Buchner, Wilhelm G. Jacobs, and Annemarie Pieper (Stuttgart: Frommann-Holzboog, 1982): 23.

25. See his letter to Hegel from 4 February 1795: "Der eigentliche Unterschied der kritischen und dogmatischen Philosophie scheint mir darin zu liegen, daß jene vom absoluten (noch durch kein Objekt bedingten) Ich, diese vom absoluten Objekt oder Nicht-Ich ausgeht. . . . Vom *Unbedingten* muß die Philosophie ausgehen. Nun fragt sich's nur, worin dies Unbedingte liegt, im Ich oder im Nicht-Ich. Ist diese Frage entschieden, so ist *alles* entschieden." *Briefe von und an Hegel*, 22.

in a practical sense, through the idea of freedom: "For me the highest principle of all philosophy is the pure, absolute I, that is, the I insofar as it is simply I, not yet conditioned by objects at all, but rather posited through *freedom*" (Schelling to Hegel, 4 February 1795 [my emphasis]).²⁶ Endowed with a freedom that is both point of departure and ultimate goal, the human subject obtains the possibility of moving beyond the limitations of a world conditioned by objects and attaining the infinite, the "supersensual" (*übersinnliche*) world.

It is with respect to this question of freedom that Schelling turns to tragedy in the tenth letter of the series; underscoring his claim that great art can represent what reason can no longer conceive theoretically, Schelling maintains that tragedy illustrates the extent to which freedom contends with necessity. Opposing human freedom with an "objective power" bent on disrupting that freedom, he manages to argue that even man's submission to the machinations of fate can affirm the force of freedom.

> You are right, one thing remains—to know that there is an objective power which threatens to annihilate our freedom, and with this firm and certain conviction in our hearts, to fight against it, to summon up the whole of one's freedom, and thus to go down (Schmidt 2001, 86).²⁷

This scenario, Schelling asserts, is thematized in the tragic situation: by allowing the hero both to struggle against the superior power of the objective world and to expiate his crime willingly, Greek tragedy affirms human freedom. It is this affirmation, in fact, that makes tragedy tolerable to its audience.

> The *reason* for this contradiction, that which made it bearable, lay deeper than the level at which it has been sought: it lay in the conflict of human freedom with the power of the objective world, a conflict in which the mortal necessarily had to succumb when that power was a superior power—a *fatum;* and yet, since he did not succumb without a struggle, he had to be punished for this very defeat. The fact that the criminal succumbed only to the superior force of fate and yet was punished all the same—this was the recognition of human freedom, an *honor* owed to freedom. (Schmidt 2001, 86)²⁸

---

26. *Briefe*, 22: "Mir ist das höchste Prinzip aller Philosophie das reine, absolute Ich, d.h. das Ich, inwiefern es bloßes Ich, noch gar nicht durch Objekte bedingt, sondern durch Freiheit gesetzt ist."

27. "Sie haben Recht, noch Eines bleibt übrig—zu *wissen*, dass es eine objective Macht giebt, die unsrer Freiheit Vernichtung droht, und mit dieser festen und gewissen Ueberzeugung im Herzen— *gegen* sie zu kämpfen, seiner ganzen Freiheit aufzubieten, und *so* unterzugehen" (*Werke* 106).

28. "Der *Grund* dieses Widerspruchs, das, was ihn erträglich machte, lag tiefer, als man ihn such-

With this logic, the tragic universe becomes recognizable from within the framework of Idealism. It is not merely the fact that the tragic hero is subject to fate that ensures his downfall; he is punished *because* he exerts his freedom by fighting against necessity. His punishment is thus a (negative) recognition of freedom: only a subject who possesses freedom—and exercises it—can be deprived of it by fate. This represents tragedy's great insight for Schelling: where philosophy exhausts itself, the "highest in art"—tragedy—allows us to "think" beyond the limits placed on freedom by a higher power.

> It was a great thought to willingly bear punishment even for an inevitable crime; in this way he was able to demonstrate his freedom precisely through the loss of this freedom, and still to go under with a declaration of free will. (Schmidt 2001, 86; trans. modified)[29]

Schelling's invocation of the hero's freedom here is clearly marked by the dialectical force of its time, as Lacoue-Labarthe has argued: insofar as the tragic subject invokes his freedom in the very moment of losing it, a negative is transformed into a positive, and the struggle, however futile it has appeared, proves productive.[30] The tragic conflict, by itself intolerable for Schelling, thus offers through this force of negativity the possibility of a resolution, and the "'idealist' interpretation . . . of tragedy" is born (Lacoue-Labarthe 217).

By virtue of this opening towards resolution, however, Schelling's interpretation runs counter to the notion that tragic art has the potential to exceed the limits of philosophy; in fact, this model embeds tragedy deeply *within* philosophy. As Szondi has discussed, the tragic comes into play here as a "third way" between dogmatism and criticism, representing the space in which those two poles come into conflict with one another.[31] But precisely by making tragedy recognizable within this intellectual context, Schelling

---

te, lag im Streit menschlicher Freiheit mit der Macht der objectiven Welt, in welchem der Sterbliche, wenn jene Macht eine Uebermacht—(ein Fatum)—ist, *nothwendig* unterliegen, und doch, weil er nicht *ohne Kampf* unterlag, für sein Unterliegen selbst *bestraft* werden mußte. Daß der Verbrecher, der doch nur der Uebermacht des Schicksals unterlag, doch noch *bestraft* wurde, war Anerkennung menschlicher Freiheit, *Ehre* die der Freiheit gebührte" (*Werke* 106f.).

29. "Es war ein großer Gedanke, willig auch die Strafe für ein unvermeidliches Verbrechen zu tragen, um so durch den Verlust seiner Freiheit selbst eben diese Freiheit zu beweisen, und noch mit einer Erklärung des freien Willens unterzugehen" (*Werke*, 107).

30. See Lacoue-Labarthe, "Caesura," 217. Schellings emphasis on the hero's freedom runs counter to the view of classicists with respect to the possibility of deliberate action in tragedy. As Vernant argues, the Greeks had no word to denote the category of "will," hence the question of individual action or choice becomes more delicate than Schelling allows here. See Vernant, "Intimations of the Will in Greek Tragedy," in Vernant and Vidal-Naquet 49–84.

31. See Szondi's analysis in *Versuch über das Tragische*, 13–16. See also Pfau 1994, 35.

clips its wings. While in Schelling's view the tragic spectacle allows contradiction to become tolerable (if not entirely reconcilable), the performative dissonances endemic to tragedy—the divisions and tensions on which Hölderlin will soon train his eye—remain unconsidered.[32]

While Schelling places Oedipus' plight in the service of the Idealist project, then, for Hölderlin the central question of the tragedy is rather how Oedipus reflects—or rather attempts and fails to reflect—the Idealist "will to system." If Oedipus' suffering remains for Hölderlin "indescribable, unspeakable, inexpressible," its semblance in language necessarily involves the containment, within the limits of reflection, of a confrontation that cannot be wholly absorbed. However, Hölderlin also opens up another path by evoking an image that exceeds its own representational form. By disrupting the subject's relation to the mirror with his "one eye too many"—a human form that suggests its own unrecognizability—Oedipus presents the negative side of the post-Kantian problem of the unmistakable, yet unknowable difference that shatters the mirror of speculation.[33] In the figure of Oedipus, Hölderlin gives form to a difficult suspension within the subject between the grounding of self-consciousness in reflection and a negativity that cannot be contained by that ground. His conception of the tragic hero thus implies that this negativity reveals itself as an other that can never be known.[34]

In this respect, it is appropriate that Oedipus appears as disfigured in a text written near the end of Hölderlin's productive life, a point at which tragedy had already for some time been the focal point of a protest and a shift with respect to attempts to contain subjectivity within a model of reflection. While the development of a philosophy of the tragic in speculative Idealism

---

32. See Jan Mieszkowski's concise and articulate summary of Schelling's text and Szondi's reading, "Tragedy and the War of the Aesthetic," in *Schelling and Romanticism*, ed. David Ferris (Romantic Circles Praxis Series, June 2000) http://www.rc.umd.edu/praxis/schelling/mieszkowski/mieszkowski.html.

33. For a thorough discussion of the significance of the mirror and the trope of reflection in post-Enlightenment philosophy, see Gasché, *The Tain of the Mirror*. See also Mark Taylor's substantive review, "Foiling Reflection," *Diacritics* 18:2 (Spring 1988): 60.

34. Schelling's later work can also be read in the context of this countermovement, which David L. Clark names as the "tropic of negativity": "to engage rather than sublate that which resists all pretensions to wholly systematic thought." Schelling's recognition that the structure of reflection always bears something irreducible to a self-present origin marks the entrance into a phase of self-critique that already approaches the radical thinking of "the unprescribable" characteristic of Derrida's concept of *différance* and De Man's materiality of the letter. Clark, "'The Necessary Heritage of Darkness': Tropics of Negativity in Schelling, Derrida, and de Man," in Rajan and Clark 82ff. Pfau develops a similar argument with regard to Schelling's contribution to contemporary theory in his critical introduction to a translation of three late essays by the philosopher (Pfau 1994, 1–57). See also Andrew Bowie's article in Rajan and Clark, "Non-Identity: The German Romantics, Schelling, and Adorno," 243–60.

bears witness to the rise and fall of the attempt to build a system around the subject, Hölderlin's tragic figures—Oedipus and Antigone as well as Empedocles before them—suffer precisely the untenability of the "will to system." For Hölderlin it is this suffering, voiced in a solitary lament, which situates the tragic hero with respect to the modern subject who encounters him. Insofar as our view of Oedipus' fate is defined by the margins of what can be known, the representation of suffering itself becomes another kind of suffering, one instigated—also parallel to Oedipus—by a reluctant recognition of limits. The effect that the structure of tragedy engenders, however, unlike the inexpressible suffering of Oedipus, must not necessarily bring on despair. That strange rupture, once acknowledged, in fact becomes something of a fascination, a momentary encounter with the outer reaches of comprehensibility, otherwise enveloped and disguised by the rush of signification: "that soon it is no longer the change of representation (*der Wechsel der Vorstellung*) that appears but the representation itself" (FA 16: 250). At the same time, language also comes up against an uncrossable horizon of difference from itself and expresses itself finally—and logically, even appropriately—by translation rather than figuration.[35]

This is the point at which Hölderlin's Empedocles, standing at the edge of Mt. Etna, reaches the limits of his usefulness as a figure of speculative thought and where Oedipus, perhaps, becomes necessary.[36] While Empedocles suffers from the impossibility of union with the gods—in other words, the limits of self-recognition and representation from which essentially all German Idealists suffered—Hölderlin's *Oedipus* reflects the consequences of that monstrous union. Moreover, the translation allows that problem to be reframed as an exposure to the alienation that sets in with the transfer from ancient text to modern context. The conflict, then, is not merely represented in the character of the tragic hero but interwoven into the modern subject's experience of the translated text as well.

---

35. Hölderlin often expresses despair at the limitations of poetic language to achieve the kind of revelation he sought in aesthetics, so that a final turn to translation makes perfect sense. From a letter to his friend Neuffer from 12 November 1798: " . . . und es ergreift mich oft, daß ich weinen muß, wie ein Kind, wenn ich um und um fühle, wie es meinen Darstellungen an einem und dem andern fehlt, und ich doch aus den poetischen Irren, in denen ich herumwandele, mich nicht herauswinden kann" (StA VI:1, 289 (*and it often seizes me, so that I must weep like a child, when I feel all around me how my representations lack this and that, and yet that I cannot extricate myself out of the poetic drift in which I wander about*).

36. See David Ferrell Krell, *The Tragic Absolute* (University of Nebraska Press, 2005), where he claims that both *Hyperion* and *Empedokles* should be understood as "steps *toward* Sophoclean tragedy, not departures from or progressions beyond it" (281).

HÖLDERLIN'S OEDIPUS is above all a figure that shuns limits, transgressing with the force that only his feverish desire to know his past and his parentage can produce, regardless of the consequences. Andrzej Warminski has this specifically Hölderlinian valence in mind when he describes Oedipus's dilemma as an "Empedocles complex"[37]: the imperative to know, to draw connections, that too often leads to the tragedy of misread signs. Although Jocasta, his mother and wife, implores him to halt at a limit that keeps him at a remove from his past, to accept ignorance of his identity as a safeguard against self-destruction, he presses on; the tamer of the Sphinx will not be denied access to absolute knowledge. And thus in Hölderlin's remarks on the tragedy it is not only Oedipus's knowledge that proves to exceed certain ethical limits—the discovery that, contrary to his previous assumptions, he has fulfilled the words of the oracle at Delphi by murdering his father and marrying his mother—but also that desire for knowledge itself: "because knowledge, when it has torn through its barriers, spurs itself on to know more than it can bear or grasp" (*weil das Wissen, wenn es seine Schranke durchrissen hat . . . sich selbst reizt, mehr zu wissen, als es tragen oder fassen kann* [FA 16: 253]). What he sees with his one eye too many—and, in effect, what we see him seeing—is therefore perhaps nothing more than the existence of that same, excess eye, insofar as that eye both brings a trace of the abyss into focus and names that trace as too much to bear. Hence it will be the fate of Oedipus to destroy his other eyes in the eternally futile attempt to shut this one, as if to say that, after having witnessed the return of this unspeakable excess—as we shall soon hear it called in Hölderlin's texts, the monstrous, "das Ungeheure"—no eye will ever see anything else again.

> Die goldnen Nadeln riß er vom Gewand,
> Mit denen sie geschmückt war, that es auf,
> Und stach ins Helle seiner Augen sich und sprach,
> So ungefähr, es sei, damit er sie nicht säh
> Und was er leid' und was er schlimm gethan,
> Damit in Finsterniß er anderer in Zukunft,
> Die er nicht sehen dürft,' ansichtig werden mög'
> Und denen er bekannt sei, unbekannt. (FA 16, 221)

> The golden needles ornamenting her
> He tore them from her dress and opened them

---

37. *Readings in Interpretation: Hölderlin, Hegel, Heidegger* (Minneapolis: University of Minnesota Press, 1987), 18.

> And stabbed into the bright of his eyes and said
> This thereabouts: so that he would not see them
> And not what he was suffering and what bad he had done
> So that in darkness in the future that would be
> How he saw others whom he must not see
> And those that he was known to, unbeknownst. (Constantine 55; trans. modifed)[38]

While a more correct rendering of the Greek would have Oedipus piercing his own eyes so that *they* would not see *him* in his misery, Hölderlin radically mistranslates the passage here, placing Oedipus into the subjective position of seeing (or more precisely, of not seeing) his own eyes and thus situating the view of the eyes themselves on a level with what those eyes have seen: "And stabbed into the bright of his eyes and said this thereabouts: so that *he* would not see *them* (*damit er sie nicht säh*) and what he was suffering and what bad he had done.[39] As we will see throughout our discussion of Hölderlin's translations, his choice here is a telling "mistake." Sophocles unmistakably places Oedipus in the objective position (*oth' ounek' ouk opsointo nin*), but Hölderlin's use of the nominative masculine pronoun *er* leaves no doubt that Oedipus is the subject, *sie* (referring to the eyes in accusative plural) the object. If Oedipus no longer wishes to see his own eyes ("damit er *sie* nicht säh,'" so that he should not see *them*), and if seeing with one's own eyes is analogous to knowing, then it is not only the knowing that is dangerous but also the awareness of that knowledge. What Oedipus suffers retroactively is rooted both in his will to delve too deeply into his own past and in the realization that this will confronts him finally with the simple knowledge that he has advanced too far. With the knowledge that he has propelled himself into a place of solitude, of darkness from which his eyes can no longer recognize any other, at all.

Whether it is deliberate or not, this moment of mistranslation reflects

---

38. Constantine translates the accusative object "sie" in Hölderlin's translation as "her" rather than "them," extending the reference to Jocasta rather than Oedipus's own eyes. In this case, the implication would not be that Oedipus should never see his own eyes but rather that he should not see Jocasta before him.

39. The Greek line reads "oth' ounek' ouk opsointo nin" (that they should not see him). Most modern translators get this pronoun pair right, including Solger, a near-contemporary of Hölderlin: "Denn aus der Frau Gewändern goldgetriebene / Brustspangen reißend, ihre Schmuckbefestigung, / Erhob er die, und traf der Augenkreise Paar, / Mit solchem Laut: nie sollten ihn sie wiederschaun, / Noch was er duldet, oder was er Böses that . . . " [57] (*Tearing the golden clasps from the woman's robes, he raised the jeweled fastenings and struck his pair of eyes while saying this: never should they see him again, nor what he endured, nor the evil he has done*).

something considerably larger than itself, for Hölderlin's interest in the contours and limits of knowledge—and the consequences of transgressing those limits—colors his work on tragedy from the start. Sophocles underscores the distinction between mere sight and insight, using the verb *eidon/oida*, which suggests both seeing and knowing, for Tiresias, while Oedipus is connected primarily with verbs implying discovery or a superficial kind of sight, *heurisko* and *blepo*.[40] For Hölderlin, however, Oedipus emerges as a counterpart to Empedocles, as the hero in dogged pursuit of an insight, a theoretical instance greater than the human subject can bear. *This* Oedipus, Hölderlin's Oedipus of 1804, is thus a product of both the poet's method of translation and a post-Idealist thinking inspired by his lengthy and intensive engagement with tragedy.

Hölderlin's earliest musings on the subject, from around 1794, already evince a struggle between the attempt to "unite ourselves with nature in an infinite whole" in an aesthetic realm and the theoretical awareness, gained from intensive study of Kant and Fichte at the university in Jena, that the subject is necessarily split from itself in the moment of consciousness.[41] This is Empedocles' conflict, not to mention the probable source of Hölderlin's frustration at his own inability to be "done" with the death of Empedocles (see Warminski xx). Indeed, his struggle to finish this text seems to have taken on the cast of what he calls "infinite approximation" (*unendliche Annäherung*). replicating Empedocles' distaste at existing in a world which cannot support the ultimate speculative solution in any other form than that of suicide—or, in the author's case, the killing of representation.[42] This

---

40. I am grateful to Jennifer Ballengee for this observation. See Chapter 2 of her book *The Wound and the Witness: The Rhetoric of Torture* (SUNY Press, 2009), 45f.

41. The clearest articulation of his theoretical doubts about achieving a unified self comes in his 1794 fragment *Urteil und Sein,* which directs itself in particular against Fichte's *Wissenschaftslehre* and its conception of intellectual intuition; for Hölderlin here, the "Ur-teilung" of the self-conscious subject constitutes a limit that speculative thought cannot exceed. The relationship between self and self-same image remains theoretically intact only until another view ("eine andere Rücksicht") recalls the forgotten distance that separates them. Could this "andere Rücksicht" not represent an earlier manifestation of the third eye of Oedipus? Warminski offers a thorough and excellent reading of the text, particularly of this idea of the "andere Rücksicht" in *Readings in Interpretation: Hölderlin, Hegel, Heidegger.* See also Dieter Henrich's essay "Hölderlin über Urteil und Sein: Eine Studie zur Entstehungsgeschichte des Idealismus" (*Hölderlin-Jahrbuch* 1965/66: 73–96), in which the author accords Hölderlin's fragment a nearly seminal position in the development of Idealism from Fichte to Hegel. For a contrary argument that situates Hölderlin's essay more closely in relation to Fichte, see Helmut Bachmaier, "Theoretische Aporie und tragische Negativität. Zur Genesis der tragischen Reflexion bei Hölderlin," in Bachmaier, Horst, and Reisinger, *Hölderlin: Transzendentale Reflexion der Poesie* (Stuttgart: Klett-Cotta, 1979), 105–8.

42. Corngold describes the development, in the course of the three versions, of Empedocles' self-reflexive autonomy as an *isolation* from the possibility of representation as image. "Disowning Contingencies in Hölderlin's *Empedocles,*" in Fioretos 233.

problem is already reflected in the earliest outline of the tragedy of Empedocles, the so-called Frankfurter Plan of 1797, in which the hero, dissatisfied with and contemptuous of the "one-sided existence" and "particular relations" among humans that fall short of the "great harmony with all living things" enjoyed by the gods, decides to end his life by plunging headlong into Mt. Etna.[43] His chosen mode of suicide is itself significant, for in order to become one with the gods, Empedocles needs a death that represents a total disappearance from the mortal world, that precludes the possibility of mourning.[44] If his contact with the despised "particular relations" is to dissipate as well, Empedocles must depart from the world without a physical trace, must be commemorated in no other form than signification through name and legend.

But already in this earliest sketch of the tragedy of Empedocles' death, the necessity of that pure disappearance for closure of the gap between god and man is undermined by the very human problem of a remainder that can (and thus must) be mourned.

> Soon afterward Empedocles hurls himself into the flames of Etna. His favorite disciple, who wanders about restlessly and anxiously nearby, finds soon thereafter the iron shoes of the master that the fiery emission had flung out of the abyss, recognizes them, presents them to the family of Empedocles, to his disciples among the people, and gathers with them at the volcano to mourn and celebrate the great man's death.[45]

---

43. It is in part for this drive for completion or "Ergänzung" that Hölderlin chooses the figure of Empedocles as protagonist after considering Socrates for a time. Empedocles, a pre-Socratic philosopher and physician who will also become a favorite of Nietzsche's, suffers the burden of communicating a union between god and man that humanity is in fact incapable of grasping, at least not with the tools of reflection. Thus Hoffmeister emphasizes the parallels between the communicative crisis of the poet and that of his hero, who assumes the task of conveying the presence of the divine in human existence. Johannes Hoffmeister, *Hölderlins Empedokles* (Bonn: Bouvier, 1963), 96. In this context see also Klaus-Rüdiger Wöhrmann, who reads the attempts to write an Empedocles tragedy as expressive of "the monstrous striving to be All" and its ultimate failure: *Hölderlins Wille zur Tragödie* (Munich: Fink, 1967), 162.

44. See Hoffmeister's still-relevant account, 38: "What is immortal cannot be seen as dying, having died; it cannot leave behind a mortal hull. It must simply disappear from the earth, so to speak, in a bodily ascent to heaven. . . . But Empedocles—according to the legendary reproach against him—attempted to exploit this belief in order to reach the whiff [*Geruch*] of immortality."

45. "Bald drauf stürzt sich Empedokles in den lodernden Aetna. Sein Liebling, der unruhig und bekümmert in dieser Gegend umherirrt, findet bald drauf die eisernen Schuhe des Meisters, die der Feuerauswurf aus dem Abgrund geschleudert hatte, erkennt sie, zeigt sie der Familie des Empedokles, seinen Anhängern im Volke, und versammelt sich mit diesem an dem Vulkan, um Laid zu tragen, und den Tod des großen Mannes zu feiern" (FA 13: 546).

With the discovery of the iron shoes belonging to the master, capable of resisting the intensity of volcanic heat for long enough to be spat out of the abyss, the disciples of Empedocles can mourn his death, thus claiming him as one of their own. Echoing the funereal traditions of ancient Greece, their ceremonial mourning, made possible with the discovery of an object of permanence, permits them to transform his death into "something done" (in Hegel's words, *ein Getanes*) and thereby preserve the memory, the name of their leader both as member of the community and as individual.[46] Had Empedocles succeeded in his quest to disappear without a trace, without even the physical remains that would signify his death to others, his legacy might have taken on mythic form, thus unifying him with the gods as he had wished; as it stands, however, his very real death, cast for eternity in the iron of his own sandals, is painfully, only human. Hölderlin's three unsuccessful attempts to write the death of Empedocles may also pay homage to this misfortune of being only human, even as his quest, like his Empedocles in suicide, was to achieve something more.[47]

Although the determined search for an unreflected access to union clearly contributes strongly to the shape of Hölderlin's early poetic intent, then, it is often undermined, even at the start, by his own theoretical and formal considerations. An insistent question imposes itself, therefore, upon that framework of aspiration and failure that literary criticism has often assigned to Hölderlin's dramatic texts, a question that more recent scholarship addresses:[48] what if, at least by the time he decides to formulate a second version of the *Death of Empedocles,* his attempt is not at all to represent the vicissitudes of the speculative system in tragedy, at which he clearly fails? What if, rather, his translations perform in deliberate fashion another failure, namely, the impossibility of precisely that system? What could *that* failure,

---

46. For a discussion of funeral customs in ancient Greece, see Vernant, "'A Beautiful Death and the Disfigured Corpse in Homeric Epic,'" in *Mortals and Immortals: Collected Essays,* ed. and trans. Froma Zeitlin (Princeton: Princeton University Press, 1991), 50–74. See also my discussion of Hegel in Chapter 3.

47. Eric Santner goes so far as to read the *Frankfurter Plan* as a "rather frank and astute self-analysis," but more with regard to Hölderlin's awareness of and frustration at his own limitations, linking the discussion of Empedokles' "Kulturhaß" to the poet's exploration of his own weaknesses. *Friedrich Hölderlin: Narrative Vigilance and the Poetic Imagination (New Brunswick and London* (Rutgers University Press, 1986), 63f.

48. Lacoue-Labarthe and Warminski led the attempt to figure this strain of negativity in Hölderlin in the 1980s, but Szondi seems to have instigated the move toward understanding Hölderlin's views as a poetics of difference, not totality, in his important reading of the 1801 letter to Böhlendorff, "Überwindung des Klassizismus," *Hölderlin-Studien* (Frankfurt: Insel, 1967), 85–104. For more recent work, see also Aris Fioretos, "Color Read," and Rainer Nägele, "Ancient Sports and Modern Transports," both in Fioretos 268–87, 247–67.

then, represent? It may be that it cannot represent at all, nor can it be represented, except as disruption. The failure of representation in Empedocles leads Hölderlin to translation as an experimental mode of expression, to Oedipus as the tragic figure that Empedocles could not successfully embody. Yet the distance between Empedocles and his Greek other—the failed reconciliation between ancient and modern modes of representation—must itself remain part of the performance. After the unfulfilling death of Empedocles, Hölderlin needs Oedipus—his Oedipus.

Lacoue-Labarthe called this performance the "caesura of the speculative," referring to a famous trope of Hölderlin's that we will have to examine shortly; however, it is also more than that. Hölderlin's exploration of the dynamics of difference within tragedy and in translation should not be seen to offer, as Lacoue-Labarthe's argument implies, the inadvertent interruption of the speculative dialectic.[49] Rather, they introduce and track a movement that describes both the literal crossing-over inherent in the word "übersetzen" and the trajectory of the subject itself in time, the difference that translated words continually trace and the disquieting effect of that trace on the subject who is exposed to it. In both cases, it is a difference that will be, as Bettina von Arnim sensed astutely upon reading Hölderlin's *Oedipus*, "borne with pain."[50]

IN "IN LOVELY BLUENESS," the suffering of Oedipus remained beyond description, speech, expression. The modern subject cannot see through the excess eye of Oedipus, let alone identify with his plight, and yet our view of that eye is directed toward an unrecognizable element that refuses capture within the act of seeing. This drive to comprehend that the spectator faces in confronting a figure so wholly other contains within it an element of danger that the tragedy of Oedipus itself, particularly as Hölderlin reads it, does not leave unexamined. For as he states in the remarks on *Oedipus*, this desire to see and thus to know with specificity, as irresistible as it may seem, is also what brings on the hero's tragic fall.

---

49. Although he does argue that Hölderlin's project of translation dislocates the speculative from within, Lacoue-Labarthe does not concede that it has any aim other than the speculative closure of the Kantian rift: "It is not that Hölderlin wanted it that way—he wanted, if he wanted anything at all (and for some time he did want something), the resolution of the crisis . . . " (213). Later: "Once again, I am not saying this with a view toward extricating Hölderlin from the speculative and making him, if you will, the "positive hero" of this adventure. The theory put forward by Hölderlin is speculative through and through" (224).

50. " . . . mit Schmerzen hineingetragen": Bettina von Arnim, *Die Günderode,* ed. Elisabeth Bronfen (Munich: Matthes & Seitz, 1982), 146.

Presented with the opportunity to recognize the direction of his fate, Oedipus interprets the enigmatic words of the oracle with a gesture that advances too far into specific knowledge, thereby edging too closely toward divine privilege and crossing into the space that Hölderlin deems "too infinite."

> Die Verständlichkeit des Ganzen beruhet vorzüglich darauf, daß man die Scene ins Auge faßt, wo Oedipus den Orakelspruch zu unendlich deutet, zum *nefas* versucht wird.
> Nemlich der Orakelspruch heißt:
>
> *Geboten hat uns Phöbus klar, der König,*
> *Man soll des Landes Schmach, auf diesem Grund genährt,*
> *Verfolgen, nicht Unheilbares ernähren.*
>
> Das könnte heißen: Richtet, allgemein, ein streng und rein Gericht, haltet gute bürgerliche Ordnung. Oedipus aber spricht gleich darauf priesterlich:
>
> *Durch welche Reinigung, etc.*
>
> Und gehet ins besondere,
>
> *Und welchem Mann bedeutet er diß Schicksal?*
>
> Und bringet so die Gedanken des Kreon auf das furchtbare Wort:
>
> *Uns war, o König, Lajos vormals Herr*
> *In diesem Land,' eh du die Stadt gelenket.*
>
> So wird der Orakelspruch und die nicht nothwendig darunter gehörige Geschichte von Lajos' Tod zusammengebracht. (FA 16: 251)

> To understand the whole we must above all look closely at the scene in which Oedipus interprets the oracle too infinitely, is tempted into *nefas*.
> For the oracle says:
>
> *Phoebus has bidden us, the King has, clearly,*
> *We must hunt down the shame our country's ground*
> *Has nourished, not nurture the incurable.*

That could mean: Judge, in a general way, with strict and pure judgments, keep good civic order. But Oedipus at once responds in priestly language:

Through what cleansing, . . . etc.

And goes into the particular,

And to which man does he pronounce this fate?

And so brings Creon's thoughts to the terrible utterance:

Lord of us formerly, O King, was Laius
Here in the land before you led the city.

In this way the words of the oracle are brought into a connection they do not necessarily have with the story of Laius' death. (Constantine 64f.; trans. modified)

Hölderlin's observation here suggests that the oracle's bearing on Oedipus' crime is arbitrary, thus defining the tragic conflict as a problem with the "insane" quest for knowledge and not with the cruel irony of fate.[51] In this sense it poses an intriguing contrast to Schelling's interpretation of Oedipus' fall, in which the hero, doomed by fate, is still allowed to struggle against that superior power, thereby affirming human freedom even in defeat and rendering the contradictions of fate tolerable. For Hölderlin, the hero's hubris amounts to a refusal to allow fate to take its course at all, to the desire for a forbidden choice—made without permission and subject to punishment—that makes tragedy quite *in*tolerable.

In der gleich darauf folgenden Scene spricht aber, in zorniger Ahnung, der Geist des Oedipus, alles wissend, das *nefas* eigentlich aus, indem er das allgemeine Gebot argwöhnisch ins Besondere deutet, und auf einen Mörder des Lajos anwendet, und dann auch die Sünde als unendlich nimmt. (FA 16: 252)

---

51. See Horst Turk, "Das Beispiel Hölderlins," *Hölderlin-Jahrbuch* 1988–89: 261. Beissner offers as well that Hölderlin's translation of the oracle is indeed given in more general language than the usual versions, indicating also that it could be interpreted as having less directly to do with the outcome of the tragedy (*Hölderlins Übersetzungen aus dem Griechischen*). Bernofsky expands on this idea, claiming that Hölderlin, in translating *miasma* (literally "stain," "defilement") with the relatively vague term *Schmach* ("disgrace"), transforms the specific into the general in order to emphasize the extent to which Oedipus "goes into the particular" (*gehet ins besondere*) with his interpretation (217).

[. . .] Daher, im nachfolgenden Gespräche mit Tiresias, die wunderbare zornige Neugier, weil das Wissen, wenn es seine Schranke durchrissen hat, wie trunken in seiner herrlichen harmonischen Form, vorerst, sich selbst reizt, mehr zu wissen, als es tragen oder fassen kann . . . (FA 16: 253)

Then in the very next scene the spirit of Oedipus, all-knowing, actually utters the *nefas* in furious presentiment, by mistrustfully interpreting the general commandment into the particular and applying it to a murderer of Laius, and then taking the sin as infinite.

[. . .] Hence, in the conversation that follows with Tiresias, the wondrously furious curiosity of a knowledge that it has torn through its barriers and now, as though drunk in its lordly harmonious form . . . first of all incites itself to know more than it can bear or grasp. (Constantine 65; trans. modified)

Provoking itself to know too much, knowledge spirals into excess, tearing through its own barriers, while the individual is swept along by the formidable force of this desire. As Bernofsky points out, by invoking the Latin term *ne-fas* Hölderlin already gives voice to the particular transgression of which Oedipus is guilty: the negation of *fas*, a Latin term for the divine law which derives from *fari* (to speak), is a negation of the divine word itself, a presumptuous readiness to interpret or "translate" the words of the oracle and thereby claim the status of a god (217f.). For Hölderlin the recognition of this transgression is central to the understanding of the tragedy as a whole. Yet the aims of this knowledge remain obscure, as does the motor of choice: if knowledge provokes *itself* to know more than it can bear, and if the subject must *necessarily* succumb to a "wondrously furious curiosity," how can an individual choice also bring on the hero's downfall, as the first part of the passage would suggest? More specifically, what does it mean for Oedipus to interpret "into the particular," and through what sort of limit or barrier does this particularity tear?

As the passage indicates, the limit is integrally related to speech; not only knowledge itself but the articulation of that knowledge set Oedipus' demise into motion ("the spirit of Oedipus, all-knowing, articulates the *nefas*"). This prospect of a limit to what may be *said* bears significance for Hölderlin's work in more than one sense. For Empedocles it is linked to the naming of gods, to the privileged status that allows some mortals to touch the divine—representing, in other words, an articulation of the problem of *logos*. As enunciated in the second draft of *Empedocles*, the naming of gods is depicted as the worst possible crime, not because human beings do not dwell in proximity to those gods but rather because that relationship must remain unspoken. As the priest Hermokrates explains, to give voice to that link is tantamount to the betrayal of a terrible secret:

> Verderblicher denn Schwerd und Feuer ist
> Der Menschengeist, der götterähnliche,
> Wenn er nicht schweigen kann, und sein Geheimnis
> Unaufgedekt bewahren . . .
> Hinweg mit ihm, der seine Seele blos
> Und ihre Götter giebt. . . . (FA 13: 821f.,1. 168–71, 175–76)

> More ruinous than sword or fire is the human spirit, the god-like, if he cannot be silent and preserve his secret unrevealed. . . . Cursed be he who bares his soul and its gods . . .

Is this critique of professed knowledge a protest to the aims of speculative Idealism itself, to a will which might be described, like that of Oedipus, as the desire to "know more than it can bear or grasp"? Although the parallel is certainly present, the problem as Hölderlin formulates it is also more complex, requiring an accounting of the wide temporal gap between the ancient model and its modern reflection. Hölderlin was interested in the implications of this gap well before he settled on the Sophocles project. In a footnote to the first version of Empedocles (ca. 1798), he insists that ancient and modern conceptions of a tragic figure's hubris emerge from fundamentally different attitudes about the nature of "crime." Even if there is a correspondence between these two "sins," that relation reveals little more than another insurmountable difference:

> For us, something like this is more a sin against knowledge, while for the ancients it was more excusable from this aspect, because it was more comprehensible to them. For them is was not <merely> inconsistency <but> crime. But they do not forgive it, because their sense of freedom would not bear such a statement. Precisely because they honored and understood it more, they were also more fearful of the hubris of the genius. To us it is not dangerous, because we are not affected by it.[52]

---

52. See StA IV:2 (Lesarten), *Empedokles I*,1.188: "Bei uns ist so etwas mehr eine Sünde gegen den Verstand, bei den Altern war es von dieser Seite verzeihlicher, weil es ihnen begreiflich war. Nicht <etwa bloß> Ungereimtheit, <sondern> Verbrechen war es ihnen. Aber sie verzeihen es nicht, weil ihr Freiheitssinn kein solches Wort ertragen wollte. Eben weil sie es mehr ehrten und verstanden, fürchte-

The hubris of the genius is not a source of dread for us as it was for the ancients, he argues, because we see only a strange inconsistency, a lack of judgment, perhaps, where they saw unequivocal crime. But even if we do not regard Oedipus's actions as the grave misstep that they were for the ancient Greeks, we cannot help but be struck by our own distance from him. We cannot entirely grasp the magnitude of his transgressions for the Greeks, just as we cannot entirely conceive of the unwritten law that drives Antigone to bury her brother Polynices beneath a thin layer of dust. The modern reader or spectator thus encounters a limit of her own, marked out by the immensity of the gap between Sophocles and Hölderlin (and in turn with respect to the reader herself), a limit through which she may strive to tear but ultimately must find another way to address.

This pattern of persistent limitation to what can and should be known and articulated seems to run counter to Hölderlin's earlier sentiment of revelatory potential in aesthetic representation—but does it, actually? In effect, something *is* named here, even if the gods are not. Although he attempts unsuccessfully to formulate the tragedy of Empedocles' death no less than four times, with respect to the work on Sophocles Hölderlin does not concede failure. This much we know from his correspondence, that he did consider his translations to be at least a qualified success and above all believed that success to be contingent upon his having communicated something that no previous translator had. He addresses that aim when he writes to his publisher Wilmans in September 1803 that he wishes to represent Greek art as "more alive than usual" in a modern context by emphasizing the "Oriental" and correcting its "artistic errors." Seven months later, the manuscript printed, he writes again to Wilmans: "I believe to have written in the direction of eccentric enthusiasm and thus achieved Greek simplicity" (FA 16: 19).[53]

Much has been said about these passages, especially in relation to Hölderlin's earlier letter to his friend Böhlendorff from December 1801, in which he delineates his idiosyncratic but quite complex view of the differences between ancient and modern modes of representation. In that letter, the great potential of artistic representation lies in the capacity to recognize one's "nature," which is for Hölderlin the most difficult task of all. Hölderlin provides an example of this idea with a comparison of Greek and

---

ten sie auch mehr den Übermut des Genies. Uns ist es nicht gefährlich, weil wir nicht berührbar sind dafür."

53. "Ich glaube durchaus gegen die exzentrische Begeisterung geschrieben zu haben und so die griechische Einfalt erreicht." Beissner pointed out the likelihood that "gegen" refers to "toward" rather than "against" here.

"Hesperian" modes of representation that underscores the importance of Greek art in a modern age. While the Greeks' "nature" was "fire from heaven," their culture contributed "Darstellungsgaabe," a talent for form-giving; on the other hand, the duality of nature and culture in the Hesperian mode of representation is precisely opposite: the "Junonian sobriety" that is our nature corresponds to the Greeks' culture of representation, while our culture ought to provide the "fire."[54] In the end, the Greeks are useful to us not insofar as they reflect to us our own nature—indeed, that would be impossible, since one's own nature cannot be assimilated from another source—but rather as an example of a process: just as Homer imposed sobriety on the "fire from heaven," form on chaos, thereby reconciling "nature" with acquired culture, we can learn to bring chaos into form.

However, a distinction should be drawn between the letter to Böhlendorff, written as Hölderlin was beginning to translate Sophocles in earnest after years of toying with the idea, and the letters to Wilmans that reflect on the finished product. To be sure, his interest in the possibility of achieving "Greek simplicity" by writing "in the direction of eccentric enthusiasm" carries echoes of that earlier model. However, Hölderlin has moved beyond the chiasmic structure of the Böhlendorff letter, in which each side acquires from the other the aspect of representation that it lacks. In his explanation of how he aims to render Greek art as "more alive than usual" by tracing the mistakenly repudiated "Oriental," the crossing is no longer a closed system, for the Greeks now have their own inaccessible other, the traces of which remain within tragic representation. The status of the other with respect to the self thus transforms into a relationship of slippage rather than of opposition. Even if the Greeks are "our" other, the Oriental sphere represents the other of the Greeks; thus no specular relation is possible, and no original can become present at all.[55]

Achieving Greek "simplicity," then, requires a shift in emphasis from the problem of representing tragedy's modern resonance solely within a thematic register. If the suffering borne on the body of Oedipus is unreadable, if the violence it implies is too monstrous to represent in familiar terms, then those terms themselves must be reframed through dramatic text and rhythm. As his cryptic remarks on the tragedy begin to suggest, translation itself—

---

54. The death of the modern subject, for example, is dry and soulless compared with the deaths depicted by the Greeks: "For this is the tragic to us: that, packed up in any container, we very quietly move away from the realm of the living, [and] not that—consumed in flames—we expiate the flames which we could not tame" (Pfau 1988, 150).

55. See Warminski, in particular the section "Caesura: Hölderlin and the Egyptians," in *Readings in Interpretation*, 17–22.

translation, that is, as a mode of transmission that emphatically does not erase its own traces—will bear responsibility for marking that otherwise unspeakable excess.

In the opening paragraph of the remarks on *Oedipus*, Hölderlin immediately distances himself from modern readers who would seek tragedy's beauty in material impressions or characterizations; here, the notable characteristic of tragedy emerges from a meticulousness that has less to do with the classical-Romantic idea of genius, with the Idealist attainment of a harmonious whole, or with the impressions that either gesture might leave on the spectator, than with an almost plodding exactitude of structure:

> Auch andern Kunstwerken fehlt, mit den griechischen verglichen, die Zuverlässigkeit; wenigstens sind sie bis izt mehr nach Eindrüken beurtheilt worden, die sie machen, als nach ihrem gesetzlichen Kalkul und sonstiger Verfahrungsart, wodurch das Schöne hervorgebracht wird. Der modernen Poesie fehlt es aber besonders an der Schule und am Handwerksmäßigen, daß nemlich ihre Verfahrungsart berechnet und gelehrt, und wenn sie gelernt ist, in der Ausübung immer zuverlässig wiederhohlt werden kann. (FA 16: 249)

> Other works of art, too, compared with the Greek, lack reliability; at least, until now they have always been judged according to the impressions they make rather than according to their calculable laws and their other procedures by which beauty is brought into being. But modern poetry is especially lacking in schooling and craft which would enable its procedures to be calculated and taught and once learned be always reliably repeated in practice. (Constantine 63; trans. modified)

In a post-Idealist, post-tragic age, the possibility of a repetition that is "reliable" depends for Hölderlin on the skill of the poet, more artisan than artist, to follow the "lawful calculation" of form and adhere to the "*mechane* of the ancients."[56] Yet this repetition of form does not simply accompany the echoes of a familiar plot in the form of rules, as in the neoclassical model promoted in the previous century by Gottsched. In fact, form's iterability

---

56. Norbert von Hellingrath emphasized for the first time the importance of Hölderlin's interest in this notion of *mechane;* by doing so Hellingrath is able to situate that interest within a progression that leads from its origins in Greek rhetoric all the way to Symbolist poetry and finally to the school of Stefan George. In this way, Hölderlin's poetry offers a crucial space of correspondence and transition between the legacy of antiquity and modern poetics. See Alessandro Pellegrini, *Friedrich Hölderlin: Sein Bild in der Forschung* (Berlin: De Gruyter, 1965), 60.

runs precisely counter to the textual material, which we cannot grasp and certainly should not attempt to repeat. Repetition takes place on a purely mechanical level and not a thematic one. While content is brought into "relation" with form in the body of text, the "living sense" remains incalculable even when projected into a familiar shape.

> Dann hat man darauf zu sehen, wie der Innhalt sich von diesem unterscheidet, durch welche Verfahrungsart, und wie im unendlichen, aber durchgängig bestimmten Zusammenhange der besondern Innhalt sich zum allgemeinen Kalkul verhält, und der Gang und das Vestzusetzende, der lebendige Sinn, der nicht berechnet werden kann, mit dem kalkulablen Geseze in Beziehung gebracht wird. (FA 16: 249f.)

> We have to see then in what way the content of a work differs from this law, through what procedure, and how in an infinite but thoroughly determined interconnection the particular content relates to the general calculation, and how the onward march of the work, the things it has to bring into shape, the living sense which cannot be achieved by calculation, how all that is related to the calculable law. (Constantine 63)

The relationship between classical art and its modern framework is twofold: not only does it demand a mechanical repetition of classical form, it also highlights a difference that the content of art must aim to reflect. In this respect Hölderlin echoes Herder's admonition to "steal the art of imitation" rather than merely imitating the classics; while form may not change over time, content *must* change, insofar as its relation to form is "infinite yet continuously determined." Content can neither be calculated nor naively repeated, since its effects can only be determined within a given historical context. Producing art after the Greeks thus requires the synthesis of calculable and incalculable elements, not in order to sublate their difference but rather to allow that difference itself to unsettle the work of art; as a result the work is always recognizable and at the same time hints at its own unfathomable depth.

This strict sameness of form differs significantly from the rigid application of Aristotelian unities of time, space, and plot upon which the German literary establishment insisted before the breakthrough of Lessing's dramaturgy. Notably, however, Hölderlin's model does return to another key aspect of the *Poetics*, echoing Aristotle's conception of mimesis, in which the activity of making and responding to likenesses involves the pleasurable process of "work[ing] out what each thing is," thus coming to appreciate its intrinsic rationale and the craft (*techne*) underlying its creation.[57] As Christopher Fynsk notes, Hölderlin does cite the *Poetics* (in Greek) in the third section of these remarks on *Oedipus;* could it be that Hölderlin hews more closely to the Greek model than his rather more pedantic predecessors ever did?[58] To be sure, he has grasped a different element of Aristotle's argument and incorporated it into his methodology as a translator. What is repeated here—far more insightfully than the rigidity of "unities" of space, time, and plot—is a form that itself has an effect, and not because of its absorption into the dramatic momentum of plot but precisely in spite of it. The stuff of tragedy wields power for Hölderlin largely because it is recognizable in its representative form, its "Erscheinung": "Most important for humankind is to see with respect to everything that it *is Something*, in other words that it is knowable in the medium of its appearance" (Constantine 63: *Man hat, unter Menschen, bei jedem Dinge, vor allem darauf zu sehen, daß es Etwas ist, d.h. daß es in dem Mittel (moyen) seiner Erscheinung erkennbar ist* . . . [FA 16: 249]). To be "Something" a tragic work must expose itself entirely to the light of day; not only the materiality of plot, but also the bare structure of performance, the nature of dialogic exchange, even the rhythm of language contribute to the intensity of tragic experience.[59]

For Hölderlin, this framework from which modern tragedy can emerge is *about* nothing at all: "For the transport in tragedy is of itself empty, and the most unbounded" (Constantine 65: *Der tragische Transport ist nemlich eigentlich leer, und der ungebundenste* [FA 16: 250]). Unconstrained by what Schiller called the "category of causality,"[60] tragic transport can be defined only by its relation to absence. Moreover, this movement through absence traces its trajectory not by any discernible progress toward its own completion but rather only in terms of a restoration of structural balance between two sides.

Das Gesez, der Kalkul, die Art, wie, ein Empfindungssystem, der ganze Mensch, als unter dem Einflusse des Elements sich entwickelt, und Vor-

---

57. Aristotle, *Poetics,* trans. Heath 7. The translation in the revised Oxford edition of *The Complete Works of Aristotle:* vol. 2, ed. Jonathan Barnes (Princeton: Princeton University Press, 1984) reads less emphatically than Heath's translation: "one is at the same time learning – gathering the meaning of things . . . " (2318).

58. See Christopher Fynsk, "Reading the 'Poetics' after the 'Remarks,'" in Fioretis, *The Solid Letter,* 239.

59. As Fynsk points out, Hölderlin's emphasis on the role of rhythm in his model of tragic effect also resembles aspects of Aristotle's (admittedly sparse) comments on catharsis. See Fynsk 243–45.

60. Beissner, *Erläuterungen zu Oedipus Tyrannus,* StA V, 483 (letter from Schiller to Goethe, 25 April 1797): " . . . daß der dramatische Dichter unter der Kategorie der Kausalität, der Epiker unter der der Substantialität steht."

stellung und Empfindung und Räsonnement, in verschiedenen Successionen, aber immer nach einer sichern Regel nacheinander hervorgehn, ist im Tragischen mehr Gleichgewicht, als reine Aufeinanderfolge. (FA 16: 250)

The law, the calculation, the way in which a sensuous system, the whole person, under an elemental influence develops, and representation, sensation and reason, in different sequences, but always according to a sure and certain rule, is in tragedy more a matter of weighting and balance than of pure sequence. (Constantine 63; trans. modified)

To calculate the precise point of "balance" in this model, however, is a tricky matter. Like the flow of poetic language, the events represented in the tragic form possess a rhythm for Hölderlin that resonates more rapidly and thus generates more dramatic urgency at a particular point. Hölderlin's assertion is thus that a caesura, a rupture in the rhythm of language, allows the parts of the tragedy to balance as a whole but must be placed asymmetrically, as a counterweight to the "heavier," more insistently active part of dramatic action. In *Oedipus*, the greater weight comes at the end, so that the caesura must be placed closer to the beginning, while for *Antigone*, the opposite is true. In both cases, the caesura arrests action in its path, opening a perspective to the viewing eye that would otherwise have been incommensurate with the progression of scenes on the stage: "that soon it is no longer the change of representation that appears but the representation itself" (250). What does it mean to obtain access to "the representation itself" in this arrested form? Representation, rather than effacing distance by upholding itself as the vehicle of tragic effect, is momentarily revealed as a pivotal part of the illusion, leaving the form of tragic transport to gape open in its emptiness.

Expressed in concrete terms, the words of the seer Tiresias represent for Hölderlin this doubly crucial slash in the movement of action, which both stops the tragic transport, the movement of language and form, in its path and propels the individual character, be it Oedipus or Antigone, into a solitary confrontation with death.

Er tritt in den Gang des Schiksaals, als Aufseher über die Naturmacht, die tragisch, den Menschen seiner Lebenssphäre, dem Mittelpuncte seines inneren Lebens in eine andere Welt entrükt und in die exzentrische Sphäre der Todten reißt. (FA 16: 251)

He enters the course of fate as overseer of the natural order which, in a tragic manner, removes man from his own sphere of life, from the midpoint of his inner life into another world and carries him into the eccentric sphere of the dead. (Constantine 64; trans. modified)

Rainer Nägele has described the manner in which Hölderlin's texts in general are marked by topological orders, both vertical and horizontal. The clearest analogy is the vertical relation of the mortal world to that of the gods, while the horizontal current of the river leaves its unmistakable inscription in Hölderlin's later lyric poetry (see Nägele 1988 and Binder 1981). Here, in the discussion of the caesura that interrupts the horizontal flow of rhythmic language and the march of fate, the image of the sphere introduces another topography, that of interior and exterior. The words of the seer tear one violently from one's path, revealing not the inscription of the hero as king of the text but rather his unexpected abduction from a position of centrality; the caesura orchestrates the tragic figure's bitter expulsion from internal center (*Mittelpunkt*) to ex-centric outcast. Revealing to Oedipus the inevitability of this expulsion, Hölderlin's Tiresias appeals to those senses that do not yet heed the suffering which will soon confront them:

> TIRESIAS: Gesehen hast auch du, siehst nicht, woran du bist,
> Im Übel, wo du wohnst, womit du haußest.
> Weißt du, woher du bist? . . .
> Fühlst du die Hochzeit, wie du landetest
> Auf guter Schiffahrt an der Uferlosen?
> Der andern Übel Menge fühlst du auch nicht,
> Die dich zugleich und deine Kinder treffen.
> Nun schimpfe noch auf Kreon und auch mir
> Ins Angesicht, denn schlimmer ist, als du,
> Kein Sterblicher, der jemals wird gezeugt sein. (FA 16: 123: 418–20, 428–34)

> TIRESIAS: You, having seen, don't see what you are at
> In evil, where you live, with what you house.
> Do you know where you are from? . . .
> Do you feel the marriage as you landed
> Voyaging well, along the bankless shore.
> Nor do you feel the multitude of other evils
> That strike you with your children equally.
> But scold at Creon still and also
> Into my face for worse than you there is
> No mortal man who ever will be fathered. (Constantine 28)

Hölderlin's progression of verbs describing modes of perception and knowledge (*sehen, wissen, fühlen*) at first hews closely to the Greek *blépo* (to see, to have sight) and *oida* (to know), but then he collapses *kataisthanomai* and *epaisthanomai* (both: to perceive, to understand) into the more physical *fühlen*, to feel. This shift introduces physicality as a hinge between key concepts in Hölderlin's language, perception as feeling and understanding as grasping, *greifen* or *begreifen*. If Oedipus does not feel "the multitude of other evils," he cannot grasp their significance; yet if he grasps at too much, he will feel the consequences as physical suffering. The concealment, even the foreclosure of "the multitude of other evils" in an unseen, unknown, un*felt* register may therefore allow Oedipus to enjoy a certain perception of centrality or mastery, but continuing to pursue that "multitude" threatens, in the damning words of the Chorus, to unleash the force of something previously untouched and strictly speaking untouchable.

> Wenn aber überschauend einer mit Händen wandelt, oder
> Mit Worten, und fürchtet das Recht nicht, und
> Die Thronen nicht der Dämonen verehrt,
> Den hab ein böses Schicksal,
> Unschicklichen Prangens wegen,
> Wenn nicht Gewinn er gewinnet recht,
> Und offenbares verschleußt
> Und unberührbares angreifft albern. (FA 16: 173–74: 906–13)

> But if a man lives carelessly and wanders with hands or
> With words and does not fear what is right and
> Does not honor the thrones of the daimons
> Let a bad fate have him
> For his unseemly showing
> If his winnings are not won right
> If he shuts up what is manifest,
> And seizes what is untouchable, the fool. (Constantine 43; trans. modified)

And seizes what is untouchable . . . : whether with words or with hands, it is possible to grasp at too much. And as in the example of Empedocles, there are consequences. If it is a reckless misstep on the part of the hero, a failure to maintain the enigma of the gods that brings this contact with the untouchable, then the only possible outcome—a radical, purifying separation from that contact—is also the impulse for tragedy's denouément. For Hölderlin this rupture, the doubled caesura which exposes both the hero's inherent ex-centricity and "the representation itself," becomes most necessary in the moment of his greatest hubris, when the representation has taken on its most dreadful cast.

> Die Darstellung des Tragischen beruht vorzüglich darauf, daß das Ungeheure, wie der Gott und Mensch sich paart, und grenzenlos die Naturmacht und des Menschen innerstes im Zorn Eins wird, dadurch sich begreift, daß das grenzenlose Einswerden durch grenzenloses Scheiden sich reiniget. (FA 16: 257)

> The presentation of the tragic rests chiefly in this: that the monstrousness of the pairing of God and Man, and the boundless coming together in fury of the powers of nature and man's innermost, grasps itself in the purification of that boundless union through boundless separation. (Constantine 67; trans. modified)

In the words of Tiresias, this inhuman coupling emerges most powerfully as an effect of revelation either through speech or handiwork, and Hölderlin also formulates Oedipus's self-imposed will to knowledge in terms of a burden both physical and conceptual, "to know more than it can bear or grasp." The accumulation of that burden in the text ends tragically, in the words that Oedipus has no choice but to hear, even though the words themselves, in being uttered for the first time, also initiate his downfall.

> DER DIENER: Oh! Oh! das Schrökliche selbst zu sagen bin ich dran.
> OEDIPUS: Und ich zu hören. Dennoch hören muß ich. (FA 16: 209: 1190–91)

> SERVANT: Oh! Oh! I am about to say the terrible itself.
> OEDIPUS: And I to hear it. Yet hear I must.

"Das Schrökliche selbst" (*the terrible itself*) here stands in for the Greek *deinon*, a term that will take on greater significance in Hölderlin's *Antigone*, where he translates it as "Ungeheuer," the monstrous. Here, *deinon* refers more obliquely to the coupling of god and man, the grand monstrosity that tragedy exposes in the words of its characters. And while Oedipus recognizes here that he has no other choice but to perceive that monstrosity when it is revealed to him, Antigone's chorus will face a similar dilemma—conveyed, however, by sight rather than hearing—in its confrontation with a heroine that is in many ways equally monstrous.

Jezt aber komm ich, eben, selber, aus
Dem Geseze. *Denn ansehn muß ich diß,* und halten kann ich
Nicht mehr die Quelle der Tränen,
Da in das alles schwaigende Bett
Ich seh' Antigone wandeln. (FA 16: 349: 830–34; my emphasis])

But now even I myself am brought outside of
The law. For I must look at this, and I can hold back
The spring of tears no longer,
As into the all-silent bed
I see Antigone wander.

One is unable to close one's ears or one's eyes to the monstrosity, and yet for Hölderlin there is recourse, at least at this point; with monstrosity already realized literally in the listening and speaking figure of Oedipus, and soon to be inspired by the very sight of Antigone, the purification from a proximity to the excess he embodies depends on the ability of tragic form to generate distance.[61] This saving attitude of rupture is already inscribed in form; a permanent division between the words of the Chorus and those of the hero concretizes the painful remedy for a pronouncement from which no one could possibly turn, for a relationship to the divine that could not keep its distance.

> Darum der immerwiederstreitende Dialog, darum der Chor als Gegensaz gegen diesen. Darum das allzukeusche, allzumechanische und factisch endigende Ineinandergreifen zwischen den verschiedenen Theilen, im Dialog, und zwischen dem Chor und Dialog und den großen Parthien oder Dramaten, welche aus Chor und Dialog bestehen. (FA 16: 257)

> Hence the constant to and fro of the dialogue, hence the chorus as its antithesis. Hence the all too chaste, all too mechanical interplay (ending in facts) of the different parts, in the dialogue, and between chorus and dialogue and the large passages made up of chorus and dialogue. (Constantine 67)

If Hölderlin portrays this process as dialectical in spirit—"Everything is speech against speech, one sublating the other"—it is a dialectic without

---

61. Quite plausibly, Fynsk describes this dynamics of separation as a form of catharsis, expanding on Aristotle's model to suggest that "tragic catharsis is effected at least in part through participation in a rhythmic movement" (*Fynsk* 245).

the possibility of synthetic closure, as the pattern of splitting through speech becomes the defining condition for both the hero and the representation of tragedy (the nearly untranslatable participial phrase *immerwiederstreitend* ironically lending unified form to that condition of rupture). This division represents a loss for the individual, insofar as the speaker who dares to utter the true names of the gods loses the former innocence of a tacit relation to the divine. Hölderlin compels Empedocles, like Oedipus after him, to bear the crushing burden of mourning this ephemeral object, once heard, once seen, now disappeared forever:

> . . . er achtets nicht, er trauert nur,
> Und siehet seinen Fall, er sucht
> Rükkehrend das verlorne Leben
> Den Gott, den er aus sich
> Hinweggeschwätzt. (FA 13: 823,1. 218–21)

> . . . he does not heed it, he only mourns, and sees only his dilemma; turning back, he seeks his lost life, the god that he banished from himself with his chatter.

Similarly, just as he was doomed by Tiresias' words to perceive with every sense the multitude of evils he embodies, Oedipus suffers and commemorates the depth of his own loss with every piercing blow to the eyes he destroys.

> o mir! o mir!
> Wie fährt in mich zugleich
> Mit diesen Stacheln
> Ein Treiben und Erinnerung der Übel! (FA 16: 225: 1347–50)

> oh me, oh me
> How with these stabs
> There enters into me
> At once a working and a memory of these evils. (Constantine 56)

Like Empedocles, who dared convey the monstrous god-human coupling directly in speech, Oedipus crosses a limit by articulating his own trangression, only discovering too late that the act of interpreting the oracle had initiated a process of thought that was "too infinite." In both cases, once that coupling has been put into words, it can only be taken away; only as a lost remnant of a painful but necessary split can the former aspiration to the untouchable be known. And in the interminably conflictual form of tragedy as Hölderlin understands it, it becomes possible to enact an otherwise unspoken mourning, that mourning for something of which one cannot possibly speak; so that in a final state of suffering, there is nothing left but the pure possibility of differentiation in empty space and empty time: "For at the outermost limit of suffering nothing else stands but the conditions of time and space" (258).[62] In a Kantian framework of space and time, this "nothing else" would be impossible; although temporal and spatial conditions indeed represent the pure forms of intuition *a priori*, they are literally nothing without the sensual experience to which they lend form.[63] The suffering here, however, which will resemble Antigone's suffering in the empty tomb as the space between life and death, represents precisely the pain of nothing but difference, without the solace of a positive concept to ground opposition.

Yet in this place where nothing exists other than pure differentiation, we are nowhere if not in language.[64] There can be little doubt that for Hölderlin one goal of these translations was to locate the space in which that "nowhere" of pure distancing might be most immediately felt. Comprehending words in logical relationships to one another becomes impossible when the most fundamental sense slips away from language, as it does so frequently in these translations. What emerges in the absence of "sense" in its customary form, however, is an impression of the obscurity contained in-between— between ancient and modern, source text and translation, subject and other. Hölderlin's task as translator is to surround that obscurity and preserve it in the dynamics of translation.[65] The remarks on *Antigone* will demonstrate

---

62. "In der äußersten Grenze des Leidens bestehet nämlich nichts mehr, als die Bedingungen der Zeit und des Raums" (FA 16: 258).

63. See *Kritik der reinen Vernunft, Transszendentale Ästhetik, 1. Abschnitt: Vom Raume* and *2. Abschnitt: Von der Zeit*, especially B42 and B51.

64. This formulation recalls Ferdinand de Saussure's contribution to the conception of language in contemporary theory, including both Lacanian psychoanalysis and deconstruction; the difference he posits in language, like Hölderlin's figuration of suffering here, undermines the possibility of opposition: " . . . in language there are only differences. Even more important: a difference generally implies positive terms between which the difference is set up; but in language there are only differences without positive terms." Saussure, *Course in General Linguistics*, trans. Wade Baskin (New York: Philosophical Library, 1959), 120.

65. In his 1921 essay "The Task of the Translator," Walter Benjamin follows a trajectory similar to Hölderlin's formal movement of differentiation, describing that task as the conveyance of something incommunicable ("Nicht-Mitteilbares"), namely a complicated relation to a "pure language" (*reine Sprache*) that emerges not from the representative potential of language but from a sense of its "becoming" in the spaces between languages. At its best, translation leaves those spaces intact, like "royal robes" surrounding content "with ample folds." Benjamin, *Selected Writings, Vol. 1: 1913–1926*, ed.

even more explicitly the potential effects of this preservation of obscurity in translation. As we will see next, the effects of an even more peculiar translation—a text that, in key moments, forecloses its own translatability—are inseparable from the experience of tragedy as Hölderlin conceives it from a modern standpoint.

Perhaps this obscurity, at once begotten and borne by language, ultimately resembles what Hölderlin himself perceived while examining the final proofs of the *Oedipus* translation. As he attempts to explain in a very curious letter to Wilmans just prior to publication in April 1804, he senses a strange interference with the solidity of the letters on the page—an interference which might not only undermine the ground of the text but already, as he contends with perhaps uncanny foresight, contribute to a perception of instability in the "creator" himself.

> Der rohe Druck hat mir fast besser gefallen, wahrscheinlich, weil die Züge, welche an den Buchstaben das Feste anzeigen, gegen das Modifizierende so gut aushalten in dieser Typographie, und dieses im rohen Druck noch bemerkbarer ist als im gefeilten. Der Erfinder ist oft verschämt gegen sein Publikum, und verlieret über die Galanterie dann das Eigentümliche überhaupt, besonders das Feste, was diese Typographie charakterisiert. (FA 16: 19)

> The raw printing almost appealed to me more, likely because in this typography those traits, which in the letters indicate the solid, hold out so well against the modifying, and because this is even more noticeable in the raw printing than in the finished one. The creator is often ashamed before his public, and through his gallantry loses the particular as such, especially the solid that characterizes this typography.

In the very next sentence he essentially dismisses what he has just written about the mysteriously "modifying" typeface: "Incidentally, the typography in this case has lost more in appearance than in reality." But the concern for the "solid" remains on the page here, as if removing it now would itself constitute a lack of "gallantry": "I say this in order to demonstrate to you the extent to which I comprehend this excellent notion."[66] What could this mean for his view of poetic language, if he "comprehends" here that words cannot even be grounded reliably on a page?

Marcus Bullock and Michael W. Jennings (Cambridge: Harvard University Press, 1996), 258. See also chapter 4, "The Translator's Courage."

66. "Übrigens hat die Typographie in diesem Vorzug nur mehr dem Scheine nach verloren als der Wirklichkeit. . . . Ich sage dies, um Ihnen zu bezeugen, wie weit ich diese Vortrefflichkeit verstehe."

Given the timing of the letter, the problem that appears to consume Hölderlin's thoughts could easily be attributed to the onset of his mental deterioration. However, in light of his insights into the empty movement of differentiation that inscribes "tragic transport," that concern suddenly appears very much justified. The permanence of letters becomes untenable after the disruptive force of these translations.[67] Perhaps because of this struggle with the instability of letters, Hölderlin will return to problems of signification and difference in the remarks on *Antigone*. Within that same space, however, he will introduce the degree to which the unstable ground of translation not only describes the relation between subject and world but also demarcates the subject as such.

---

67. A powerful expression of the poetic will to maintain the solidity of letters appears in Hölderlin's hymn "Patmos," written around 1803:

> Wir haben gedienet der Mutter Erd
> Und haben jüngst dem Sonnenlichte gedient,
> Unwissend, *der Vater aber liebt,*
> *Der über allen waltet,*
> *Am meisten, daß gepfleget werde*
> *Der feste Buchstab, und Bestehendes gut*
> *Gedeutet.* Dem folgt deutscher Gesang.

> We have served Mother Earth.
> And lately have served the sunlight,
> Unwittingly, *but what the father*
> *Who reigns over all loves most*
> *Is that the solid letter*
> *Be given scrupulous care, and the existing*
> *Be well interpreted.* This German song observes. (Hamburger 477)

THREE

Difference Becomes Antigone

Ungeheuer ist viel. Doch nichts
Ungeheuerer, als der Mensch. (FA 16: 299)

Much is monstrous. Yet nothing
More monstrous than the human.

THOUGH FEW are like Hölderlin, as Susette Gontard noted, and even fewer like solitary Oedipus, still we all are, unsettling as it is, like Antigone. With a judicious word choice, Hölderlin makes his Chorus of Theban elders suggest as much: as monstrous as she may appear to man in her singular determination, she cannot exceed him in this regard, for nothing is more monstrous than the human.[1] Though Hölderlin had already attempted a translation of the Choral ode in 1800, rendering these lines as "Vieles Gewaltige giebt's. Doch nichts / Ist gewaltiger als der Mensch" (FA 16: 56: *There is much that is powerful. But nothing / Is more powerful than the human*), his published translation of 1804 marks a radical shift that forms one of the most striking passages in the entire play: the word that in the remarks on *Oedipus* had described the monstrous link between human and divine—*das Ungeheure*, the monstrous—now confirms our uncomfortable likeness to Antigone.[2] And if we seem eternally tempted to identify with

---

1. Modern commentators on Sophocles' tragedy seem in general to agree with this assessment of Antigone as strange or uncanny. Besides Heidegger, whose reading will be discussed in more detail in the following chapter, Luce Irigaray describes her act of burying her brother against the decree of the state as "a perversity," linking it to her femininity and her relationship to the gods of the underworld; Lacan, arguing more closely along Hölderlin's line of reasoning (as we shall see), discusses the extent to which that act appears "inhuman" to us. Irigaray, "The Eternal Irony of the Community," trans. Gillian C. Gill, rpt. in *Feminist Interpretations of Hegel* (University Park, PA: Penn State University Press, 1996), 49; Lacan 263.

2. For a comparison of the two translations of the passage, see Louth 159–67.

Antigone's plight, if much of the modern history of her tragedy's reception reflects that effort, this may turn out to be the resemblance that drives the temptation in a most fundamental sense. A resemblance colored by shades of both universality and particularity—though we are all "ungeheuer," Antigone's own haunting justification for burying her brother Polynices insists upon a distance at its very ground—that monstrosity marks a cipher that will soon reveal itself in Hölderlin's translation and reading to be strangely familiar. While our fascination with Hölderlin's Oedipus has everything to do with his particular solitude, coded as a distance from that which can be grasped as exemplarily or timelessly human, the unique solitude with which Antigone moves toward her chosen death is exposed by Hölderlin's Chorus to inhabit each and every subject.[3]

Although they were conceived as part of a larger project and cannot easily be separated within his body of work, it is nonetheless productive to consider what makes this text distinct from the translation and remarks on *Oedipus*. (In his translation of the translations, Constantine reflects on the greater difficulty of Hölderlin's *Oedipus* compared with his *Antigone*.) Because this second translation shifts our focus from the exposure of pure difference in language and figure to a register that involves the modern subject more intimately in the tragic situation, the question of transitions comes into play: How does the confrontation with ancient text affect a modern subject? To what extent can the translation itself reflect the conflicts inherent in that temporal and conceptual crossing? On the whole, despite being involved in translating from the Greek throughout most of his productive life, Hölderlin made few comments on the practice in his theoretical writings; in this text, however—starting with the passage above—it becomes possible to map out a theory of how the significance of Greek tragedy in a modern register might be inseparable from the effects of its translation. Ultimately Hölderlin's translation achieves something of a performance of transition as such, not only as a problem of translation but as an exposure of the radical instability of modern subjectivity.

Antigone of Thebes, the daughter of Oedipus and Jocasta, sister of Eteocles, Polynices, and Ismene, acknowledges only one task at the beginning of her tragedy, one that she is determined to meet regardless of the consequences. In the aftermath of the battle waged by her brothers against one

---

3. Lacan's reading of the tragedy also takes note of this disquietude mixed with familiarity brought on by the figure of Antigone, but underlines at the same time the power of undeniable attraction that the discomfort engenders: " . . . it is Antigone herself who fascinates us, Antigone in her unbearable splendor. She has a quality that both attracts and startles us, in the sense of intimidates us [*nous interdit*]; this terrible, self-willed victim disturbs us" (Lacan 247).

another, one protecting the city and the other attacking it, both have fallen. Creon, as acting ruler of Thebes, decrees that one brother, Eteocles, will be honored in death for his heroism while the other, Polynices, will be punished for his betrayal of the city; rather than being buried within the community, his body will be left to wild dogs and birds. Yet Antigone is determined to offer Polynices a proper burial, even though that act disobeys Creon's law; plainly unconcerned with the fact of that disobedience, she acts even as she prepares to face the inevitable repercussions for that action. Even after Creon has sentenced her to her own death for doing so, she makes it clear that she had no other choice.

No other figure on the stage claims to agree with Antigone's decision, and no one else is a party to it. Though Karl Reinhardt has taken note of the special solitude characterizing all of Sophocles' heroes—the abandonment that all are ultimately forced to recognize[4]—Antigone's solitude may be most special of all. To be sure, her situation presents a compelling ethical dilemma, a universally felt tension, perhaps, between being good, if "the Good is what the Law says,"[5] and being loyal to a brother who otherwise has no one to defend his position. Yet a closer look at her moving words upon entering the tomb reveal not universality but something strangely other, for they form an elegy to that brother alone:

> Nun, Polynikes,
> Indem ich deke deinen Leib, erlang' ich diß,
> Obgleich ich dich geehrt, vor Wohlgesinnten.
> Nie nemlich, weder, wenn ich Mutter
> Von Kindern wäre, oder ein Gemahl
> Im Tode sich verzehret, hätt' ich mit Gewalt,
> Als wollt' ich einen Aufstand, dies errungen.
> Und welchem Geseze sag' ich diß zu Dank?
> Wär' ein Gemahl gestorben, gäb' es andre,
> Und auch ein Kind von einem andern Manne,
> Wenn diesen ich umarmt. Wenn aber Mutter
> Und Vater schläft, im Ort der Todten beides,
> Stehts nicht, als wüchs' ein andrer Bruder wieder.
> Nach solchem Geseze hab' ich dich geehrt . . . (FA 16: 359: 936–49)

---

4. For Reinhardt, the "Sophoclean situation"—the conflict that develops on multiple levels within the tragedy—involves above all the hero's recognition of his own utter solitude. Reinhardt 1947, 10.

5. Deleuze, *Kant's Critical Philosophy*, x. Lacan has pointed out the similarity between Creon's position as arbiter of the law and Kant's articulation of the forms of practical reason (259).

> Now, Polynices,
> Covering your corpse I have come to this,
> Though in well-minded eyes I honoured you.
> For never had I either been a mother
> Of children or if in death a husband
> Had lain rotting would I with force,
> As though wanting revolt, have brought this off.
> And to what law do I say thanks for this?
> A husband dying there would be other husbands
> And even children by another man,
> If I embraced that man. But when the mother
> And father sleep both in the place of death
> It cannot be another brother will grow.
> According to that law I honoured you. (Constantine 98)

Here is the claim that shocked Goethe, that Lacan declared a "scandal," that in its stark simplicity resists so much of what is held dear in the community of humans organized around Christian declarations of universal love and charity:[6] Antigone values her brother, *this* brother, above all others, because unlike all others she regards his particularity as irreplaceable and his ethical position as otherwise indefensible. In justifying her actions before the Theban community she invokes no other law than this one, which applies to their relationship alone. At no point in her tragedy does Antigone claim to stand for anyone but herself and her own, particular, fallen brother. Not even Ismene, who offers her advice to Antigone in their exchange in the very first scene, may take part in the relationship that her sister defends, and Hölderlin's translation underscores this insistent solitude:

> Magst du so etwas sagen, hass' ich dich,
> Hasst auch dich der Gestorbene mit Recht.
> Laß mich aber und meinen irren Rat
> Das Gewaltige leiden. (FA 16: 273: 95–98)

> If you can say that and the like, I hate you,
> Also the dead man hates you and is right to.
> But let me and my errant counsel
> Suffer the violent/the powerful.

---

6. Lacan discusses Goethe's apparent hope that this passage would prove corrupt (255).

Yet to leave Antigone to suffer her fate alone has hardly ever been as self-evident as she would wish here, as countless revisions of her tragedy and invocations of her character in every conceivable context evince.[7] Nor was Hölderlin any less susceptible to her allure; his first attempt at translating the second choral ode goes back five years previous to the publication of the Sophocles project, to 1799.[8] However, the particular attraction of this "most Greek of tragedies," as Lacoue-Labarthe calls *Antigone* in contrast to *Oedipus*, must have lain for Hölderlin in its sheer conceptual distance from modernity, its status as "not 'reconstitutable'—if not wholly untransposable" (Lacoue-Labarthe 1998, 220). While Oedipus acts excessively in his reliance upon *logos*—a point of departure more recognizable to a modern audience— Antigone calls upon laws ancient and unwritten even in Sophocles's time. And Hölderlin, to a far greater extent than many contemporary readers, seems to have understood the importance of maintaining this distinction. Rather than coaxing Antigone into a form that would resonate with the experience of modern subjectivity, Hölderlin's translation and remarks preserve in their central figure a difference that remains unquestionably alone, thwarting readers who would seek to make an example of her—that is, until Antigone exposes difference itself to be oddly exemplary, even as she continues to claim it as her very own.

Indeed, it is precisely within this exposure of exemplarity in difference that Hölderlin locates the special resonance of Antigone's tragedy for modernity: on one hand in what one critic has called its enactment of the "tragedy of being human,"[9] but at the same time in its strict particularity, its insistence that the pivotal act to which her tragedy bears witness has in its essence nothing to do with anyone else. This sentiment already emerges in the passage cited at the start of this chapter, drawn from one of the most discussed passages in any Greek tragedy. While most translators fashion out of the second choral ode a paean to the magnitude of humankind in the face of adversity,[10] Hölderlin's rendering guides the proceedings of the tragedy in

---

7. For an exhaustive account of numerous examples, see Steiner, *Antigones* (New York: Oxford, 1984).

8. Hölderlin first reflects upon Antigone as an exemplary figure in his philosophical fragments on religion at approximately the same time.

9. Kathleen Wright, "Heidegger's Hölderlin and the Mo(u)rning of History," *Philosophy Today* 37: 4 (Winter 1993): 430. Wright adds "among the Greeks," which will become unnecessary in a discussion of *das Unheimliche* as Heidegger poses it with respect to Hölderlin; the translation from Greece to modernity even doubles the experience of this notion of monstrosity.

10. Compare, for example the Loeb edition, translated by Hugh Lloyd-Jones: "Many things are formidable, and none more formidable than man!" (Cambridge, MA: Harvard University Press, 1994):35. In the introduction to his translation of Antigone, Robert Fagles describes the ode as "celebrat[ing] Man's progress and powers" (Fagles 42); meanwhile, his translation captures some of the

a more unsettling direction: "Ungeheuer ist viel. Doch nichts / Ungeheuerer, als der Mensch" (299: 349–50: *Much is monstrous. Yet nothing more monstrous than the human*).

The word "ungeheuer" is an astute translation choice for the Greek *deinon*, as the two terms share a fundamental ambiguity that cuts to the heart of the Chorus's words. In describing the human being as *deinon*, Sophocles famously evokes both man's greatness and his dreadfulness, his autonomy and his excessiveness in his interactions with nature and the gods. This conflicting range of meanings in a single term underscores the fundamental tolerance of contradiction inherent in ancient Greek cosmology, as Oudemans and Lardinois have argued.[11] Indeed, Sophocles employs contradictory imagery and language throughout the entire stasimon in order to emphasize the extent to which *deinon* is both the precondition for human achievement and a transgression of the boundaries that separate humans from the gods; again, Oudemans and Lardinois point out how Sophocles uses multivalent terms (not just *deinon* but also *perao*, to traverse or transgress, and *tolma*, daring but also recklessness) to convey the idea of the human being's tendency to overreach in his confrontations with nature (Oudemans and Lardinois 126).[12] Even the reference to man's venturing and advancing in the notion of seafaring has an ambiguous status, as Mark Griffith points out in the Cambridge edition of the *Antigone*, "as a positive symbol of adventure and technical mastery, but also a negative one of temerity, violation of boundaries, and unnatural greed."[13]

Unlike many modern translators, including his contemporaries, who tend to emphasize in their translations the "wonders" of human achievement, Hölderlin manages to convey this broad and ambivalent range of human characteristics with an understanding of its significance as the essential marker of a tragic universe. While the customary choice of German translators of the nineteenth century, *gewaltig*, evokes above all a sense of power, *ungeheuer* signifies both strength and excess, immensity and mon-

---

ambiguity of Hölderlin's: "Numberless wonders/terrible wonders walk the world but none the match for man" (76). *Sophocles, The Three Theban Plays*, trans. Robert Fagles (New York: Penguin, 1982).

11. Th. C. W. Oudemans and A. P. M. H. Lardinois, *Tragic Ambiguity: Anthropology, Philosophy, and Sophocles' Antigone* (Leiden: Brill, 1987), 4.

12. See also Darien Shanske's discussion of the concept of *deinon* from its pretragic manifestations in Homer to its role in the historical writings of Thucydides. Shanske argues that for Sophocles, the relation of the human to *deinon* is "not just a question but a leitmotiv, that is, a question that must be answered." *Thucydides and the Philosophical Origins of History* (Cambridge 2006), 85.

13. Sophocles, *Antigone*, ed. Mark Griffith (Cambridge: Cambridge University Press, 1999), 185.

strosity.[14] If by valuing her brother uniquely and refusing any other earthly contingency Antigone approaches the limits of what is commonly understood to be human nature, this statement's open appeal to the monstrosity of humankind indicates that the rest of us might share her taste for transgression. Indeed, Hölderlin's adjectival phrases throughout the passage emphasize the disturbance caused by the actions of humankind, continually marking contrasts between the untouched, raw status of nature and the ambition and industry of humans:

> Und der Himmlischen erhabene Erde,
> Die unverderbliche, unermüdete,
> Reibet er auf; mit dem strebenden Pfluge,
> Von Jahr zu Jahr.
>
> And the noble earth of the gods in heaven
> The unspoilable, unweary,
> He rips up with the striving plough
> From year to year. (Constantine 81; trans. modified)

Hölderlin's use of the term *aufreiben* for the Greek *apotribo* points up with intense physicality the negative repercussions of human ambition; *aufreiben*, to tear up or ream out, implies the annihilation of its object, here the "unperishable" earth.[15] The form of the passage redoubles this destructive intensity, as Hölderlin modifies the tonal continuity of the passage in Greek (*aphthiton, akamatan apotruetai*) in favor of a visual and acoustic disruption: he begins with a pattern similar to the Greek (*unverderblich, unermüdet*), only to break it with the phrase "reibet er auf," in which a verb with a separable prefix (*aufreiben*) is itself literally torn in two.

Hölderlin's rendering certainly demonstrates his unusually keen comprehension of the ambiguities inherent in both the language and the worldview of the ancient Greeks, yet there is more at stake here than a "correct" translation. *Deinon*, which Hölderlin translates elsewhere and at other times as "das Gewaltige" (signifying, more univocally, the powerful or the great) now disturbs in the very act of signifying; its translation into the ambiguous

---

14. Hölderlin begins here as well, translating the passage in 1799 as "Vieles Gewaltige giebt's. Doch nichts Gewaltiger, als der Mensch" (*There is much that is powerful. Yet nothing as powerful as the human being*). Compare K. W. F. Solger's translation from 1824: "Vieles Gewalt'ge lebt, und doch / Nichts gewaltiger, denn der Mensch..." (*Des Sophokles Tragödien* [Berlin 1808], 159).

15. Griffith and others point out the oxymoron of this passage in Greek, in which man wears out the unwearying earth (Griffith 186; see also Joan O'Brien, *Guide to Sophocles' Antigone* [Carbondale: Southern Illinois University Press, 1978], 54).

"ungeheuer" produces an effect of foreignness in the same gesture that ought to render it comprehensible. At the same time, Greek wordplay (the oxymoron of man wearing out the unwearying earth) gives way to a translation that performs visually and aurally what it also represents conceptually. In a striking enactment of what his remarks will ultimately explore, translation begins to take action here, to speak its own name even as it stands in for an other that will not be silenced; for rather than approximating (and thereby flattening) the Greek text in terms unproblematic to a modern context, the translation maintains and even intensifies the disquieting movement, staged in tragedy, through which man will become unrecognizable to himself: Much is monstrous, but nothing is more monstrous than the human.

To be sure, this choral passage is not the first place where Hölderlin articulates the problem of accounting for an unrecognizable element within the self. As a host of Hölderlin scholars have noted, his December 1801 letter to friend Böhlendorff already invokes the imperative of approaching that which is one's own, a lesson that is an infinitely greater challenge than the encounter with the foreign: "But that which is one's own must be learned just as well as the foreign. . . . The free use of that which is one's own is the most difficult" (FA 16: 16).[16] However, the remarks on *Antigone*, completed nearly three years later, extend this point to an unsettling (and unsettled) conclusion, indicating that the shock of exposure to one's own "character" may reveal the consequence of this difficult lesson in the simple discovery that one is not at all "one" with oneself.

> Der kühnste Moment eines Taglaufs oder Kunstwerks ist, wo der Geist der Zeit und Natur, das Himmlische, was den Menschen ergreift, und der Gegenstand, für welchen er sich interessirt, am wildesten gegeneinander stehen [. . .] In diesem Momente muß der Mensch sich am meisten festhalten, deswegen steht er auch da am offensten in seinem Karakter. (FA 16: 412).

> The boldest moment in the course of a day or a work of art comes when the spirit of time and nature, the divine/heavenly that seizes hold of the human being, and the object in which he is interested are most wildly opposed to one another. [. . .] At that moment the human being must keep the firmest hold on himself, for which reason he also stands most openly there in his character. (Constantine 114; trans. modified)

---

16. "Aber das Eigene muß genau so gut gelernt seyn, wie das Fremde. . . . [Der] freie Gebrauch des Eigenen [ist] das Schwerste" (FA 16: 16).

Whether it happens in the work of art or the course of an ordinary day, Hölderlin's subject finds herself not only isolated but suspended in a gap between her own experience of the phenomenal world ("the object in which he is interested") and the divine spirit of time and space that frames that experience ("the spirit of time and nature"). However, while the former represents the subject's "interest"—the object that she herself has determined, "her" other—the force of the latter guarantees that this appropriative gesture is eternally accompanied by a disruption that seizes the subject and shows her, otherwise, the extent to which that other exceeds her.

Hölderlin's *Antigone,* precisely insofar as it is at once tragedy *and* translation, proposes to make that event happen; exposing the subject's character will demand the effects of both separate dynamics. Although the remarks on *Oedipus Tyrannus* similarly emphasize the hero's solitude in the context of the tragedy, they leave aside the crucial question of how translation itself may become involved in that process of exposure. In effect, the formidable temporal lag between Sophocles' text and Hölderlin's age itself becomes a player, as characters' words mark not a form of privileged access but a glimpse into the experience of transition as such. While Hölderlin's friend and classmate, G. W. F. Hegel, produces an account which places Antigone on one side of an ethical impasse in the ascent towards universal Spirit, then, Hölderlin's version of the tragedy (published three years before Hegel's *Phenomenology*) anticipates a different ethics that tragedy and translation together have the potential to enact. In this model difference *becomes* Antigone; that is, the interplay between familiar and foreign that the heroine embodies in the text—not coincidentally, the exchange that also describes the relationship between original and translation—defines, suits, and illuminates her as a source of potentially limitless fascination. And as a final consequence, it becomes the modern subject as well.

Long before Hölderlin's remarks begin to sketch the outline of this difference expressed in translation, she is there. And some of the most compelling moments of the translation actively nourish a lasting fascination with her, the mysterious girl who has for so long brought this tragedy to life. Unlike the necessary distancing that informed the reading of *Oedipus,* however, Antigone's allure is meant directly to engage the subject who makes contact with it, seizing him with the force of an ancient passion returning—perhaps, as Hölderlin will soon specify, through nothing more than the utterance of a single word. Just as it seizes the Chorus, which soon enough has little choice but to look on, through tears aroused from a distant and forgotten source, as a figure roams its field of vision like a wandering spirit.

Jezt aber komm' ich, eben, selber, aus
Dem Geseze. Denn ansehn muß ich diß, und halten kann ich
Nicht mehr die Quelle der Tränen,
Da in das alles schwaigende Bett'
Ich seh' Antigonä wandeln. (FA 16: 349: 830–34)

But now even I myself am brought outside of
The law. For I must look at this, and I can hold back
The spring of tears no longer,
As into the all-silent bed
I see Antigone wander.

Early in the remarks on *Antigone*, Hölderlin reiterates a crucial element of his argument from the remarks on *Oedipus* by insisting that the "lawful calculus" (*gesezlicher Kalkul*) fundamental to tragic form must be reproduced in modern terms, culminating in the caesura that marks the balance between two irreconcilable halves.[17] In this passage from the translation, however, we seem to have reached a space in which laws no longer apply. Before the vision recognized by my very own eye—for I must look at this—even I myself am brought outside of the system of laws through which I constitute myself, and hence I myself am shattered. In fact, I do it to myself, *ich, eben, selber;* echoed in the jagged rhythm of the Chorus's lines, culminating in the visually and aurally arresting "aus / Dem Geseze," the disturbance emerges not from without but from *within* the subject who sees Antigone enter her tomb.[18] This production of an internal "outside" is clearly distant from Lessing's influential reformulation of tragic catharsis, in which the viewing subject identifies with the figure onstage through pity and its self-reflexive component, fear. If the possibility of identifying with the tragic heroine in Lessing's view is contingent upon our recognition of her likeness to us (and even the extent to which we "like" her), the attraction that the Chorus describes here does not replicate that movement into the sphere of familiarity. Rather, a process is initiated in the opposite direction: because it is

---

17. "Die Regel, das kalkulable Gesez der Antigonä verhält sich zu dem des Ödipus, wie __/__ zum ____, so daß sich das Gleichgewicht mehr vom Anfang gegen das Ende, als vom Ende gegen den Anfang zu neigt" (FA 16: 411) (*The rule, the calculable law of the Antigone relates to that of Oedipus as __/__ to ____, so that the balance leans more from the beginning towards the end than from the end towards the beginning*).

18. In his 1948 adaptation of Hölderlin's *Antigonä*, Bertolt Brecht accentuates the rhythmic caesura of these lines—"Jetzt aber komm ich, eben, selber/Aus dem Takte" (*Now even I myself am put off the rhythm*)—while inexplicably failing to retain the formal line break that performs it. See Brecht, *Die Antigone des Sophokles*, 44.

impossible to tear one's eyes from the sight of her, we must follow Antigone, like the Chorus, "outside of the law." Something other than identification brings one outside of the comprehensible here, and not only as an effect of tragic form and poetic language, where one would expect to find it after his remarks on *Oedipus*. To be sure, that resonance of form is again essential to the tragedy's potential for affirming an uncrossable distance between subject and world, self and other; however, an equally powerful kind of difference comes to be expressed directly by the fascinating and haunting figure we see before us: *Ich seh' Antigonä wandeln*. . . . The German word "wandeln" refers here to her movement into the tomb, but it also denotes change, thus evoking the idea of a crossing from life into the "all-silent bed" of death. What brings one "outside of the law" here—hence beyond the potential for understanding or "grasping" (*begreifen*) that underlies the speculative effort—is precisely this captivating vision confronting the Chorus, the vision of a wandering, changing Antigone. Thus it cannot wrest its tearful eyes from the sight of her, despite that sight's evocation of something almost chilling, something so marked by the allure of its difference that Heidegger will eventually describe it as "unheimlich": *For I must look at this*. . . .

The Chorus is not alone in its bewilderment, for the reader of Hölderlin's remarks on the tragedy cannot help but find herself similarly unsettled in facing the density of these articulations. In this sense, translation and interpretation also initiate a movement "outside of the law" in the challenging language of this *Antigone*. While in *Oedipus* Hölderlin allows text to decenter itself through translation and form, disrupting and endlessly deferring the dialectical resolution that other modern readers would wish to give it, here the word and its form affect the subject directly, with translation as the vehicle of that effect. As Hölderlin theorizes it in the remarks, it is ultimately the word that seizes ("ergreift") the subject, compelling it to murder, instigating tragedy; and the experience through translation of this word's force and its proximity to death both undermines the solid ground on which the subject believes itself to be standing and establishes that vertiginous difference itself as constitutive. Thus every subject becomes at once as particular, as exemplary and as monstrous as Antigone.[19] This, as we will see, brings

---

19. Derrida's discussion of the singular and the universal is significant in this context, see for example "Passages—from Traumatism to Promise" (in *Points . . . Interviews, 1974–1994*, ed. E. Weber, trans. P. Kamuf [Stanford University Press, 1995], 378). In his discussion of the date here as well as in *Shibboleth*, singularity is both kept and lost by virtue of the fact that a unique moment repeated, made readable is no longer entirely unique; a similar structure would correspond to the figure of Antigone here, except that in this case what is readable and iterable must stand alongside that which cannot be read but imposes itself onto the text nevertheless. Derrida also treats this element of unreadability in the same interview by introducing—like Hölderlin—the figure of the monster (385ff.).

the whole operation all the more proximate to that space between life and death in which Antigone will choose to linger.

STRICTLY SPEAKING, the chronology of my discussion of Hölderlin's reflections on tragedy is both right and wrong; although the translation of *Oedipus* appears first in print in 1804, Antigone makes her first entrance into Hölderlin's writings several years earlier.[20] She enters the scene, like the Oedipus figure of "In lovely blueness . . . ," not yet in the specific context of Sophoclean tragedy but rather as a disruption within a moment of philosophical posturing by the poet, again with respect to the nature of speculative reflection.

This initial link to Antigone appears in a period in which Hölderlin, first studying with Fichte in Jena and then living in close proximity to Hegel in Frankfurt, was concerned not only with poetic production but also the very current problem of accounting for a fundamental self-recognition.[21] As he describes a new set of philosophical letters to Niethammer early in 1796, he intends to coax the conflictual tones of reflective subjectivity into pulling a disappearing act.

> In the philosophical letters I wish to find the principle that will explain for me the separations in which we think and exist, that however is also capable of making the conflict vanish, that conflict between subject and object, between our self and the world, yes even between reason and revelation.[22]

The unlikely image of conflict being made to vanish into thin air suggests that even at this early juncture, Hölderlin poses these questions with more desire than conviction; not only must the principle he seeks elucidate the nature of division but must also, in order to repair that division, perform something like a feat of magic. The desire to formulate a philosophical system thus continues to be irritated by his awareness of an ineffaceable distance defining self-consciousness. As a result, in the philosophical letters he mentions to Niethammer, Hölderlin resorts to a bizarre grammar of

---

20. Hölderlin first confronts that unsettling choral ode from the *Antigone* ("Ungeheuer ist viel . . . ") in 1800. At that time, his translation is closer to the traditional one: "Vieles gewaltige gibt's. Doch nichts / Ist gewaltiger, als der Mensch" (FA 16, 56).
21. See Henrich, "Hölderlin über Urteil und Sein," 73–77.
22. "In den philosophischen Briefen will ich das Prinzip finden, das mir die Trennungen, in denen wir denken und existieren, erklärt, das aber auch vermögend ist, den Widerstreit verschwinden zu machen, den Widerstreit zwischen dem Subjekt und dem Objekt, zwischen unserem Selbst und der Welt, ja auch zwischen Vernunft und Offenbarung" (24. February 1796, StA VI:1: 203).

relativity in which a subject's approach to the unreflected absolute is never defined by what it is or is not, but rather by that which it is constantly becoming: "then there exists, in every sphere that is proper to him, a more than necessity-based, higher life, thus a more than necessity-based, a more infinite satisfaction (Pfau 1988, 90; trans. modified) (*so giebt es für ihn, in jeder ihm eigentümlichen Sphäre, ein mehr als nothdürftiges, ein höheres Leben, also eine mehr als nothdürftige, eine unendlichere Befriedigung* [StA IV: 275]). As such this approach is not different from a rigorously dialectical structure of patient ascension toward absolute "satisfaction." However, while for Hölderlin aesthetic representation had previously formed, at least in his direct address of the problem, the means to enable the disappearance of conflict, in this text that same work of art—specifically, tragedy—will exemplify conflict's permanence. Within this context, Antigone appears as a foreign entity, wholly unassimilable to the thinking subject who is confronted with her.

> . . . those infinite, more than necessary relations of life can be thought, to be sure, but not *merely* thought; thought does not exhaust them . . . and if there exist unwritten divine laws of which Antigone speaks, . . . then they are *insufficient* insofar as they are grasped, represented only by themselves and not in life because . . . the law and the particular world in which it is enacted interrelate more infinitely; and because the law, even if it were universal for civilized people, could never be conceived of abstractly without a particular case unless one were to take away from it its peculiarity, its intimate relation with the sphere in which it is enacted. (Pfau 1988, 91; trans. modified)[23]

In Hölderlin's view, Antigone's unwritten laws cannot be grasped or even thought in the abstract, outside of their own lost particularity; modern thought and religion simply cannot account for what emerges in this representation of a tragic hero, for a difference that cannot be known in the terms constituting a speculative approach to knowledge, even knowledge of

---

23. "... jene unendlicheren mehr als nothwendigen Beziehungen des Lebens können zwar auch gedacht, aber nur nicht blos gedacht werden; der Gedanke erschöpft sie nicht . . . und wenn es ungeschriebene göttliche Gesetze giebt, von denen Antigonä spricht, . . . so sind sie, in so fern sie blos für sich und nicht im Leben begriffen werden, vorgestellt werden, *unzulänglich,* einmal weil . . . das Gesez, und die besondere Welt in der es ausgeübt wird, unendlicher verbunden ist und eben deswegen das Gesez, wenn es auch gleich ein für gesittete Menschen allgemeines wäre, doch niemals ohne einen besonderen Fall, niemals abstract gedacht werden könnte, wenn man ihm nicht seine Eigentümlichkeit, seine innige Verbundenheit mit der Sphäre in der es ausgeübt wird, nehmen wollte" (StA IV: 277).

"difference." Understanding her law as universally legitimate thus becomes impossible, her experience too particular to be grasped as fuel for the dialectical force of history. Tragedy reveals not proximity but rather the formidable presence of a barrier to the absolute in the structure of thought itself. The dynamics of endless approach, already familiar in Hölderlin's reflections by this time, are replicated in the text of *Antigone* by the permanent division between us and her, between familiar self and a radically foreign other.

This view of the inaccessible laws that govern Antigone's actions remains largely unchanged for Hölderlin, even as his approach to tragedy continues to evolve from philosophical reflection to translation. Despite his emphasis on "lawful calculus" in the remarks on *Oedipus*, Hölderlin's *Antigone* demonstrates that this evolution will remain distant from the question of legitimacy in any conventional sense. It is with respect to this question that the differences between his and Hegel's accounts come to a distinct point. While Hegel lets Antigone and Creon exemplify the ethical divide between the equally legitimate duties of family and community, the divine and human laws embodied by woman and man, Hölderlin manages to call into question the demand of legitimacy as such.

In the sixth chapter of the *Phenomenology of Spirit*, Hegel situates the tragic universe as a vital step within the dialectical advance toward universal spirit, where the ethical conflicts that both define and divide the community are confronted in stark and brutal terms. Every human being within the tragic universe has a legitimate duty upon which he or she, of necessity upholding one or the other aspect of the ethical order, must act without reservation; the human law of the community and state is consciously maintained by man, whereas the divine law, that of the family, is intuitively, unconsciously preserved by the woman.[24] The guardian of the divine law—for Hegel, the sister—has as her only responsibility precisely that which Antigone is compelled to perform: in the name of an individual helplessly facing the threat of a return to pure universality in death, she must see to it that this death become an act of consciousness, that the very destruction of the body not be left to nature but be transformed into "something done" (*ein Getanes*).[25] Although in carrying out this duty the sister violates the human law, this in no way alleviates its necessity. Indeed, as in Antigone's case,

---

24. Hegel's structure of opposing laws is, however, far from simple division. The two sides of the law and the groups they represent cannot be seen as mutually exclusive in the lives of individuals but rather intersect necessarily and constantly, that law which constitutes the *positive* side for each individual determines his or her fundamental duty. See Chanter, "Antigone's Dilemma," 138.

25. G. W. F. Hegel, *Phänomenologie des Geistes*, ed. J. Hoffmeister (Hamburg: Felix Meiner, 1952), 321. Subsequent page number references will be given in parentheses directly after citations.

precisely when her brother is excluded from the community and denied a public funeral before the state, it is the duty of the sister alone, made necessary by bonds of blood, to make death into an act of consciousness, to ensure that her brother's singular place will be maintained at least in memory.[26]

Ostensibly at least, these two divisions of the law remain equally legitimate for Hegel, because they represent the two equally necessary elements of the ethical order: family and community, woman and man, singularity and universality. What is more, though Antigone may be guilty of violating the law of the state, that guilt is inevitable; in the Hegelian system, pure innocence only equals inertia, in the manner of nothing but a stone.[27] In fact, as it turns out the crime itself is unavoidable, irreversible in any case; as Derrida asserts in *Glas,* by the very nature of the Hegelian system that introduces sexual difference as intrinsic conflict, the crime constitutes a "fatal necessity."[28] There is no other means to act within the ethical world but through crime. Thus Creon, too, must act criminally, and even if Hegel does not discuss this prospect explicitly, the tragedy itself supports it; in the end he, too, will acknowledge his guilt and bear his punishment in the loss of his entire family. Merely by acting, both man and woman are guilty by definition; meanwhile, ethical consciousness benefits dialectically from the eventual restoration of an equilibrium which Hegel calls "justice" (*Gerechtigkeit*).[29]

Yet even as Hegel insists that the two sides are equal in their culpability as well as their legitimacy, his conception of that guilt takes on various forms in his use of tragic material. In fact, one man and one woman in particular, Oedipus and his daughter Antigone, embody the limits of those forms in a manner that curiously seems to contradict his previously universal distinctions of gender. Citing a passage from Antigone's final lament before she enters the tomb out of which she will never return, Hegel argues that her guilt is purer ("reiner") than her father's, insofar as she is fully aware at the

---

26. The other possibility in death, a "dishonoring" operation of unconscious desires, would constitute, as Derrida points out in *Glas,* desecration and decomposition "at the mercy of every lower individuality and the forces of abstract material elements," an expression that would destroy the dead one in his being *für sich,* would leave him an "empty singular"; this desire is suppressed by the act of the sister for her brother [145]. Derrida also links this "dishonoring operation" to what he calls a "probably cannibal desire" that the family must suppress by taking on this duty.

27. Hegel, *Phänomenologie,* 334: "Unschuldig ist daher nur das Nichttun wie das Sein eines Steines, nicht einmal eines Kindes."

28. Derrida, *Glas,* 172.

29. Lacan openly questions this possibility of reconciliation, echoing the critical voice of Erwin Rohde, who argues against the view that the outcome of tragedy is "ennobling"; in disagreement with what he calls "conventional literary interpretation." Rohde, *Psyche: The Cult of Souls and Belief in Immortality among the Greeks* (London: Routledge & Kegan Paul, 1950), 431. See also Lacan 249ff.

same time that she must obey the law that constitutes her "intuition" of the divine law and that this act of obedience violates the human law that governs the community:

weil wir leiden, anerkennen wir, daß wir gefehlt—(336)

because we suffer we acknowledge that we have erred—(Miller 284)

Because she can acknowledge the certainty of her crime, yet still proceeds with her duty under the divine law, Antigone represents a higher level of self-consciousness than her father Oedipus, who remained blind to the possibility that his actions, which in this model appear "right" according to his duty to the human law, might inscribe into him a terrible, unavoidable guilt:[30] "the ethical consciousness is more complete, its guilt more inexcusable, if it knows *beforehand* the law and the power which it opposes, if it takes them to be violence and wrong, to be ethical merely by accident, and, like Antigone, knowingly commits the crime" (Miller 284).[31]

Miller's translation poses a semantic problem for nonreaders of German here by presenting Antigone's "reinere Schuld" (literally, *purer* guilt) as "more inexcusable." The question of "excuse" does not actually arise in Hegel's account. What is clear in the German text is that Antigone's act represents a more complete ethical consciousness than her father Oedipus, to whom Hegel obviously alludes here. Since in Hegel's system one is guilty as soon as one acts, acting with awareness is more productive, for then one may turn a temporary, personal loss into a gain in the universal direction of Spirit.[32] Her guilt involves two independent movements: on the one hand, she acts without question in the name of the divine law, which she has (been) chosen to represent; on the other hand, she recognizes that another (in this system, equally just) side exists, a law of the state that she grasps but nevertheless must violate for the sake of the laws of the family.[33] Still, Derrida emphasizes

---

30. This sharply contrasts Hegel's view of effective tragedy with Aristotle's; while it is clear, of course, that for Hegel the question of guilt extends far beyond the scope of Aristotle's poetics, still it is interesting to note the exact reversal of Aristotle's view of *Oedipus* as the most successful tragedy precisely because the hero remains until the end completely unaware of his guilt.

31. " . . . das sittliche Bewußtseyn ist vollständiger, seine Schuld reiner, wenn es das Gesetz und die Macht vorher kennt, der es gegenüber tritt, sie für Gewalt und Unrecht, für eine sittliche Zufälligkeit nimmt, und wissentlich, wie Antigone, das Verbrechen begeht" [336]).

32. Antigone's act thus illuminates, in Derrida's words, an opposition between two laws that is of the order of universality, even if the crime is committed in the name of singularity (*Glas*, 173). Within Hegel's logic of sexual difference, as Judith Butler notes, she thus acts more like a man. See Butler 8f.

33. Binder, by contrast, valorizes Antigone's act as divinely inspired and condemns Creon's as excessive, thus curiously naming him as the hero whose hubris leads to his ruin. "Ein gotterfüllter und

that Antigone remains "in the middle of the ascent," that her act does not yet constitute "ethical plenitude"; while her recognition for itself represents an advance toward self-conscious understanding of the ethical system as evolving unity of opposing factors, she herself remains only the "figure of the fall"—the individual who disobeys even as she obeys, who even as she performs this advance also ensures that the subsequent fall on both sides of the law will restore equilibrium through justice (*Glas* 174f.). Nevertheless, for Hegel the consequences of both her act and her acknowledgment of it offer signs that, in its advancement toward universal Spirit, the ethical realm of community and individual is certainly getting somewhere.

To be sure, Antigone's acknowledgment of her own guilt here does not exonerate her, since her act still reflects the disruptive status of womankind—Hegel's famous internal enemy, the "eternal irony of the community"—that unsettles the community's stability from within. One might wonder, however, if another force of irony doesn't play havoc with Hegel's own approach to the universal conflict of laws he presents; for precisely in this turn to the tragedy that ought to exemplify a crucial step in his progression, the structure of his argument begins likewise to unravel. That single reference to Antigone's recognition of her guilt is taken badly out of context, while Hölderlin's translation of the passage emphasizes that context as crucial to any inquiry into Antigone's relation to the law. Citing a passage from Antigone's final lament (his only direct reference to Sophocles' text in translation), Hegel notes her recognition that an act of obedience to her "intuition" of the divine law would at the same time violate the human law that governs the community, a recognition brought on by the suffering she endures: "because we suffer we acknowledge that we have erred" (Miller 284). In contrast to the apparent clarity of Hegelian oppositions, however, for Hölderlin Antigone's statement expresses neither intuitive conviction nor acceptance of inevitable guilt, but rather bitter frustration with the gods and their power to force their laws arbitrarily upon the acts of individuals.

> Was soll ich Arme noch zu himmlischen
> Gewalten schaun? Wen singen der Waffengenossen?
> Da ich Gottlosigkeit aus Frömmigkeit empfangen.
> Doch wenn nun dieses schön ist vor den Göttern,
> *So leiden wir und bitten ab, was wir*
> *Gesündiget* . . . (359: 958–963; emphasis added)

---

ein selbstherrlicher Mensch stehen sich gegenüber und also nicht mehr Wille gegen Wille, sondern Wissen gegen Ichsucht, religio gegen Hybris" (*Hölderlin und Sophokles: Turmvorträge* [Tübingen: Hölderlin-Gesellschaft, 1992], 151).

Poor girl, why look henceforth
To heavenly powers? What comrade sing for help?
Since I from piety got godlessness.
But if this thing is lovely to the gods
*We suffer it and beg forgiveness for
How we have sinned.* (Constantine 99; emphasis added)

As we saw in the previous chapter, an inquiry into the problem of exercising free will shapes Hölderlin's reading and translation of the oracle in *Oedipus;* for Hölderlin, it is not the force of fate or the will of the gods but Oedipus' own unfortunate interpretation of the oracle that places him on the path of despair. But while Oedipus' downfall comes with his excessive drive to interpret what ought to have remained general, Antigone is trapped finally by her refusal of the arbitrary exercise of law and punishment: her act is neither sanctioned by the state nor "beautiful to the gods," and yet still she makes her choice, like Oedipus, without that permission. If her action were beautiful to the gods, circumstances would be simpler, the outcome more conventionally acceptable; she could atone for her sins by suffering and be excused for them. The passage that Hegel cites to establish Antigone's conscious guilt therefore signifies in Hölderlin's reading nothing more than her assurance that suffering in a manner pleasing to the gods would constitute (and encompass) atonement; meanwhile, she also recognizes that her own suffering will be far more abysmal. Indeed, Hölderlin locates the foundation of Antigone's law neither in intuitive adherence nor in strict opposition to *any* law, whether just or arbitrary, human or divine. Rather, his translation points the question of legitimacy in quite another direction.

> KREON: Was wagtest du, ein solch Gesez zu brechen?
> ANTIGONE: Darum. Mein Zevs berichtete mirs nicht;
>   Noch hier im Haus das Recht der Todesgötter,
>   Die unter Menschen das Gesez begränzet . . . (309: 466–69)

> CREON: Why did you dare to break a law like that?
> ANTIGONE: Because. *My* Zeus did not tell it to me;
>   Nor did the justice of the gods of death,
>   Here in the house who limit human laws. (Constantine 84; trans. modified)

These lines have inspired some controversy among Hölderlin's critics, for Antigone's justification for her action may be understood in different ways.

Neither Zeus nor the gods of the underworld instructed her to follow *Creon's* law; that much is clear. (This is consistent with the prevalence of negatives in the Greek original [Griffith counts nine negatives in the passage, 200]). However, her position here is not a mere conflation of the laws of "her own" Zeus and those of Hades, as some critics have unproblematically stipulated in citing Hölderlin's proximity to Hegel's model on this point.[34] Given the dramatic quality of Hölderlin's punctuation in this passage, in fact, it is possible to read Antigone's response here in direct defiance of her image in Hegelian eyes: by insisting that she transgressed the law "Darum" (followed by a striking full stop); she refuses to appeal to any formal law at all, only to the "Satzungen," the unwritten customs or principles that the gods represent and that the law of the state keeps at bay.[35] If she is beholden to anything, it is only to rights which remain forever unwritten and untraceable.[36]

In the remarks on *Antigone* Hölderlin elaborates further in comparing the tragedy's two protagonists, describing the conflict between Creon and Antigone more precisely as the perception of the law and its absence.

> Einmal das, was den Antitheos karakterisirt, wo einer, in Gottes Sinne, wie *gegen* Gott sich verhält, und den Geist des Höchsten gesezlos erkennt. Dann die fromme Furcht vor dem Schiksaal, hiemit das Ehren Gottes, als eines gesezten.[. . .] Im ersten Sinne mehr Antigonä handelnd. Im zweiten Kreon. (FA 16: 416)

> First in what characterises the *antitheos*, where one, after God's own mind, acts, as it seems, *against* god and recognises the spirit of the highest with-

---

34. See in particular Wolfgang Binder's lecture, *Hölderlin und Sophokles. Turmvorträge*, where the speaker's adherence to a dialectical model of tragedy leads to a strange reversal of Hölderlin's actual translation: "Jetzt aber, in dem Moment, da sie im Streit mit Kreon sich auf den höchsten Gott beruft, wird ihr auf einmal klar, daß hinter dem allgemeinen Brauch der einmalige Wille des Gottes steht. Und der meint sie und verlangt hier und jetzt von ihr das Unerhörte. Deshalb übersetzt Hölderlin: 'Mein Zeus' hat mir's befohlen'" [150]. (*But now, in the moment in which she, in her struggle with Creon, calls upon the highest god, it becomes clear to her that the singular will of the god stands behind the common practice. And this refers to her and demands from her, here and now, the inconceivable. For this reason, Hölderlin translates: "'My Zeus commanded me to do it.'"*)

35. Jean Beaufret acknowledges very carefully in his reading of Hölderlin's translations that it would be possible to read the Greek text in light of Antigone's independence from laws of any kind—"Il est, à l'extrême rigeur, théoretiquement possible de lire ainsi le texte de Sophocle"—although in his view it is the translation alone that represents this independence as hubris in direct relation to that of Oedipus: "Comme Œdipe solicitant d'une manière 'trop infinie' la parole d'oracle, l'hérétique Antigone s'arroge le partage des dieux." *Hölderlin et Sophocle* (Brionne: Monfort, 1983), 36ff.

36. Griffith points out that Antigone's formulation of "unwritten law" here, *agrapta nomima*, is the earliest extant reference to a concept that "by the late fifth and early fourth century are frequently invoked in appeals to universal codes of morality" (201).

out laws. Then, the pious fear of fate, and with it the honouring of God as something set in law ... Antigone acting more in the first sense. Creon in the second. (Constantine 116; trans. modified)

Even if Hölderlin's translation of the relevant passage in the tragedy remains ambiguous, then, here he responds directly to those who would legitimize Antigone's act as divinely ordained, by introducing a "pious" (*fromm*) fear that is not Antigone's impulse but rather Creon's: he views the divine as *gesetzt*, grounded both in law and in a sense of destiny. Meanwhile, Antigone embodies an outlaw recognition (*gesezlos*). (Thus she also leaves the chorus no choice but to follow her "outside of the law.") She asserts her position in the absence of law, and that position does not claim conventional legitimacy any more than it can contribute to the dialectical advancement of Spirit's ethical substance. Antigone's conviction, at least as Hölderlin presents it, leads her elsewhere.

Having moved beyond questions of legitimacy, then, we are left with an empty space at the very heart of this model: while it is evident that the human is equated with the "monstrous" in Hölderlin's account just as tragic experience is aligned with the experience of being "outside of the law," that double experience is thus far discernible only in a negative sense, only as that which it is not—the *Un-geheuer* of the human as un-recognizable, ex-centric, un-speakable. In Hölderlin's translation both Antigone and her act of defiance are at first couched in words that defy signification, for the messenger bearing the news of Polynices' burial is clearly at a loss to say anything at all about her:

> DER BOTE: Ich sag' es dir. Es hat den Todten eben
> Begraben eines, das entkam, die Haut zweimal
> Mit Staub bestreut, und, wies geziemt, gefeiert.
> KREON: Was meinst du? Wer hat diß sich unterfangen?
> DER BOTE: Undenklich. Nirgend war von einem Karst
> Ein Schlag; und nicht der Stoß von einer Schaufel,
> Und dicht das Land; der Boden ungegraben;
> Von Rädern nicht befahren. Zeichenlos war
> Der Meister, und wie das der erste Tagesblik
> Anzeigte, kams unhold uns all' an, wie ein Wunder. (FA 16: 289: 255–
> 64)

> MESSENGER: I'll tell you. Just now something which escaped
> Has buried the dead man, twice sprinkled the skin

> With dust, and in the fit way honoured him.
> CREON: What do you mean? Who was it dared do this?
> MESSENGER: Unthinkable. Nowhere had any mattock
>   Gone in or any shovel thrust, the land
>   Was solid, the earth nowhere dug up;
>   Not ridden over by wheels. Without sign was
>   The master, and when the day's first glimpse denounced it
>   It seemed monstrous [*unhold*] to us, like a miracle. (Constantine 78;
>   trans. modified)

Thus Antigone's act is "unthinkable" from the start. Not only is the messenger at a loss to identify for Creon the one who has done the deed, but that "something" (*eines*) which has acted is itself inconceivable. And that is not all. The prominent absence of any trace, already so striking in the images of untouched ground, extends to the "master" herself; Antigone does not only *leave* no sign in this translation, she literally *is* no sign ("Without sign [*Zeichenlos*] was / The master"]). The messenger describes her lack of sign or trace as *unhold*, fiendish or monstrous where the Greek *duscheres* signifies something that is difficult to handle or manage. The valence of both terms is more unequivocally negative than *deinon* and *Ungeheuer* were in the earlier choral passage, but Hölderlin's choice of *unhold* here—along with the messenger's judgment of the events as *undenklich*, unthinkable—establishes more plainly a relationship between this passage and the earlier reference to monstrosity. *Un-geheuer, un-denklich, un-hold:* Antigone is pressed firmly into the service of the negative even before she is identified as the one who has left no trace. Just what does Antigone reach? When she finally does appear before Creon and the Chorus, what does her vision inspire? Hölderlin attempts to theorize it, again with a negative signifier: Sophocles' language, he writes, brings human understanding to wander "amidst the unthinkable" (*unter Undenkbarem wandelnd* [FA 16: 413]).[37] As we shall see, it is the responsibility of the translation to sustain that inconceivable moment, that trace of nothing that is visible in Antigone yet monstrous (*unhold*) to all.[38]

---

37. The tendency to translate this phrase as "wandering *beneath/below* the unthinkable" (cf. Pfau 110, and Schmidt 2001, 153) obscures Hölderlin's image unnecessarily, since "unter" can denote "amongst" or "amidst" as well as "under" or "beneath."

38. In his reflections on the role of Eros in and for the translated text, Nägele discusses how Antigone is first presented in the text in a "curious mixture of an appeasing familiarity (*hê pais*) and disconcerting strangeness (*ornythos oxyn phthoggon*)." When she does finally appear to the Chorus, she is described as a "demonic sign" (*es daimonion teras*); Hölderlin, in fact, elides that direct description of Antigone as sign by translating the passage as "wie Gottesversuchung" (*like a temptation of the gods*) (*Echoes of Translation*, 106).

But what does it mean to produce such a trace in intelligible form? We have seen how Antigone's act of burying her brother attains universal significance for Hegel, translated into an operation representative of familial duty and legitimized as tacit intuition. By contrast, Hölderlin is more apt to leave Antigone in peace to do what she must.

> Laß aber mich und meinen irren Rath
> Das Gewaltige leiden. (FA 16: 273: 97–98)

> But leave me and my errant counsel
> To suffer the powerful/violent.

As we already know, Hölderlin's Antigone speaks these words in the opening dialogue with Ismene, in which she reveals her determination to disobey Creon's edict. This time *deinon*, Hölderlin's *Ungeheuer*, is translated as *Gewaltiges* (the powerful), and even if elsewhere it describes the human being as such, here Antigone states unequivocally that she intends to suffer it alone. But she will not suffer passively. Rather, her suffering is the result of a certain choice (although not exactly of a free will, since Antigone asserts from the start that she has no *other* choice): *leave me to suffer the powerful*. Antigone asks for a suffering, asks to endure it, and thus takes it actively upon herself.

The sensible Ismene already knows that her sister's plan is impossible, and she tells her so: "Gleich Anfangs muß niemand Unthunliches jagen" (FA 16: 273, *No one need pursue the impossible from the start*). And while every indication is that Antigone knows it as well, that knowledge does not stop her. Nor does the certainty that by pursuing the impossible—by taking on a suffering that no one else will assume—she is acting improperly, against the law of the state and solely in the name of a brother whose identity, as she also knows, might otherwise crumble to dust. Suffering the powerful and the violent implies being exposed to that impossibility, recognizing it as such and taking it on nonetheless.

> Nein, denke du, wie dir's gefällt; doch ihn
> Begrab' ich. Schön ist es hernach, zu sterben.
> Lieb werd' ich bei ihm liegen, bei dem Lieben,
> Wenn Heiligs ich vollbracht. (FA 16; 271)

> No, you think as you like; but I
> Will bury him. To die after is beautiful then

And lovely to lie by him then, my loved one,
When I've done what is holy. (Constantine 73)

While it is arguably possible to discern an erotic tone to this passage in German—which would stand in stark contrast to Hegel's central assertion that the relation of sister to brother is devoid of desire, hence pure in its ethical obligation—it is perhaps even more striking that the desire expressed by the figure of Antigone here is linked to her suffering ("To die after is beautiful then"). Her desire is to suffer *deinon* in the name of her brother, and nothing else. And if the Chorus follows her "outside of the law," once it is captivated, as Lacan emphasized, by "the powerful plea on the eyelid of the bridal girl" (*das Mächtigbittende am Augenliede der hochzeitlichen Jungfrau*), it already finds itself implicated in that suffering as well.[39]

For Hölderlin, then, the tragedy of *Antigone* stages the confrontation with an impossibility beyond limits and "outside of the law"; it is this confrontation that Antigone fiercely desires and for which she "powerfully begs." Hölderlin describes the effects of this confrontation in terms of time. In a single eventful moment—the *deinon* moment in which Antigone begs and we have no choice but to follow—the subject finds itself implicated in the flow of time, in which it has only to hang on, powerless, for dear life. In this moment of "wildest opposition," the subject is utterly decentered, in the first place insofar as she is not even active in the struggle that engulfs her; the "spirit of time and nature" contends with the object, while the subject is seized by that same spirit.

However, the opposition Hölderlin posits here no longer has solely the character of an insurmountable distance between subject and world, as it did in his reading of a solitary Oedipus. In the remarks on *Antigone*, the most compelling threat to the self-posited unity of the subject takes the form of what Hölderlin will call the "tearing spirit of time" (*der reißende Zeitgeist*). Where the "lawful calculus" of tragedy required a careful evaluation of the order and timing of oppositions between nature and culture, Greek and Hesperian worlds, the tearing spirit of time introduces the chaos of a close encounter with the untamed wilderness of death: "not, like a ghost in daylight, sparing man at all, but quite pitiless, as the spirit of the always alive, unwritten wilderness and the world of the dead" (Constantine 114: *nicht, dass er die Menschen schonte, wie ein Geist am tage, sondern er ist schonungslos,*

---

39. See Lacan 281: "And it is from the same place that the image of Antigone appears before us as something that causes the Chorus to lose its head, as it tells us itself, makes the just appear unjust, and makes the Chorus transgress all limits.... Nothing is more moving than the *himeros energes*, than the desire that visibly emanates from the eyelids of this admirable girl."

als Geist der ewig lebenden ungeschriebenen Wildniß und der Todtenwelt [FA 16: 266]).

Unwritten, unsparing, infinite: the world of the dead and of its "Geist," the conceptually unthinkable world to which Antigone opens herself in performing the forbidden funeral rites for her brother, can only be represented oppositionally, as darkness in contrast to daylight, obscurity to clarity. And yet its effects are most sharply felt not in this simple opposition of dark and light, but rather in the mysteries of the movement that encompasses both, that of time. The most uncompromising expression of this "tearing spirit of time"—onrushing like an angry river, but also tearing, as through a single piece of cloth—is that moment of wildest opposition in which the subject is revealed "in his character." Like the caesura in the remarks on *Oedipus,* which interrupted the flow of "tragic transport" with the exposure of "representation itself," wild opposition interrupts the dramatic order with the unsettling proximity of the limit zone between life and death.

The "wilderness" represented by both formal interruption and conceptual liminality is also expressed in dramatic language. The structural point of caesura itself for Hölderlin—the scene in which Tiresias berates Creon for his failure to understand the importance of maintaining the separate registers of life and death—contains as its dominant image the beasts that enable the blind man to "see" by means of a signification that scorns representation by either word or image.

> Du weist es; hörst die Zeichen meiner Kunst.
> Denn auf dem alten Stuhle, Vögel schauend,
> Saß ich, wo vor mir war ein Hafen aller Vögel,
> Da hört' ich unbekannt von denen ein Geschrei,
> Mit üblem Wüthen schrien sie und wild,
> Und zerrten mit den Klauen sich einander,
> In Mord, das merkt' ich, denn nicht unverständlich war
> Der Flügel Sausen. (FA 16: 369: 1034–42)

> You know it, you hear the signings of my art.
> I sat in the ancient chair, scrying the birds
> And had before me a haven of all the birds
> And heard an unknown screaming out of them,
> Wildly in an evil raging they were screaming
> And tearing at one another with their claws
> In murder, I marked that, for the rush of the wings
> Were not incomprehensible (Constantine 102; trans. modified)

With its description of the birds' cry and their untamed, violent behavior, Tiresias' speech enacts its own disruption; the birds' wail, the center of his reading of "signings," is both "unknown" (*unbekannt*) and "not incomprehensible" (*nicht unverständlich*), outside of the limits of language and yet still signifying. Once again, Hölderlin employs negative (and even double negative) terminology to evoke an otherwise unattainable "outside." However, the reverberations set off by the intrusion of a beastly sound here also contribute in a different way to the events of the tragedy. They form a layer over an earlier scene in which Antigone herself signifies in the same doubled tone as Tiresias' birds, both "unknown" and "not incomprehensible."

> DER BOTE: So wird das Kind gesehn und weinet auf,
> Mit scharfer Stimme, wie ein Vogel trauert,
> Wenn in dem leeren Nest verwaist von Jungen er
> Das Lager sieht. So sie, da sie entblößt
> Erblikt den Todten, jammerte sie laut auf,
> Und fluchte böse Flüche, wers gethan,
> Und bringet Staub mit beiden Händen, schnell,
> Und aus dem wohlgeschlagnen Eisenkruge kränzt
> Sie dreimal mit Ergießungen den Todten. (FA 16: 307: 440–48)

> MESSENGER: The child was seen and she was weeping loudly
> With a sharp voice the way a bird will grieve
> When in an empty nest orphaned of young
> She sees the sleeping place. So she when she
> Espied the dead man bare, she howled
> And cursed whoever had done it with bad curses
> And in both hands brought dust, quickly,
> And from the jug of hammered iron three times
> With waterings she wreathed the dead man. (Constantine 83)

Thus a chorus of beastly cries does not only disrupt the otherwise uneventful movement of time, revealing the ruptures inherent in representation; by evoking the plaintive wail and mournful countenance of the girl as she pursues the impossible, this event approaches not only the limits of language but also—foreshadowing her later banishment to the tomb—the very margin of life and death.

Yet the solitude of Antigone's pursuit of that limit zone need not imply that her inscription in the movement of time, and that of her tragedy, are likewise solitary. If Hölderlin insists upon the singularity of Antigone's suffering, that is not to say that he refuses to translate it, only that his translation aims to convey what remains of that solitude. As a result, Antigone's unflinching movement toward the impossible will expose a curious communion among subjects, both in spite of and because of the act of translation. In spite of translation we are nothing like Antigone, and yet because of translation we follow her; and in the process, something is disclosed to us even as we find nothing. To be sure, the modern subject discovers *something* in viewing Antigone; condemned to a live burial, she stands between life and death, facing the inevitability of this end with open eyes: "I, poor girl! Not among mortals, not among the dead" (*Ich Arme! Nicht unter Sterblichen, nicht unter Todten* [353: 880–81]). Advancing without question towards the liminal space of her tomb, she lends credence to the words of Hölderlin's Chorus in the second choral ode, in which the human, perhaps revealing the monstrosity at its heart, is indelibly marked by its own relation to death: "Only the future place of the dead / He does not know how to flee" (Constantine 81: *Der Toten künftigen Ort nur / Zu fliehen weiß er nicht* [301: 377–78]). The Chorus already makes it clear: human beings cannot escape the encounter with their own finitude, no matter what crafts they employ to avert its inevitability—not as long as the "tearing spirit of time" holds dominion over subjective experience.

However, even as Antigone leads us to an end that takes the form of *something*, death, in this translation she also defies any merely teleological description. The Chorus's reference to human beings' inability to escape "the place of the dead" is followed closely by a call to a different register: "All-traveled, untraveled. He comes to nothing" (*Allbewandert, unbewandert. Zu nichts kommt er* [301: 376]). Strictly speaking, this translation is, once again, inaccurate; the logic and syntax of the Greek passage suggest a separation or pause between *pantoporos* and *aporos*, not a pairing as Hölderlin would have it here, and most modern translators recognize this, resulting in a more stable reading: "He meets nothing in the future without resource" (Lloyd-Jones 37; see also Solger 159, Fagles 77).[40] The logic underlying Hölderlin's incorrect syntax resonates with his overall reading of the Choral passage, however, leaving the parallel terms *allbewandert, unbewandert* to encapsulate

---

40. Stathis Gourgouris notes this translation error in Heidegger's discussion of the same passage in his lecture on "Der Ister," a reading which was almost certainly inspired by Hölderlin's translation. In both cases the incorrect juxtaposition of *pantoporos aporos*, rather than its separation, implies an echo effect with the phrase *hypsispolis; apolis* (high in the city; cast out of the city). Gourgouris emphasizes in convincing fashion the productivity of this error for Heidegger's reading of *deinon* as ontological condition; I would merely argue that although it clearly represents a misreading of Sophocles' *Antigone*, it responds directly to Hölderlin's *Antigone*. *Does Literature Think? Literature as Theory for an Antimythical Era* (Stanford University Press, 2003), 138.

the ambiguity that describes human beings, who have traveled much but nevertheless must reach the conclusion that they have arrived nowhere at all.

Even more revealing in the context of Hölderlin's view of the tragic is the second part of that descriptive phrase: "He comes to nothing." While the expression *zu etwas kommen* signals an arrival at a destination, a conclusive "getting somewhere" (and the reflexive *zu sich kommen* implies a moment of self-conscious realization) the human's only destination here is nowhere—or more precisely, nothing.[41] Advancing towards nothing as she faces her inevitable death in the tomb, Antigone confronts that impossible, unthinkable suffering that she chose at the very start. She takes a step that the Chorus attributes to the human being as such, a step "to nothing" that brings a subject to the precipice of meaning, to a limit that can only be represented as death. All fascination aside, it seems that Antigone's suffering means "nothing" to us after all.

Yet it is a nothing that is not meaningless, far from it. It is inseparable from a tragic experience made possible in translation alone. In fact, for Hölderlin it is only because of this particular experience of translation that the tragedy can *be* "vaterländische Sache," of concern at all to his time and place. Translation, like Antigone's tragedy, brings the subject to arrive at no place—at nothing; translation will both trace and intensify a movement that Antigone already enacts. Whatever may be "lost" in translation in a conventional sense, therefore, pales in comparison to what may be gained.

THIS INTENSIFYING MOVEMENT of translation is delineated in some of the most challenging passages of the remarks; in fact, reading these reflections often demands something of a translation in its own right. Nevertheless they remain crucial to any understanding of the project's model of tragic experience. Its movement is based on an exchange of structural generality and material specificity, and in this sense follows logically from Hölderlin's slightly more legible remarks on *Oedipus*, where, as we have already seen, he takes a similar point of departure. Arguing in those remarks for a rigidity of form, a "lawful calculus" that would permit the modern poet, artisan-like, to create beauty with the tools of antiquity, Hölderlin resists (or at least rethinks) the lure of imitation to which his contemporaries often succumbed.[42] For although the mathematical markings of tragic form bear repeating in a modern era, the words that give life to that form remain necessarily specific,

---

41. On the semantic implications of *zu sich kommen* within the discourse of tragedy and classical drama see Nägele 1991, 11.

42. Lacoue-Labarthe has shown this convincingly in "Hölderlin and the Greeks," 237–38.

a "living sense that cannot be calculated"; from age to age the content of a text cannot bear the same resonance. A tension thus arises between form and content, and the moments in which the translated text conveys this distinction shed light from another angle—as we will see, from an "askew perspective"—on that which brings tragedy to "life" for a modern audience.

At its heart, this model of linguistic and discursive exchange is a theory of tragic experience, of how ancient tragedy may "translate" into a modern context. Hölderlin specifies that the effects of tragedy change with the introduction of language that moves the modern subject differently, bringing facets to light that were only implicit in the Greek text. In the passage from antiquity to modernity, Hölderlin asserts that something has solidified "in the course of events, in the grouping of characters against one another" (*in die Art des Hergangs, in der Gruppierung der Personen gegeneinander* [419]), something which may have underlain the movement of Greek tragedy in its time, but which only becomes readable in our time.

> Vorzüglich aber bestehet die tragische Darstellung in dem factischen Worte, das, mehr Zusammenhang, als ausgesprochen, schiksaalsweise, vom Anfang bis zum Ende gehet; in die Art des Hergangs, in der Gruppirung der Personen gegeneinander; in der Vernunftform, die sich in der furchtbaren Muße einer tragischen Zeit bildet, und so wie sie in Gegensätzen sich darstellte, in ihrer wilden Entstehung, nachher, in humaner Zeit, als feste aus göttlichem Schicksal geborene Meinung gilt. (FA 16: 419)

> However, tragic representation principally consists of the factual word which, being more a relation than something that is stated explicitly, moves by means of fate from beginning to end; in the specific course of events, in the grouping of characters against one another; in the form of reason that constitutes itself in the dreadful idleness of tragic time, and just as at its wild origin it represented itself in oppositions, afterwards, in human time, it counts as a firm opinion born of divine fate. (Pfau 1988, 114; trans. modified)

If what was formed (*gebildet*) in a "tragic time"—Antigone's solitary suffering unto death, here the "dreadful idleness of tragic time"—is solidified into a "firm opinion" that counts (*gilt*) only in *our* time, then that experience must logically make itself felt as a consequence of not only tragedy but also translation. Translation has the potential to expose the subject to the very effect of difference upon which Antigone's tragedy always already insists. Familiarity gives way to foreignness, and vice versa, in a most radical sense when the subject's own representative mode (*Vorstellungsart*) confronts him with an experience that is profoundly other.

This experience lies at the core of Hölderlin's distinction of the "Greek" word from the "Hesperian," and given the stakes of Antigone's own pursuit, it is perhaps fitting that the distinction on the level of words takes shape with respect to the representation of death.[43] Where once the Chorus was seized by the haunting vision of a wandering Antigone, now the viewing subject is likewise seized simply by a word—and here, the context of that seizure, whether Greek or modern, makes all the difference. In the "Greek" sense, words seize the physical body in a mediated way, bringing that body to kill: "The Greek-tragic word is deadly-factual, because the body that it seizes actually kills" (Pfau 116; trans. modified: *Das griechischtragische Wort ist tödtlichfaktisch, weil der Leib, den es ergreifet, wirklich tödtet* [FA 16: 417f.]). Meanwhile, in "our" time and mode of representation, words seize the spirit *im*mediately, so that the word *itself* kills by seizing the "more spiritual body." Admittedly, this train of thought is extremely opaque, but upon reflection it becomes clearer. In the "more Greek" sense, words always bring a body to kill on the tragic stage, always mediate the theatrical representation of murder, insofar as killings are never actually shown on stage but rather described by a messenger. Particularly the deaths of women in Sophocles, including Jocasta, Eurydice, and Antigone, remain fiercely private scenes only "visible" to an audience through description.[44] When the word itself kills, however, it has a more immediate effect on the tragic heroine as well as the viewing subject:

> Eine vaterländische mag . . . mehr tödtendfactisches, als tödtlichfactisches Wort sein; nicht eigentlich mit Mord oder Tod endigen, weil doch hieran das Tragische muß gefaßt werden, sondern mehr im Geschmake des Oedipus auf Kolonos, so daß *das Wort* aus begeistertem Munde schreklich ist, und tödtet, nicht griechisch faßlich, in athletischem und plastischem Geiste, wo das Wort den Körper ergreift, daß dieser tödtet.

> Such an art of our homeland . . . may be a language that is killingly-factual rather than deadly-factual; so not actually ending with murder or death as that through which tragedy must be apprehended, but more in the manner of *Oedipus at Colonus*, where the words spoken by a mouth inspired

---

43. Hölderlin confronts this tension between the "Vorstellungsarten" of different ages in other texts as well, particularly the letter to Böhlendorff discussed in the last section and the 1799 essay "Der Gesichtspunct, aus dem wir das Altertum anzusehen haben" (FA 14: 95–96).

44. In this context, see in particular Nicole Loraux's detailed and interesting study, *Tragic Ways of Killing a Woman*.

are terrible, and kill, but not in a graspable Greek way, in an athletic and plastic spirit, where the words seize the body so that it kills. (Constantine 117; trans. modified)

In modern tragic experience, initiated as thinking spirit is seized by a word that kills when "spoken by a mouth," words lead one *in thought* along a certain trajectory that ends in death. That ends, perhaps, in nothing but the space of the unthinkable that houses Antigone's suffering. As the Chorus concludes, "Thinking is more, much more / Than happiness" (*Um vieles ist das Denken mehr, denn / Glükseeligkeit* [FA 16: 405: 1397–98]).

If, however, the disclosure of this tragic movement unto death is to become particularly evident "in human time," in what form does it reveal itself to the modern subject? For if Hölderlin is justified in suggesting that our experience of Antigone's suffering is intensified through something which only counts (*gilt*) in this time, "standing as we do under a Zeus more our own" (Constantine 116; *da wir unter dem eigentlicheren Zeus stehen*), then the form of that experience must make itself felt as a consequence of not only tragedy but also translation. In these remarks, that trajectory takes the form of what he calls "infinite reversal" (*unendlicher Umkehr*).[45] Reversal here does not refer, as it did in other contexts in Hölderlin's age, to the return to Greek ideals or to a mythic national origin. As Hölderlin already explains in the remarks on *Oedipus,* the reversal characteristic of tragedy in translation cannot possibly resolve itself in a return to an origin, if only for the epidemic of forgetting that accompanies it.

> In dieser (i.e. der äußersten Grenze des Leidens) vergißt sich der Mensch, weil er ganz im Moment ist; der Gott, weil er nichts als Zeit ist; und beides ist untreu, die Zeit, weil sie in solchem Momente sich kategorisch wendet, und Anfang und Ende sich in ihr schlechterdings nicht reimen läßt; der Mensch, weil er in diesem Momente der kategorischen Umkehr folgen muß, hiermit im Folgenden schlechterdings nicht dem Anfänglichen gleichen kann. (FA 16: 258)[46]

---

45. Reversal or "Umkehr" frequently appears in Hölderlin's writings as "patriotic" reversal (vaterländische Umkehr), which as Szondi discusses often construed in the earlier part of this century to refer to the German ability to supercede the legacy of antiquity ("Überwindung des Klassizismus," 89ff.) Henning Bothe points out in contrast that George and his school celebrated in Hölderlin the German proximity to the greatness of Greece, the "heilige Heirat" of *Nüchternheit* (sobriety) and *Heiterkeit* (exhilaration). *"Ein Zeichen sind wir, deutungslos . . . " die Rezeption Hölderlins von ihren Anfängen bis zu Stefan George* (Stuttgart: Metzler, 1992), 108ff.

46. For Heidegger in "Der Ister," this notion of forgetting becomes significant, since it describes the human in relation to *Sein*. However, while Hölderlin demonstrates here that the hero and the god

At that limit the human being forgets himself, because he is wholly in the moment; and the god forgets himself, because he is nothing but time; and both are unfaithful, time because in such a moment it is a categorical turning-point in which beginning and end cannot rhyme at all; the human being, because at that moment he must follow the categorical moment of turning but in what follows he cannot at all match what was there in the beginning. (Constantine 68; trans. modified)

While the process of reversal in this tragic context is a must—it is our only concern, "vaterländische Sache"—its destination remains unknown; the subject has forgotten itself in the force of the moment, the god in the rush of time, and thus neither has the possibility of returning to anything familiar.[47] No origin remains to which reversal could refer here; what remains is only the movement that reversal generates, only the recognition that in and through this movement everything has changed, irrevocably: "For patriotic reversal is the reversal of all modes and forms of representation" (Constantine 117; trans. modified: *Denn vaterländische Umkehr ist die Umkehr aller Vorstellungsarten und Formen* [FA 16: 419]).

How, then, is this movement of reversal directed, if not to a conceptual origin? Perhaps it leads to nowhere but that space of nothingness which Antigone already occupies, to the possibility that the subject somehow partakes of her final, solitary confrontation with impossibility. For as it turns out, it is a space that she shares with another. While at the moment of her death the god is already present "in the figure (*Gestalt*) of death," another human literally shares Antigone's tomb; and he is also one prototype for the man who, forgetting himself in the event, finds himself moving suddenly and inexplicably in reverse. In the remarks on *Oedipus*, Hölderlin describes the moment of *Umkehr* as personified by two characters in particular: "Hämon stands thus in *Antigone,* and Oedipus himself thus in the centre of the tragedy of *Oedipus*" (Constantine 68; *So stehet Hämon in der Antigonä. So Oedipus selbst in der Mitte der Tragödie von Oedipus* [FA 16: 258]).

---

both "forget," Heidegger suggests that Antigone represents a relation to Being that the rest of humanity has forgotten (para. 18, "Das Herd als das Sein," 134ff.).

47. In a discussion of the ode "Patmos," Warminski addresses the notion of "wiederkehren" in Hölderlin as a nonsymmetrical relation, arguing that the verb "wiederkommen" would more clearly communicate absolute return: "But for that which is human such a coming back would be mere identity, sterile one-sidedness; only the God can come back: 'Denn wiederkommen sollt es / Zu rechter Zeit" (StA II:168). The poem's wiederkehren is a re-turning: a going over and a turning again. . . . The asymmetry of 'hinüberzugehen' and 'wiederzukehren' is a loss of identity and a gain of meaning" (Warminski 89). "Umkehren" is an even more ambiguous, less symmetrical action than "wiederkehren," for it signifies only a turning "around" without any implication of an absolute reversal.

The prospect of reversal as the exposure of the impossible is perhaps more intuitively at hand in *Oedipus,* since the process of unveiling information in his tragedy clearly turns the proceedings in a previously inconceivable direction. Within this context it is also more clearly related to Aristotelian *peripateia,* which generates its effect through the development of plot structure.[48] In *Antigone,* however, reversal is less evident. Only her betrothed, the son of Creon—only Haemon, whose name occurs neither before nor after this point in any of Hölderlin's remarks—follows its trajectory. What status does Haemon take on in the tomb, what direction is he compelled to follow that will also concern Hölderlin's age? And what does his reversal have to do with Antigone, who after all maintains her solitude to the end?

A messenger's description of Haemon's confrontation with his father in the tomb—the Greeks' "real" killing through speech that will soon drive Eurydice to suicide—begins to shed light upon these questions, which finally lead to a reversal even more shattering than that of Oedipus the King.

Schnöd blikend, nichts entgegensagend, starrt
Mit wilden Augen gegen ihn der Sohn;
Und zieht das Schwert, zweischneidig, gegen ihn erst.
Und da der Vater, aufgeschrökt, zur Flucht
Sich wandte, fehlt' er. Grimmig dann im Geiste,
Der Unglückliche sties, so wie er ausgestrekt stand,
Die Spize mitten sich in seine Seite.
Den feuchten Arm, bei Sinnen noch, küßt er
Der Jungfrau . . .
Das Todte liegt beim Todten, bräutliche
Erfüllung trifft es schüchtern in den Häußern
Der Todtenwelt, und zeigt der Menschen rathlos Wesen,
Und wie als größtes Übel diß der Mann hat. (FA 16: 393–95: 1285–98)

---

48. Aristotle's introduction of the term *peripateia* in the *Poetics* appears together with that of recognition (*anagnorisis*) in the section dealing with "simple and complex plots" (Aristotle 2322–27). In general, Aristotle argues that plot should be just long enough to show "the hero passing by a series of probable or necessary stages from bad fortune to good, or from good to bad . . . "[2322]; however, a peripatetic shift comes about when an action has an effect opposite to what was expected, thus taking both the hero and the audience by surprise. Combined with the effect of recognition—a "change from ignorance to knowledge" (36)—*peripateia* will excite feelings of pity and fear in the spectator. The difference from Hölderlin's notion of reversal, as we will see soon, is that "recognition" in Hölderlin's sense takes place with regard to a different register of knowledge; the question is no longer one of identification with the hero in his misfortune, which would excite pity and fear in the spectator, but rather of an experience of isolation that seizes the viewer directly, *not* through the mediation of plot, and with the same force that it enacts a reversal for the hero.

> With baleful eyes and saying nothing in return
> Wildly the son stared back at him
> And drew his two-edged sword against him first.
> But when the father, frightened into flight,
> Turned, he failed. Then savage-mindedly,
> Outstretched, standing there, the unhappy man
> Thrust with the point of it full in his side.
> Before his senses went he kissed the girl's
> Moist arm, on her white cheek he frothed
> Sharp breaths of bloody droplets out.
> The dead one lies by the dead one, shyly they came to
> Their wedding's consummation in the houses in
> The world of the dead and show how lost for counsel
> Humans are and how the man has this as greatest ill (Constantine 109; trans. modified)

The messenger's monologue forms one of the most affecting passages in Sophocles' text as well as Hölderlin's translation, insofar as it bears witness to a transformation unprecedented in a text that relies otherwise on the stony resolve of its central figures. After bitterly raising his sword against his terrified father, Haemon demonstrates concretely why he may occupy the place of infinite reversal for Hölderlin. Now sharing the tomb with his bride Antigone is the son who had once sought to achieve a balance, to quell through words of persuasion his father's fatal obsession; from his proclamation that "Father, I'm yours" (Constantine 90; *Vater, dein bin ich*) in his first line of the play, Haemon has literally reversed his allegiance. And consequently, a marriage is consummated in the world of the dead rather than of the living, a tardy union of bride and groom being one result of this double suicide. Just as this union hints at a moment of reconciliation, however, the linguistic neutralization of gender in the very next line stands as a stark reminder of the death's anonymity: "the dead one lies by the dead one" (*das Todte liegt beim Todten*). Given that both the Greek word for corpse, *ho nekròs*, and the German term, *der Leichnam*, are masculine, Hölderlin's choice of the neuter term *das Todte* is surely not coincidental; rather, it represents a striking transformation of gendered beings into neutral bodies.

Hölderlin's play with gender in his rendition of the messenger's words also complicates the reversal that Haemon enacts in another way, by virtue of an astute choice in the disclosure of "how lost for counsel (*rathlos*) humans are and how the man has this as greatest ill." For in contrast to the un-gendering of the dead in the tomb, here Hölderlin maintains the gender specificity of Sophocles' language, naming the bearer of greatest ill as masculine: *der Mann*. Allowing the other, more universal masculine term for humankind, der Mensch, to stand in for the Greek *ho anēr* here would link the passage to the second Choral ode (where, however, the human is not *anēr* but *anthropos*) as part of a larger statement about the status of humankind. (For example, the translator for the Loeb edition, Hugh Lloyd-Jones, uses "mortals" [117].). *Ho anēr* refers specifically to a man, however, and for Hölderlin this point was important enough not to elide; *der Mann* can only refer to a man or husband, never a woman or wife. What this implies for his rendition of the line is that of the three human beings in the tomb, only Antigone is exempt from the greatest ill of being "lost for counsel." While Sophocles' language seems to refer to Haemon here, Hölderlin's version maintains a more ambiguous stance, so that it is not entirely clear which man is called to recognize how "lost for counsel" he is. Is it the would-be husband Haemon? the man, father, and king Creon?

If it is the man's greatest ill that he is at a loss at this limit, that the prospect of facing the "wilderness" that Antigone confronts leaves him despairing of his next move, as Hölderlin's translation implies with the word *ratblos*, then this tragic uncertainty must characterize Creon in particular, for it stands in stark contrast to the determination with which Antigone—and now Haemon—act. Evident from the first scene has been Antigone's own certainty that she must take on and pursue the impossible without question; this is what makes her appear solitary, unsettling, monstrous to a modern audience. However, in the reversal enacted by Haemon, precisely this tension between acting decisively and being at a loss comes to light, along with the direction that reversal must take as a consequence, even if it does not know its destination. If Antigone unsettles us for reasons we do not entirely grasp, therefore, Haemon demonstrates the *process* of this destabilization for the subject, the shocking reversal that also succeeded in unsettling and unseating Oedipus the King. Indeed, by unveiling this process of destabilization Haemon also demonstrates that the trope of reversal as Hölderlin describes it may itself be a radical form of translation. That the movement of translation, in a fundamental sense, thus generates the essence of tragic effect from the very start.

The reversal that represents "our" concern in tragedy, therefore, involves nothing less than the discovery of an abysmal form of thinking—call it "thinking in translation"—that not only preserves an irreducible difference with which the translated other refuses to part but also reveals a monstrous aspect at the very heart of both subject and text that is itself, in effect, untranslatable—and signifies precisely *as* the untranslatable. In our time and in translation as Hölderlin conceives of it, the word kills in tragedy by compelling us to *think* this process that seizes and shocks us, to be shaken by that recognition, to be led along the same trajectory that Antigone traces and Haemon follows unto death, into an infinite nothing that bears no other name, no other sign. It compels us to experience radically, in other words, tragedy's particular form of rebellion:

> Die Art des Hergangs in der *Antigonä* ist die bei einem Aufruhr, wo es, so fern es vaterländische Sache ist, darauf ankommt, daß jedes, als von unendlicher Umkehr ergriffen, und erschüttert, in unendlicher Form sich fühlt, in der es erschüttert ist. (FA 16: 419)

> The course of events in the *Antigone* has the form of an unrest/rebellion where, so far as it is a matter for the nation, it is essential that every thing, caught up in infinite reversal and shattered by it, feels itself in the infinite form in which it is shattered. (Constantine 117; trans. modified)

Had Antigone moved alone in the direction of death, one could almost have left her to her solitude. With Haemon joining her in that sheer determination, however, and with the emergence of the word's potential to compel spirit to conceive of the limit between life and death through the introduction of translation, the link to the human being in general can no longer be denied. If the Greek subject in Hölderlin's model suffered this course of events along with the figures on the stage, a subject "in human time" has the potential to think through that suffering in its own infinite relation to itself. This is *vaterländische Sache,* of concern to Hölderlin's time and place; it is the "established opinion, born of a divine fate," the ethical experience that counts in Hölderlin's presentation of tragedy in translation: May the subject's "character," its "highest consciousness" be awakened at the moment in which it is confronted with the infinity both outside and within; may it call attention to the impossible, unthinkable movement "to nothing" to which Antigone, and with her the human being as such, is always subject, "this most steadfast abiding in the passage of time" (Constantine 115). Translation presents the modern subject with a glimpse into the infinite from another perspective, not unlike the perspective that allows one to view the intensity of the sun in eclipse: "For us such a form is exactly suitable, because the infinite, like the spirit of states and of the world, can in any case only be grasped from an askew perspective [*aus linkischem Gesichtspunkt*]" (Constantine 118; trans. modified).[49]

---

49. Für uns ist eine solche Form gerade tauglich, weil das Unendliche, wie der Geist der Staaten und der Welt, ohnehin nicht anders, als aus linkischem Gesichtspunkt kann gefaßt werden. (FA 16: 421)

Only when implicated in this peculiar dynamics of translation can the modern subject come to recognize this unsettling communion with each and every subject, because any other vantage point would leave it beyond our grasp. The limits of translatability, laid bare in both the awkward spaces in which translation speaks and the idiosyncratic beauty of Hölderlin's "mistakes," do not place this recognition into doubt; indeed, they set it in motion. Through Hölderlin's model of translation, a strange and solitary girl escapes the status of Hegel's internal enemy, exceeds the visceral fascination that attracts us inexplicably to her strange plight, to expose the slippage fundamental to the human as such. Acting "outside of the law," she embodies a relation to the other that exists alongside the experience of selfhood as it is posited within speculative thought. As we recognize through the lens of translation, Antigone performs the impossible movement "to nothing" for us, and yet we must also acknowledge the responsibility we bear for her solitude, for a common thread of untranslatable difference that both isolates and sustains, that penetrates subject and text alike, that no act of interpretation can entirely bridge and yet no dialectics can fully dismiss. Difference becomes Antigone, to be sure, but in her solitude she proves to be anything but alone.

FOUR

The Translator's Courage

IN 1806, just two years after publishing the Sophocles translations, Hölderlin was institutionalized at the Autenrieth clinic in Tübingen. A year later he was released into the care of the Zimmer family and spent the next thirty-seven years—half of his life—in a small tower overlooking the Neckar river. Until his death in 1843 he remained an object of considerable fascination and sentimentalization among fellow poets and thinkers of his age (to whom he often introduced himself as "Scardanelli").[1] As poetic and cultural phenomenon, then, Hölderlin hardly spent the nineteenth century in an enchanted sleep. The later decades of the nineteenth century saw the publication of several editions of his poetry, and he came to be regarded as one of the major poets in the German literary tradition, the so-called "Werther of the Greeks," tragically brought low at the height of his creative powers. The Sophocles project, however, did languish in obscurity as the German penchant for all things Greek moved on to other discussions and controversies, notably the excavation program promoted by the archaeologist Ernst Curtius, Heinrich Schliemann's discovery of the lost city of Troy, and academic disputes initiated by the classical philologist Ulrich von Wilamowitz-Moellendorf with Nietzsche and Wagner.[2]

---

1. Hölderlin attracted numerous prominent visitors to the tower, including Achim and Bettina von Arnim, the young Eduard Mörike, and the editor Christoph Theodor Schwab. On the history of Hölderlin reception see Lawrence Ryan, *Friedrich Hölderlin* (Stuttgart: Metzler, 1962), 1–4. Today the Hölderlin tower in Tübingen is the seat of the Hölderlin-Gesellschaft, the literary society founded on the hundredth anniversary of his death in 1943. See http://www.hoelderlin-gesellschaft.info.

2. For a fascinating and detailed discussion of these developments, see Marchand's chapter 4, "Trouble in Olympus" (116–51).

Indeed, Hölderlin's translations and late poetry garnered little attention until the start of the next century, when the reception of his work was marked by a genuine turning of fortune. Critical and popular interest blossomed after the Munich doctoral student Friedrich Norbert von Hellingrath published a dissertation on the previously unpublished Pindar translations in 1910. A celebrated critical edition followed, including a volume of the late poetry (also heretofore unpublished), which was popular reading material among the troops stationed at the front in the Great War.[3] Hellingrath edited two other volumes, one containing Hölderlin's earliest writings and the other his translations from the Greek, before falling at Verdun in 1916. This critical edition (completed by Friedrich Seebass and Ludwig von Pigenot after Hellingrath's death) has had considerable cultural resonance, and considering the progression of thinkers that has engaged with Hölderlin in direct and measurable response to Hellingrath's edition, it is fair to say that there would be no twentieth-century Hölderlin without him. One of the primary thrusts of Hölderlin scholarship in the twentieth century, the examination of his engagement with the Greeks and its influence on the composition and revision of his late poetry, is particularly indebted to the framework of Hellingrath's doctoral thesis.[4]

One of the earliest respondents to Hellingrath's critical reintroduction has also proved, in belated fashion, to be one of the most noteworthy: in 1914 a 22-year-old philosophy student in Berlin named Walter Benjamin took up a direct challenge from the pages of Hellingrath's dissertation. Reflecting on the potentially rich vein of poetic development contained in Hölderlin's habitual revisions of earlier poems, Hellingrath writes: "One has only to compare 'Timidity' with the first version of 'The Poet's Courage' to see that each passage acquires a fullness of being only as a result of these changes."[5] The product of Benjamin's acceptance of this assignment is the essay "Two Poems by Friedrich Hölderlin" (*Zwei Gedichte von Friedrich Hölderlin*), at once a close and often exemplary reading of the two poems mentioned by Hellingrath and a primer for a concept of literary criticism

---

3. Friedrich Hölderlin, *Sämtliche Werke: historisch-kritische Ausgabe,* ed. Norbert von Hellingrath, Friedrich Seebass (Berlin: Propyläen, 1923).
4. See Rudolf Speth, *Wahrheit und Ästhetik: Untersuchungen zum Frühwerk Walter Benjamins* (Würzburg: Königshausen & Neumann, 1991), 10.
5. "Man vergleiche nur Blödigkeit mit der ersten Fassung von Dichtermut, um die Veränderung in Hölderlins Dichtung anschaulich machen zu können." Friedrich Norbert von Hellingrath, *Hölderlin-Vermächtnis,* ed. Ludwig von Pigenot (Munich: F. Bruckmann, 1936), 65. Stanley Corngold considers Benjamin's acceptance of this explicit challenge in light of his development of the idea of the "task" in *Complex Pleasure: Forms of Feeling in German Literature* (Stanford: Stanford University Press, 1998), 152.

that informs Benjamin's thought in a much larger sense.[6] Unpublished in his lifetime, the essay represents a kind of youthful exuberance of expression that is both impulsive and derivative in its approach to the material; the sometimes breathless characterization of the poet as purveyor of a higher truth marks the influence of Stefan George's reception of Hölderlin, for example, and also looks forward, as critics have pointed out, to Heidegger's "elucidations" (*Erläuterungen*) on the poet.[7] Yet despite its stylistic shortcomings—Stanley Corngold describes the essay as "in places written in a German whose tortuousness defies deciphering" (Corngold 1988, 152)—Benjamin himself saw the essay as more than the relic of an youthful phase, later deeming his reflections there as one of the "magnificent foundations" (*herrliche Grundlagen*) of his thought.[8]

Like so much of Benjamin's work today, the "Two Poems" essay has been exceptionally well covered by many of the lions of literary scholarship.[9] My aim here is not to add to that rich collection of commentary on the essay as a textual whole. Rather, I wish to follow a delicate thread, interlaced within the complex web of associations in Benjamin's thought here and yet clearly central to it, implicit within the lines of poetry that Benjamin cites yet also, clearly, extending beyond them. Benjamin demonstrates in the essay that he has read more of Hölderlin than just the two poems that anchor his discussion, and this peripheral reading illuminates connections that otherwise remain obscure within the text's stated motives. At the same time, by taking a closer look at a few briefer and apparently more spontaneous references to Hölderlin's work in Benjamin's later writing I hope to show how the texts at the center of this book project—the translations and remarks on Sophocles—form a crucial link among several of Benjamin's key concepts in his theory of the work of art.

---

6. Speth cites a letter to Ernst Schön in which Benjamin states that he intended to send the essay to Hellingrath before learning that he had been killed (9).

7. See Lacoue-Labarthe, "Poetry's Courage," in which he compares Benjamin's discussion of the poet's courage with Heidegger's "arche-ethical" quality of courage as outlined in his "Letter on Humanism." While Heidegger's definition of the poet's courage relies on a theological-political model that reinforces the mythological basis of fascism, Benjamin's theological-*poetical* project posits the failure of the theological in poetry and the "conquest of objectivity and the concrete" (88). In Fioretos 88–93.

8. Michael W. Jennings, "Benjamin as a Reader of Hölderlin: The Origins of Benjamin's Theory of Literary Criticism," *German Quarterly* 56:4 (Nov. 1983): 545. Corngold speculates that the timing of the essay, composed when "only an ultimately high seriousness could make a contribution suited to . . . world war" (153), indicates its author's desire to "secure the very idea of a foundation" (154).

9. See, for example, Corngold, *Complex Pleasure;* Lacoue-Labarthe, "Poetry's Courage"; Michael W. Jennings, "Benjamin as a Reader of Hölderlin"; Rainer Nägele, "Benjamin's Ground"; David Wellbery, "Benjamin's Theory of the Lyric"; Beatrice Hanssen, "'Dichtermut' and 'Blödigkeit': Two Poems by Hölderlin Interpreted by Walter Benjamin," *MLN* 112:5 (Dec. 1997): 786–816. Jennings also devotes a chapter to the essay in *Dialectical Images*.

Little would indicate at the start of "Two Poems" that Benjamin intends to engage with Hölderlin's writings on tragedy at all, let alone with the Sophocles project. In fact, he distances himself from tragedy in the very first lines of the essay, stipulating that the type of aesthetic commentary he is about to attempt more typically applies to the "great works of classical literature," such as tragedy, but that he will apply it instead to Hölderlin's lyric. In the pages that follow, Benjamin outlines the emergence, within each of the poems and between the lines of their development, of what he calls "das Gedichtete" (only awkwardly translatable as "the poetized"), a term meant to describe the *a priori* truth content contained within, but not openly expressed by, poetic language: the poem's "task (*Aufgabe*) *and* precondition." The basic thrust of his very complex argument is that the second, revised poem, "Blödigkeit," succeeds in revealing the truth content that the first poem represents only in a limited sense, the "poet's courage" (*Dichtermut*). Toward the end of the essay, however, he makes the allusion that is most interesting for our purposes here. Reflecting on how the development of the poem from the first to the final version represents a more nuanced relation to the forms of classical Greece, he writes:

> Dies Leben [i.e., *the life traced out in the second version of the poem*] ist in Formen des griechischen Mythos gebildet, aber—das ist entscheidend—nicht in ihnen allein; gerade das griechische Element ist in der letzten Fassung aufgehoben und ausgeglichen gegen ein andres, das (zwar ohne ausdrückliche Rechtfertigung) das orientalische genannt war. Fast alle Änderungen der spätern Fassung streben in dieser Richtung . . .(GS II:1,126)

> This life is shaped in the forms of Greek myth, but—this is crucial—not in them alone; the Greek element is sublated in the last version and balanced against another element that (without express justification, to be sure) was called the Oriental. Almost all the changes in the later version strive in this direction . . . (SW 1: 35).

The formulation is peculiar: this expression of life *was called* the Oriental, and Benjamin himself is only relaying the news. His use of the passive voice here is consistent with a stylistic tendency within the essay, perhaps reflective of Benjamin's attempt to sound academic in response to Hellingrath's challenge.[10] However, the passive construction also removes the speaker from responsibility for a naming that took place "without express justification"; as

---

10. As Corngold writes, to "go one better than the academic source of his 'assignment,'" Hellingrath (153).

Benjamin clearly states here, the term "Oriental" is not of his own invention. The one who did the naming is, of course, Hölderlin, in a letter to his publisher Friedrich Wilmans from September 1803; what *is named* is a particular quality that he attempted to lend to his translations of Sophocles. The letter appears in the volume of Hellingrath's edition devoted to the translations from the Greek, and in light of Benjamin's obvious interest in Hellingrath's work, his familiarity with this particular letter is not only possible but likely:

> Ich hoffe, die griechische Kunst, die uns fremd ist, durch Nationalkonvenienz und Fehler, mit denen sie sich immer herum beholfen hat, dadurch lebendiger, als gewöhnlich dem Publikum darzustellen, dass ich das Orientalische, das sie verläugnet hat, mehr heraushebe, und ihren Kunstfehler, wo er vorkommt, verbessere. (FA 16: 19)[11]
>
> I hope to represent Greek art, which is foreign to us through the conformity to the native and the flaws to which it has always resorted, as more alive than usual to the public by bringing out the Oriental element that it has disavowed and by correcting its artistic flaw where it occurs.

Perhaps surprisingly, given the prominence of the Oriental as an organizing principle in Benjamin's essay, this letter to Wilmans is the only place in his body of work where Hölderlin calls that term by its name. Benjamin has a point, moreover, in stating that he names it "without express justification," as Hölderlin does not offer any further explanation for his use of the term. In other letters and essays Hölderlin constructs similar oppositions, such as in the letter to Böhlendorff, where he compares the Greeks' "fire from heaven" with our "Junonian sobriety," or in the discussion of Greek vs. Hesperian "modes of representation" (*Vorstellungsarten*) in the remarks on *Antigone*. At no other point, however, does Hölderlin invoke the exact term "Oriental," which indicates that already in 1914, Benjamin was not only familiar with the apparatus surrounding the translations of Sophocles but considered it a key to understanding the logic and process of Hölderlin's late poetic production. From the start of his engagement with Hölderlin, then, Benjamin regards him not merely as a poet but also, always, as a translator. By placing the Oriental alongside the Greek as an organizing principle of Hölderlin's process of revision, he casts the poet, in a sense, as translator of his own poem.[12]

---

11. See *Hölderlins Sämtliche Werke: Fünfter Band*, ed. Norbert von Hellingrath (Berlin: Propyläen, 1923), 325f.

12. Lacoue-Labarthe calls Hölderlin's process of revision as Benjamin describes it "*internal trans-*

Benjamin's introduction of the term "Oriental" warrants closer examination here, as it plays a subtle role at several points in the essay. He brings it into the discussion literally at surface level, *as* surface, in his reading of Hölderlin's revision of the second line of the poem, from "Does not the Parca herself nourish you for service?" (first version, *Dichtermut*) to "Does not your foot stride upon what is true, as upon carpets?" (in the final version, *Blödigkeit*).[13] Throughout the essay Benjamin aims to demonstrate that the poem in its initial version, with its primarily Greek imagery and static, mythic quality, needs the transition to a less form-giving, more independent poetic language in order to allow for the emergence of its truth, *das Gedichtete*. The first version of the poem is limited by its dependence on Greece as a model, since the principle that underlies Greek beauty and mythology cannot become fully manifest in the modern world. The final version, on the other hand, accomplishes (as Corngold discusses) a transition from the mythic world of Greece to the "myth of modernity," "to a modernity that *reflects on* Greece . . . [and] whose essential shape must be produced by poetry . . ." (Corngold 161; my italics).

That transition as Benjamin theorizes it is already apparent in the first lines of the poem; he points out the telling shift from dependency (being nourished) to positing (striding) and the image, "with a vastness evoking the oriental" (SW 1: 26) (*an Orientalisches gemahnender Weitläufigkeit* [GS II:1, 113]), of a carpet spreading out beneath the feet of the poet, connecting the living as " . . . the extension of space, the plane spread out, in which . . . destiny extends itself" (SW 1: 26) (*die Erstreckung des Raumes, der gebreitete Plan, in dem sich das Schicksal erstreckt* [GS II:1, 113]). The exemplarity of the image of the carpet (its *Musterhaftigkeit,* a term that also plays on the idea of its woven pattern) also reflects for Benjamin "a great deal, a very great deal, of Hölderlin's cosmos . . . once again foreign-sounding, as if from the world of the East, and yet much more primordial than the Parca . . ." (SW 1: 26) (*viel, sehr viel über den Kosmos Hölderlins . . . wieder fremd wie aus östlicher Welt und doch wieviel ursprünglicher als die griechische Parze . . .* [GS II:1, 114]). The same stanza continues its representation of the poet's striding forth in the final version: "Therefore, my genius, only step / Naked into life and have no care!" (*Drum, mein Genius, tritt nur / Bar ins Leben und sorge nicht!*) As the poet strides forward and enters naked, vulnerable, into life, he also acknowledges for Benjamin an underlying sense of connection, of interweaving, with the living. This, too, is the legacy of the Oriental carpet:

---

lation." "Poetry's Courage," in Fioretos 82.

13. In the original, "Nährt zum Dienste denn nicht selber die Parze dich?" becomes "Geht auf Wahrem dein Fuß nicht, wie auf Teppichen?" (GS II:1, 114)

" . . . it [life] is not the precondition but the object of a movement accomplished with a mighty freedom: the poet *enters into* life; he does not wander forth in it," revealing "connectedness, in destiny, between the living and the poet" (SW 1: 28).[14] The Oriental, as a tone emerging in balance with the Greek, form-giving gesture, thus makes it possible to grasp the essential relation between this poem and its "life-context" (*Lebenszusammenhang*) (SW 1: 20). In a sense crucial for Benjamin's way of thinking, this life-context is not determined by the "individual life-mood (*Lebensbestimmung*) of the artist" (SW 1: 20) but rather marks the poem as an effect of historical experience.[15] The courage named in the first poem's title, then, emerges in the second poem as a willingness to allow this connectedness—the "innermost identity of the poet with the world" (SW 1: 34)—to appear without intervention.

This mode of reading, which Benjamin here calls "aesthetic commentary," is not only a fine example of literary criticism in its own right but also underscores the role of criticism for the fulfillment of the poetic task. For Benjamin, criticism allows relationships to unfold that are only implicit in the original text, shedding light where the poetic text only testifies to its relation to the poetized; it reveals a "life-context" that the text bears silently within itself.[16] But this belated unfolding of something intrinsic yet unarticulated within the work of art is *also* the fundamental logic of Hölderlin's "Oriental" as he applies it to his translations. His letter to Wilmans contains its own references to the "life" contained within poetic texts, for by incorporating the Oriental in his translations he hopes to render the Greek text "more alive than usual." His line of argumentation is strikingly similar to Benjamin's: Greek art is foreign to us, and when we try to make it conform to our mode of representation (making mistakes "durch Nationalkonvenienz," for the sake of the native), we only highlight the flaws that this process creates.[17] By bringing out what he perceives as the "Oriental"—a

---

14. " . . . es ist in der neuen Fassung nicht Voraussetzung, sondern Gegenstand einer mit mächtiger Freiheit vollzognen Bewegung: der Dichter *tritt* ins Leben, er wandelt nicht in ihm fort" (GS II:1, 116).

15. Jennings thus describes the essay as "Benjamin's first attempt to formulate an anti-subjective position" (Jennings 1983, 553).

16. Although he does not use the term *Kritik* in the essay on Hölderlin, there is ample evidence that the "aesthetic commentary" he describes here represents an early formulation of that concept. For a discussion of Hölderlin's influence on Benjamin's theory of literary criticism (*Kritik*), see Jennings 1983, 550f.

17. On the other hand, Benjamin's comparison of tragedy and *Trauerspiel* follows something of a reverse trajectory in the *Origin of German Tragic Drama:* modern readers of tragedy have tried for too long to understand the Baroque and modern mourning play as the heirs of classical Greece, whereas Benjamin regards each form as the product of the specific historical moment in which it emerges. When we attempt to make sense of tragedy as a primordial form of modern drama and a representa-

mode disavowed by the Greeks, but nevertheless persistent as an undertone within the Greek text—he means to let the text become more relevant, hence "more alive," to a modern audience. Although Hölderlin speaks nowhere of what Benjamin calls the balance between Greek and Oriental registers, the idea of a balance is implicitly necessary; the Greek text will appear (to us) more authentic, more alive, more *Greek*, if a foreign element is introduced into it, making the text not just objectively foreign to us moderns but also foreign to itself, in its very linguistic essence.

The complexity of the relationship between languages and the reawakened "life" of the text in Hölderlin's model once again evokes the interwoven threads of the Oriental carpet, the "life-context determined by art" (*durch die Kunst bestimmter Lebenszusammenhang* [GS II:1, 107]) at the heart of Benjamin's reflections here. Languages, modes of representation, the passage of time—all must interact dynamically for the text to come alive in a given moment, and the text must bear the traces of that interaction. The weaving of an imagined past and present, of Greek and Hesperian and "Oriental," *is* the life of the text, and only a translator who recognizes this and brings it to bear upon the process of translation can render a text "more alive" to a modern audience. Conventional measures of a translation's quality since the age of Luther—its rendering of the sense of the original, or its lyrical beauty—thus become irrelevant, as the key task of the translator, at least in Hölderlin's model, involves the rejuvenation of the text through the careful retention—even restoration—of its polyvalence as an object of history. Translation (in Hölderlin's sense) and aesthetic commentary (in Benjamin's sense) may have the potential, therefore, to achieve a similar goal. Moreover, if we return to the initial point that Benjamin regards Hölderlin's final revision of *Dichtermut* as likewise Oriental in tone, then the pieces fall together: revision, criticism, and translation all appear as facets of the same stone.[18]

Given its fleeting appearance in the essay, it is not entirely certain whether his reference to Hölderlin's concept of the "Oriental" only functions for Benjamin as an offhand allusion, a convenient point of departure, or if he means for the term to underlie his commentary as a foundation of

---

tion of something "universally human," he argues, we lose sight of the separate logics underlying both tragedy and *Trauerspiel*. See Benjamin, *The Origin of German Tragic Drama*, 53–54 and 100–101; *Gesammelte Schriften* I:1, 234–35 and 279–80.

18. Critics have noted the circularity of Benjamin's argumentation here, that in the end he conveniently achieves what he has just defined at the start of the essay as the poetological "task" at hand, namely, the constitution of *das Gedichtete* as the truth of poetry through the work of aesthetic commentary (see, for example, Corngold 157). In a slightly different vein, Wellbery discusses Benjamin's "strategy of displacement," his habit of invoking classical technique to create a foundation for his own argument and at the same time to break out of its limits. "Benjamin's Theory of the Lyric," 42.

Hölderlin's poetic project. (To be sure, there is little reason to believe that the "Oriental" even plays this role for Hölderlin, since he only uses the term once, as we have seen, and with reference to the Sophocles translation rather than a poetic text.) If Benjamin's interest is based on the latter, however—if the Oriental represents a fundamental term in his reading of "Hölderlin's cosmos," as his language here would indicate—then there is ample justification for asking about the larger significance of Hölderlin's Sophocles translations for Benjamin's thought. For there is no doubt that Benjamin frequently taps into Hölderlin's Sophocles when he is in need of exemplary material. Upon closer consideration it reveals itself as something of a shadow text, lending substance to and revealing connections among key concepts: the life of the work of art, history, criticism, translation.

Benjamin, of course, had more explicit thoughts of his own about the status of translations and their role in the life of texts, and those remarks again bear a heavy debt to Hölderlin, though they also venture further. His 1921 essay "The Task of the Translator" (*Die Aufgabe des Übersetzers*), published in 1923 as a foreword to his own translations of Baudelaire's *Tableaux Parisiens,* may already represent in its form an homage to Hölderlin's esoteric remarks. It also contains several direct references to the Sophocles project, and its theoretical justification of translation bears unmistakable echoes of Hölderlin's thoughts on rendering a text "more alive than usual." However, already at the start of the the essay, Benjamin draws a fundamental distinction between his train of thought and Hölderlin's idea of the text come "alive" for its audience, for in Benjamin's estimation the translation's quality of being "alive" has little to do with its audience or, for that matter, the poet or the translator.[19] Any translation concerned with the quality of communicating to its audience represents in his estimation "the inaccurate transmission of an inessential content" (SW 1: 253) (*eine ungenaue Übermittlung eines unwesentlichen Inhalts* [GS IV:1, 9]). Instead, translation itself marks a text's "stage of continued life" (SW 1: 254), if a life can be conceived in terms of the history of a thing rather than its status as organic matter. In the case of translations produced in the historical moment of a text's "fame," "the life of the original attains its latest, continually renewed, and most complete unfolding" (SW 1: 255) (*das Leben des Originals [erreicht] seine stets erneute späteste und umfassendste Entfaltung* [GS IV:1, 11]) in the form of an "afterlife" (*Fortleben,* literally "living on") that reinscribes a text's contemporary relevance.[20] For Benjamin translation as *Fortleben* marks not

---

19. See Carol Jacobs, "Letters from Walter Benjamin": The translator is given up and abandoned as a matter of course . . . " *In the Language of Walter Benjamin* (Baltimore: Johns Hopkins, 1999), 13.

20. This concept of "fame" is reminiscent of what Franz Rosenzweig called the "miraculous" mo-

only the passage from one language to another but also the passage of time, effecting for the original text the expansion of its significance within a new historical context. Although he will state later that translations themselves cannot be re-translated, the possibility of continual renewal inheres in the production of new translations that extend a text's lifespan.

In this sense translation is once again a gesture akin to criticism within his theory of the work of art as bearer of its own history; both are not simply a reaction to a text but a continued exploration of, even a crystallization of, its relation to an abstract notion of truth.[21] Just as criticism (and revision, in Hölderlin's case) bear the potential of unlocking the relationship to *das Gedichtete*, the poem's fundamental connection to its particular "life-context," so too a translation can begin to illuminate the source text's fundamental connection to what Benjamin calls "pure" language. Pure language is that which all individual languages "want to express" (SW 1: 255) but cannot quite achieve *as* individual languages, because each single language, being alive, is in a "constant state of flux" (SW 1: 256) that changes its relation to the ideas it means to express. Even the words of dead languages undergo a process of change as they emerge into the light of the present day. Translation, "of all literary forms," is "the one charged with the special mission of watching over the maturing process of the original language and the birth pangs of its own" (SW 1: 256);[22] it bears responsibility not only for the transfer of a text's meaning to another language but for marking the space between languages, for illuminating the fact that language exists at all. Pure language makes itself heard most distinctly here, in the looser relation between language and content that a translation represents—in place of the organic connection of language to content in the original ("like a fruit and its skin"), we find in translation the "royal robes" that envelop content "with ample folds" (SW 1: 258, GS IV:1, 15).

The task of translation is of a piece, then, with the role of criticism, which opens a path from the poem to the poetized: whereas in criticism the poem itself is displaced by "the world beyond the poem," the "meta-

---

ment in which a foreign work becomes part of the receiving culture, when "the receiving people comes forth of its own desire and in its own utterance to meet the wingbeat of the foreign work." "Scripture and Luther," in Martin Buber and Franz Rosenzweig, *Scripture and Translation,* trans. Lawrence Rosenfeld and Everett Fox (Bloomington: Indiana University Press, 1984), 53.

21. In a similar vein, De Man notes the resemblance between translation and philosophy "in the sense that it is critical, in the same way that philosophy is critical, of a simple notion of imitation . . . " (*The Resistance to Theory,* 81). Both translation and philosophy, De Man claims, fulfill Benjamin's notion of the ironic gesture, undoing the stability of the original that would otherwise go unnoticed.

22. " . . . daß gerade unter allen Formen ihr als Eigenstes es zufällt, auf jene Nachreife des fremden Wortes, auf die Wehen des eigenen zu merken" (GS IV:1, 13).

physical substructure upon which the poem is based" (Jennings 1987, 192), translation as the transfer from one language to another reveals the interdependence among languages and their various ways of expressing the same thing: "the totality of their intentions supplementing one another: the pure language" (SW 1: 257).[23] Both forms point in their internal logic toward the obliteration of the artist (and the audience) in favor of a concept of the work as "organ of history";[24] both suggest that the unfolding that takes place in the engagement with a literary work is as much a part of the life of that work as the original composition. Criticism and translation, far from diluting or complicating the work's access to its own truth content, offer another way of looking (what Hölderlin called an "askew perspective," *ein linkischer Gesichtspunkt*) that can render that truth more evident, if only fleetingly.[25]

In each case, to be sure, this access to truth remains a theoretical construct, "a purely methodological, ideal goal" (SW 1: 21) (*das rein methodische, ideele Ziel* [GS II:1, 108]). Not unlike Hölderlin's characterization of intellectual intuition as "infinite approximation," the project of both the critic and the translator is a task in the true sense of the German word *Aufgabe*, which implies both the imposition of duty and resignation (*aufgeben*, to give up).[26] Any tentative step in the direction of truth is fleeting, fragmentary; nevertheless, there is no possibility of access other than by means of such fragments.[27]

In contrast to criticism, however, Benjamin's mode of translation allows this relation to truth to unfold not by way of meaningful engagement but by a radical fidelity to individual words at the expense of meaning. Because "ripening the seed of pure language in a translation" (SW 1: 259) has noth-

---

23. "... dass dennoch keiner einzelnen von ihnen, sondern nur der Allheit ihrer einander ergänzenden Intentionen erreichbar ist: die reine Sprache" (GS IV:1, 13). Benjamin describes the Romantics' concept of criticism as "another, if lesser factor in the continued life of literary works" compared with translation (SW 1: 258). He justly points out as well that the Romantics, though not explicitly concerned with translation in their theoretical writings, produced great translations that "testify to their sense of the essential nature and the dignity of this literary mode" [SW 1: 258].

24. Benjamin's formulation in the 1931 essay "Literaturgeschichte und Literaturwissenschaft," cited in Jennings 1987, 142. The entire passage is instructive: "Works must be considered quite as much according to the totality of their afterlife and reception as according to the history of their composition. We must interest ourselves in their destiny, their contemporary reception, their translations, their fame. Only thus does the work form itself internally into a microcosm, or rather, into a microaeon. . . . Literature in this way becomes an organ of history."

25. Contemporary translation theory tends to embrace Benjamin's point about the displacement of origins; see Bachmann-Medick 2009 and Buden and Novotny, *Translation Studies* Forum 2009.

26. On this dual notion of 'aufgeben" see Nägele, "Benjamin's Ground," 25.

27. In a sense this is the basis of Jennings's whole book-length argument: "His [Benjamin's] entire project can be read as the attempt to recognize these revelatory shards and, in particular, to exploit their revolutionary potential" (Jennings 1987, 128).

ing to do with the reproduction of a text's meaning, moreover, the translator need not aim at achieving sense, for revelation occurs on a level other than the semantic.[28] On the contrary, what is essential is what happens when a word-for-word translation, divorced from the demands of making sense, allows language to speak. Fidelity to the literal word (*Wörtlichkeit*), rather than to the "sense" of a text at the sentence level, brings a transparency to the translation that lets the spaces between languages shine through instead of smoothing over those gaps. The fragments that represent the potential access to truth are directly related to this fragmentation of sense in translations, for only by breaking up the coherence of language and content in the source text is it possible to discern the interaction among the elements that make up pure language. This attitude allows Benjamin to recast the translator's traditional categories of fidelity and freedom as operating in concert with one another rather than as conflicting tendencies; while fidelity conveys a connection to pure language through literalness, freedom is associated with the liberation of one's own language from within its "decayed barriers." Benjamin's well-known image of a collection of fragments (*Scherben*) that makes both original and translation "recognizable as fragments of a greater language" (SW 1: 260) thus describes a radical form of fidelity as literalness, which finds its highest expression in the translation of Holy Writ, where "meaning has ceased to be the watershed for the flow of language and the flow of revelation" (SW 1: 262) (*in dem der Sinn aufgehört hat, die Wasserscheide für die strömende Sprache und die strömende Offenbarung zu sein,* GS IV: 1, 21). At the same time, however, the imperative that these broken pieces somehow fit together—like "fragments of a vessel that are to be glued together" (SW 1: 260)[29]—also underscores the significance of freedom, of relaxing the boundaries of the receiving language to allow the breathing room necessary to "release . . . that pure language which is exiled among alien tongues, to liberate the language imprisoned in a work in his re-creation of a work" (SW 1: 261).[30]

Benjamin's reconsideration of the categories of fidelity and freedom at this point—as both divorced from the limitations of making sense and

---

28. On this point see Beatrice Hanssen, "Language and Mimesis in Walter Benjamin's Work," in *The Cambridge Companion to Walter Benjamin,* ed. David S. Ferris (Cambridge University Press, 2004), 62–63.

29. Carol Jacobs is rigorously literal in claiming that Benjamin's twin notions of a) fragments as the *broken part* of a vessel (*Scherben als Bruchstück eines Gefäßes* [18]) and b) translation and original as the *broken part* of a greater language (*Bruchstück einer größeren Sprache*) suggest together that language remains broken, incomplete in the passage from original to translation. "The Monstrosity of Translation," 84f.

30. "Jene reine Sprache, die in fremde gebannt ist, in der eigenen zu erlösen, die im Werk gefangene in der Umdichtung zu befreien, ist die Aufgabe des Übersetzers" (GS IV:1, 19).

pressed into the service of releasing pure language—also opens up more space for his reading of Hölderlin's translations, which now represent an extreme example of the linguistic fragmentation that Benjamin names as essential to the "task of the translator." Early in the essay he relates how in the nineteenth century the Sophocles translations were characterized as "monstrous examples" of the literalness that leads to incomprehensibility, apparently casting them as an intriguing yet failed project. Yet near the end of the essay he refines this description to complement his own theory of translation:

> Hierfür wie in jeder andern wesentlichen Hinsicht stellen sich Hölderlins Übertragungen, besonders die der beiden Sophokleischen Tragödien, bestätigend dar. In ihnen ist die Harmonie der Sprachen so tief, daß der Sinn nur noch wie eine Äolsharfe vom Winde von der Sprache berührt wird. Hölderlins Übersetzungen sind Urbilder ihrer Form; sie verhalten sich auch zu den vollkommensten Übertragungen ihrer Texte als das Urbild zum Vorbild . . . (GS IV:1, 20f.)

> Confirmation of this as well as every other important aspect is supplied by Hölderlin's translations, particularly those of the two tragedies by Sophocles. In them the harmony of the languages is so profound that sense is touched by language only the way an aeolian harp is touched by the wind. Hölderlin's translations are originary images/prototypes (*Urbilder*) of their form; they are to even the most perfect renderings of their texts as a originary image/prototype is to a model . . . (SW 1: 262)

As *Urbilder*, originary images or prototypes, the translations take on a very different status from that of the "monstrous": they become both representative and inimitable. All other translations of Sophocles—even those that are "most perfect"—are mere approximations of the *Urbild* that is Hölderlin's translation.

Here Benjamin performs a twofold gesture that implicitly explains his particular, even personal interest in Hölderlin's project: he marks Hölderlin's Sophocles as "originary," as the first of its form, and claims at the same time that this translation confirms the essence of his own argument. Could we then regard Benjamin's essay as something of a translation (*qua* criticism, the illumination of that which inheres silently in the original) of that "originary" form? To be sure, Benjamin would not be the only reader of Hölderlin's translations to suggest that they might require a translation of their own. Whatever he has said here, he claims, finds confirmation in Hölderlin's

Urbild, yet the language of the translations only maintains the most delicate contact with the sense of the Greek text: "in them meaning plunges from abyss to abyss until it threatens to become lost in the bottomless depths of language" (SW 1: 262) (*In ihnen stürzt der Sinn von Abgrund zu Abgrund, bis er droht in bodenlosen Sprachtiefen sich zu verlieren*, GS IV:1, 21). In an obvious and extreme way, the translation cannot shed light on its own truth content, because its translator has stretched the boundaries of his language so far that its gates "slam shut and enclose [him] in silence" (*zufallen und den Übersetzer ins Schweigen schließen* [GS IV:1, 21]). Given his evident interest in and even identification with Hölderlin as thinker, poet, and translator, we could indeed see Benjamin's response to Hölderlin's Sophocles as a dynamic expression of that text's "living on"—not a translation of a translation (which, as he states, would be impossible) but an engagement with it that extends and expands its historical relevance.[31]

Benjamin's apparent tendency to identify with Hölderlin throughout the early stages of his scholarly career also sheds light on some intriguing weaknesses in his argument here. Like so many readers both before and after him, he indulges in an overly neat conflation of the "monstrous" translation with the fallen translator. He does not miss the opportunity to point out that the translations are Hölderlin's "last work" (SW 1: 262), thus suggesting that the "monstrous (*ungeheure*) and originary danger" to which he exposed himself in the process also made it impossible for him to fend off madness. Benjamin's tendency to valorize this translator in particular begins to undermine his view that the subject is relatively unimportant in the process of producing a text's truth content; here, Hölderlin rather heroically obliterates himself for the sake of the text (and, one could argue, for the sake of his audience). Perhaps it is no coincidence, then, that Benjamin invokes one of Hölderlin's most prominent terms from the translations here, *ungeheuer*, to describe the "originary danger" that the translator faces. In Hölderlin's translation of *Antigone*, *ungeheuer* stood in for the Greek *deinon* and nearly matched its ambivalent complexity, evoking at once the exalted and the monstrous: "Ungeheuer ist viel, doch nichts ungeheurer als / Der Mensch" (*Much is monstrous, but nothing is more monstrous than the human*).

---

31. Samuel Weber reflects astutely on Benjamin's concept of origin, outlined in the *Trauerspielbuch*, as it relates to translation. The origin is "the springing-forth that emerges out of coming-to-be and passing-away" (*dem Werden und Vergehen Entspringendes*), thus not a static moment but a relation to historical time, always in flux: "Its historicality resides . . . in its power to return incessantly to the past and through the rhythm of its ever-changing repetitions set the pace for the future." Translation is similarly the "stopping place of an ongoing movement," a gesture that touches the text without taking possession of it. "A Touch of Translation: On Benjamin's 'Task of the Translator,'" in Bermann and Wood, *Nation, Language, and the Ethics of Translation* (Princeton, 2005), 73.

This term, which the Chorus first used to describe humankind in general, came to be embodied by Antigone in our stead; *ungeheuer* encompassed the unfamiliar, unsettling quality that, through Antigone, the human subject is brought to recognize in himself. If Hölderlin as translator exposed himself to a danger within language that was *ungeheuer*—monstrous, enormous, disconcerting—then by Benjamin's logic he, like Antigone, could only withdraw from the world as a result. His "last work" causes the gates to shut, just as Antigone's ceremonial act of burial effectively causes the tomb to be sealed.

Like Antigone, then, the translator in Benjamin's view has already taken on a sacrificial role—"for the sake of pure language, he breaks through decayed barriers (*morsche Schranken*) of his own language" (SW 1: 261) —and if Benjamin associates Hölderlin in particular with this mode of sacrifice, that gesture only reveals a certain consistency in his method. Though not in such an explicit form, he has already made this association in "Two Poems," where he develops, in conversation with Hölderlin's poetry, a radical concept of the poet's courage. The implicit characterization of the *translator* as heroic—as attempting a task both dangerous and necessary—thus demands that we wind our way back to Benjamin's very first engagement with Hölderlin. In the earlier essay, Benjamin finds that the poet's courage in facing the danger of death and the dissolution of the self in pure relatedness (the revelation of *das Gedichtete,* the truth content of the text) brings salvation to the world. Benjamin first rejects the notion of *Dichtermut* that lends Hölderlin's first version its title, claiming that its lack of clarity places it in line with vulgar locutions such as *Weibertreue,* too close to the plasticity of life to attain the purity of connection to the poetized that Benjamin's concept requires. Courage as he conceives of it, on the other hand, may *be* the primary stance of both versions of the poem but only reaches the level of intellectual *insight* in the final version, where courage is not merely a static quality ("Man and death stand rigid, opposing one another") but a dynamic recognition of relationship in the poet's surrender to death, "the innermost identity of the poet with the world" (SW 1: 34). With this gesture of surrender, which in the context of the poetic text is also recognition and revelation, "the poet does not have to fear death; he is a hero because he lives at the center of all relations."[32]

The authentically "heroic" stance of the poet is thus not that of the first version, *Dichtermut,* in its static confrontation with death, but of *Blödigkeit,*

---

32. "Der Dichter hat den Tod nicht zu fürchten, er ist Held, weil er die Mitte aller Beziehungen lebt" (II:1, 124).

timidity, a characteristic that does not automatically invite associations with boldness or risk. The courage that Benjamin locates in timidity seems to inhere in the willingness to do nothing at all.

> In die Mitte des Lebens versetzt, bleibt ihm nichts, als das reglose Dasein, die völlige Passivität, die das Wesen des Mutigen ist; als sich ganz hinzugeben der Beziehung. (GS IV:1, 125)

> Since he has been transposed into the middle of life, nothing awaits him but motionless existence, complete passivity, which is the essence of the courageous man—nothing except to surrender himself wholly to relationship. (SW 1: 34)

One result of this surrender is the dissolution of the poet as subject, the collapse of poet and poetry at the "untouchable center of all relation" (SW 1: 35).[33] The form-giving gesture of Greek art, the realm of the first version, thus makes space for the Oriental, the overcoming of the limits and boundaries of form. The distance the poet has traveled, from being an individual part of the world of form to the formlessness of the center, ultimately finds expression, Benjamin claims, in the "intrusive caesura" of the poem's final lines:

> Gut auch sind und geschikt einem zu etwas wir,
>   Wenn wir kommen, mit Kunst, *und von den Himmlischen*
> *Einen bringen. Doch selber*
> *Bringen schikliche Hände wir.*

> Good, too, are we and skillful for [*or* sent to] someone to some end,
>   When we come, with art, *and bring one*
> *From among the heavenly beings. Yet we ourselves*
> *Bring suitable [or appropriate, fitting] hands.* (SW 1: 22; my italics)

Benjamin's use of the poetic term "caesura" (*Zäsur*) here doubtless refers at surface level to enjambments in the last two lines, but the term has a loaded significance for Hölderlin's Sophocles project as well, as Benjamin surely knew: in the remarks on *Oedipus,* the caesura underlay Hölderlin's theory of the relation between the structure of tragedy and its effects, marking that point of "counter-rhythmic rupture" at which the tragic hero is

---

33. On understanding the poet's courage in relation to passivity see Corngold 1998, 163–64.

banished from the centrality of life into the "excentric sphere of the dead." At this moment, which for Hölderlin coincides with the appearance of the seer Tiresias, "representation itself appears." Benjamin is a bit cryptic here, however, and the single mention of the caesura is perhaps not truly helpful unless we understand it through another lens. Although in this passage "caesura" seems to refer primarily to a rhythmic disruption, Benjamin makes evident in other writings that he understands the depth that the concept possessed for Hölderlin. In the essay on Goethe's *Elective Affinities,* he invokes Hölderlin's definition of the caesura as "the pure word, the counter-rhythmic rupture" (*das reine Wort, die gegenrhythmische Unterbrechung*) to describe a moment in which "something beyond the poet interrupts the language of the poetry" (SW 1: 341) (*etwas jenseits des Dichters der Dichtung ins Wort fällt* [GS I:1, 182]—literally, it *falls* into language, underscoring the poet's inertia in that process).[34] And here we find a deeper connection to the notion of courage expressed as passivity; at the point of caesura the poet's primary role, for Benjamin, is to give room to something larger than himself: "Every expression comes to a standstill, in order to give space to an expressionless power inside all artistic media" (SW 1: 340f.; trans. modified) (*in der . . . zugleich jeder Ausdruck sich legt, um einer innerhalb aller Kunstmittel ausdruckslosen Gewalt Raum zu geben*).

Benjamin goes on to draw a logical parallel, which for our purposes possesses an almost tantalizing potential:

> Solche Gewalt ist kaum je deutlicher geworden als in der griechischen Tragödie einer-, der Hölderlinschen Hymnik andererseits. In der Tragödie als Verstummen des Helden, in der Hymne als Einspruch im Rhythmus vernehmbar. (GS I:1, 182)

> Such power has rarely become clearer than in Greek tragedy, on the one hand, and in Hölderlin's hymnic poetry, on the other. Perceptible in tragedy as the falling silent of the hero, and in the rhythm of the hymn as objection. (341)

Composed in 1919–1922 and published in 1924–5, the essay on *Elective*

---

34. Lacoue-Labarthe offers another highly evocative image of the caesura in an interview in the documentary film "The Ister," where he describes it as an historical moment in which "humanity is all of a sudden short of breath." This is, in a sense, another dimension of the "expressionless" moment of which Benjamin speaks; Lacoue-Labarthe ultimately associates the caesura as historical phenomenon with the reality of the Shoah, as an inexpressible moment after which "we will always have trouble catching our breath." In Barison and Ross, "The Ister," Black Box Sound and Image, 2004.

Affinities marks almost exactly the chronological span between the "Task of the Translator" (1921) and Benjamin's habilitation, the *Origin of German Tragic Drama* (*Ursprung des deutschen Trauerspiels*), which he completed in 1925. Perhaps it is fitting, then, that this passage incorporates elements of the earlier essays (Benjamin's interest in Hölderlin's writings on translation and his poetry) as well as the later study. The "falling silent" of the tragic hero to which Benjamin refers here is a trope identified by Franz Rosenzweig in the *Star of Redemption,* and it will play a significant role in Benjamin's reading of Greek tragedy in contrast to the Baroque *Trauerspiel.* In the *Trauerspiel* book, the tragic conflict marks a transitional and ambiguous moment in which the hero must sacrifice himself for the sake of the world, and that sacrifice is both "first and final," because at once he moves to invalidate the gods and to announce the onset of a new order:

> Die tragische Dichtung ruht auf der Opferidee. Das tragische Opfer aber ist in seinem Gegenstande—dem Helden—unterschieden von jedem anderen und ein erstes und letztes zugleich. Ein letztes im Sinne des Sühnopfers, das Göttern, die ein altes Recht behüten, fällt; ein erstes im Sinn der stellvertretenden Handlung, in welcher neue Inhalte des Volkslebens sich ankündigen. (GS I:1, 285)

> Tragic poetry is based on the idea of sacrifice. But in respect of its victim, the hero, the tragic sacrifice differs from any other kind, being at once a first and a final sacrifice. A final sacrifice in the sense of the atoning sacrifice to gods who are upholding an ancient right; a first sacrifice in the sense of the representative action, in which new aspects of the life of the nation become manifest.[35] (*Origin,* 106f.)

In the midst of this turmoil of transition, the tragic hero remains notably silent, confined for Rosenzweig within "the icy loneliness of the self" (*Origin* 107). The hero is emphatically not an object of identification for the audience but rather embodies change; his silence is the "sublime element" that generates a tipping point from the gods' complete dominion to their decline, as the audience sees "not the guilt of the accused but the evidence of speechless suffering" (*Origin* 109) (*nicht die Betroffenheit des Angeschuldigten, sondern das Zeugnis sprachlosen Leidens,* GS I:1, 288). In tragedy Rosenzweig recognizes the "paradox of the birth of the genius in moral speechlessness,

---

35. Walter Benjamin, *The Origin of German Tragic Drama,* trans. John Osborne (London and New York: Verso, 2009), 106f. Hereafter cited in body of text as *Origin.*

moral infantility" (*Origin* 110) (*Das Paradoxon der Geburt des Genius in moralischer Sprachlosigkeit, moralischer Infantilität*, 289).[36]

A sustained reading of the *Trauerspiel* book would take me too far afield here, but surely it is impossible not to be tempted by the apparent similarities between the respective portraits of the tragic hero in *Trauerspiel* and the poet in "Zwei Gedichte." Indeed, when in the *Elective Affinities* essay Benjamin calls attention to the caesura's convergence in the falling-silent of the tragic hero and the rhythm of Hölderlin's late poetry, he more or less invites that comparison. To what extent, however, can we push the analogy? Can it lead us from Hölderlin as poet to Hölderlin as translator of Greek tragedy—the Hölderlin who, for Benjamin, stands alongside the poet from the very start?

Both Jennings and Beatrice Hanssen have noted the proximity of the poet in "Zwei Gedichte" to the character of the tragic hero, though not in direct relation to the *Trauerspiel* book. Jennings draws a specific parallel to Hölderlin by pointing out the similarities between the courageous poet and the tragic hero Empedokles, both of whom must save the world by surrendering their own subjectivity:

> [T]he poet and Empedokles are at once privileged and condemned to lead a life above and outside that of the 'Volk.' And again like Empedokles, the poet in Benjamin's reading is able by virtue of his song to impose a new order and meaning on the lives of the people. . . . And finally, just as the problem of Empedokles' death stands at the center of the drama, so, too, does the death of the poet in Benjamin's interpretation figure as the major and necessary event in the realization of the new order. The poet's death frees his song from the bounds of his subjectivity and thus objectifies and universalizes it. (Jennings 1983, 554)

This comparison is compelling and largely persuasive but does not go far enough. In Hölderlin's dramatic text Empedocles is heroic not just because he speaks but because he first speaks too much—articulating too clearly his own privileged status as conduit to the divine—and then falls silent. He does not "impose a new order and meaning on the lives of the people" merely

---

36. Rainer Nägele associates this pivotal quality of Greek tragedy in Benjamin's view with Hölderlin's distinction of Greeks and moderns in the relationship between word and body (the Greeks' more physically mediated relation [deadly-factual, *tödlichfaktisch*] vs. the moderns' more spiritual and *un*-mediated relation ["killing-factual," *tödtendfaktisch*]); both describe the "scene of the formation of the yet unformed, of giving language to the yet unspoken," linking them to Kant's concept of becoming *mündig*, that process of coming to consciousness that amounts literally to receiving a mouth. Nägele, *Theater, Theory, Speculation*, 38. The discussion of Kant appears on pp. 7–8.

because of his song but also by his silencing of that song. The thrust of the tragedy rests on his recognition of this very point, as the priest Hermocrates describes:

> Verderblicher denn Schwert und Feuer ist
> Der Menschengeist, der götterähnliche,
> Wenn er nicht schweigen kann, und sein Geheimnis
> Unaufgedekt bewahren . . . (FA 13: 821f.,1. 168–71)

> More ruinous than sword or fire is the human spirit, the god-like, if he cannot be silent and preserve his secret unrevealed . . .

While Empedocles achieves heroic status not just through his song but also through his silence, we also find a similar situation in Oedipus, whose self-blinding is another expression of the silencing which follows too much speech (where "the spirit of Oedipus, all-knowing, articulates the *nefas*" [FA 16:252]). This is the aspect of tragic heroism that Rosenzweig elides but Hölderlin underscores: in the end, the hero's silence is a necessary consequence of having said too much.

How can this description of the tragic hero's silence possibly relate to the poet, as Benjamin suggests? By definition, after all, a poet cannot be silent. For Benjamin, however, he does embody "timidity," and the association with the tragic hero may offer insight into the question of how to understand the somewhat problematic formulation *Blödigkeit*. Corngold calls it a "troublesome word . . . which while unquestionably meaning 'timidity,' also, like *Blödheit*, suggests short-sightedness and, in certain contexts, stupidity" (162). And indeed, at least in a contemporary sense it is difficult to separate the word *Blödigkeit* from the common exhortation *blöd*, meaning stupid.[37] (Grimms' dictionary, by the way, includes both *infirmitas* (feebleness) and *timiditas* as possible definitions along with *hebetudo*, mental dullness.[38]) The quality of timidity or weakness that Benjamin locates in Hölderlin's poem, however, implies above all a receding from the spotlight into a realm of insignificance: "The poet is nothing but a limit with respect to life, the point of indifference . . . " (SW 1: 35) (*Er ist nichts als Grenze gegen das Leben, die Indifferenz* . . . [II:1, 125]). The kind of courage denoted by *Blödigkeit* is the

---

37. See Avital Ronell's commentary in *Stupidity* (University of Illinois Press, 2002, where she discusses the "tradition" among commentators since Benjamin "of diverting the title from its disturbing implications" [7], whereas she sees Hölderlin's shift from the poet's courage to his *Blödigkeit* as "bringing forth stupidity as a crucial poetic sign" [8] in the tradition of Rousseau.
38. See the Grimm's dictionary online at http://germazope.uni-trier.de/Projekte/DWB.

courage to withdraw into the marginality of death for the sake of a truth that will bestow itself on the living. The courage, in effect, to be tragically, heroically silent.

This concept of courage strongly recalls Hölderlin's remarks on *Oedipus,* where he identifies the caesura as the moment in which Tiresias banishes the hero from a position of centrality to one of excentricity:

> Er tritt in den Gang des Schiksaals, als Aufseher über die Naturmacht, die tragisch, den Menschen seiner Lebenssphäre, dem Mittelpuncte seines inneren Lebens in eine andere Welt entrükt und in die exzentrische Sphäre der Todten reißt. (FA 16: 251)

> He steps into the course of fate as overseer of the natural order which tragically displaces the human being from his own sphere of life, from the midpoint of his inner life into another world and tears him into the excentric sphere of the dead. (Constantine 64; trans. modified)

While the instance of caesura in tragedy denotes the hero's silencing in the case of Oedipus (and Empedocles by association), it also represents in the remarks on *Antigone* "the moment of greatest risk in the course of day or a work of art"—the moment in which "the human being must hold onto himself the most" and therefore also "stand most openly there in his character." In that moment of risk, which the human being confronts by holding on more tightly, the tragic hero, by contrast, must let go. Benjamin's poet, with his stance of passive courage, must effectively do the same.

The weak and distant pulse that remains as mark of Hölderlin's tragic hero thus links him conceptually to Benjamin's poet, who lets go of his own form for the sake of the relatedness of the whole; both figures succumb to silence rather than "holding onto themselves" in the way that the human being typically must, at least for Hölderlin. Yet if letting go of oneself is related, for both Hölderlin and Benjamin, to accepting silence as opposed to maintaining one's own voice—*not* being silent—then we find ourselves facing yet another intriguing triangulation. For who is more silent in this sense than the translator? Much more obviously than the poet, after all, he is meant to be as silent as possible in the course of fulfilling his task—silent not in the sense of creating a smooth and seamless translation (for that degree of intervention would in fact be the opposite of silence), but in the manner that Benjamin describes: as a surrender of control over the sense of a text in the name of a radical fidelity to its language. Perhaps one could even go so far as to say that the translator has no choice but to make himself "blöd," if he wants to achieve a translation of the peculiar quality that both Hölderlin and Benjamin demand.

Interestingly enough, Schleiermacher realized this a hundred years before Benjamin.

> The attempt seems to be the most extraordinary form of humiliation that a writer, who is not a bad writer, could inflict upon himself. Who would not like to have his native tongue appear everywhere in its most enticing beauty, of which every literary genre is capable? Who would not rather beget children who are in their parents' image rather than bastards? Who would like to show himself in less attractive and less graceful movements than he is capable of, and at least sometimes appear harsh and stiff, and shock the reader as much as is necessary to keep him aware of what he is doing? . . . These are the sacrifices that every translator must make; these are the dangers to which he exposes himself. . . . (Schulte and Biguenet 46f.)

The translator, in "keep[ing] the reader aware of what he is doing" and sacrificing his own poetic capacity for the sake of the text before him, must be willing to face humiliation, not just to accept the passive silence of *Blödigkeit* but also to risk the exposure of *Blödigkeit* in its other sense: to look stupid. At least in the eyes of many of his contemporaries, Hölderlin as translator certainly exposed himself in this respect. Schleiermacher recognizes and sheds light upon the injustice of such characterizations: the translator looks stupid, yes, but it is probably not his fault. Benjamin, on the other hand, takes that charge of stupidity, as it was applied specifically to these translations and this translator, and reformulates it as an asset. Hölderlin's translations look stupid because as a translator he is *blöd*, and with respect to the "living-on" (*Fortleben*, the afterlife) of both the text and the languages that mark a crossroads within it, that is courage *par excellence*.

This process is in no way effortless, and a hint of the tragic hero's "speechless suffering" is implicit in the stance of the poet or translator who gives space to a truth that otherwise defies expression. Much later, in a text of 1936 entitled *German Men and Women*, Benjamin revisits the idea of a suffering that this translator-poet must bear; taking up the language of a second letter to Casimir Ulrich Böhlendorff from 1802 (subsequent to the more famous letter of 1801 regarding the interplay of the foreign and that which is one's own, *das Fremde und das Eigene*) he describes the suffering that connects Hölderlin's world to that of ancient Greece, not as "blossoming idealized world" but as "the desolate real one": "This suffering is the secret of the historical transformation, the transubstantiation, of the Greek spirit, which is the subject of Hölderlin's last hymns" (SW 3:181). In historical transformation we find the same insufficiency with which the "desolate real" world of the Greeks would have met alongside its idealized image. For Hölderlin the best solution was to embed that suffering within his poetry by marking out, in language, the distance that this "Greek spirit" would have traveled.

In an interview in the fascinating documentary film "The Ister," the filmmaker Hans-Jürgen Syberberg describes his visual concept of Hölderlin's relation to Greek sources, which offers a similar, but more affirmative version of transubstantiation than the one Benjamin constructs: the image of a "little," empty model of a stage marks the insufficient reflection of an idealized Greece, juxtaposed by Hölderlin's words.

> To have Greek theater in our life . . . the best . . . is . . . as a little model, not too small, but very precisely made, full in light. And if you then hear the words of Hölderlin, together with this empty stage, and see this piece, this model of Greece, then you have it. You have what he means.[39]

Taken as a reflection on the challenges of historical transformation, Syberberg's concept is no pessimistic statement on translation's impossibility. Nor does this process of reconstruction demand, as it does for Benjamin at the endpoint of the "Task of the Translator," submitting to a strictly literal mode of translation. The reconstruction may be of smaller stature than its idealized source, but it is precise, and its contours are brightly illuminated. This offers a worthy counterpoint to the model of "invisible" translator and "transparent" text, effectively redefining the set of values that traditionally underlie perceptions of "good" translation: Hölderlin's translations of ancient text—as well as their transubstantiation in poetic form, which for Benjamin involves a similar process—make no particular claim to transparency, and that is their virtue. What they do claim instead is the reconstruction of a text that *lives on*. The translator's courage, the courage to be small, perhaps, and to allow one's words to echo around an empty stage, is ultimately a stance more liberating than constrictive. It sheds light on language as language, on the unexpected relationships between languages and between texts and contexts that let a text live and breathe; and at the same time, it ennobles the gesture of *Aufgabe* as surrender, perhaps, but not failure. Translation in this sense is essential to the living-on (*Fortleben*) of texts in new contexts, and the translator bears responsibility for that living-on; like the tragic hero, she is the silent pivot that lets the source text cross barriers, whether temporal or spatial, and resonate anew.

---

39. David Barison and Daniel Ross, *The Ister* (Black Box Sound and Image, 2004).

Only a few years after Benjamin reflects in *German Men and Women* on the rupture between the distant, idealized world of the Greeks and the harsh glare of the "real"—implicitly situating the translator-poet, once again, as ethically bound to a purely passive courage—Martin Heidegger takes on the question of courage as well, also binding it to the figure of the translator-poet (and particularly the poet who engages in an exchange with classical Greece) in his 1943 lecture "Hölderlins Hymne 'Der Ister.'" As we will see in the next chapter, Heidegger brings together Sophocles' Antigone and Hölderlin's late hymn "Der Ister" to consider the exchange or "conversation" (*Zwiesprache*) between the two texts as well as to engage in his own dialogue with them. In some ways, Benjamin and Heidegger are intriguingly close to one another in their respective assessments of the role of translation and the "foreign" in the development of one's own language. The two seem to agree, for example, that the exchange with the foreign should remain transparent, that the translator-poet ought never to erase the tracks that lead him outward into the unknown and back to the "Eigenes," that which is one's own. For Heidegger, however, the ultimate goal of the "conversation" with ancient text is not, as it was for Benjamin, a glimpse of the connection to a universal truth inherent in the space between languages; rather, insofar as the poet represents the voice of his people, the Germans, his expression of courage serves a political rather than an ethical purpose, standing in the service of consolidating national identity during the crisis of wartime. This concept of identity, moreover, is not universal but rather originates precisely in the specific relationship of the Germans and the ancient Greeks—the idealized Greeks, once again, and not their "desolate real" world, in harmony with a no less idealized version of the Germans. Yet however emphatically Heidegger attempts to embed patriotic sympathies in his lecture, delivered in the period of the siege at Stalingrad, his reading and simultaneous performance of the concept of dialogue or *Zwiesprache* renders problematic any possibility of triumphant homecoming.

FIVE

Out of Tune?
Heidegger on Translation

Die Gedichte [Hölderlins] sind im Lärm der "undichterischen Sprachen" wie eine Glocke, die im Freien hängt und schon durch einen leichten, über sie kommenden Schneefall verstimmt wird. Vielleicht deshalb sagt Hölderlin in späteren Versen einmal das Wort, das wie Prosa klingt und doch dichterisch ist wie kaum eines (Entwurf zu Kolomb IV, 395):

Von wegen geringer Dinge
Verstimmt wie vom Schnee war
Die Glocke, womit
Man läutet
Zum Abendessen.

Vielleicht ist jede Erläuterung dieser Gedichte ein Schneefall auf die Glocke.[1]

Amidst the noise of "unpoetic languages"(IV, 257) the poems (i.e., Hölderlin's) are like a bell, hanging in the open air and already brought out of tune by a light snowfall that is coming over it. Perhaps this is why Hölderlin once, in later verses, speaks the word that sounds like prose and yet is poetic in a way that few others are (Draft for "Colombus," IV, 395):

Put out of tune
By humble things, as by snow

---

1. Martin Heidegger, "Vorwort zur zweiten Auflage [1951]," *Gesamtausgabe 4: Erläuterungen zu Hölderlins Dichtung* (Frankfurt: Klostermann, 1944), 7f. Henceforth abbreviated as GA, with volume and page number. Unless otherwise indicated, translations are my own.

> Was the bell, with which
> The hour is rung
> For the evening meal.
>
> Perhaps every elucidation of these poems is a falling of snow on the bell.
>
> Sage mir, was du vom Übersetzen hältst, und ich sage dir, wer du bist.
>
> Tell me what you think of translation, and I will tell you who you are. (GA 53: 76)

JUST AS SNOW falls softly upon a bell, reading touches lightly upon a text. And leaves a trace, however faint. A *Verstimmung,* a disordering, resounds from within, leaving the voice of the bell out of tune, the tenor of the text inescapably other than it was before—allowing existing forms to be unsettled by "humble things," revealing a new dimension of the past that only becomes audible through its echoes in the present, in the moment of reading. In the 1951 foreword to his *Elucidations of Hölderlin's Poetry* (*Erläuterungen zu Hölderlins Dichtung*), Martin Heidegger claims that the act of reading Hölderlin (and, by extension, of attempting to illuminate his poetry amid the clamor of "unpoetic languages") requires the active engagement with a poetic text that both demands elucidation and resists mere ordering. Indeed, these preliminary remarks suggest that when confronted with those most conceptually distant examples of Hölderlin's poetry, the late hymns, interpretation can perhaps only take place as dis-ordering.[2]

And yet, as Heidegger goes on to insist in this same passage, the task of the interpreter—"the last, but also the most difficult step of each interpretation"—is to erase every vestige of that dismantling operation she has only just undertaken. While a reader's elucidations may let the poem ring out otherwise than before, they may not make themselves heard as such; after her attempts at clarification the reader must aim to disappear without a trace.

---

2. Dirk de Schutters argues similarly that for Heidegger, the "Umstimmung" that characterizes reading in an authentic sense requires a "Verstimmung," a disordering in the act of reading: in order for the text to give itself "the law according to which it can be." "The Parergonality of Reading: Heidegger reading Hölderlin," in *Die Aufgabe des Lesers: On the Ethics of Reading,* ed. L. Verbeeck and B. Philipsen (Leuven: Peeters, 1992), 126.

> . . . damit das im Gedicht rein Gedichtete um einiges klarer dastehe, muß die erläuternde Rede sich und ihr Versuchtes jedesmal zerbrechen. Um des Gedichteten willen muß die Erläuterung des Gedichtes danach trachten, sich selbst überflüssig zu machen. (GA 4: 8)

> . . . so that what has been composed purely into a poem may stand forth a little clearer, the elucidating speech must each time shatter itself and what it had attempted to do. For the sake of preserving the poetized, the elucidation of the poem must strive to make itself superfluous.

In other words, the lucidity of the poem must appear to have always been there, in spite of the many steps, however arduous, taken to attain it. The practice of reading as Heidegger describes it here is thus not so distant from a historically stable concept of translation that bears the similarly impossible demand of seamless transfer: like translation, *Erläuterung* remains suspended between the inevitable disturbance of the text—its *Verstimmung*, its status out of tune—and the imperative to preserve its pristine integrity.[3]

There is a point at which Heidegger does not only aim to elucidate Hölderlin's writings but also acknowledges the need to "translate" them—and thus to reveal the nearly imperceptible layers of a text's history that interpretation must uncover. In his 1942 lecture on Hölderlin's hymn "Der Ister," Heidegger asserts that the interpretation or laying-out (*Auslegung*) of any great work (he includes the *Phenomenology* and the *Critique of Pure Reason* in this category) amounts to "a translating within our German language" (75). To designate such works as "in need of translation" (*übersetzungsbedürftig*) is not at all to suggest, as one might intuitively guess, that they suffer from a lack of clarity; quite the contrary, their "need of translation" only underscores their significance insofar as it confronts us with other possible ways in which to "understand."

In translating Sophocles, as we have seen, Hölderlin performed a double gesture that preserved intact a tension between fidelity and transformation, oscillating between a pure, often nearly absurd fidelity to the ancient text and an unsettling reorganization that, in the eyes of most of his contemporaries, hardly approximated the source text at all. As we have also seen, Ben-

---

3. Although the German word *Erläuterung* is commonly translated as "elucidations," it is worth mentioning in this context that it derives from the verb "läuten," to sound or ring out, rather than from the description of an action implying visual clarification. Thus the practice of interpretation implicitly (perhaps even explicitly, given Heidegger's close attention to language and etymology) involves the process of allowing a text not only to become "lucid" but to ring out more clearly. This emphasis on sound extends in Heidegger's discourse to terms like "Anklang."

jamin identified this mode of translation, informed by the relation to "pure language" as such, as the most dangerous and hence most courageous of its kind. Thus it may appear upon first glance that what Heidegger describes as *Erläuterung* here—that stroking of the text that leaves no fingerprint behind—hews more closely to conventional modes of translation, insofar as they construct order from the artifacts of the past and reestablish it in the form of untainted identity. After all, for many of its practitioners the ideal translation has always been one that, like Heidegger's ideal elucidation, leaves no trace at all. Yet in laying out the text of Sophocles' *Antigone* in his "Ister" lecture, Heidegger turns to no other translation than Hölderlin's (and, ultimately and with more satisfaction, his own). If, as Heidegger asserts in this lecture, all interpretation is a form of translation, all translation a form of interpretation—an interpretation that, moreover, must constantly cover its own tracks—why does he consult a translation that never ceases to speak its name? For there is no question that Hölderlin's *Oedipus* and *Antigone* are far from pitch-perfect; one might even say that their status of being out of tune is what defines them.

One approach to the question may lie in the contrast of the second citation above, culled from the 1942 lecture: "Tell me what you think of translation, and I will tell you who you are." Here it is not translation itself that secures identity—*who you are*—but the act of reflecting on it. Heidegger's rather audacious statement claims the authority to interpret not merely a translated text but a reader of translation as well. The evaluative gesture concerns the manner in which translation ought to take place rather than the product of that taking-place; the rhetorical tone, meanwhile, mimicking the syntax of both the distinguished professor and the seer, conveys a sweeping command that nullifies the discordant complexity of the interpretive process and leaves one with—clarity. Yet it is a clarity that ultimately rings false within the larger framework of this text, which repeatedly indicates that the apparent simplicity of this exchange—*tell me, and I'll tell you*—can only result from the stifling of an inherent discord that both tempts and vexes the lecturer throughout his lecture. In short, despite first appearances it is a highly ambivalent piece of work.

In this chapter I wish to focus on the stakes inherent in that ambivalence as they bear upon the reading Heidegger produces: a reading of tragedy and translation, of poetry and history, and finally of reading itself. The tension contained there may be most clearly expressed in a conflict, already evident in this single statement about translation, between a certain argumentative position—a position that might at best be called exclusionary, at worst totalizing—and a tendency to undermine that position's stability in the rhetorical form of the lecture. While the practice of transmission from one language to another as well as that from text to elucidation hardly appears from the perspective of his discussion to be an object of debate, the demonstrative specimen that Heidegger produces emerges precisely in the form of, if not debate, then at least dialogue: *Tell me, and I'll tell you.* Interpretation—*qua* translation—is in this sense not a usurpation of difference but an exchange with it, and that exchange with the foreign elements of text and language has lasting consequences. Consequences that cannot be swept away without a trace, that prove to extend far beyond the limits of what that initial promise of identity, of discovering "who you are," may have indicated.

The remarks that frame this statement on translation contain both familiar and foreign elements, endowing the text itself with a somewhat fractured identity. On one hand, Heidegger's lecture represents yet another chapter in his decades-long effort to articulate the singular status of Hölderlin's poetry within a metaphysical tradition that had, in his view, thus far failed to comprehend it. It is not the first place in which he argues that Hölderlin's writing offers a departure from the discourse of metaphysics that has shaped not only the course of philosophy but those of history and technology as well. And it will not be the last place; Hölderlin plays a crucial role in Heidegger's thought up until his interview with *Spiegel* magazine in 1966.[4] However, in this particular lecture Heidegger's commentary on Hölderlin's later work is unique insofar as it takes shape as an extended reflection on translation, even featuring Heidegger's own practical attempts to render Sophocles' Greek into his particular formulation of German. This foray into translation happens not only because Hölderlin's texts require, as Heidegger puts it, a translation within their own language. Rather, Heidegger attempts to demonstrate how the poetic texts he considers here articulate a relationship between the foreign and the familiar that both dovetails with Hölderlin's simultaneous work of translation, particularly his work on Sophocles, and allows the concept of translation itself to resonate distinctly with the experience of language and history. Hölderlin's often obscure practice of carrying ideas and words across millennia in translated and otherwise transmitted forms demonstrates for Heidegger the radical expression of a language not at home with itself. This, in turn, evokes the ebb and flow of history as it shapes and is shaped within modernity. As a mode of representation, translation expresses in language an unsettling, disordering movement underly-

---

4. The volume *Erläuterungen zu Hölderlins Dichtung* (GA 4) alone contains a collection of essays and lectures published between 1936 and 1963. In addition, the *Gesamtausgabe* includes three lectures on Hölderlin's poetry, "Germanien/Der Rhein" (GA 39), "Der Ister" (GA 43) and "Andenken" (GA 52).

ing Heidegger's concept of history and the status of the modern subject within it.

Not surprisingly, this reading brings Heidegger well beyond Hölderlin's poetry and indeed beyond the poet himself, to the ancient texts that make themselves heard in his work. Reading Hölderlin's late hymns demands at the same time an engagement with the Greek text that dominates his work of translation, and thus an interpretation of Sophocles' (and Hölderlin's) *Antigone* constitutes the central portion of this lecture.[5] For Heidegger, not only Hölderlin's theories of translation and modern tragic experience but also the poetry he composed at approximately the same time find agreement or *Anklang* (harmony) with Sophoclean language; the Greek text sets a tone that Hölderlin's work echoes, both in active interlocution with Sophocles and in more subtle moments of influence.[6] The difference between these registers of translation and contemporaneous poetic production is only slight, for both are part of a body of work that comes to acknowledge the foreign as crucial to the recognition of that which is one's own. Reading and writing take place within a dynamics of exchange or dialogue (*Zwiesprache*) in which the foreign touches lightly upon the ownmost and changes it irrevocably, in which the distant past is brought to bear upon the present and leaves its own disturbance there. And at the same time, the concurrent acts of turning back to that past and reaching out towards the foreign together open another dimension that reveals the momentary convergence (*Anklang*) of past with present, of the foreign with that which is one's own. The exchange between

---

5. Because I am primarily interested in the interplay between translation and tragedy structuring the "Ister" lecture, I have chosen not to foreground my discussion with Heidegger's comments on *Antigone* from his *Einführung in die Metaphysik*. Although many of the same issues arise in that earlier text, such as the relationship of history to the *deinon* or *Unheimliches*, Heidegger does not relate them to Hölderlin's poetry, nor to the dynamics of *Zwiesprache* as it informs his conception of both translation and history. For a thorough discussion of the role of tragedy and particularly sacrifice in the *Einführung*, see Schmidt, *On Germans* and 245–54, as well as his "Ruins and Roses: Hegel and Heidegger on Sacrifice, Mourning, and Memory," in *Endings: Questions of Memory in Hegel and Heidegger*, ed. Rebecca Comay and John McCumber. (Evanston: Northwestern University Press, 1999), 97–113.

6. With his concept of "Anklang" Heidegger means to distance his reading from one of "influence" in a conventional sense, and the result seems to epitomize the dynamics of "Zwiesprache": "What we must keep constantly in mind is this: It is the prerogative of great poets, thinkers and artists that they alone are capable of letting themselves be influenced. . . . What the great ones give they do not have by way of their originality, but rather from another origin, one that makes them sensitive to the 'influence' of that which is originary in the other great ones" (I 50: *Bedenken müssen wir stets dieses: Es ist das Vorrecht der grossen Dichter, Denker und Künstler, dass sie allein das Vermögen haben, sich beeinflussen zu lassen. . . . Die Großen haben das, was sie geben, nicht aus ihrer Originalität, sondern aus anderem Ursprung, der sie empfindlich macht für den 'Einfluss' des Ursprünglichen der anderen Großen"* [62]).

Sophocles and Hölderlin, with its staggering heights of poetic achievement alongside glaring and often baffling insufficiencies, may therefore represent in many ways a literary anomaly within the modern tradition of imitating Greek tragedy, but the regenerative process that it also models proves for Heidegger to be a fundamental characteristic of modernity experienced authentically. The concept of *Zwiesprache* that Heidegger develops in his readings of Hölderlin and Sophocles becomes in this lecture the primary trope of poetic production, of translation, and of history itself.

This emphasis in the lecture on the role of translation as means of exchange between present and past, identity and difference, tends to produce at least two distinct results. On a substantive level, the discussion of *Zwiesprache* inspires Heidegger to ever greater hyperbole regarding the special affinity of the Germans with the Greeks. It is on this point that the lecture has been most widely, and deservedly, criticized.[7] As with his authoritative claim to know "who you are" on the basis of "what you think of translation," this attitude clashes with the notion of *Zwiesprache* as he develops it in the lecture.[8] At the same time, however, the modality of *Zwiesprache* also lends the lecture its shape and movement in another sense, for ultimately Heidegger will be unable to keep his distance from the dialogic structure that he identifies. As a result his lecture does not merely present a detached account of the exchange between Sophocles and Hölderlin (and thus of the symbiotic relationship between modern Germany and ancient Greece) but participates in that exchange, allowing points of reference to shift in the process of reading, owning the possibility—even the necessity—of being moved, unsettled, dis-ordered by the past (both ancient and modern) and its foreignness in the act of interpretation.[9] In this respect his lecture constantly undermines what it argues, indicating that precisely those attempts to account for a more concrete relationship between difference and identity,

---

7. See, for example, Véronique Foti, *Heidegger and the Poets* (New Jersey: Humanities Press, 1992), 47 and 54, and Kathleen Wright, "Heidegger's Hölderlin and the Mo(u)rning of History," *Philosophy Today* 37:4 (Winter 1993): 423–35.

8. In a similar vein, his presentation of the form of "Gespräch" in the later "Aus einem Gespräch von der Sprache zwischen einem Japaner und einem Fragenden" (*Unterwegs zur Sprache*, 83–157) implies an absurdly obvious manipulation of the interlocutor. See Hans Ulrich Gumbrecht, "Martin Heidegger and His Japanese Interlocutors: About a Limit of Western Metaphysics," *Diacritics* 30:4 (Winter 2000): 83–101.

9. Fred Dallmayr describes Heidegger's understanding of the Hölderlinian concept of recollection ("Andenken") in similar terms, "not as a return to a finished past but rather as a meeting ground where past or alien experience reveals itself as also an impending prospect." Rather than representing something "gone or vanished," "the recollected experience returns to the greeting poet in a vivid countergreeting, one not confined to the given moment." Fred Dallmayr, *The Other Heidegger* (Ithaca and London: Cornell University Press, 1993), 153.

the foreign and the ownmost, are fundamentally troubled by the disordering that must accompany its expression.

To revisit once again Heidegger's encounter with Hölderlin's poetry requires some justification. Few intersections of poetry and philosophy have been more closely examined, more exhaustively analyzed, and more painstakingly criticized than this one. One result of this scrutiny has been a frequent discrediting of Heidegger's work on Hölderlin as reductive, decontextualizing, even violent. Heidegger strikes a dissonant chord for both readers approaching his texts on Hölderlin from a literary standpoint and those rooted in philosophy, and that dissonance has itself become the irresistible center of many analyses.[10] Consequently, the practice of reading Heidegger reading Hölderlin has consisted virtually from the start in calling Heidegger's controversial interpretations into question.

As Heidegger himself insists in his own defense, however (and not only in this lecture), his concern with Hölderlin's writings has nothing to do with the "science of literature" (*Literaturwissenschaft*) in any conventional sense. With respect to this distinction, the lecture on "Der Ister" may represent something of a specimen piece. Leaving open more obvious questions regarding the content of the poem, Heidegger introduces the concept of attentiveness (*Aufmerksamkeit*) to describe his technique of reading in these remarks: "attentiveness in the sense of a fundamental attunement, out of which we have a sense only for the essential and have the sole vocation of marking out the essential from everything else so as to retain it in the future, to 'attend' to it (*die Aufmerksamkeit im Sinne einer Grundstimmung, aus der wir stets und nur den Sinn haben für das Wesentliche, die Bestimmung, dieses Wesentliche aus dem Übrigen herauszumerken, um es künftig zu behalten, zu "merken"* [GA 53: 14]).[11] "Merken" appears in quotes here, as if to emphasize its dual valence in this context, where it refers to both the need to "take note" of the essential in an attitude of *Aufmerksamkeit* and the gesture of remembrance, of "marking," that allows the essential to be preserved for itself. In contrast to a method, grounded in metaphysics, that

---

10. The critical voices are legion and include Christopher Fynsk, *Heidegger: Thought and Historicity* (Ithaca: Cornell, 1986), who locates in Heidegger's early readings of Hölderlin the stabilizing gesture of "mimetic violence" (194); Warminski, "Monstrous History"; Foti, *Heidegger and the Poets;* Wright, "Heidegger's Hölderlin"; Lacoue-Labarthe, "Poetry's Courage," in *The Solid Letter: Readings of Friedrich Hölderlin,* ed. Aris Fioretos (Stanford, 2000), 74–93.

11. *Hölderlin's Hymn "Der Ister,"* trans. William McNeil and Julia Davis (Bloomington: Indiana University Press, 1996), 13f. Henceforth designated in the body of text as I, with relevant page number reference. Since, however, Heidegger's writings are understandably difficult to translate in a manner that maintains the peculiar polyvalence of his German, it will often be necessary for me to modify the published translation or even depart from it completely.

would seek to decide the undecidable rather than engage with it—a "calculating, discovering, and conquering measurement of the world" (I 48, trans. modified: *eine rechnende, entdeckende, erobernde Durchmessung der Welt* [GA 53: 59])—Heidegger follows a mode of reading that does not generate understanding so much as submit to a moment in which understanding falls short. (This submission indicates an astute interpretive perspective in its own right, for it acknowledges and reiterates Hölderlin's gesture of allowing the untranslatable to represent itself as such.) Insofar as Heidegger confronts the pitfalls of translation—and the translation of Greek tragedy in particular—this lecture might constitute nothing less than a reorganization (and reenactment) of Hölderlin's own remarks on translation; yet it is a reorganization not based on the attempt to comprehend that earlier text but rather constructed around the impossibility of comprehension. Thus Heidegger preempts criticism of his interpretive practice by implicitly making his reading call itself into question as a reading, call reading as such into question insofar as he insists on an ineffaceable element of unreadability. As a result, while he consistently resists the call to formulate an ethics per se (as in the *Letter on Humanism,* for example), this lecture carves out another kind of ethical stance in the place of translation and finally in that of interpretation as such: a stance that questions the violence inherent in a practice of reading that erases its own tracks, that affirms instead, through the concept and technique of *Zwiesprache,* the excess gathered along the path. The snow on the bell. The subtle slide out of tune. Translation, as he writes elsewhere, should be a passing-on (*Überlieferung*) rather than a transformation; should reflect that which it collects along the trajectory of its history.[12]

If his lecture on "Der Ister" holds as a central insight the ambivalent practice of reading (and writing, or lecturing) as *Zwiesprache,* however, it is not long before he retreats from this insight. Only a year later, in a lecture commemorating the hundredth anniversary of Hölderlin's death in 1843, he reduces the encounter with the foreign to the process of bringing the Germans "home." The swiftness with which Heidegger backpedals to a more stable position in "Homecoming/To Kindred Ones" (*Heimkunft/An die Verwandten*), which appeared along with "Hölderlin and the Essence of Poetry" (*Hölderlin und das Wesen der Dichtung*) in the first edition of the *Elucidations* (1944), will ultimately highlight the radicality of his process in the "Ister" lecture. For—as this lecture illustrates both conceptually and rhetorically—if reading must engage in a dialogue with its object, then it always leaves a trace, on reader and text alike, that cannot be erased or made "one's own."

---

12. *Der Satz vom Grund* (Frankfurt: Klostermann, 1997), 164.

The subsequent fading of that trace does not imply that the process of reading as *Zwiesprache* has reached its culmination but rather indicates the unfortunate retreat to another kind of reading altogether.

HÖLDERLIN'S POETRY FLOWS. It does not posit, nor does it attempt to situate itself on solid ground. For Heidegger, this is the sole characteristic of the late hymns, their only concern (*Sorge*); they comprise what he describes as the "poetry of streams" (*Dichtung der Ströme*), of movement without halt, of incessant wandering for its own sake. In contrast to the metaphysical tradition extending from Plato to Kant, in which the artist depicts a series of "symbolic images" (*Sinnbilder*) whose representations of the physical world remain subordinate to the ideas and values they approximate (GA 53: 19), Hölderlin's poetry presents the reader with an image that is not at all "sinnbildlich," whose sense or "Sinn" remains an enigma encompassed by the river in its glorious flow:

> Wenn nun aber die Ströme in Hölderlins Dichtung in Wahrheit keine "Sinnbilder" sind, was sollen sie dann sonst sein? Wie sollen wir dann noch von ihnen etwas wissen können, wo doch all unser Wissen, und die Wissenschaft erst recht, in der Metaphysik Grund und Halt hat? Fast scheint es so, als sagte der Dichter selbst, dass wir von den Strömen nichts wissen können. Die Ister-Hymne schliesst, genauer: sie hört auf, mit dem Wort:
>
> *Was aber jener thuet der Strom*
> *Weis niemand.* (GA 53: 21)

> But if the streams in Hölderlin's poetry are in truth not "symbolic images," then what else can they be? How are we to know anything of them when all of our knowledge, and especially scientific knowledge, has its ground and foothold in metaphysics? It almost seems as though the poet himself were saying that we can know nothing of the streams. The Ister hymn closes, or more precisely, it comes to a halt, with the word:
>
> *But what that one does, that stream*
> *No one knows.* (I 19; trans. modified)

Despite attempts to define it in symbolic terms, the enigma remains intact, loosening knowledge's every potential foothold. In fact, no knowledge can contain it—or rather, as we will see, it challenges the possibility of knowledge as such. In Hölderlin's poetry, that enigma takes shape conceptually as the river and rhetorically as a flow to which the reader can only succumb, even if she cannot know to what foreign soil it might convey her. For Heidegger, it is this perpetual motion that counts, that passage into the unknown that models the peculiar dwelling-place of humankind as a locus without rest, an "Ortschaft der Wanderschaft" (GA 53: 39).[13] The stream is utterly foreign to the human being, "dem Menschen fern und fremd," and yet at the same time it is irresistible, inciting a "going along" (*ein Mitgehen*) that undermines any stable or static notion of locality, *Ortschaft*. Indeed, it tears the human being away from that notion of locality in a most Hölderlinian sense: "The tearing and the certainty of the streams' own path is precisely what tears human beings out of the habitual center of their lives" (*Das Reissende und Gewisse der eigenen Bahn der Ströme ist es gerade, was den Menschen aus der gewöhnlichen Mitte seines Lebens herausreisst* [GA 53: 32]). Hölderlin's familiar image of the "eccentric path" becomes for Heidegger the unsettled dwelling-place of the human. And there is no other *Ortschaft* to which one might aspire.

From the start, then, Heidegger's discussion of the "poetry of streams" alludes to sources other than the hymn featured in the lecture's title, and these alternate sources soon assume center stage. Upon closer examination, the outline of geographical space in the lecture—the shape of the river, the curve of the path—reveals a relationship to time, to the conveyance of a lifetime, and in this sense Heidegger's remarks begin to converge even more closely with Hölderlin's own theory of tragedy; from this point, in fact, that convergence takes on a certain primacy. Heidegger's assertion that the human being is torn out of a position of centrality by the sure motion of poetry is a close paraphrase of Hölderlin's own remarks on *Oedipus*, drawn from a passage in which he names the poetic caesura as the rhythmic interruption upon which the entire balance of the tragedy turns. After this point in dramatic time—the point at which the blind seer Tiresias enters the scene—nothing will ever be the same again.

> Er tritt ein in den Gang des Schicksals, als Aufseher über die Naturmacht, die tragisch, den Menschen aus seiner Lebenssphäre, dem Mittelpuncte seines innern Lebens in eine andere Welt entrückt und in die exzentrische Sphäre der Todten reisst. (FA 16: 251)

---

13. The published translation "locality of journeying" (I 33) is perfectly serviceable but does not present the internal relationship of these two opposing terms, captured in the doubling of the suffix "-schaft." The juxtaposed words in German evoke both the stark difference between situatedness (*Ortschaft*) and restlessness (*Wanderschaft*) and the oscillating movement linking the two in Heidegger's reading.

> He (i.e., Tiresias) steps into the course of fate as overseer of the natural order which tragically displaces the human being from his own sphere of life, from the midpoint of his inner life into another world, and tears him into the excentric sphere of the dead. (Constantine 64; trans. modified)

Where Tiresias steps in to stand guard over nature's powerful force, presented elsewhere in Hölderlin's remarks as the "tearing spirit of time" (FA 16: 370), the familiar march of fate is permanently disrupted, the direction of the tragic hero's future derailed in a single moment. Yet it is a temporal shift not entirely fulfilled by its forward orientation; for not only the future assumes a different shape, but the past—most plainly evident in the havoc of Oedipus' own memories when he learns the truth of his heritage—takes on an unexpectedly malleable texture. Remembered events, however distant, words spoken, sins committed with and without awareness signify something quite other than they once did. In this sense they only illustrate further the extent to which the tragic hero's perception of centrality has always already been a false assumption.

In these passages, the remains of the past thus contain within them a potentiality not yet realized, not yet unleashed; and this acknowledgment, as we have seen, lies not only at the core of Hölderlin's theory of tragic experience but also in his practice of translation. As we have already seen, the temporal disruption staged before an audience in Greek tragedy is reflected and intensified in Hölderlin's translation through the experience of a fractured syntax, neither Greek nor German, and of an "Oriental" element that is explicitly foreign to both registers but brought to light through a particular attitude of translation. Within that emergent dimension of "the Oriental," Hölderlin aims to reveal within the tragedy something older than the Greek text—something *other* than that text—and that expression of internal difference proves to be integral both to tragic effect and to its redoubled intensity in translation. Once the exclusive referentiality of original and translation, the tragic text's perceived origin and its proper afterlife, become as unsettled as the hero they depict, there is no turning back to a familiar understanding of the past, for it has become as uncertain as the future.

For Heidegger in the "Ister" lecture, the streaming motion that epitomizes the dynamism of Hölderlin's river poetry inscribes a similarly unmistakable temporality, for the streams too are "zwiefach gerichtet" (GA 53: 33) (*oriented in a twofold direction* [I 29]): "The stream is a wandering of a singular kind, insofar as it goes simultaneously into what has been and what is to come" (I 29; trans. modified: *Der Strom ist eine Wanderung von einziger Art, sofern sie zumal in das Gewesene und in das Kommende geht*). Yet identity proves to be even more elusive than it was for Oedipus, who does ultimately survey the ruins of his once-unknown past. Like the tragic hero wrenched out of his perceived centrality, the human being who cannot help but go along—whose ensuing *Wanderschaft* proves simultaneously to be his *Ortschaft*—becomes subject to a temporality that changes remembrance as well as anticipation, ebb as well as tide. Anticipation opens up not only that which is to come but also what has been; and even more crucially, remembrance in a genuine sense is no longer encompassed by the mere orientation toward past events. Rather, it confronts an inwardness whose meaning is still to come, that retains within it a hint of the undecided: "Genuine remembrance is a turning toward the undisclosed inwardness of what has been" (*Echte Erinnerung ist Zuwendung zum unerschlossenen Inwendigen des Gewesenen* [GA 53: 34]). The contradictory movement (*gegenwendige Bewegung*) that Heidegger views as inherent in both Hölderlin's poetry of streams and his remarks on tragedy thus figures human experience in flux, *as* flux: as the continuous wandering both toward and away from an untapped interiority "to come," as the endless oscillation between the familiar and the unknown, even if that unknown proves to be part of that which is most one's own. Thus the movement of *Heimischwerden im Unheimischsein* (an awkward but close translation is "coming to be at home in not being at home"), constantly set into motion through the encounter with the foreign essential to translation, also describes the process by which history comes to be grasped.

At the same time, however, this dynamics of a poetry of streams also opens a radically other dimension of reading. For Heidegger's discussion of the fluidity of Hölderlin's poetry in relation to the contradictory movement of history is also a reflection on a particular mode of interpretation that he both names and performs in this text. If the poetry's only concern is "coming to be at home within that which is one's own" (*Heimischwerden im Eigenen*)—within that which is, in Heidegger's paraphrase of Hölderlin, most difficult to find—then its flow must logically lead the human being in the direction of that "home." Yet that movement, like the *Gegenwendigkeit* of the streams, proves to be far more elusive. Drawing explicitly on the terminology of Hölderlin's letter to Casimir Ulrich Böhlendorff of December 1801, in which he discusses the difficulty of confronting not only the foreign (*das Fremde*) but also that which is one's own (*das Eigene*), Heidegger describes the turn of *Heimischwerden* as a "passage through the foreign" (*Durchgang durch das Fremde*). Thus the poet's orientation towards *Heimischwerden* can only come about as the result of a dialogue (*Zwiesprache*) with foreign voices, and the process of interpreting the poetry that results must involve this dialogue. Not a relationship of influence per se, Heidegger describes the dynamics of *Zwiesprache* as a confrontation with difference that ultimately conveys the ownmost back to itself. Within this model, Hölderlin engages in a particular mode of exchange with the Greek poets Pindar and Sophocles, and not only in his translations of their work; his dialogue with the Greeks, particularly Sophocles, resonates throughout the hymns he produced during that period of translation.

But what does this "ownmost" turn out to be? In the course of Heidegger's lecture it tends to diverge into two distinct directions—one determined by a static relationship of *Eigenes* to *Fremdes* (evident in his reductive comments on the letter to Böhlendorff), the other by a more dynamic concept of translation as the fluid dialogue that maintains the locality of wandering, the *Ortschaft der Wanderschaft*.[14] Indeed, this latter concept seems even to infect Heidegger's style of argumentation, which is not precisely linear but rather more spiral; in the first and second parts of the lecture, every forward advance is interrupted by a repetition (*Wiederholung*), producing an effect of halting momentum not unlike Hölderlin's own description of the Ister river itself: "Der scheinet aber fast/Rükwärts zu gehen . . . " (4) (*But it [the river] seems nearly to go backwards . . .*). By the conclusion of the lecture, this more fluid mode of conceiving the ownmost seems to have assumed precedence—even if Heidegger does not quite acknowledge it—as the possibility of reaching mastery of so much "foreign" material is foreclosed again and again.

Hölderlin's letter to Böhlendorff from December 1801 has long inspired commentaries on its theory of the relation between the foreign and that which is one's own, and Heidegger eagerly takes up the discussion in the "Ister" lecture as well as in the essay "Andenken," published in 1943. For Heidegger, the letter articulates what he terms Hölderlin's "law of history": for a people to approach that which is proper to it, it must first encounter that which is foreign. Citing the famous lines from the letter, "but that which is one's own (*das Eigene*) must be learned just as well as the foreign (*das Fremde*)," he describes the conflict between foreign and ownmost among the Greeks as a process of attaining ownership, effectively of both elements: "Only through that which is foreign to them . . . does that which is their

---

14. The former conception of "Eigenes" is the one found more frequently in Heidegger's writings on Hölderlin, including the essay "Andenken," which was written in the same period as the lecture and published in 1943 during the National Socialists' highly publicized commemoration of the hundredth anniversary of Hölderlin's death. For extensive comments on the relationship of the foreign to the ownmost in that lecture, see Fynsk, *Heidegger: Thought and Historicity*, 198–205.

own become theirs" (*Durch das ihnen Fremde hindurch . . . wird ihnen erst ihr Eigenes zum Eigentum* [GA 4: 87]).[15]

Heidegger's assertions with respect to this interplay of the foreign with the ownmost leave his presentation at some distance from Hölderlin's actual statements in the letter. At no point, for example, does Hölderlin claim directly that the encounter with the foreign will result in a greater understanding of what is one's own. Rather, his primary argument is that modernity cannot simply adopt the aesthetic principles of the Greeks as its own, since their "culture"—the "talent for representation" that he calls "Junonian sobriety"—is our "nature" and cannot be assimilated from another source.[16] Precisely this impossibility of obtaining that which is most our own from the experience of the foreign ensures that achieving our "nature" will remain our most difficult task.

Heidegger's model is not Hölderlin's. In fact, structurally it often appears closer to Schleiermacher's notion of authentic translation as the openness to the foreign in the interest of expanding the self, as the practice of bringing the reader to the author while "leaving the author alone" as much as possible.[17] However, Heidegger explicitly denies this particular provenance, insisting that his model of translation operates not in the interest of *Bildung* but rather the movement of history and the unconcealment of "the concealed essence of our own historical commencement (I 66: *das verborgene Wesen unseres eigenen geschichtlichen Anfangs* [GA 53: 81]). Moreover, the inherently expansive tone of the Romantic model also contrasts sharply with Heidegger's narrower notion of *Zwiesprache*. For while Schleiermacher's proposed methodology of negotiating difference in translation stipulates an openness to the foreign conceived universally, in the terms of Goethe's notion of *Weltliteratur, Zwiesprache* for Heidegger is a gesture that is "removed from all coincidence" (*jedem Zufall enthoben*) by an unmistakable claim to historical specificity. "What is one's own is that which belongs to the fatherland of the Germans" (I 49: *Das Eigene ist das Vaterländische des Deutschen* [GA 53: 60]), and its interlocutor in a proper sense is "the foreign that relates to the

---

15. See Dallmayr's discussion of the Böhlendorff letter, which focuses on the significance of estrangement in the recognition of the self (153–55).

16. See Warminski 26–37.

17. Miguel de Beistegui notes this similarity as well in a footnote to his interesting discussion of Heidegger's conception of translation. He perceives a difference, however, in the two thinkers' views of how the foreign affects the ownmost: while Schleiermacher's perception of translation remains governed by a logic of appropriation (even if it is impossible) and hospitality ("the other idiom is *invited* to penetrate the sphere of my own"), for Heidegger it's the other way around: "my own language is to become other, foreign to myself; translation is an experience of dis-propriation." *Thinking with Heidegger: Displacement* (Bloomington: Indiana University Press, 2003), 203n.

return home, that is, is one with it" (I 54: *das auf die Heimkehr bezogene, d.h. mit ihr einige Fremde* [GA 53: 67]), the foreignness *precisely of* that which is one's own—in other words, of the Greeks vis-à-vis the Germans.[18] The proper negotiation of difference in Heidegger's reading does indeed depend on the preservation of the foreign as such, but only insofar as that foreignness already stands in intimate relation to identity. Which raises the suspicion that, in its current form, it may not be so foreign after all.

> Weil der Bezug Hölderlins zum Griechentum . . . weder klassisch, noch romantisch, noch metaphysisch ist, deshalb wird die Bindung Hölderlins an das Griechentum nicht lockerer, sondern umgekehrt inniger. Denn erst dort, wo das Fremde in seiner wesenhaften Gegensätzlichkeit erkannt und anerkannt ist, besteht die Möglichkeit der echten Beziehung, und d.h. der Einigung, die nicht wirre Vermischung, sondern fügende Unterscheidung ist. (GA 53: 67f.)

> Because Hölderlin's relationship to the Greek world is . . . neither classical nor Romantic nor metaphysical, his tie to the Greek world does not loosen; on the contrary, it becomes more intimate. For only where the foreign is recognized and acknowledged in its essential oppositeness do we find the possibility of a true relationship, i.e., of a union that is not a confused mixing but a conjoining in differentiation. (I 54)

Though he depicts their difference as a juxtaposition rather than a blurring of boundaries, Heidegger still continues to insist upon the "essential oppositeness" of German and Greek worlds. By arguing for the fundamental union of the two in Hölderlin's work, he lets their relationship function as a mirror, while for Hölderlin the relationship was far more complex.[19] From this perspective his description of the specific dialogue between Germany and Greece appears at odds with his presentation of Hölderlin's poetry of streams as an ambivalent movement through the foreign, an infinite movement without clear origin or destination.

However, another strain of his argument begins to develop alongside this predominant oppositional structure, one that underscores the movement of infinite differentiation proposed by Hölderlin:

---

18. "For Hölderlin, that which is foreign to the historical humankind of the Germans is the Greek world" (I 54: *Dieses Fremde des geschichtlichen Menschentums der Deutschen ist für Hölderlin das Griechentum* [GA 53:67])

19. Fynsk notes Heidegger's tendency to overstabilize the complexity of Hölderlin's insights, particularly in the later writings and the work on tragedy. See *Heidegger: Thought and Historicity*, 187–88.

> Weil Hölderlin wie keiner seiner Zeitgenossen das innere Vermögen besitzen durfte, von Pindar und Sophokles beeinflusst, d.h. jetzt, dem fremden Ursprünglichen aus dem eigenen Ursprung ursprünglich hörig zu sein, deshalb hat auch Hölderlin allein aus der geschichtlichen Zwiesprache und Entsprechung es vermocht, uns diese Dichter und ihre Dichtung in einem ursprünglicheren Lichte zu zeigen. (GA 53: 62)

> Because Hölderlin was able to possess, like no other of his contemporaries, the inner capacity to be influenced by Pindar and Sophocles—and that now means, of being subject, out of one's own origin, to a foreign originariness in an originary sense—for this reason Hölderlin was also alone in his ability to reveal these poets and their poetry to us in a more originary light, out of historical dialogue and approximation. (I 50; trans. modified)

To be sure, the emphasis here on "Hölderlin alone" continues to support the problematic assertion that Sophocles and the Greeks are the privileged counterpart of Hölderlin and the Germans, that they present a "more originary" sense of history that will bring German identity back to itself. However, the passage also begins to undermine that relation. The purpose of the exchange with the foreign here is not only to search for one's ownmost origin; if it were, perhaps that origin would not be as difficult to find as Hölderlin asserts. Rather, the origin itself becomes pliable in the process of searching; the ancient poets appear not in a more accessible form but "in a more originary light" as a result of their exchange with modernity. In alluding to Hölderlin's contribution within the discourse of modern tragedy and of tragedy in a modern age—the idea that, even as the present is continually permeated by its relationship to the past, the past is not static—Heidegger begins to suggest that its translation as a mode of reading can shed another light, can send tremors through both the ancient edifice and its modern remains. That the oscillating movement to and from the past, the search altering both past and present—and not the return to a specific historical origin—may define both the act of reading and the experience of history within modernity.

Read along these lines, Heidegger's account of Hölderlin reading Sophocles begins to take shape as something other than the violent appropriation of poetry in the interest of philosophical posturing. Like Hölderlin's dialogue with Sophocles, it is also a moment of participation, a *performance* of *Zwiesprache* that has the potential to effect change in both past and present; Heidegger's remarks both reflect and perpetuate the gesture they describe. And since that description presents a mode of interpretation and translation that refuses to be done with its source, that lets itself be disordered by their contact, the effect of its continuation here is to undermine any definitive status of reading as such. This slippage becomes particularly evident in passages in which Heidegger must confront Hölderlin's reading of Sophocles with his own, for in doing so he is forced to construct a reading of a reading, to take on a double original that always already exists both in Greek and in German and therefore maintains its own internal dissonance. In hearing this dissonance as it bears upon Heidegger's own efforts here, one cannot help but observe how it tends to subvert the other, more dominant strain of thought at the heart of the text: that of the dynamics of foreign and familiar, *Fremdes* and *Eigenes*, in the interest of establishing the special affinity between Germany and Greece. And if that subversive reading occasionally comes across as violent, it is in a sense other than the blind appropriation of the other into the economy of identity; rather, it is a violence through which the other makes itself counted.

Given the path that leads him through the texts in this lecture, Heidegger has no choice: he must translate Sophocles via Hölderlin, by involving himself in the same form of dialogue that he wishes to investigate. This involvement already becomes evident on more than one level in his extensive account of a single key passage, where he reflects on both Sophocles's and Hölderlin's renditions of the choral ode *Polla ta deina* . . . , *Ungeheuer ist viel*. . . . Rather than simply using Hölderlin's version of the passage to augment his discussion, Heidegger argues that that particular version is comprehensible only in the context of Hölderlin's translation (literally his carrying-over, *Übertragung*) of the tragedy as a whole, and he indicates that his more serviceable translation will effectively "translate" that incomprehensible element left by Hölderlin. Warminski unpacks the complexity of Heidegger's justification: "In order to *think* the same of what Hölderlin says, it is necessary to say what he leaves unsaid, in other words, to say it differently, to say it otherwise" (Warminski 1990, 199).

Yet precisely by attempting to "say the unsaid" in the act of translation, Heidegger invokes the precedent of Hölderlin's own emphasis on the "Oriental" element that had remained silent in the Greek. That link is further reinforced insofar as Heidegger describes his commentary as "remarks" or *"Anmerkungen"* (appearing in quotes in the text) in contrast to the ostensibly fuller notion of *Auslegung*, laying out.[20] Consequently, the expected result of his translation and "remarks" also carries familiar echoes:

---

20. Heidegger clearly distinguishes between the remarks he intends to present here and the more encompassing notion of an interpretation, further suggesting that his practice of reading will remain distant from conventional modes: "That an adequate interpretation of his choral ode . . . is beyond our capabilities in all respects, requires no further elaboration. Here too, remarks must suffice" (I 59: *Dass eine zureichende Auslegung dieses Chorliedes . . . unser Vermögen nach allen Hinsichten übersteigt, bedarf keiner umständlichen Versicherung. Auch hier müssen Anmerkungen genügen* [GA 53:72]).

> ... wir müssen uns aber im Aufgaben-Bezirk dieser "Anmerkungen" zur Isterhymne mit einer Aushilfe begnügen, d.h. mit einer Übersetzung, die im Hinblick auf das, was es zu durchdenken gilt, einiges deutlicher umschreibt und heraushebt. . . . (GA 53: 70)

> ... yet within the context of our task in these "remarks" on the Ister hymn, we must be content with some makeshift assistance; that is, we must make do with a translation that, with respect to what we have to think through, demarcates and emphasizes some things more clearly. . . . (I 57; trans. modified)

What must be more clearly "demarcated" and "emphasized" in Heidegger's version of translation? "Some things" (*Einiges*) may not only refer here to difficult sections of the Greek text but also that which he deems less than comprehensible in Hölderlin's own version, for otherwise there would be no need for clarification, let alone for (re)translation. This raises the intriguing possibility that Heidegger aims to locate within Hölderlin's work on Sophocles a line of inquiry that has thus far remained untranslated, unarticulated, unthought. Does Hölderlin's constellation of poetry and translations after 1800 contain, like the Greek text with which it is constantly engaged, its own "Oriental" shadows? Heidegger, after all, deems not only the work of Sophocles but also of Hölderlin to be "in need of translation," and of a peculiar sort of translation at that: one that itself might be called Hölderlinian, for as Heidegger explains, it "can even bring connections to light that lie within the translated language but are not laid out" (*kann sogar Zusammenhänge ans Licht bringen, die in der übersetzten Sprache zwar liegen, aber nicht herausgelegt sind* [GA 53: 75]). Heidegger's "remarks"—his confrontation with both the text of Sophocles' *Antigone* and Hölderlin's complex process of working through that same text—aspire to illuminate those shadows, to set into motion just such a (Hölderlinian) translation. But what does that process of illumination imply for the shadowy texts it "translates"?

Here again, Heidegger displays an unexpected affinity with the Romantic model of translation and with Schleiermacher's hermeneutics in particular.[21] Translation is an act of interpretation, and every interpretation is a translation. Even within a single language there is need of translation, insofar as translation figures a space in which understanding is necessarily negotiated

---

21. Schleiermacher's view of translation was influenced to a great extent by his interest in hermeneutics; therefore the negotiation of meaning and the affirmation not only of commonality but also of difference are his central concerns. See his lecture "On the Different Methods of Translating" in Schulte and Biguenet 36–54.

rather than presupposed or even superimposed. However, for Heidegger the result of such negotiations is an understanding of an unusual sort: more precisely, it is an understanding that does not establish itself on solid ground but rather calls itself constantly into question. For as with knowledge when faced with the poetry of streams, the foothold given to understanding here proves to be extremely precarious.

> Verständlichmachen darf nie heißen, eine Dichtung und ein Denken jedem beliebigen Meinen und dessen Verständnis-Horizont anzugleichen; verständlich machen heißt, das Verständnis dafür wecken, daß der blinde Eigensinn des gewöhnlichen Meinens gebrochen und verlassen werden muß, wenn die Wahrheit eines Werkes sich enthüllen soll. (GA 53: 76)

> Making understandable can never be the same as assimilating a poetry and a thought to any arbitrary opinion or its horizon of understanding; making understandable means awakening our understanding that the blind obstinacy of conventional opinion must be broken and abandoned if the truth of a work is to unveil itself. (I 63; trans. modified)

The approximation of understanding is not understanding. Securing a place for the exchange between text and translation within the domain of what is already known, what is comprehensible, is tantamount to bringing its incessant and ambivalent movement, *zwiefach gerichtet*, to a grinding halt. On the other hand, if understanding comes to be aligned with attentiveness (*Aufmerksamkeit*) rather than knowledge—if, far from gaining mastery over the inherent difference of the foreign, understanding implies being radically exposed to, and learning to listen to, its offering of the not-known—then translation, and hence reading, itself becomes unsettling, or as he will soon name it, *unheimlich*. This is for Heidegger the "own and only element" (*eigenes und einziges Element* [81]) of translation and interpretation; the possibility of the "truth" of the work revealing itself, of "the true reading of the true word" (*das echte Lesen des echten Wortes*), depends on this exposure of and in the unsettling process of reading.[22]

---

22. Heidegger gives a very clear definition of translation as a gesture that moves well beyond the literal approximation of one language for another: "Translating is not so much a "trans-lating" and passing-over into a foreign language with the help of one's own. Rather, translating is an awakening, clarifying, unfolding of one's own language with the help of an encounter with the foreign language (I 66: *Übersetzen ist gar nicht so sehr ein "Über-setzen" und Hinübergehen in die fremde Sprache mit Hilfe des eigenen. Das Übersetzen ist vielmehr eine Erweckung, Klärung, Entfaltung der eigenen Sprache durch die Hilfe der Auseinandersetzung mit der fremden* [GA 53:80]). This is not quite as close to Benjamin as it might appear at first glance; in the "Task of the Translator" (SW 1, GS IV:1) Benjamin is not

Within this context, both Sophocles and Hölderlin are exemplary for Heidegger because they produce texts that not only incite this unsettling reading but articulate it as well. Do not only perform in a structural sense the contradictory movement of which Heidegger speaks but reflect upon it as human experience at the same time. Their exchange, as conceived in the "Ister" lecture, demonstrates that the logic of translation *is* the fundamental movement of *Heimischwerden* in one's own language and identity, yet that that movement's only real effect is to underscore the extent to which one is "not at home" (*unheimisch*) within those registers. It is thus a movement that represents not the mere expansion of acquired knowledge through *Bildung*, as Schleiermacher's model of translation once promised, but a dialogue with the foreign that brings the ownmost to what it *is* but cannot *know*: *das Unheimliche, to deinon*.

> Vielfältig das Unheimliche, nichts doch
> Über den Menschen hinaus Unheimlicheres ragend sich regt. (GA 53: 71)
>
> Manifold is the unsettling, yet nothing
> More unsettling looms beyond the human.[23]

NO LONGER is the human being merely monstrous; now, in Heidegger's language, he is *unheimlich*, and in fact the most *unheimlich* of all things. While the centrality of the second choral ode of the *Antigone* (*polla ta deina* . . .) was implicit in Hölderlin's translations, Heidegger explicitly identifies the passage as exemplary not only for the poetic dialogue between ancient and modern texts but also for the historical movement, the *Ortschaft und Wanderschaft* that their exchange names. The focal point of this assertion is his emphasis on the Greek word *to deinon*, which Hölderlin rendered as "das Ungeheure" and Heidegger retranslates, with ardent justification, as "das Unheimliche."[24] In his reading an "inner relation" (GA 53: 84) emerges

---

primarily concerned with the expansion of one's own language but rather with the possibility that translation can illuminate the relation of each individual language to a "pure" language. I would argue instead that Heidegger remains, as he has throughout this lecture, more proximate to the tradition of translation within German Romanticism.

23. In what follows, I have chosen to translate *unheimlich* as "unsettling." To be sure, this exchange erases some crucial nuances of the German concept; however, I choose "unsettling" here over "uncanny" insofar as it evokes the concept of "heim"—the home, that which is "settled"—which is central to Heidegger's representation of the term.

24. As we will see below, Heidegger submits that this translation may be technically "wrong" but it is also "true." This distinction highlights another one crucial to his thought, namely, that between truth as correctness ("adaequatio") and truth as unconcealment, historically determined (*aletheia*). See

between the concern for "coming to be at home" (*Heimischwerden*) expressed in Hölderlin's poetry—a movement of endless deferral that logically implies a state of "being not-at-home" (*Unheimischsein*)—and the *Unheimlichkeit* of the human in Sophocles' tragedy, expressed in the choral ode and incarnated by Antigone herself. Thus the same passage that revealed for Hölderlin the strange but universal relation of the human to the monstrous now represents for Heidegger both the founding moment of the poetic *Anklang* between Hölderlin and Sophocles and the very condition of being human—for the Greek word that marks the human as a monstrosity is also revealed to be its unsettling "ground."

Not surprisingly, then, Heidegger makes a case for a translation that expresses the choral passage's intimate relation to the ambivalence at the heart of his concept of *Zwiesprache*, a translation in which "the contradictory holds sway" (*das Gegenwendige waltet*) (GA 53: 76). *To deinon* as he defines it reflects an internal structure of contradiction as such:

> Es bedeutet das Dreifache: das Furchtbare, das Gewaltige, das Ungewöhnliche. Jedesmal ist es gegensätzlich bestimmbar: das Furchtbare als das Fürchterliche und als das Ehrwürdige; das Gewaltige als das Überragende und als das nur Gewalttätige; das Ungewöhnliche als das Ungeheure und als das in allem Geschickte. (GA 53:78)

> It signifies all three: the terrible, the powerful, the uncommon. Each time it can be determined oppositionally: the terrible as the dreadful and the venerable; the powerful as the overwhelming and the merely violent; the uncommon as the monstrous and as that which is destined in all.

For Hölderlin, the articulation of *to deinon* had everything to do with this final opposition: "the uncommon as the monstrous and as that which is destined in all." Indeed, what is unsettling for Hölderlin *is* that unexpected contradiction, the recognition that the monstrous is also "destined in all." Monstrosity beyond is perhaps bearable, comprehensible; monstrosity within, repressed and returning, is nothing less than awe-inspiring. And yet it also cannot be destroyed, only guarded carefully to thwart its inevitable emergence, only left to exist, in the nearly-silent form of a trace, alongside what we know as identity.[25]

Beistegui's excellent discussion in *Thinking with Heidegger: Displacements*, 170–74.
   25. Also in the context of this notion of trace, see Adorno's critique of Heidegger's early reading of Hölderlin in "Parataxis—Zur späten Lyrik Hölderlins," 166. Interestingly enough, Adorno, though

Heidegger's insistence on the term *Unheimliches* likewise evokes the internal dissonance within the experience of being human, but in far more concrete and calculated terms. As articulated by the Chorus of Theban elders, the movement of *Heimischwerden,* in its indivisible relation to *Unheimischsein,* is hardly an Odyssean journey of exploration and return, nor is it a quest that can have any particular destination at all. Indeed, the "adventurer" who thrives on the state of being "not-at-home," of being, according to the Chorus, *pantoporos—überallhinausfahrend* is Heidegger's translation—ultimately comes to nothing, because for him there is no essential difference between being at home and not being at home; he finds a "home" (in an inauthentic sense) in the foreign as such and takes that wilderness as his absolute.[26] The authentically "not-at-home," on the other hand, assumes the *Heimisch* as a point of reference despite its inaccessibility, thus remaining in a perpetual state of "not-attaining" (*Nicht-Erlangen* [91]). Presence prevails in the form of absence (*Abwesung in der Art der Anwesung*) as "doing without" (*das Entbehren*) becomes the only authentic relation to *Heimischsein.*

For Heidegger the Chorus's revelation of *das Unheimliche* is crucial both in the context of the play and as an homage to the unique elasticity of the Greek language itself. With the invocation of *deinotaton,* he claims, Sophocles names precisely the contradictory tension which the human being bears as identity.[27] Though he readily concedes that his translation is "falsch" in a conventional sense, Heidegger asserts that the polyvalence of his chosen term is not at all a modern superimposition upon the Greek text. On the contrary, he argues that by unifying the manifold possibilities inherent in *to deinon, das Unheimliche* throws into relief a frame that already delimits the Greek concept, if only implicitly; meanwhile, it is our reluctance to bring this frame to light in interpretations and translations of these lines that stems from modern interference. In fact he claims that an "internal contradiction" (*inwendige Gegenwendigkeit* [103]) was fundamental to the Greek sense of

---

explicitly and often sharply critical of Heidegger, presents a very similar argument to that of "Der Ister," figuring the vestiges of poetic language, "'die Waffen des Worts,' die dem Dichter übrig bleiben," not as "Stiftung" in the (early) Heideggerian sense but rather as unassimilated memory traces which remain "überschattet" but ever-present, perhaps not unlike the wandering figure of Antigone from which the Chorus cannot turn away.

26. Hans Sluga claims that this (for Heidegger, inauthentic) form of being "not-at-home" in fact describes the modern condition as outlined by Nietzsche: "it is in the wilderness that we construct our shelters." However, this distinction relies upon a somewhat reductive reading of Heidegger's idea of *Heimischwerden im Unheimischsein* as the mere precursor to "coming home"—which is, if one reads Heidegger carefully, itself an impossibility here. "Homelessness and Homecoming: Nietzsche, Heidegger, Hölderlin," in *India and Beyond: Aspects of Literature, Meaning, Ritual and Thought,* ed. Dick van der Meij (London: Kegan Paul International, 1997), 509.

27. See the discussion of the Greek term *deinon* in Chapter 2.

being; not at all a dilemma to be overcome, ambiguity was preserved and valued:

> Das Negative [der Griechen] behält sein eigenes Wesen und steht nicht in der Rolle dessen, was beseitigt und überwunden werden könnte und sollte. Weil es als Gegenwesen eigenen Wesens ist, muß es mit seinem Gegenwesen aus dem Grunde ihrer Einheit getragen und gewürdigt werden. (GA 53: 104)

> The negative [for the Greeks] retains its own essence and does not exist in the role of that which could or ought to be cast aside and overcome. Because it exists as the counteressence of its own essence, it must be sustained and respected along with its counteressence on the basis of their unity. (I 84; trans. modified)

The status of being "unheimlich" in a Greek sense, therefore, retains for Heidegger a more measured connotation than the Christian notion of banishment from paradise. Only since Plato and the birth of metaphysics has Western culture given up this willful preservation of ambiguity, this tolerance of the negative in a radical sense, in favor of a "reductive and negating conception of the negative" (79: *herabsetzende negierende Fassung des Negativen* [GA 53: 95])—in other words, dialectics *par excellence*.[28] Only with the essential privilege of the positive in metaphysical terms has the negative become intolerable. Thus *das Unheimliche*, insofar as it is framed by contradiction, names what is contained but not yet explicit in *to deinon*, a non-dialectical coextensivity of identity and difference: "in such a manner that the concealed ground of the unity of the manifold significations of *deinon*, in its concealed being, is grasped within *das Unheimliche* (*so, dass mit dem Unheimlichen der verborgene Grund der Einheit der mannigfaltigen Bedeutungen des deinon und dieses so in seinem verborgenen Wesen gefasst wird* [GA 53: 78]).

Ultimately, however, Heidegger's translation is not merely concerned with the Greek word here but also with the German; for he expressly intends his line, "Vielfältig das Unheimliche," to be a "translation" of Hölderlin's "Ungeheuer ist viel" as well (GA 53: 85–86). In this sense he deliberately confronts the original in doubled form, effecting a displacement that leaves his version simultaneously at a greater remove from the Greek and more involved in its afterlife. For while his choice in rendering *to deinon* as *das*

---

28. Nussbaum is not far from this argument in her study of ethics and luck in Greek tragedy, in which she also claims that Greek culture tolerated a more ambiguous stance with respect to the tragic hero's fate, a stance that from a modern perspective seems "repugnant to reason" (Nussbaum 25).

Unheimliche aims to expose a facet heretofore concealed by its conventional translation, concealed even in its original language, his "translation" of Hölderlin is no less an attempt to bring to light what its "original" had not yet said: "[We] must learn to recognize the concealed essence of the monstrous" (*[Wir] müssen . . . das verborgene Wesen des Ungeheuren erkennen lernen*):

> Das "Ungeheure" braucht nicht notwendig nur im Sinne des Riesenhaften gedacht zu werden. Das Ungeheure ist zugleich und eigentlich das Nicht-Geheure. Das Geheure ist das Vertraute, Heimische. Das Ungeheure ist das Un-heimische. (GA 53: 86)

> The "monstrous" need not necessarily be thought only in the sense of the enormous. The monstrous is properly and at the same time the not-ordinary (*das Nicht-Geheure*). The ordinary [*das Geheure*] is the familiar, that with which one is at home. The monstrous is the not-at-home.

The reductiveness of this equation, the readiness with which it dispenses with the possibility that Hölderlin's translation may express something other than what Heidegger now offers with his, presents a frustrating problem in Heidegger's approach, to be sure. The implication is clear: if Hölderlin alone possessed the capacity to reveal Sophocles in a more originary light, so it must be for Heidegger alone in his exchange with Hölderlin. For Heidegger, Hölderlin evokes in his dialogue with Sophocles the same contradictory movement of history that he recognizes in both the choral ode and the "poetry of streams." If that gesture remained unspoken in the "original," it is the task of the "translator"—this particular translator—to release it into language.

However, while the acute violence of his transformation is barely concealed, Heidegger's remarks here also demonstrate as much an engagement with the problematics of that violence as an exercise of it. It is in this sense that he describes *to deinon* as a "real word" (*ein echtes Wort*) that also names what it says, "itself an unsettling (*unheimliches*) word" (GA 53: 83); in the very polyvalence in which it revels, the word itself breaks down the possibility of resting upon understanding, undermines the stabilizing effects of violent translation—remains, at its heart, untranslatable. The translation that bears this foreign body within itself is the only kind that does not do away with the unsettling effect of the "real word." *Das Unheimliche* thus no longer only describes the human being in Sophocles' choral ode; it also gives a name to Heidegger's practice of translation as a form of reading that disrupts what precedes it, brings on a *Verstimmung* that changes its original from within—and thereby leaves itself vulnerable to change as well. The movement of *Heimischwerden im Unheimischen* may inhabit the choral ode on a denotative level, but it guides its "translation" on a structural level as well; Heidegger's double translation of Sophocles and Hölderlin performs what it also purports to expose.

Perhaps that very performance, insofar as it enacts on a rhetorical level the epistemological engagement inherent in Heidegger's notion of *Zwiesprache*, is essential in bringing human beings to the limit that the choral passage describes. Indeed, for Heidegger there may be no other way to present it. Taken alone, *Unheimliches* is "named poetically with the word *deinon*, but not unfolded on the level of thought" (I 91; trans. modified: *dichterisch mit dem Wort deinon genannt, aber nicht denkerisch entfaltet* [GA 53: 114]), relegated to the domain of "the scarcely sayable" (*kaum Sagbares*). Its very reticence marks an inaccessibility to knowledge in any conventional sense; *Unheimliches* can only only come to light as a "poetic knowledge" (*dichtendes Wissen*), as a particular aesthetic relation that renders useless all overtures of consciousness and lets its effects be heard only alongside a remainder which must remain silent, evoked in the negation of *un-* in Heidegger's leading term. It is an aesthetic relation of imperfect "translation," in other words, one that transmits its own lacunae rather than its abundance. In Heidegger's view, Hölderlin achieved this form of translation—perhaps it was the only kind of which he was capable—and thus constructed a mode of reading and writing that took that incompletion, rather than the negotiation of sense in representation (the *Sinnbild*), as its framework. As a reader of those texts alone and in dialogue with Sophocles, has Heidegger any choice but to follow suit? For if a knowledge established solely in a poetic register cannot be entirely grasped by consciousness (let alone by philosophy), it is conceivable only as that which signifies simultaneously as the translated and the untranslatable, and therefore it cannot entirely "make sense." What it communicates can emerge only in dialogue with the poetic text—in a dialogue that leaves room for that unheard element to remain as such.

But what would such a dialogue resemble, and what would it communicate? Turning from Sophocles' Chorus to the first scene of the tragedy, Heidegger expands upon these questions by attending to the particular literariness of the tragic text. As with the Chorus's unsettling invocation of the *Unheimliches*, the opening scene between Antigone and Ismene presents for Heidegger what it names at the same time, causing its thematic content to double over into its form. In underscoring this duality Heidegger both indicates what *Zwiesprache* is not—namely, a stable dialogue between two immutable sides—and begins to point towards what it might be, within both the process of reading and, in a larger sense, the movement of history.

IMMEDIATELY EVIDENT from his discussion of the choral ode is that Heidegger's reading of the *Antigone* approaches the text from a different point of departure than that of other modern readers. As he asserts unequivocally, his concern is not with the conflict of state and family laws as represented by the opposing figures Antigone and Creon, but rather with an internal conflict that Antigone bears in an exemplary fashion.[29] That different emphasis is reflected in the passages he chooses to discuss, for not only does he give primacy to the Chorus's invocation of *to deinon*, he also bypasses the traditional focus on the clash between Antigone and Creon in favor of Antigone's initial confrontation with her sister in a section entitled "The introductory dialogue (*Zwiesprache*) between Antigone and Ismene." Whether it is by coincidence that Heidegger describes this textual exchange as "Zwiesprache" remains to be considered.

As in his remarks on the choral ode, Heidegger frames the section by distancing his account of the scene from Hölderlin's translation, claiming repeatedly that the latter "does not attain the essential (*das Wesentliche*)" (GA 53: 122, 125). This "essential" element apparently inheres in the stark, graphic style of the Greek dialogue between the sisters:

> Wort und Gegenwort der beiden Schwestern ist hier wie das Begegnen zweier Schwerter, deren Schärfe, Glanz und Wucht wir erfahren müssen, um etwas von dem Blitz zu vernehmen, der aus ihrem Ineinanderschlagen leuchtet. (GA 53: 122)

> The word and counter-word of the two sisters is here like the meeting of two swords, whose sharpness, luster and force we must experience in order to apprehend something of the lightning that flashes when they strike one another. (I 98; trans. modified)

Within the scope of a literary exchange between sisters, then, we encoun-

---

29. GA 53: 147: "Von hier aus wird deutlich, daß das Gegenspiel dieser Tragödie nicht spielt in dem Gegensatz zwischen 'Staat' auf der einen und 'Religion' auf der anderen Seite, sondern zwischen dem, was die innerste Gegenwendigkeit des *deinon* selbst ausmacht, sofern dieses als das Unheimische gedacht wird . . ." (*From here it becomes clear that the counterplay of this tragedy is not played out in the opposition between the "state" on the one hand and "religion" on the other, but between what constitutes the innermost counterturning of the deinon itself, insofar as the deinon is thought as the unhomely* . . . [I 118]).

ter a violence that is essential, *wesentlich*. Their dialogue must strike us with the force of clashing swords in order to have its proper effect. The sisters' language may not cohere, or complement, or meet in compromise; their exchange is defined by its bellicose character. Yet it, too, is named as *Zwiesprache*, dialogue, just like the poetic-historical relation exemplified by Hölderlin and Sophocles, the exchange that inscribes reading in writing, the past in the present. Can the essential violence of this single textual example—Antigone's dialogue with Ismene—extend to the dynamics underlying poetic *Zwiesprache*?

If the progress of Heidegger's argument is any indication, the two modes of exchange may indeed have something in common. In his translation Ismene and Antigone do fire intense reproaches at one another—Ismene accuses Antigone of having a "hot heart" (*heißes . . . Herz*) turned only towards "the cold one" (*den Kalten*, i.e., her dead brother), while Antigone denounces her sister for standing before her and Polynices "in hate" (GA 53: 123)—but their altercation is also balanced in a specific passage by the familiar notion of *Anklang* (126). In a single verse, Ismene invokes for Heidegger both the urgency that drives her sister to act and the thrust of the entire tragedy:

> Als Anfang aber jenes zu erjagen, unschicklich bleibt's,
> wogegen auszurichten nichts. (GA 53: 124)

> But it remains improper to start out in pursuit of
> that against which nothing can be done.

As Heidegger points out, the image of pursuit here recalls the gesture already described in the choral ode as characteristic of the human being, his tendency to be *pantoporos*, "überall hinausfahrend": the improper pursuit (*Erjagen*) of this passage and man's *Jagen* in the later one are both derived from the Greek *theran*, and therefore represent a hinge connecting Ismene's words to the Chorus's song: "Everywhere venturing forth, underway experienceless without a way out, he comes to nothing" (I 59; trans. modified: *Überall hinausfahrend unterwegs erfahrungslos ohne Ausweg kommt er zum Nichts* [71]). Yet the object of pursuit in Ismene's claim is something quite other than the *machanóen* (*Gemache*, machinations) of the human in that example. What Antigone pursues (and what Ismene deems "improper," *unschicklich*) is *ta amechana*, that against which nothing can be done (*wogegen auszurichten nichts*, GA 53: 126). While the human being with all of his might and machinations may have the power to cheat sickness and ill fortune, only death leaves him "without escape" (*ohne Ausweg*). This much is clear from the choral ode; quite literally, nothing can be done to stop death from taking its inevitable place. But Antigone, far from struggling to escape, pursues that inescapable end. What does it mean for her to do this?

To be sure, it takes her in another direction than that of the human beings who are *pantoporos*. It is thus tempting, Heidegger concedes, to hold Antigone's deed separate from the actions of other human beings and in particular from that which renders them *unheimlich* (GA 53: 121). She is, after all, a heroine, a selfless figure who protests with her own body and her own life the injustice imposed upon her brother by her uncle the king. Yet in light of her insistence on pursuing the impossible in the exchange with Ismene, Antigone is hardly excluded from the realm of the unsettling. On the contrary, Heidegger submits that with a single gesture she reveals herself to be the most unsettling of all, *das höchste Unheimliche*. That gesture is simply the taking-on, the enduring, the suffering of *to deinon*.

> Doch überlaß dies mir und jenem, was aus mir Gefährlich-Schweres rät, ins eigene Wesen aufzunehmen das Unheimliche, das jetzt und hier erscheint. (GA 53: 127)

> Yet leave this to me and to that in me that counsels the dangerous and difficult, to take into my own essence the unsettling that appears here and now. (I 103; trans. modified)

The human being has no means by which to orchestrate this taking-on, the Greek *pathein*, as an act of will; rather, it is a gesture intimately linked to what he is: "the not-at-home is nothing that human beings make themselves but rather the converse: something that makes them into what they are and who they can be (I 103; trans. modified: *das Unheimische [ist] nichts, was der Mensch selbst macht, sondern was umgekehrt ihn macht zu dem, was er ist und der er sein kann* [GA 53: 128]). Yet by undertaking this pursuit of the impossible, that against which nothing can be done, Antigone takes *das Unheimliche* into her essence (*ins eigene Wesen*) and thereby supersedes all others in her *Unheimlichkeit*. She is "ausgenommen," an exception, but not as a figure excused from that unsettling quality which the Chorus invokes; on the contrary, she is the most authentic representative of it insofar as she takes *deinon* into her very being (GA 53: 146).[30]

---

30. In a brief reading of the lecture, Schmidt points out that this reading of Antigone's *Unheimlichkeit* suggests Heidegger's attempt to understand "the nature which drives us into catastrophe," by means of a rigorous thinking beyond good and evil; in this regard Heidegger's reading is "exquisitely

Thus, like the *Anklang* that echoes through the poetic relation between Hölderlin and Sophocles, Ismene's admonition against pursuing *das Unausrichtbare* resonates both with Antigone's essence (*Wesen*) and the essential character (*das Wesentliche*) of the piece as expressed by the Chorus: that pursuit, precisely insofar as it is both impossible and irresistible, makes Antigone most *unheimlich* from the very start. While that resonance remains at this point "not yet grasped" (*noch unbegriffen*) (GA 53: 124), the dissonant language of the scene between Antigone and Ismene allows it to flash momentarily in its keenness.

What is modeled in this first literary *Zwiesprache* is therefore a violence other than that instigated by the act of interpretation *qua* appropriation, the violence of translation. That violence would involve the erasure of difference within the economy of the same. But the discord of this exchange between the sisters, like a translation that clashes starkly and on equal ground with its original, lets its uncomprehended (and perhaps incomprehensible) essence make itself heard. The opening dialogue of the tragedy thus takes preliminary shape as a literalization—"not yet grasped"—of the disordering dynamics of *Zwiesprache* that for Heidegger both provide the central theme of the tragedy and underlie its reception in modern poetry and history.

If the very first scene alludes to an awareness not yet grasped, however, how does that consciousness emerge poetically in the course of the tragedy, and from where? Heidegger locates it again within the Chorus's words:

Nicht werde dem Herde ein Trauter mir der,
nicht auch teile mit mir sein Wähnen mein Wissen
der dieses führet ins Werk. (GA 53: 74)

Such shall not be entrusted to my hearth,
Nor share their delusion with my knowing,
Who put such a thing to work. (I 61)

The hearth (*der Herd, hestia*) that the Chorus evokes here is for Heidegger the site of being-at-home (*Heimischsein*); yet, as he points out, this would logically imply that the Chorus of Theban elders possesses some knowledge of that place—in contrast to the remainder of humankind, which remains suspended within the movement of *Heimischwerden* and is therefore *unheimisch*—for they speak of banishing from the hearth those who do not share

---

'Greek'" insofar as it avoids placing the tragedy within the context of Christian morality (Schmidt 259).

their insight. Is the Chorus not made up of human beings? Does its knowledge endow it with a status other than that of the human?

In fact, the Chorus remains entirely human, Heidegger states, because it does not *know* the knowledge of which it speaks, if knowledge refers to the certainty of consciousness. A distinct kind of knowledge of *Unheimliches* emerges in the Chorus's words, but it is an *Ahnen*, a sense—an awareness not entirely aware of itself, because its materiality always withdraws in the very moment of its emergence. Though as the central figure of the tragedy the Chorus speaks the "poetic truth" (*die dichterische Wahrheit* [GA 53: 148]), "what is properly to be said" (I 106) (*das eigentlich zu Sagende*) remains unsaid in any explicit sense: "The 'content' of what is enunciated does not exhaust the truth of what is said" (I 106: *Der 'Inhalt' des Ausgesprochenen erschöpft nicht die Wahrheit des Gesagten* [GA 53: 132]). The spoken word conceals within itself something other than its own meaning that eludes any representation, however precise; whatever it *means* to say, therefore, language constantly speaks of its own *Unheimlichkeit*. And it is at this point that Heidegger stops, withdraws: "So no account of the 'content' of what is expressed, however precise, can bring us to the truth of this poetry's word" (GA 53: 133: *Also bringt uns auch keine noch so genaue Angabe des 'Inhaltes' des Ausgesprochenen zur Wahrheit des Wortes dieser Dichtung*). Though his interpretation of the passage goes on after this statement, it has no place to go any longer. And yet in this moment in which reading exhausts itself, there is insight: "it is only with this insight that we arrive at the true beginning of understanding" (. . . *mit dieser Einsicht kommen wir nun erst an den echten Beginn des Verstehens* [GA 53: 134]).

What the Chorus finally presents us with, then, is a moment of failed reading, a moment at which no attempt to understand the meaning of words will find resolution, at which no consideration of the work's content will generate a satisfactory account of the knowledge that these last lines of the choral ode convey. That knowledge "does not express itself immediately" (*spricht sich nicht unmittelbar aus* [GA 53: 134]), but remains at the level of *Ahnen*, where there is no possibility of translation—at least not of a translation that insists upon its own seamless completion. Yet even if it does defy the negotiation of understanding in a conventional sense, knowledge as *Ahnen* is no vague intuition: "It has its own lucidity and decisiveness and yet remains fundamentally distinct from the self-assuredness of calculative understanding" (I 108: *Es hat seine Helle und Entschiedenheit und bleibt doch von der Selbstsicherheit des rechnenden Verstandes grundverschieden* [GA 53: 134]). It is, to put it plainly, possible both to know and not to know at the same time. Both to hear what is said in the act of reading and to absorb what is not said, even if it remains beyond one's conscious grasp.

So what does this "knowledge" know? Above all, it knows a difference, for there are fundamentally distinct modes of being "not at home." And that difference, expressed poetically by the Chorus, reflects a relation to the ontic-ontological difference at the very heart of Heidegger's thought: the relationship of being (*Seiendes*) to Being (*Sein*) itself. For Heidegger, the hearth is the center, the "at home"—is Being (GA 53: 140), and the Chorus's reflection on *das Unheimliche* sheds light upon "the Being of all beings" (*das Sein alles Seienden* [GA 53: 135]). Though being "not at home" in no way implies exclusion from the sphere of Being—indeed, as Heidegger notes, there are no limits on the movement of "hinausfahren," however extreme—the human being that the Chorus describes as "überall hinausfahrend unterwegs erfahrungslos" (*pantoporos aporos*) has adopted a way of being "not at home" that leaves him blind to any relation to Being. And it is this particular blindness, this inauthentic way of *Unheimischsein* that merits his banishment from the hearth; it is of this human being that the Chorus speaks in the final lines of the crucial ode.

Yet there is another course of *Unheimischsein*, one that entails far more risk and reveals its subject as far more unsettling—in fact as the most unsettling of all things. This is the course that Antigone takes in pursuing that against which nothing can be done (*das Unausrichtbare*) despite not knowing the outcome of that pursuit, in taking *Unheimliches* into her very being despite its futility. The risk (*tolma, Wagnis*) of taking on *das Unheimliche* ennobles her and excludes her from the Chorus's condemnation, for precisely in that state of uncertainty lies the relation to Being. Her determination to confront that risk, already evident in the very first scene of the tragedy, points to the possibility of authentic experiencing itself, *das eigentliche Erfahren*.

> Das Schlusswort verbirgt in sich den Wink auf die unentfaltete und noch unvollzogene, aber im Ganzen der Tragödie sich vollziehende Wagnis, zwischen dem eigentlichen Unheimischsein des Menschen und dem uneigentlichen zu scheiden und zu entscheiden. Antigone selbst ist diese höchste Wagnis innerhalb des Bereichs des deinon. Diese Wagnis zu sein, ist ihr Wesen. (GA 53: 146)

> The closing word conceals within itself the sign toward that risk that has yet to be unfolded and accomplished but that is accomplishing itself in the tragedy as a whole, the risk of distinguishing and deciding between the

authentic and the inauthentic not being at home of the human. Antigone herself is this supreme risk within the realm of the *deinon*. To be this risk is her essence. (I 117; trans. modified)

Where the human being takes on this risk—takes it into her being, as Antigone does—there is a possibility, still undeveloped, but nevertheless in motion: the possibility of being "at home," the "not yet awakened, not yet decided, not yet assumed potential for being at home and coming to be at home" (I 115; trans. modified: *das noch nicht erweckte, noch nicht entschiedene, noch nicht übernommene Heimischseinkönnen und Heimischwerden* [GA 53: 144]). It is a mode of experiencing that demands "doing without" (*das Entbehren*) with respect to its center, however, for any knowledge of that center can only consist in the revelation of a contradictory movement (*gegenwendige Bewegung*) from the nearness to being "at home" to the withdrawal from that relation. At the center, it turns out, there is nothing that can be found; the authenticity of *Heimischwerden im Unheimischsein* consists of the decision to pursue a particular mode of approach that allows for the experience of being unsettled, of taking on the risk in that which is unsettling and owning its central role in what we understand as being.

Sophocles' tragedy reveals all of this—or rather points toward it in its refusal to reveal—but it is not alone in doing so. Poetry as such has the potential to participate in this refusal to be "found," standing as a moment in which a question is posed and a "searching" is founded precisely where there is no hope of finding anything: "this poetizing finding-out . . . is the purest find of a purest searching that does not restrict itself to being" (*dieses dichtende Er-finden . . . ist das reinste Finden eines reinsten Suchens, das sich nicht an das Seiende hält* [GA 53: 149]). Like the possibility of being at home (*Heimischseinkönnen*), the poetic knowledge that a reader seeks in text always remains "to come," "to be poetized" (*zu-dichtend*) even if it already appears on the page to be read.

And it is precisely this prefatory status of poetic knowledge as "the undecided, but still to be decided, for this poetry and in it" (*das Unentschiedene, aber erst zu Entscheidende für diese Dichtung und in ihr* [GA 53: 151]) that leaves it open to *Zwiesprache*, indeed marks that underlying process of exchange as a task both essential and infinite. The dialogic approach to the poetic text demands the same assumption of risk that Antigone takes on, the risk both of being unsettled and of unsettling the text in the act of reading. That Sophocles' choral ode not only demands such a precarious relation to its reader but also *depicts* it allows that ode to resonate with the poetic-historical dialogue that will follow it, whether the reader is Hölderlin or anyone else, into infinity.

Und wenn demnach dieses Chorlied die höchste Dichtung des höchsten Dichtungswürdigen ist, dann könnte das wohl der Grund dafür sein, daß dieses Chorlied dem Dichter Hölderlin in der Zeit seiner Hymnendichtung immer neu zugesprochen wurde. (GA 53: 152)

And if, accordingly, this choral ode is the supreme poetic work of what is supremely worthy of poetizing, then this might well be the reason why this choral ode came to speak ever anew to the poet Hölderlin during the period of his poetizing of the hymns. (I 121f.)

The authentic relation to Being that the Chorus invokes in negative form, that Antigone embodies in her tragedy thus finds an analogue in the practice of reading as *Zwiesprache,* in the open development of possibility and the perpetual subversion of interpretive certainty.

Despite the assurance with which Heidegger outlines this task "to come" in the act of reading as well as poetizing (indeed, both are now part of the same process), therefore, his lecture ultimately offers anything but a resolution of that task. To do so would be to forfeit a responsibility inherent in the task itself. Thus the final section of the lecture is in some ways the most subversive of all; with its recurrent withdrawal from any conclusive position, it succeeds in undermining much of what it also attempts to construct. In the end, it shifts the focus of the lecture towards an essentially ethical dimension of reading, one based upon a curious conception of love.

THE THIRD and final portion of Heidegger's lecture on "Der Ister" was never delivered. The semester in Freiburg ended with the conclusion of the second part, and part III, entitled "Hölderlins Dichten des Wesens des Dichters als Halbgott" (*Hölderlin's Poetizing of the Essence of the Poet as Demigod*) languished in a drawer until the lecture's belated publication in 1984. If, as Hans Sluga has asserted, the form of the lecture course itself resembles the movement that it describes—a wandering from the origin (Hölderlin's poetry) toward the foreign (Sophocles) and back to the ownmost[31]—then this premature ending suggests that its final journey back to *das Eigene* was never entirely accomplished, because it was never heard, only implied by what preceded it. As it turns out, of course, this state of incompletion is oddly appropriate within the logic of *Heimischwerden im Unheimischsein* as Heidegger has already outlined it, for it only underscores the notion that the authentic relation to the hearth as Being cannot be

---

31. Sluga, "Homelessness and Homecoming," 506.

"known" in any conventional sense. Interestingly enough, what Heidegger *does* say within this strange echo chamber both represents an attempt to return to the origin—not only to the start of this lecture, but to his other writings on Hölderlin as well—and forecloses the possibility of that return, now that, as Hölderlin writes in another context, what follows cannot resemble the beginning at all.

Consistent with the ongoing structure of forward motion and circling repetition that characterizes the lecture, the third section begins by returning—in this case to the Böhlendorff letter, which, as Heidegger states now, does not simply outline an aesthetics of "literature" but calls attention to a fundamental responsibility native to the poets: the responsibility to speak of the "coming-to-be-at-home of the historical mankind of the Germans within the history of the West" (I 124; trans. modified: *das Heimischwerden des geschichtlichen Menschentums der Deutschen innerhalb der abendländischen Geschichte* [154]). The "law of history" itself is this movement of coming to be at home, and history is accomplished in this movement, which *must be; for Heidegger,* Hölderlin is the first poet to "experience poetically" the "German necessity of being not-at-home" (*die deutsche Not des Unheimischseins* [155]). Throughout this section, however, Heidegger also clearly vacillates between statements that affirm the concept of "homecoming" as the destiny of the Germans and those that emphasize the practical impossibility of such a return.

Virtually every page in which Heidegger discusses the law of *Heimischwerden* seems to treat the subject differently. At times he emphasizes the dynamism of a return to *das Eigene* with active verbs of opportunity such as "lernen" and "heimisch werden" (GA 53: 156),[32] while only a few pages later he appears to retract that enthusiasm with verbs of stasis ("sein," "bleiben"):

> Das Finden des Schicklichen um Unheimischsein ist das Heimischwerden. . . . Das Zugeschickte und Schickliche aber bleibt für den Menschen stets das auf ihn Zukommende, Zukünftige. . . . Das Zugeschickte schickt sich so und anders und bleibt stets im Kommen. (GA 53: 159)

---

32. "The law of being-at-home as coming-to-be-at-home consists in the fact that historical human beings, at the beginning of their history, are not intimate with what is at home, and indeed must even become not-at-home with respect to this, in order to learn the proper appropriation of that which is one's own in venturing to the foreign, and only to come to be-at-home in the return from the foreign. [. . .] For history is nothing other than this return to the hearth" (I 156: *Das Gesetz des Heimischseins als eines Heimischwerdens besteht darin, dass der geschichtliche Mensch im Beginn seiner Geschichte nicht im Heimischen vertraut ist, ja sogar unheimisch zu diesem werden muss, um in der Ausfahrt zum Fremden von diesem die Aneignung des Eigenen zu lernen und erst in der Rückkehr aus ihm heimisch zu werden. [. . .] Denn Geschichte ist nichts anderes als solche Rückkehr zum Herde* [GA 53: 125]).

Finding what is fitting in being not-at-home is coming-to-be-at-home. . . . Yet what is fitting and fittingly destined for them always remains for human beings that which is coming toward them, that which is futural. . . . What is fittingly destined for us sends its destining in one way and another and always remains in coming. (I 128)

At the midpoint of a sort of ontological to-do list (the "zu"-prefix in German here indicating both completed and future tasks), Heidegger situates the poet; that which is to be realized, "das Kommende in seinem Kommen," can only be preserved in poetry. Thus the poet speaks from between two possibilities, that of *Heimischwerden* and that of *Unheimischsein,* and the constant oscillation between the two implies the "doing-without" (*Entbehren*) that has already characterized the only authentic relation to *Heimischsein* (GA 53: 91). The poet must have the "courage" ("Mut," also in quotation marks in Heidegger's text) to record this movement, the trajectory of "historically grounding spirit" (I 128) (*der geschichtlich gründende Geist* [GA 53: 160]).

How does this "courage" express itself? In contrast to Benjamin, who located his concept of courage in the poet-translator's self-sacrifice for the sake of the poetic truth to which the work of art inherently refers, Heidegger locates the poet's courage in an internalizing, even self-motivated gesture. He calls this motivation "love"—a love that emerges as a longing for one's own essence (*Sehnsucht zu seinem eigenen Wesen*), a desire to move outward into the foreign in order to return from a distance to that which is one's own. Love is thus not entirely self-love, but it is also not entirely altruistic. Above all, it is the poet's responsibility to channel that love into a preservation of "what is coming in its coming" (I 128) (*das Kommende in seinem Kommen* [GA 53: 160]). How can poetry express and preserve within it such a movement? And to what extent can it become intelligible in the process of reading?

Calling upon one of his favorite passages from "Brod und Wein," Heidegger turns to this problem of love as it bears upon the experience of the foreign with a reading of the line "Kolonie liebt, und tapferes Vergessen der Geist . . . " (*The spirit loves colony, and bold forgetting*). Here true love—spirit's devotion to the "colony" as well as the particular sort of forgetting endemic to it—is distinct from a mere infatuation with difference.

> Den Geist befällt nicht eine zufällige Lust nach dem Fremden. Der Geist "liebt" Kolonie. Liebe ist der wesentliche Wille zum Wesentlichen. (GA 53: 164)

Spirit is not befallen by some arbitary desire for the foreign. Spirit "loves" colony. Love is the essential will for the essential. (I 131; trans. modified)

The thrust outward into the foreign thus also reflects a desire to attain "the essential," *das Wesentliche,* thus in some sense to lay claim to it—in effect, to colonize it. For Heidegger, "love" refers to the desire to recognize within the foreign the ownmost, which has not yet been disclosed but can only be "won" upon returning.[33] "Love" for the foreign thus implies a commitment to being "not at home" for the sake of coming to be at home (GA 53: 164). It is for this reason, moreover, that Spirit (Hölderlin's *Geist,* which for Heidegger remains distinct from the Idealists' *Geist*) has the courage to "forget" its origin in the interest of recognizing the foreign:

> Die Tapferkeit des Vergessens in der Liebe zur Kolonie ist die Bereitschaft, im Fremden vom Fremden um des eigenen Willen zu lernen und dergestalt das Eigene, bis es die Zeit ist, hintanzustellen. (GA 53: 165)

> The boldness of forgetting in the love of colony is the readiness, while in the foreign, to learn from the foreign for the sake of what is one's own, so as to defer what is one's own until it is time. (I 132)

The very idea of the foreign as "colony" obviously renders problematic the idea of an encounter on equal terms. "Colony" for Heidegger here refers to the "the daughter-land that is related and refers back to the motherland" (I 131, trans. modified: *auf das Mutterland zurückbezogene Tochterland* [GA 53: 164]); foreign and ownmost remain symbiotically linked, ensuring not only their fundamental relatedness but also their unequal standing in a relation of dependency. There would be no foreign, in other words, if it did not in some way give the ownmost back to itself.

This raises the question of how Heidegger thinks the concept of turning-back (*Rückkehr*) in his discussion of Hölderlin's writings here. Insofar as it implies a return to the source, the "motherland," the "hearth," it inappropriately stabilizes one of Hölderlin's key concepts in his reading of tragedy. As we have already seen, Hölderlin's tragic vision ends in a moment of frightening stasis, in which "nothing more (exists) but the conditions of time and space," in which suffering prevails and offers no path back to a more innocent state:

---

33. I 131: "in the foreign, Spirit essentially wills the mother who . . . is indeed "difficult to attain: the closed one (*Der Geist . . . will im Fremden wesentlich die Mutter, die freilich . . . 'schwer zu gewinnen: die Verschlossene'* [GA 53: 164]).

> In dieser (i.e. der äußersten Grenze des Leidens) vergißt sich der Mensch, weil er ganz im Moment ist; der Gott, weil er nichts als Zeit ist; und beides ist untreu, die Zeit, weil sie in solchem Momente sich kategorisch wendet, und Anfang und Ende sich in ihr schlechterdings nicht reimen läßt; der Mensch, weil er in diesem Momente der kategorischen Umkehr folgen muß, hiermit im Folgenden schlechterdings nicht dem Anfänglichen gleichen kann. (FA 16: 258)

> In this [i.e., the outermost limit of suffering] the human being forgets himself, because he is entirely in the moment; the god, because he is nothing but time; and each one is disloyal: time, because in such a moment it turns itself round categorically and does not allow beginning and end to rhyme in it at all; the human being, because he must follow the categorical reversal in this moment and thus in what follows cannot resemble the beginning at all.

The end cannot resemble the beginning at all; the reversal that Hölderlin describes in tragedy explicitly forecloses the possibility of returning to familiar ground, for that ground has become unrecognizable. Strictly speaking, this is the only way to conceive of reversal ("Umkehr") as Hölderlin presents it in his writings on tragedy.

Strangely enough, although his remarks here often contradict it, Heidegger seems to know this. Or if not to "know" it in an explicit sense, perhaps to know it in the spirit of *Ahnen*, that poetic knowledge (*dichtendes Wissen*) that acknowledges the unknown. For although he initially turns back to his own earlier writings in the attempt to stabilize his reading, he soon arrives at a recognition that this lecture, this mode of reading, does not resemble those others at all. In a discussion of the "poetic spirit" as the "Stromgeist" (*spirit of the stream*), Heidegger returns to the river poem he had scrutinized nine years earlier, "Der Rhein." That which the poets must express, *das Zu-Dichtende*, is the holy (*das Heilige*), the determination of both the gods and the dwelling of humankind, which emerges from *Heimischwerden im Unheimischsein* (GA 53: 175). The poet who presents this structure as such must therefore stand between gods and men as a demigod (*Halbgott*), as an outsider capable of measuring the distance, and the difference, between mortals and immortals. Heidegger sums up and concretizes as follows:

> Das "Dichterische" ist der Geist und das Wesen der Ströme. Der Dichter des Dichterischen ist der Halbgott. Diese Bezüge sind von Hölderlin in der Einfachheit ihrer Wesensvollendung klar geschaut und gesagt in dem

vollendetsten der Stromgesänge, in der Hymne "Der Rhein." (GA 53: 173)

The "poetic" is spirit and the essence of the streams. The poet of the poetic is the demigod. Hölderlin clearly perceives these relations in the simplicity of their essential completeness and tells of them in the most complete of the river songs, in the hymn "The Rhine." (I 139)

The terms are all present, front and center: simplicity, clarity, completion. Whereas the "Ister" leaves no one, neither the poet nor the reader, invulnerable to the unsettling effects of *Zwiesprache,* the "Rhein" offers everyone a place from which to take measure of others. "Der Rhein" simplifies what the "Ister" complicates; it clarifies what the "Ister" conceals. And perhaps, therefore, it offers, in contrast to its unruly counterpart, the possibility of a "complete" (*vollendet*) reading. This is the difference.

Aber gleichwie die Rheinhymne im Wesen des Rheins das Wesen der Ströme dichtet, so dichtet die Isterhymne im Wesen des Isters das Wesen der Ströme, und d.h. Wanderschaft und Ortschaft. (GA 53: 175)

Yet just as the Rhine hymn poetizes according to the essence of streams in the essence of the Rhine, so too the Ister hymn poetizes according to the essence of streams in the essence of the Ister, that is, journeying and locality. (I 140; trans. modified)

That is to say: in the movement from stream to stream, the essence of the streams itself has changed. Has presented itself otherwise. The source has divided itself in two, and in this sense it has unsettled its own status *as* source. The poetry of streams now contains within it a fundamental dissonance.

However, that dissonance cannot be reduced to mere opposition, for the "Ister" hymn insists on its own internal difference as well in its relationship to the foreign, which Heidegger now terms "hospitality" (*Gastlichkeit*).

So wundert
Mich nicht, dass er (der Ister)
Den Herkules zu Gaste geladen. . . . (GA 53: 175)

Thus it surprises
Me not, that he [the Ister]
Invited Hercules as guest. . . . (I 140)

By inviting the Greek Heracles to itself, the Ister does not only continue to distinguish itself from the quintessentially German Rhine but underscores the distance traveled between the age of tragedy and the age of Reason; in this sense the hymn "thinks an entirely different and new relation" (GA 53: 177) between ancient and modern registers, a relation that is only possible through *Zwiesprache*.³⁴

But what exactly is "hospitality," and how does it relate to the question of return that Heidegger continues to pose in this section? The "guest" is the one who remains who he is: the foreigner in his foreignness. *Gastlichkeit* refers to the capacity to recognize that foreignness and the decision to allow it to remain as such.

> Herkules ist vom Ister nur zu Gast geladen. Er bleibt, der er ist, und ist doch als der Fremde "vom heißen Isthmos" aus dem Lande des "Feuers" im deutschen Lande gegenwärtig. In dieser Gastlichkeit des Isters liegt die Bereitschaft der Anerkennung des Fremden und seiner Fremde. . . . In der Gastfreundschaft liegt aber zugleich die Entschiedenheit, das Eigene als das Eigene nicht mit dem Fremden zu mischen, sondern den Fremden sein zu lassen, der er ist. (GA 53: 175f.)

> Hercules has been invited by the Ister only as a guest. He remains the one he is and yet, as the foreigner "from the sultry Isthmus," from the land of the "fire," is present in the German land. In this hospitality on the part of the Ister there lies the readiness to acknowledge the foreigner and his foreignness. . . . In guest-friendship, however, there also lies the decisiveness not to mix what is one's own, as one's own, with the foreign, but to let the foreigner be the one he is. (I 141)

What the "Ister" hymn says in its *Zwiesprache* with the foreign is thus analogous to Hölderlin's notes on the modern encounter with ancient Greece; crucial in both cases is not only the recognition of the foreign but the *decision* to bear its traces *as* difference. That decision, in effect, represents the ethical dimension of *Zwiesprache,* where the act of reading amounts to a renunciation (*Entbehren*, doing-without) of certainty, of stability, of *Ortschaft:* "The presence of the guest in the homely locale tells us that even in, indeed precisely in the locality of the homely, journeying still prevails and

---

34. Thus it would seem that Heidegger states the obvious when he claims that such a relation would have been both unnecessary and impossible for the Greek poets to conceive. However, if one takes seriously Hölderlin's thoughts on the role of the "Oriental" in Greek tragedy, it becomes likelier that what he was attempting to uncover in Sophoclean language was precisely the trace of such a relationship to the foreign.

remains determinative, albeit in a transformed manner" (I 142: *Die Gegenwart des Gastes im heimischen Ort sagt, daß auch und gerade in der Ortschaft des Heimischen noch die Wanderschaft west und bestimmend bleibt, wenngleich gewandelt* [GA 53: 177]). Approaching that which is one's own "*is* only as the encounter and guest-like dialogue with the foreign" (I 142: *ist nur als die Auseinandersetzung und gastliche Zwiesprache mit dem Fremden* [GA 53: 177]).

With the introduction of this idea of hospitality, Heidegger's concept of return has changed. His own attempt to return to the "source" (Hölderlin's poetry and his own earlier lectures) after the encounter with the foreignness of Greek tragedy leaves the certainty of the ownmost very much in doubt. This is true not least because the Ister hymn locates the foreign at its very source; its strange current, which seems almost to flow backward (*Der scheinet aber fast / Rückwärts zu gehen . . .*), gives the river a different relationship to itself:

> Hier, in diesem Fast-rückwärts-gehen, ist noch ein anderes Nicht-vergessen-können des Ursprunges. Hier wohnt einer so nahe dem Ursprung, daß er ihn schwer verläßt . . . ; nicht weil er nur im Heimischen . . . verharrt, sondern weil er *schon an der Quelle das Unheimische zu Gast geladen hat* und vom Unheimischen ins Heimische gedrängt wird. Der Ister *ist* jener Strom, *bei dem schon an der Quelle das Fremde zu Gast und gegenwärtig ist,* in dessen Strömen die Zwiesprache des Eigenen und Fremden ständig spricht. (GA 53: 182; my emphasis)

> Here, in this almost going backwards, there is yet another not being able to forget the origin. Here someone dwells so near to the origin that he abandons it with difficulty . . . not because he simply remains at-home . . . but because *already at the source he has invited the not-at-home as guest* and is pushed toward the at-home by the not-at-home. The Ister *is* that stream *in which the foreign is already present as guest at its source,* that stream in whose flowing the dialogue between one's own and the foreign constantly speaks. (I 146; trans. modified; my emphasis)

If the "Ister" hymn speaks of a way back to the source, then, that return does not only require the journey outward into the foreign. It demands that we recognize the presence of the foreign guest already at the source, "schon an der Quelle." *Zwiesprache* itself is not a matter of choice; it speaks continually, whether we hear it or not. But to hear that speaking whether or not it is understandable, to allow for its unsettling effects, is to act as Antigone does in taking *das Unheimliche* into her very being. There is nothing more *unheimlich* than the human, as Antigone shows in the highest sense, for the *Zwiesprache* that guarantees its permanent instability also describes its very ground. Heidegger's early promise to tell his listeners "who they are" on the basis of their thoughts on translation thus attains another level of significance, as translation presents this logic of *Zwiesprache in nuce*.

Perhaps it is because he reaches this unstable place that Heidegger cannot reach a conclusion, except for the conviction that it would be impossible to conclude. In the final pages of the lecture (again, pages that were never delivered to their addressees *as* a lecture) he struggles to qualify the essential incompletion that his reading represents: "Nor should the opinion arise that these remarks might in themselves suffice in order to think the truth of this poetry, or even to experience the poetic word and the word itself in its own essential space (*Wesensraum*)" (I 166).[35] If the reading is incomplete, however, that is not to say that Heidegger regards the poetry in question as having exhausted itself; on the contrary: "This poetry demands of us a transformation in our ways of thinking and experiencing, one that concerns Being in its entirety" (I 166: *Diese Dichtung fordert von uns eine Umwandlung der Denkungsart und des Erfahrens, die das Ganze des Seins angeht* [205]). There is still much "to do" before we can think the exchange with the foreign in relation to the movement of history, to the determination of Being.

Yet the task that reading poses here, the task of "turning over" (*umwandeln*) our way of thinking and experiencing, is one that Heidegger soon abandons. His next turn to Hölderlin's poetry, the lecture and essay "Homecoming/To Kindred Ones (*Heimkunft/An die Verwandten)*, shuts down the subversive operations of the "Ister" lecture by eliminating the problem of the tragic and thus stabilizing two key terms essential to *das Unheimliche;* grounding "homecoming" in understanding (*Verstehen*), he lets Hölderlin's poetry once again speak of the special destiny of the Germans.

THE ENEMY is foreign. The Germans are "the thinking and poetizing people" (*das Volk des Dichtens und des Denkens,* GA 4: 30). In 1943, the year that marked the hundredth anniversary of Hölderlin's death and the end of the siege of Stalingrad, there is a certain urgency in that distinction. Now Heidegger no longer speaks of *Heimischwerden,* of the idea that Hölderlin's poetry speaks of the incessant exchange with the foreign while preserving its essential difference; now another poem enacts a literal homecoming:

---

35. "Auch soll nicht die Meinung aufkommen, diese Anmerkungen reichten schon aus, um die Wahrheit dieser Dichtung zu denken oder auch nur dafür, das dichterische Wort und das Wort selbst in seinem eigenen Wesensraum zu erfahren" (GA 53: 204f.)

> Die Elegie 'Heimkunft' ist nicht ein Gedicht über die Heimkunft, sondern die Elegie ist als die Dichtung, die sie ist, das Heimkommen selbst, das sich noch ereignet, solange ihr Wort als die Glocke in der Sprache der Deutschen läutet. (GA 4: 25)

> The elegy "Homecoming" is not a poem about homecoming, but rather the elegy is, as the poetry that it is, homecoming itself, that still comes to pass as long as its word peals as the bell in the language of the Germans.[36]

The semantic difference between *Heimischwerden* and *Heimkommen*, coming-to-be-at-home and homecoming, may seem small and easily explainable; the idea of homecoming corresponds more viscerally to lived experience, to the fact that hundreds of thousands of young men had already fallen for the sake of the homeland, all the while remaining oriented toward that "home." However, the difference is far from insignificant. While *Heimischwerden im Unheimischen* reveals itself as a possibility that is basically untenable, *Heimkommen* directs itself to a destination that remains secret (*ein Geheimnis*). And secrets can be told, though they must be guarded until the proper moment.

The absence of the foreign is as conspicuous in this text as its presence was dominant in the earlier lecture. Whereas in the "Ister" lecture, ethical responsibility lay primarily within the notion of hospitality, in the decision to preserve difference as such even at the source, here the "care" (*Sorge*) of the poet inheres in the preservation of the secret held by all Germans, the secret of proximity to the source (*das Geheimnis der Nähe zum Ursprung* [24]). *Sorge*, in fact, here comes to replace the love that expressed the poet's courage as a fundamental openness, as hospitality to that which is unsettling, *unheimlich*. All that remains of the foreign is a sense of the burden placed upon those who have proven themselves worthy of the journey home.

> Wiederkehren kann nur, wer vordem und vielleicht schon eine lange Zeit hindurch als der Wanderer die Last der Wanderung auf die Schulter genommen hat und hinübergegangen ist zum Ursprung, damit er dort erfahre, was das Zu-Suchende sei, um dann als der Suchende erfahrener zurückzukommen. (GA 4: 23f.)

---

36. *Elucidations of Hölderlin's Poetry*, trans. Keith Hoeller (Amherst, NY: Humanity Books, 2000): 44 (translation modified). Henceforth designated as Hoeller, with page number.

Only he can turn back who previously, and perhaps for a long time, has wandered as a traveler and borne upon himself the burden of the journey upon his shoulders, and has crossed over into the origin, so that there he might experience what is to be sought, in order then as the seeker, to come back more experienced. (Hoeller 42; trans. modified)

Those who are worthy of returning have learned to hear the *Sorge* that the poet speaks: "'The others' must first learn to think the secret of sparing nearness" (*'Die anderen' müssen erst lernen, das Geheimnis der sparenden Nähe zu bedenken* [GA 4: 29]). And it is in this regard that the "others" become the poet's relations (*Verwandte*). Caring for the secret thus implies insularity—and guarantees the exclusion of the foreign. For those with their eyes trained towards the homeland, not even a death on foreign soil can preclude the inevitability of return.

> . . . sind dann nicht die Söhne der Heimat, die fern dem Boden der Heimat, aber mit dem Blick in die Heitere der ihnen entgegen leuchtenden Heimat ihr Leben für den noch gesparten Fund verwenden und im Opfergang verschwenden—sind dann nicht diese Söhne der Heimat die nächsten Verwandten des Dichters? Ihr Opfer birgt in sich den dichtenden Zuruf an die Liebsten in der Heimat, der gesparte Fund möge ein gesparter bleiben.
> Er bleibt es, wenn aus denen, "die im Vaterlande besorgt sind," die Sorgsamen werden. Dann ist die Verwandtschaft mit dem Dichter. Dann ist Heimkunft. Diese Heimkunft ist aber die Zukunft des geschichtlichen Wesens der Deutschen. (GA 4: 49f.)

> . . . then are not the sons of the homeland, who though far distant from its soil, still gaze into the gaiety of the homeland shining toward them, and devote and sacrifice their life for the still reserved find, are not these sons of the homeland the poet's closest kin? Their sacrifice shelters in itself the poetic call to the dearest in the homeland, so that the reserved find may remain reserved.
> So it will remain, if those who "have cares in the fatherland" become the careful ones. Then there will be a kinship with the poet. Then there will be homecoming. But this homecoming is the future of the historical being of the German people. (Hoeller 48)

Whereas Antigone's destiny in Heidegger's view was to take das *Unheimliche* into her very being, the destiny of the Germans only one year later is quite opposite: the preservation of the center, the source, will bring the Germans back to themselves, bring them back home. Previously, in the logic of *Ortschaft* und *Wanderschaft*, the center could not hold; now it is held dear.

The conclusion to this piece, then, is very different from that of the "Ister" lecture; whereas in the latter text Heidegger appears in the end to back off from the notion that he has modeled any sort of understanding at all, calling attention only to the limits of understanding, in "Homecoming" he concludes with a call to action:

> Darum wendet der Dichter sich zu den anderen, dass ihr Andenken helfe, das dichtende Wort zu verstehen, damit im Verstehen für jeden je nach der ihm schickliche Weise die Heimkunft sich ereigne. (GA 4: 30f.)

> That is why the poet turns toward the others, so that their remembrance may help in understanding the poetizing word, so that in understanding homecoming might take place in a fitting sense for each one of them. (Hoeller 49; trans. modified)

Significantly, it is not only through the saying of poetry but through the help of understanding that homecoming is possible, an understanding that takes place by means of a form of thought (*Andenken*). We are very far here from the notion of "poetizing knowledge" that Heidegger developed in the "Ister" lecture, as a moment in which understanding falls short in the face of the "hardly sayable"; we are far from his assertion that "truth" may lie in the recognition that thought cannot exhaust its poetic object:

> Sind wir aber stark genug zum Denken, dann kann es genügen, daß wir die Wahrheit der Dichtung und ihr Gedichtetes nur aus der Ferne, und d.h. kaum, bedenken, um von ihr plötzlich betroffen zu sein. (GA 53: 205)

> Yet if we are strong enough to think, then it may be sufficient for us to think upon the truth of this poetry and what it poetizes, merely from afar, that is, scarcely, so that we may suddenly be struck by it. (I 167; trans. modified)

In "Heimkunft," reading as *Zwiesprache* has been displaced by reading as prelude to thought. This is where the violence of interpretation begins anew. Despite the rhetoric of homecoming, it is a shift that signifies no return to an origin but a retreat into insularity, a flight from the possibilities of the foreign, a silencing of *Verstimmung*.

Only a few years later, Bertolt Brecht will himself experience an unsettling sort of "homecoming." Returning to Europe in 1947, he will be confronted with a "home" that had not only become unrecognizable in the aftermath of world war but also bore the fresh scars of unrepresentable events. His foray into tragedy at precisely this moment of return is significant insofar as he considers, not unlike Heidegger, the potential explosion of historical complacency inherent in the confrontation with the unsettlingly foreign.

SIX

Ruined Theater
Adaptation and Responsibility in Brecht's *Antigonemodell*

> in der tat scheint es die hauptsächliche wirkung einer produktion
> wie der meinen heute zu sein, soviel wie möglich vom theater
> niederzureißen und zu ruinieren (AJ 20 Dec. 1947: 797).
>
> In fact it seems that the primary effect of a production like mine
> today is to tear down and ruin as much of the theater as possible.
>
> Known, don't know, over known
> day after day, moon after moon,
> overfull, pain after pain,
> horrors of hate abate not
> ever.[1]

BERTOLT BRECHT returned in late 1947 to a shattered Europe. To a Europe in which memory would be forced to bear the "horrors of hate," in which art would have to confront incessantly the contours of that hatred and to place itself at odds with a tainted history. In 1947, to be sure, art could do little else. A mere five years after Heidegger had insisted on the concurrent flow, the *Zwiesprache* of poetry and history evidenced in Hölderlin's *Dichtung der Ströme*, their dialogue had been irrevocably changed, leaving irruption and discord as the artist's only tenable position. For the dramatist returning out of fifteen years of exile, that rupture expressed itself in an existential as well as an aesthetic register. Even Brecht's initial overtures towards a post-war, divided Germany required an intermediary, Switzerland,

---

1. Ezra Pound and Rudd Fleming, *Elektra* (Princeton: Princeton University Press, 1987), 35f.

that maintained (however questionably) its own status as neutral bystander; likewise, even his first commissioned production for the Berlin theater, *Mutter Courage und ihre Kinder*, required the intervention of another theatrical vehicle in order to come to fruition.

That supplemental production, conceived as a second role for Helene Weigel during rehearsals for the lead in *Mutter Courage,* was a new adaptation of Sophocles' *Antigone* as translated by Hölderlin. It was hardly a rousing success in its first incarnation; the production closed a mere four weeks after its premiere at the Stadttheater in Chur in January 1948. Yet the materials Brecht generated out of that initial production—beyond his rendering of the play itself, a visual and textual record consisting of script, photography, sketches, and commentary collectively published in 1949 as the *Antigonemodell*—have maintained an intriguing afterlife as an example of critical debate over the function and practice of modern theater. In December 1947, Brecht outlined his objectives for this project in typically irreverent fashion: "In fact it seems that the primary effect of a production like mine today is to tear down and ruin as much of the theater as possible."(AJ 797) But what does it mean to "ruin" theater, precisely in the moment in which the rest of the world is occupied with picking up the pieces? What is at stake for Brecht—embittered by years of exile and dismayed by post-war Germany's reticence with respect to the recent past—in positing the idea of a theater in ruins?

On a very superficial level, it would be immediately possible to say that Brecht's *Antigone* "ruins" its source text twice over, insofar as the play is situated at some distance from the plot and structure of both Sophocles' drama and Hölderlin's translation. Yet elements of Sophoclean and Hölderlinian drama prove effective nevertheless in producing an essentially Brechtian text, and not only in the sense of the anti-Aristotelian epic theater. By adapting a text steeped in classical tradition (again, twice over—the Greek and the German) Brecht weaves a sense of historicity directly into the fabric of the text, not merely by bringing the material into the present day but by showing the process by which stories are recorded and performed. In doing so, he allows both violence and its resistance to rise to the play's surface on a structural level, making form resonate with the political themes of the piece.

This exposure of the process of "making history" takes tangible form in what Brecht calls the "Modell," a collection of script, notes, photographs, and sketches that create a record of the play's performative genesis and development. Beginning with initial rehearsals and extending potentially into infinity is a gathering of materials—in effect, a history—meant to serve as both an example and an impetus for future productions. In its multimedial incarnation as the first installment in a planned series of *Modelle*, the *Antigone* represents for Brecht the genesis of a new "way of doing theater" (*eine neue Spielweise*) far more than it suggests a return to the dramatic stuff of ancient Greece. Brecht's adaptation develops from a concept of translation as a quintessentially modern paradigm: his *Antigonemodell* blends the remains of a distant, even inaccessible aesthetic tradition with the novelty of modern methods of artistic production, effectively offering a prototype for translation in the age of technological reproducibility.

What this implies for Brecht's work will prove not to be so distant from Benjamin's discussion of the potential effects of the photographic image as mass medium in his essay *The Work of Art in the Age of Its Technological Reproducibility*. For Brecht as for Benjamin, concepts such as authorship, immortality, and genius had been co-opted and thus corrupted by fascist ideology, leaving entirely unsettled—but also entirely open—any remaining possibilities for artistic production. By using photography alongside extensive textual commentary to record the ongoing adaptation of a "classic" play (not to mention a legendary translation), Brecht attempts to achieve the "shattering of tradition" that Benjamin sees in the decline of the primacy of the singular art work.[2]

Taken as a whole, then, Brecht's *Antigone des Sophokles* marks an intriguing if little-examined moment in the development of a modern concept of tragedy, a moment of transition in which the classical text morphs into what Brecht describes as a "theater of the scientific age" (*Theater des wissenschaftlichen Zeitalters*). In its "through-rationalization" (*Durchrationalisierung*) through the lens of scientific inquiry, the concept of authorship will be more closely related for Brecht to the piecework of the assembly line than to the toils of the individual genius: "The modern division of labor has recast the idea of creativity in many significant areas . . . so that the isolated, original invention has lost significance" (*Die moderne Arbeitsteilung [hat] auf vielen wichtigen Gebieten das Schöpferische umgeformt . . . so daß die isolierte ursprüngliche Erfindung an Bedeutung verloren hat* [BFA 25: 76]). Embedding this challenge in his radical reformulation of tragedy—a genre whose founders had been revered literally for millennia—Brecht takes on the task

---

2. Interestingly enough, in a twist that leaves Brecht's engagement with tragedy even more proximate to Benjamin's essay, the consequence of this destructive moment for Benjamin will be nothing less than a new kind of catharsis. With respect to film as the "most powerful agent" (*machtvollster Agent*) of mass movements, Benjamin writes in the artwork essay: "Seine gesellschaftliche Bedeutung ist auch in ihrer positivsten Gestalt . . . nicht ohne diese seine destruktive, seine kathartische Seite denkbar: die Liquidierung des Traditionswertes am Kulturerbe." Benjamin, *GS I:2*, 478 (*The social significance of film, even—and especially—in its most positive form, is inconceivable without its destructive, cathartic side: the liquidation of the value of tradition in the cultural heritage* [SW 4, 254]).

of formulating the stakes of a theater in ruins. It is a project that demands a confrontation with the violence of literary and historical transformation, with the urgency implicit in the attempt to represent through art a history that has become unrepresentable. In a new "time of need" (*dürftige Zeit*), a time in which, as Hannah Arendt notes, Brecht struggled openly with the notion "that he felt himself unequal to the formidable task of being a poet in a time such as this," both Antigone and the text she inhabits offer the expression *par excellence* of responsibility to the dead, to the signs of the past both written and unwritten, both remembered and forgotten.[3]

It was not his idea. Hans Curjel, director of the Stadttheater in Chur, had previously collaborated with Brecht in 1927 at the Kroll-Oper in Berlin and now offered him a choice of several pieces, including *Macbeth* and Racine's *Phaedra* (BFA 8:489). Brecht opted for *Antigone*—Antigone in a new adaptation, the ancient Greek text reimagined in his own epic theatrical vision and recorded as both text and image in the photographs, sketches, and remarks that make up the *Antigonemodell*. Following the suggestion of his collaborator Caspar Neher, he chose Hölderlin's translation as his German source.[4] In opting for *Antigone* he joined a trend, most famously taken up at the time by the avant-garde dramatist Jean Anouilh, of adapting Greek tragedy in the context of anti-Fascist politics. Anouilh's own *Antigone* (1945), which transformed the heroine essentially into a modern resistance fighter and Creon into a puppet of the totalitarian state, was markedly more successful than Brecht's was in 1948, perhaps due to its wholly contemporary, thus more immediately accessible context.[5] Brecht's version is partly consistent with this overall inclination, for he also modified the details of Sophocles' plot in ways that render its conflicts more contemporary: most notably, in his version the war in Argos has not yet ended, and Polynices

---

3. Arendt, *Walter Benjamin, Bertolt Brecht. Zwei Essays* (München: R. Piper, 1971), 82. Arendt also describes Brecht's "list of losses" (*Verlustliste*), constructed in exile in the forties, with Walter Benjamin, Karl Korsch, and others who did not survive. Brecht writes of the self-loathing he experienced with the awareness that he had somehow survived those others: "Ich weiß natürlich; einzig durch Glück / Habe ich so viele Freunde überlebt. Aber heute nacht im Traum / Hörte ich diese Freunde von mir sagen: 'Die Stärkeren überleben.' / Und ich haßte mich" (81: *Of course I know that I survived so many friends by pure luck. But last night in a dream I heard these people say of me: "The stronger survive." And I hated myself*).
4. Ruth Berlau claims in her memoirs that Brecht went through various translations and even consulted a Greek text, "having found someone with a slight knowledge of Greek." According to Berlau, Brecht viewed Hölderlin's rendering as "'the strongest and the most amusing.'" *Living for Brecht: The Memoirs of Ruth Berlau*, ed. Hans Bunge, trans. Geoffrey Skelton (New York: Fromm, 1987), 167.
5. For a comparison of the two Antigone plays, see Gisela Dibble, "Antigone: From Sophocles to Hölderlin and Brecht," *Legacy of Thespis: Drama Past and Present*, v. IV, ed. Karelisa V. Hartigan (Lanham, MD: University Press of America, 1984), 1–12.

(rather than falling in battle with his brother) is a deserter whom Creon himself kills for failing to stand firm against the enemy; moreover, not only Polynices' corpse is left to decompose in the open, but the bodies of all Argaean soldiers are mutilated and left on the battlefield as well.[6] Brecht also adds a prologue in the initial version that plainly aims to link the events of the tragedy to the present day: below a hand-lettered sign that reads "Berlin, April 1945, daybreak," a scene plays in which a deserter is killed and strung up in front of his home, where his two sisters discover him and argue bitterly over whether to endanger their own lives by claiming his body.

Yet even as Brecht's adaptation maintains a political stance unmistakably tied to the contemporary critique of power and its abuse, he also insists in his opening remarks on the ancient text's essentially insuperable distance from any modern events whatsoever, despite superficial resemblances.[7] In fact, it will be this distance that, in properly epic-theatrical fashion, helps to engender the Greek tragedy's effect on a modern audience:

> For the theatrical undertaking before us, the Antigone drama was chosen, because from a thematic standpoint it could achieve a certain currency and because it presented formally interesting tasks. With respect to its political material, to be sure, its analogies to the present emerged as more disadvantageous than originally thought: the great figure of resistance in the ancient drama does not represent the German resistance fighters, who must appear as most significant to us. Their poem could not be written here. . . . It will not be immediately clear to everyone that this play is not about those resistance fighters, and only those to whom it is clear will be able to muster the degree of foreignness necessary to see with profit (*mit Gewinn*) that which is worth seeing in *this* Antigone play: namely, the role played by the assertion of power in the disintegration of the state. (BFA 25:74; my emphasis)[8]

---

6. This is implicitly true of Sophocles' version as well, where in line 10 Antigone refers to the treatment of *philoi* as enemies, indicating that all have been left unburied (*tôn echthrôn kaka*, "that evils belonging to (proper for) our enemies are coming upon our friends" [Jebb 1.10]). However, that implication is not emphasized in Hölderlin's translation; Antigone speaks merely of the "enemy's ills" (*Feindesübel*) that have befallen "the dear ones" (*die Lieben*), without suggesting that the enemies have been treated likewise (FA 16: 265).

7. See Wilfried Barner's account of the project's development from a complete transformation of the Greek source to an engagement with its mythic content; he argues that Brecht's early interest in rendering the story current by showing the effects of political resistance ultimately proves untenable, leading Brecht, through a "process of working-through and testing-out" (*Prozeß des Erarbeitens und Erprobens*), to call this knee-jerk connection to the present into question [192f.]. Barner, "'Durchrationalisierung' des Mythos? zu Bertolt Brechts 'Antigonemodell 1948,'" *Zeitgenossenschaft: zur deutschsprachigen Literatur im 20. Jahrhundert: Festschrift für Egon Schwarz zum 65. Geburtstag* (Frankfurt A.M. 1987), 192f.

8. "Für das vorliegende theatralische Unternehmen wurde das Antigonedrama ausgewählt, weil

The "poem" dedicated to German resistance could not be written in the end over the abiding marks of Antigone's own resistance, of her defiant refusal to allow a brother to depart from this earth unburied and unmourned. Although Brecht's and Neher's original goal had been a contemporary recasting of the play's representation of resistance, that actualization has met with its own resistance. As a result, the tragic text remains detached from the new and rooted in a particular history that will likewise not go gently in the transformation to contemporaneity; for Brecht the text itself in its ancient form resists such transformation, and it is precisely *this* resistance that helps to generate an alienating effect on the audience. That critical element which for Brecht makes the play "worth seeing"—its enactment of both the abuse of power and its resistance in a moment of political crisis—will thus extend to the formal process of adaptation itself and its assumption of a certain defiance for the sake of the ancient text it references. While the content of the tragedy resists its potentially new configuration into a version of modern-day events, its formal demands will model a new "way of doing theater" that takes into account the ruined landscape in which dramatic art will have to situate itself. Insofar as the "profit" to be procured from theatrical representation rests in the viewer's capacity to take note of that which is "worth seeing," moreover, that *Spielweise* will be integrally linked to the economy of seeing that Brecht attempts to distill and reproduce in the photographic images of his *Modell*. Seeing theater—and seeing, in turn, precisely how theater is constructed as an event—makes possible not only a critical understanding of the aesthetic space but a new ethico-historical awareness as well.

What Brecht describes in his introductory remarks to the *Antigonemodell* as the desire to slake the vague "thirst for the new" (*Durst nach Neuem*) in post-war European culture represents for him nothing more than an overdetermined response to the "fear of the return of the old" (*Furcht vor der Rückkehr des Alten*), which might refer to the dread of memories returning as well as of history repeating itself (BFA 25: 73). The task of a "theater of the scientific age" will lie in this double confrontation with the past and the apprehension that accompanies its remembrance; in short, it must call

---

es stofflich eine gewisse Aktualität erlangen konnte und formal interessante Aufgaben stellte. Was das stofflich Politische betrifft, stellten sich die Analogien zur Gegenwart . . . freilich als eher nachteilig heraus: die große Figur des Widerstands im antiken Drama repräsentiert nicht die Kämpfer des deutschen Widerstands, die uns am bedeutendsten erscheinen müssen. Ihr Gedicht konnte hier nicht geschrieben werden. . . . Daß von ihnen auch hier nicht die Rede ist, wird nicht jedem ohne weiteres klar sein, und nur der, dem es klar ist, wird das Maß von Fremdheit aufbringen, daß nötig ist, soll das Sehenswerte *dieses* Antigonestückes, nämlich die Rolle der Gewaltanwendung bei dem Zerfall der Staatspitze, mit Gewinn gesehen werden."

into question how history is to be remembered. As he writes in his *Kleines Organon für das Theater*, written in 1948 just after the Chur production of the *Antigone*, "stories can be told very differently" (*Geschichten sind sehr anders zu erzählen*), and it is this telling difference that will make it possible not only to relate historical events on the dramatic stage but also, more importantly, to lay bare the process by which the past is itself reconstructed and transformed as history. The *Modell* attempts to produce and reproduce this process, to make certain that it is seen, acknowledged, confronted. By compelling the critical stance so vital to Brecht's epic theater, then, the persistence of a gap in the modern viewing of classical tragedy—and, in particular, the reception presented by Brecht's own *Modell*—will allow the spectator to survey the ruins of theater both ancient and modern and consider the passage of time and ideological investment that rendered it as such.

As I will argue here, however, the ethical and critical sway of the *Modell* proves ultimately to be much less self-evident than Brecht's comments let on. For at the same time that the play's form encourages its audience to reflect critically on the brutality of the modern state, Brecht commits a violence of a different kind—namely, an overstabilization of his sources—in the (perhaps irresistible) gesture of leaving his own signature. In some ways, the result is not entirely distant from the motives Brecht aims to criticize.

IF BRECHT'S DECISION to stage a Greek tragedy appears surprising at first glance, his choice of Hölderlin's translation over any other in 1947 ought to seem at least as curious, despite his explicit affinity for its "Swabian cadences and schoolish Latin constructions" (*schwäbische tonfälle und gymnasiale lateinkonstruktionen*) (AJ 795 [16. Dec. 1947])[9] The National Socialist party, drawing rhetorical support from the youth movement inspired by Hölderlin at the turn of the century, had all but usurped the poet's image in the service of the *Vaterland;* already enthroned by Stefan George as the voice of German destiny, already linked to the war heroism of Norbert von Hellingrath (to whom Heidegger dedicated one of his first published essays on Hölderlin, the 1936 "Hölderlin and the Essence of Poetry"), Hölderlin the radical revolutionary had risen under the Nazi regime to a legendary status as icon of a luminous cultural past, as heroic beacon of hope for Germany's future resurrection as a *Kulturnation*.[10] Perpetuated not least by

---

9. Berlau confirms Brecht's affection for Hölderlin's "folklorish Swabian idiom, which he was constantly pointing out as he read it to me…" (Bunge 167)

10. See Claudia Albert, "'Dient Kulturarbeit dem Sieg?' Hölderlin-Rezeption von 1933–1945,"

Heidegger, the cultic image of Hölderlin as messenger, as seer—even as messiah—had overshadowed his more dubious history: his enthusiasm for the French revolution, his madness, even the daunting nature of the poetry itself. Meanwhile, his complex relationship to classical Greece had been reduced to the conviction that a more profound study of the ancients served the sole purpose of solidifying national identity.

To be sure, Brecht was hardly unaware of this heritage of ideological appropriation; in conversations with Hanns Eisler (who set Hölderlin's poetry to music) he clearly expressed his general distaste for Hölderlin's poetry, particularly in light of what had been done to it in the twentieth century.[11] Why, then, when presented with the opportunity to stage an adaptation of Sophocles' text, did he follow Neher's suggestion and turn to Hölderlin's translation? The decision may have proven even more personally motivated than Brecht's comment about the familiar appeal of "swabian tones" lets on, for Hölderlin's *Antigonä*—an eccentric text at the very least, at most a translation that undermines the very possibility of establishing identity of any sort, national or otherwise—mobilizes an experience of the foreign that mimics the acute dislocation of the recent exile.[12] While still in America, Brecht had already considered problems of translation when he recorded in textual and photographic form the painstaking process of developing a theatrical performance, that of Charles Laughton in a Los Angeles (Beverly Hills) production of *Galileo Galilei* (1947). Entitled *Aufbau einer Rolle: Laughtons Galilei* (*Constructing a Role: Laughton's Galilei*) the published text shows how the challenges of bringing his own work to the American stage shed light upon the parallel problems of negotiating between two languages and bridging the gap between text and performance.[13] The

---

in *Hölderlin und die Moderne*, ed. Gerhard Kurz et al. (Tübingen: Attempto, 1995), 157–59. Albert focuses her highly informative discussion on the year 1943, in which the hundredth anniversary of Hölderlin's death served as a crucial marker of the resilience of German culture. In an historical moment in which resources were scarce, the event was given the highest priority, and its commemorations remain influential even today; it was the year that Goebbels founded the Hölderlin-Gesellschaft and Beissner published the first volume of the *Stuttgarter Ausgabe*.

11. See "Fragen Sie mehr über Brecht! Hanns Eisler im Gespräch," ed. Hans Bunge (Munich: Rogner & Bernhard, 1970).

12. See Albert's discussion of how German exiles likewise adopted Hölderlin as their own: "Wie die Exilanten schien er auch ein 'Fremdling im eigenen Haus'" (155: *Like the exiles he seemed to be a "stranger in his own house"*). Within exile culture, Albert claims, the fragmentation and "Zerrissenheit" (*torn-up, disrupted quality*) of Hölderlin's character represented a contrast to the totalizing aims of National Socialism. See also Bruce Cook, *Brecht in Exile* (New York: Holt, Rinehard and Winston, 1982).

13. See Patrick Primavesi's discussion of the *Aufbau* in relation to Benjamin's conception of translation in *Die Aufgabe des Übersetzers*. "The Performance of Translation: Benjamin and Brecht on the Loss of Small Details," *The Drama Review* 43:4 (1999): 53–59.

collaboration between Laughton and Brecht, as Brecht stresses, demanded an almost constant recourse to these interconnected modes of translation:

> Wir trafen uns zur Arbeit gewöhnlich in L.s großem Haus über dem Pazifischen Ozean, da die Kataloge der Synonyme zu schwer zum Herumschleppen waren. Er gebrauchte diese Folianten viel und mit unermüdlicher Geduld und fischte dazu noch Texte der verschiedensten Literatur heraus, um diesen oder jenen Gestus oder eine besondere Sprachform zu studieren, den Äsop, die Bibel, Molière, den Shakespeare. . . . Dies waren Übungen, und er verfolgte sie mitunter in mannigfache Richtungen, sie seinem übrigen Werk einverleibend. . . . Wir benötigten solche ausgebreiteten Studien, da er kein Wort Deutsch sprach und wir uns über den Gestus von Repliken in der Weise einigen mußten, daß ich alles in schlechtem Englisch oder sogar in Deutsch vorspielte, und er es sodann auf immer verschiedene Art in richtigem Englisch nachspielte, bis ich sagen konnte: Das ist es. Das Resultat schrieb er Satz für Satz handschriftlich nieder. Einige Sätze, viele, trug er tagelang mit sich herum, sie immerfort ändernd.
>
> We usually met to work at L's big house overlooking the Pacific Ocean, since the catalogs of synonyms were too heavy to lug around. He used these folios often and with tireless patience and even fished other texts out of the most various literature—Aesop, the Bible, Molière, Shakespeare—in order to study this or that gesture or a particular linguistic form. . . . These were exercises, and he pursued them at times in numerous directions, incorporating them into the rest of his work. . . . We needed such extended studies, since he did not speak a word of German and we had to agree on the gesture of each bit of dialogue by my acting it all out in bad English or even in German and his acting it back in proper English in different ways until I could say: That's it. He wrote down the result by hand, sentence by sentence. For days he would carry some sentences, many, about with him, changing them constantly. (BFA 25: 11)[14]

Resulting from this negotiation were what Brecht called "theatrical thoughts" (*theatralische Gedanken*), new insights into the possibilities posed by the text

---

14. As Ruth Berlau notes in her memoirs, however, Laughton had far less confidence than Brecht indicates here in the process of developing an epic-theatrical performance, to the point that the clicking of Berlau's camera shutter during rehearsals drove him to distraction. This apprehension led him to attempt numerous changes in the New York production of *Galilei*, staged after Brecht's departure from the United States. Brecht dispatched Berlau to photograph and record the performance in detail, including phonograph recordings of Laughton explaining the changes he had made. Berlau claims to have sent over three thousand photographs to Brecht in Switzerland (Bunge 1987, 155–57).

in performance. As an attempt to harness in text and image the manifestations of these "theatrical thoughts," the *Aufbau* amounts to a translation from text to performance (and ultimately to published record) that not only allows the process of adaptation to advance in new directions but tracks, both visually and textually, the steps that led to that creative result (cf. Primavesi 57).

By showing the dialectical process of crafting a performance, moreover, Brecht's *Aufbau* means to proffer a new, critical way of taking pleasure in the experience of theater: "the spectator, particularly the sophisticated type, enjoys in art the making of art, the active element of creating" (*Der Zuschauer, besonders der bewanderte, genießt in der Kunst das Kunstmachen, das aktive Element des Schaffens* [BFA 25: 9]). Thus it brings to light the framework of theatrical performance as a negotiation of existing, written material with a more ephemeral *Aktualität*, the result of which is constantly in flux (*immerfort ändernd*), and it posits that negotiation as a creative act vital to the piece's effectiveness on stage. This does not at all imply that a performance referencing the past must merely place that past into a contemporary context; rather, the dimension of creativity lies in illuminating the delicate links between past and present. That these tears and sutures must remain *visible* in particular is clear in Brecht's recourse to a photographic record of Laughton's performance;[15] the still images of various scenes, which were viewed in Los Angeles and in a brief run on Broadway by barely ten thousand spectators, became, along with Brecht's commentary, an integral part of the play's textual fabric. Though the production failed as a piece of popular theater, then, its physical remains express Brecht's hope for its future potency: "Thus such productions must be viewed as examples of a theater that could be possible under other political and economic circumstances" (BFA 25: 69).[16]

---

15. By this time Brecht relied on photography as a means to record the progress of his work, for purposes of collaboration and creative development as well as the establishment of an archive. His 1948 versification of the *Communist Manifesto*, also photographed by Berlau in various stages of completion, represents another interesting example of his attempt to record the dynamics of writing and rewriting, this time not demonstrated by the actors' performances but inscribed within the text itself. Berlau further describes Brecht's striking method of textual correction, which he called *Klebologie ("stickology")*: "In order to avoid the task of recopying corrected pages in full, he would write the new text on a fresh page, cut it out neatly, and stick it to the old manuscript" (183). These attempts to mark textual modifications as such reflect a more intriguing dynamic than Berlau indicates in describing Brecht's "weakness for clean, uncorrected manuscripts" (183); I would argue that they record for Brecht in physical form the sedimentary, fragmented nature of writing that underlies the illusion of teleological linearity.

16. "So müssen solche Aufführungen als Exempel eines Theaters betrachtet werden, das unter anderen politischen und ökonomischen Verhältnissen möglich sein könnte."

And indeed, Brecht's theatrical production in Switzerland and later with the Berlin Ensemble would adopt this framework as an example for the *Modellbücher,* though with an important difference: what appears here, often at close range, as the singular performance of a renowned, if fading, actor (in this sense the vestige of an "auratic" event) soon develops into a more distanced perspective with respect to *Antigone,* where for the most part the individual actors are so far away from the camera that they are barely recognizable. Despite the photographer Ruth Berlau's retrospective laments about the poor quality of her photographs, this distancing constitutes a refinement of the *Modellbuch* as it reflects Brecht's project; the actors, after all, should recede behind their gestures, that "grouping of characters against one another," as Hölderlin put it (FA 16: 419), which is all the more visible from a distance. Even Weigel's Antigone, clearly the focal point of the production, only rarely assumes center stage in the photographs; on the other hand, Berlau stood so close to Laughton that the clicking of the shutter unnerved him, forcing her to snap the images behind a glass partition (Bunge 1987, 155).

Brecht returned to Europe from America, as he states in his work journal, intending to "ruin" what was left of its theater; yet given this recently demonstrated commitment to making visible the constructedness of theatrical performance, it is impossible not to think that his new way of doing theater means to be an engagement with those ruins and not a blueprint for their total erasure. Even a ruined past speaks volumes (as Brecht's friend Benjamin knew), if only about its own corrupt premises. Hence Brecht's turn to Hölderlin with the *Antigonemodell* might represent an engagement with ruins in its own right: while his adaptation of the tragedy and the record of its performance lay bare the process by which the politics of historical transformation shape the receptive act, the choice of Hölderlin's translation represents his encounter with the remains of a poetic corpus long enslaved by political motive. And insofar as the *Modell* attempts to narrate that encounter at the same time that it presents the result, the transformative process it undertakes will this time not negate its own past. Consequently, as Brecht writes in his notes to the 1951 production in Greiz, even the most difficult passages of Hölderlin's translation must be preserved for their dialectical possibilities:

> The choral passages, into which new thoughts have likewise developed, have also been adapted. These choruses, like some other passages in the poem, can hardly be fully understood in a single hearing. Parts of the choruses sound like riddles that demand solutions. Yet their outstanding feature is

that, when studied a bit, they give back more and more beauty. The adaptation was not merely supposed to eliminate this difficulty, the overcoming of which brings so much pleasure—particularly since the *Antigone* has the good fortune of having been translated by one of the greatest formers (*Gestalter*) of the German language, Hölderlin (AB 114).[17]

Like the "theatrical thoughts" that resulted from his collaboration with Laughton, the new thoughts ("neue Gedanken") emerging out of this ongoing process of adapting the *Antigone* constitute an exchange between text and something intangible, something that happens in the course of developing a particular adaptation; thus creative responsibility never rests solely in the authorship of an "original" text or even, in this specific case, in Hölderlin's act of producing a uniquely challenging translation. We will have to return to the question of how Brecht marks or effaces the specificity of language that Hölderlin has "formed" (*gestaltet*) in the translation, for it is here, in the text of Brecht's *Antigone*, that his theoretical remarks may be most in tension with their product. In structural terms, however, his *Antigonemodell* presents its public with a clear, critical purpose: it illustrates the ongoing practice of translating a translation in original terms, both bridging and problematizing the gaps between text and adaptation and between past events and present perceptions. "Copying," insofar as it becomes the basis for a new concept of creativity as a collective and collaborative act, must be a fluid art rather than a static exercise.[18] It must not only destabilize the place of an "original" per se, but it also subvert any possibility of claiming finality; every adaptation is at once part of the "original" and a product of translation, subject to the "continuum of a dialectical sort" (BFA 25: 76) that enabled it in the first place.

By disavowing the tyranny of origin in the creative process, moreover, the theatrical material produced out of this position aims to achieve not only

---

17. "Bearbeitet sind auch die Chöre, in welche ebenfalls neue Gedanken kommen. Diese Chöre, wie auch manch andere Stellen des Gedichts, können bei einmaligem Anhören kaum voll verstanden werden. Teile von den Chören klingen wie Rätsel, die Lösungen verlangen. Es ist jedoch das Vortreffliche bei ihnen, daß sie, ein wenig durchstudiert, immer mehr Schönheiten herausgeben. Die Bearbeitung wollte diese Schwierigkeit, deren Überwindung soviel Freude macht, nicht einfach beseitigen—um so mehr, als das Werk "Antigone" das Glück hat, einen der größten Gestalter der deutschen Sprache, Hölderlin, zum Übersetzer zu haben."

18. Werner Hecht, *Brecht im Gespräch: Diskussionen, Dialoge, Interviews* (Frankfurt: Suhrkamp, 1975), 86: "Man muß sich frei machen von der landläufigen Verachtung des Kopierens. Es ist nicht das 'Leichtere.' Es ist nicht eine Schande, sondern eine Kunst. Das heißt, es muß zur Kunst entwickelt werden, und zwar dazu, daß keine Schablonisierung und Erstarrung eintritt" (*One must free oneself from the common disdain for copying. It is not "easier." It is not a scandal, but rather an art. That is to say, it must be developed into an art, to the extent that it avoids [mere] templates and congealment*).

the ruination of an entire theatrical tradition but also something like the destruction of totalitarianism as an aesthetic system. It attempts to initiate, in other words, what Benjamin named as the antidote to National Socialism: in response to the aestheticization of politics, it presents, particularly on a structural level, the politicization of art.

EPIC THEATER is the antithesis of the poetry of streams. The flow of the river as Heidegger described it in Hölderlin's poetry, the fluid interchange it models between dynamism and stillness, *Wanderschaft* and *Ortschaft*, suggests a synergy—if not necessarily a union—between the foreign and of that which is one's own; the subject submits to an uncertain movement of history and memory that moves in two directions (*zwiefach gerichtet*), to a transport that leaves no place for a foot to take hold. Epic theater, on the other hand, consists precisely in the process of taking hold, of stopping, of refusing to submit to the flow of events staged before the audience: "Since the audiences is not being invited to fling itself into the plot as into a river, to let itself be borne here and there indeterminately, the individual events must be connected so that the knots become evident" (BFA 23: 92).[19] The pattern Brecht describes here is familiar in the context of his dramatic theory; far from being swept away, the spectator takes firm hold of the knots that disrupt the flow of performance, allowing the productive stoppage Brecht finds exemplified in the iconography of technological progress—or, more precisely, in the force of technology in the service of discontinuation.

> The attitude is a critical one. With respect to a river it consists in the regulation of the river; with respect to a fruit tree, in the grafting of the fruit tree; with respect to forward movement, in the construction of driving and flying machines; with respect to society, in the overturning of society. (BFA 23: 73)[20]

If a river's current can be regulated, made productive through redirection by technological means, Brecht goes on to suggest, the dynamics of theatri-

---

19. The passage is from the *"Kleines Organon für das Theater":* "Da das Publikum nicht eingeladen werde, sich in die Fabel wie in einen Fluß zu werfen, um sich hierhin und dorthin unbestimmt treiben zu lassen, müssen die einzelnen Geschehnisse so verknüpft sein, daß die Knoten auffällig werden."

20. "Die Haltung ist eine kritische. Gegenüber einem Fluss besteht sie in der Regulierung des Flusses; gegenüber einem Obstbaum in der Okulierung des Obstbaums; gegenüber der Fortbewegung in der Konstruktion der Fahr- und Flugzeuge, gegenüber der Gesellschaft in der Umwälzung der Gesellschaft."

cal performance can likewise be made more "productive" through its own disruption. Dramatic effect in a "scientific age" finds its stimulus not in the spectator's propensity to let herself be swept away but precisely in the caesurae that render that affective participation impotent.

In this attitude of interruption, Brecht's project finds itself in unexpected congruence with its two *Vorbilder,* both Sophocles' "original" and Hölderlin's translation. In his introduction to the *Antigonemodell,* Brecht notes the "formally interesting tasks" particular to producing Sophocles' tragedy in modern form, claiming that the "historical remove" (*historische Entrücktheit*) of the piece precludes the possibility that a modern audience might identify with its heroine, and asserting that "formal elements of an epic sort," including the structural and visual insertions of the Chorus, guarantee that viewers will remain at distance from the action as well (BFA 25: 75). Neher's stage itself replicates that distance, as the model shows: it is divided into two realms, one small area in which the action of the play takes place and the remainder of the stage surrounding it, where actors who are not part of the current scene are seated facing the action, presenting to the spectator a model of her own activity (see BFA 25: 93).[21] Meanwhile, center stage is surrounded by tall pillars topped by the skulls of horses, what Brecht describes as "barbarische Kriegskultpfähle" (*barbarian war cult stakes*). As cultic death tokens, these delineate the space in which the mythic action of the play diverges from any possible modern-historical context.[22]

Two disruptions, then, two examples of displacement (*Entrückung*)— one temporal, one structural—are characteristic of the tragic drama as it plays itself out before a modern audience. And for Brecht, those disruptive elements potentiate the "freedom of calculation" (BFA 25:75) necessary to make theatrical performance productive. If tragic representation once generated its effect, in Aristotelian terms, by evoking the powerful emotions of fear and pity—or even, for that matter, by exhausting itself in Nietzsche's Dionysian intoxication—Brecht's reformulation of tragedy aims to mobilize its audience toward a moment of reflection by making use of the very same elements, now skewed to such an extent that it becomes impossible not to

---

21. For a detailed account of Neher's stage layout, see Jochen Schmitt-Sasse, "Zwischen barbarischen Kriegskultpfählen: Antigonemodell 1948—Bild und Text—Brecht und Neher," *Theater ZeitSchrift* 26:4 (Winter 1988–89): 128. Schmitt-Sasse presents a very helpful discussion of the relationship between text and image in the *Antigonemodell,* in particular how its photographic images form a layer of meaning independent of the play itself, ultimately offering an interpretation of the dramatic text.

22. As Barner asserts, this structural preservation of the drama's "sinnlich-physische Dimension" (*sensual-physical dimension*) serves as a visible and omnipresent contrast to the "Entideologisierung des alten Mythos" (*de-ideologization of the old myth*) undertaken in a thematic sense (Barner 196).

notice their acute foreignness. Like Ezra Pound's translation of *Elektra,* in which entire choral passages left in the original Greek intensify the disorienting experience of taking in ancient tragedy with modern senses, Brecht's and Neher's visual and aural dramatization of the gap between actors and spectators reveals the temporal disjunction that other modern interpreters aim to bridge.[23]

At the same time, Brecht's desire to exploit the productive effects of discontinuity reveals on a textual level a certain affinity with Hölderlin's translation in particular. Passages in which Brecht remains particularly close to Hölderlin reflect the eccentricity that voices that translation's instability, its "madness."[24] And while Hölderlin's translation emphasized this instability conceptually in the words of the Chorus ("Jetzt aber komm ich, eben, selber aus dem / Geseze"), Brecht—as if he recognized the crucial synthesis of content and form in Hölderlin's model—transfers the stakes to a linguistic dimension of pure rhythm: "Jetzt aber komm ich eben selber / Aus dem Takte . . . " (*But now even I myself step out of* meter [BFA 8: 224]). Instead of articulating the disruption of the "outlaw" subject inspired by the sight of a wandering, changing Antigone, language now speaks of its own rhythmic rupture. This is at once both a metaphor for the destabilizing force of tragic experience and the radical refusal of metaphor in the service of translation; for even in Hölderlin's version, it is always already the "Takte," the meter disrupted by the caesura, that affects the modern audience in the most immediate sense.

Such small but extremely weighted modifications to Hölderlin's text— the measured transformation of a different sort of "original"—present the reader with a challenge, insofar as they further undermine the conventions of authorship already shaken to the core by a transforming translation. In effect, Hölderlin's text proves to be the first text of the *Antigonemodell*—subject, like all others that will follow it, to the dialectical process of adaptation— while Brecht's, from its inception, is already a modification. Moreover, in

---

23. See Richard Reid's introduction to Pound's translation of *Elektra,* in which he discusses Pound's concept of "logopoiea" as the abrupt intrusion of the unexpected in language, through which his translation depicts not only a house divided but "language at war with itself" (Pound xvii).

24. Thus it is unfounded to claim, as Ulrich Weisstein has, that Brecht's adaptation of Hölderlin's language constitutes a return to a "more Sophoclean spirit, without indulging in the use of eccentricity" ("Imitation, Stylization, and Adaptation: The Language of Brecht's Antigone and Its Relation to Hölderlin's Version of Sophocles," *German Quarterly* 46:4 [November 1973]: 585). Indeed, in the materials that make up Brecht's *Antigone* project there is little evidence that he is at all interested in the stylistic recovery of a "Sophoclean spirit" that would efface the "indulgence" of Hölderlin's translation; on the contrary, he leaves much of Hölderlin's most "eccentric" language intact (the most obvious example being, as even Weisstein notes, Ismene's opening observation that Antigone "schein[t] ein rotes Wort zu färben").

proposing the continuation of this process (potentially into infinity), Brecht places himself, as one adaptation's "author," in an equally precarious position. The *Modell* is "to be regarded from the start as unfinished (*unfertig*)," its development as much at the mercy of accident as dramaturgic intention. The remarks that frequently interrupt the script of Brecht's *Antigone*, often in the form of questions posed and answers given by unknown interlocutors, stylize this state of incompletion:

> FRAGE: Die Darstellerin der *Ismene* hat diese Szene ohne jeden Stellungswechsel oder besondere Geste gespielt. Aber sollte nicht wenigstens zwischen der Haltung vor dem Spielfeld und der auf ihm ein Unterschied sein, da sonst das Warten auf den Auftritt und das Warten auf *Antigones* Anliegen nicht verschiedenartig ist?
> ANTWORT: Ja, *Ismene* könnte, ausgehend von Vers 21, beim Betreten des Spielfeldes das Gesicht verhüllen.
> FRAGE: So war, was ihr machtet, unrichtig?
> ANTWORT. Ja. (BFA 25: 90)

> QUESTION: The actress portraying Ismene played this scene without any change of position or particular gesture. But shouldn't there at least be a difference between the posture/attitude before the field of action and the one in it, since otherwise her waiting for her appearance and waiting for Antigone's request would not be different?
> ANSWER: Yes, Ismene could, according to line 21, conceal her face upon entering the field of action.
> QUESTION: So what you did was incorrect?
> ANSWER: Yes.

Even errors discovered in hindsight are now meant to serve a dialectical purpose; plainly interwoven into the text's recorded history, they signal both its evolution and its potentiality. Moreover, the reproduction of a performative moment in visual form permits contemplation from an angle that can catch hold, in the very same instant, of what Brecht calls "the before and the after," *das Vorher und das Nachher:* the evidence of a text's fractured history and the questions it continues to pose. This in-between status reflects not only the content of the piece but its very structure. Its dynamics of pure mutability—indeed, of the impossibility of standing still—again brings the *Modell* into surprisingly close proximity to its own "Vorher" by recalling the "tragic transport" of Hölderlin's translation, which was likewise unlimited (*ungebunden*); Hölderlin's Antigone, too, was perpetually in the process of "wandeln." And yet at the same time the text anticipates its own "Nachher;" the visual component of the *Antigonemodell*, made possible by technological means, ensures that the text will also be continually marked as a product of its own time. This intervention by the future into the past opens new possibilities, just as it does for Benjamin in the artwork essay, where "process reproduction can bring out those aspects of the original that are unattainable to the naked eye yet accessible to the lens. . . . "[25]

Brecht's series of *Modelle,* from *Laughton's Galilei* to *Antigone* to *Mutter Courage,* demonstrates that photography offers an ideal means to represent this momentary status, this position between "the before and the after." As stop-action mode it reveals to the naked eye those ephemeral moments in performance that would not otherwise have come to such evident light. Compared with Neher's preliminary sketches for the stage, which have the static two-dimensionality of primitive line drawings, there is even a kind of indeterminacy to the photographs, as if they were taken at random and in unguarded moments; they convey a mobility and an imperfection that hint more generally at the provisional status of the *Modell* (see BFA 25: 139).[26] (This random quality begins to disappear in the *Couragemodell*, where the photography is of uniformly higher quality than in the previous *Modelle;* what this may mean, however, is that the model places greater emphasis on facial expressions rather than gestures, the actions of individuals rather than their attitudes towards one another.)

Perhaps as a direct result of his increasingly sophisticated work with photographs from the *Aufbau* to the *Modelle,* Brecht eventually conceived of this provisionality in an explicit sense (even if, ironically, the images begin to look more posed). In the *Couragemodell 1949* he notes the extent to which art after 1945 cannot help but reflect a new environment, a new life characterized by its own destruction:

> If life continues after the great war in our ruined cities, then it is a life of another kind, the life of others or at least that of groups that are otherwise put together, and it is both hampered and governed by our new surroundings, the new part of which is its destroyed state. Where the great piles of rubble lie, we also find valuable underground structures, the sewer system and the gas and electricity grids. Even the large, untouched building is drawn into sympathy with the half-destroyed ones and the debris it stands

---

25. Benjamin, "The Work of Art in the Age of Mechanical Reproduction," first version, in *Illuminations,* ed. Hannah Arendt, trans. Harry Zohn (New York: Schocken Books, 1968), 220.

26. Berlau: "If the takes are posed, the pictures that emerge may be very sharply focused, but they are unrealistic, counterfeit" (Bunge 1987, 232).

between, and under some circumstances can be a hindrance to planning. Structures must be built provisionally, and yet the danger is that they will remain. Art reflects all of this; ways of thinking are part of our ways of living. As it pertains to the theater, we fling the Models into the breakage. (BFA 25: 171)[27]

This rich passage, with its allusions to the parallel destruction of cities, their subjects, and the art they produce—and the concomitant potency that lies beneath the rubble—establishes not only a rationale for the *Modelle* but a set of working hypotheses. Even if the past, the *Vorher*, has been ruined, art must work with what remains to ensure a *Nachher*. Must build provisionally, and yet never stop building for so long that the provisional becomes permanent. Must allow the "sympathetic" engagement between the ruins and that which, right next door, remains intact. Where fragmentation represents future possibility, the "untouched building" may even become the "hindrance to planning;" the implication is that it, too, must be destroyed before it can be of use. This emphasis on the primacy of destruction even finds its way into Brecht's conception of how Greek tragedy might be productively compared with the present; unsatisfied with the contemporary prologue he and Neher presented in the initial production of the *Antigone* in Chur, Brecht suggests that it be replaced with "a panel with the representation of a modern city in ruins" (*eine Tafel mit der Darstellung einer modernen Trümmerstadt*).[28]

Brecht posits his *Modelle* as likewise broken, fragmented bodies that must be put back together again. Between creation *ex nihilo* (which would secure the sacred status of the "original," the "author") and overly reverent imitation, they represent a way of working with extant materials that produces something both new and alert to its relation to the past. Brecht as "creator" of the *Modell* insists over and over that the copy need not be an inherently restrictive medium: "There are slavish and sovereign ways of imitating."[29] The collective dread of the past returning should not hinder

---

27. "Wenn in unsern Ruinenstädten nach dem großen Krieg das Leben weitergeht, so ist es ein anderes Leben, das Leben anderer oder wenigstens anders zusammengesetzter Gruppen und gehemmt und geleitet von der neuen Umgebung, an der neu die Zerstörtheit ist. Wo die großen Schutthaufen liegen, liegen auch die wertvollen Unterbauten, die Kanalisation und das Gas- und Elektrizitätsnetz. Selbst das unversehrte große Gebäude ist durch das Halbzerstörte und das Geröll, zwischen denen es steht, in Mitleidenschaften gezogen und unter Umständen ein Hindernis der Planung. Provisorisches muß gebaut werden, und die Gefahr besteht, es bleibt. Die Kunst spiegelt all dies wider; Denkweisen sind Teil der Lebensweisen. Was das Theater betrifft, werfen wir in den Bruch hinein die Modelle."
28. Cited in Barner 192.
29. "Es gibt eine sklavische und eine souveräne Nachahmung" (*Hecht* 87).

the confrontation with the intact remnants of history, however scattered and irreconcilable they may be; out of the "Trümmerstadt" emerges the possibility of the new. To rebuild without this open link to history would be to deny its raw impact. To erase the remains of totalitarianism, then, would be to replicate its own founding gesture. For Brecht, art is effective as a political instrument only insofar as it depicts that which it rejects along with everything else.

Thus Brecht remained unperturbed by the howls of protest provoked by the *Modelle* among theater companies who were accustomed to adapting and modifying dramatic texts as their players saw fit. The notion that all subsequent productions of a particular play would have to refer to a single specimen project was profoundly unappealing to many, and there was little enthusiasm for participating in a rigidly conceived dialectics of imitation and variation where total creative freedom ought to be the norm. As Brecht states in his own defense, however, every theatrical production of an existing text has an element of imitation to it; in fact, every theatrical text is always already an imitation of human behavior (*menschliches Verhalten*), constrained by its own set of imperatives. There is essentially no difference between reproducing the small details of the script and those of the *Modell*:

> What difference does it make if you find in the script that Courage gave the peasants money for burying the mute Kattrin before departing, or if you find in studying the model that she counted it out in her hand and put a coin back into her leather pouch? In truth you'll find only the former in the script, the latter in Weigel's figure in the model. Should you keep the former and forget the latter? (Hecht 86).[30]

However, in arguing for the creative potential of copying, Brecht neglects to distinguish between the decision to copy (his, for example) and the externally imposed command to follow a rigidly conceived example. The former is a creative device employed not only by Brecht but by countless theatrical predecessors, from Gottsched and Lessing to Goethe and Kleist to Karl Kraus; by contrast, not even Brecht can claim to have followed the latter concept in his adaptation—except insofar as he follows his own *Modelle* in subsequent productions.[31]

---

30. "Was macht es für einen Unterschied, ob Sie im Stücketext finden, die Courage habe den Bauern Geld für die Beerdigung der stummen Kattrin gegeben, bevor sie wegzog, oder beim Studium des Modells auch noch, sie habe es in der Hand abgezählt und eine Münze wieder zurück in die Ledertasche gesteckt? In der Tat finden Sie im Stücketext nur das erstere, das zweite bei der Weigel im Modell. Sollen Sie das erstere behalten, das zweite vergessen?

31. Cf. Brecht's *Anmerkungen zur Bearbeitung*, which accompany the second production of his

Nonetheless, for Brecht the desire to create something new in theatrical production is not a sufficient reason to break with a text's performative history. Rather, with the concept of the *Modell* he insists that history must be permitted to find its own way into that which is new. The point is thus to reconsider in a radical sense the place of creativity, to claim that place not for the "original" text, nor for any single director's vision of the *mise-en-scène* but for the observing eye itself, the sophistication of which had been neglected: "Our theater [i.e., German theater] is not realistic precisely because it underestimates observation" (*Unser Theater ist schon deshalb nicht realistisch, weil es die Beobachtung unterschätzt*) (Hecht 86).[32] The witnessing eye must take note of the fragments before it and make something of them. As a result, the *Modell* ultimately introduces another dimension of historical transformation by assuring at its very foundation its own infinite variability, thus the impossibility of ever being "finished" with the past. The dramatic confrontation with a textual and performative history—the self-conscious presentation of its ruins—becomes an affirmation of the relationship to the past not as something to be overcome but rather as a means of comprehending one's own responsibility for the survival of that history. Seeing *is* authorship—is participation. It is up to the one who examines the *Modell*—the witness to its history—to view the process by which a story comes to be told and find his or her own position with respect to that story. The *Modell* is, as Brecht puts it, "not meant to spare us from thinking, but rather to stimulate thinking; not meant to replace artistic creation, but rather to compel it" (BFA 25:172).

Not all of Brecht's modifications evince such a delicate intervention into Sophocles' and Hölderlin's texts, however. Indeed, many of his changes reflect not an engagement with the "difficulties" of the texts, as he professes in his remarks on the adaptation, but a neutralization of their unsettling power. To begin, the drastic plot alterations clearly flatten the complexity

---

Antigone in Greiz, 1951: "*Adaptations of this kind are nothing unusual in literature. Goethe adapted Euripides' Iphigenie, Kleist Molière's Amphitryon. These adaptations do not impede enjoyment of the original works*" ("Bearbeitungen dieser Art sind in der Literatur nichts Ungewöhnliches. Goethe bearbeitete die 'Iphigenie' des Euripides, Kleist den 'Amphitryon' des Molière. Diese Bearbeitungen verhindern nicht den Genuß an den Originalwerken" [BFA 25: 216]).

32. "*Our actors look within themselves rather than at their environment. They take interactions between people, on which everything depends, purely as a vehicle for the display of temperament and so on. The directors use the theater pieces as motivation for their "visions." . . . We should stop this, today rather than tomorrow*" (*Unsere Schauspieler schauen in sich hinein, anstatt auf ihre Umwelt. Sie nehmen die Vorgänge zwischen Menschen, auf die alles ankommt, lediglich als Vehikel für die Zurschaustellung von Temperament und so weiter. Die Regisseure benutzen die Stücke als Anregung für ihre 'Visionen.' . . . Damit sollten wir lieber heute als morgen aufhören*). "Hemmt die Benutzung des Modells die künstlerische Bewegungsfreiheit?" interview with Erich-Alexander Winds, *Hecht* 86).

of the Greek conflict. Brecht's crude and despotic Creon, rather than representing a theoretically legitimate instance pushed beyond its own limits, now occupies a clearly indefensible position, making Antigone's the only tenable stance in the play. Creon's command to leave Polynices unburied is no longer transgression enough, since Brecht emphasizes that he orders his army to leave all enemy soldiers unburied;[33] thus Creon must kill Polynices as well. Precisely because Brecht's Creon is so wicked, Antigone's once singular act takes on the milder character of a more general protest against the injustice of state violence.[34]

What does this tendency to generalize the tragic conflict do with Hölderlin's translation, which, as we have seen, bears the full weight of Antigone's solitude in its very foreignness, in the monstrosity of its language? The shift is nearly a full reversal: while for Hölderlin Antigone's ethical stance was grounded in the imperative to preserve the dignity of difference, Brecht's heroine acts in the name of unity, for the sake of a larger community of which she is unquestionably part. The Chorus even chides Antigone for not recognizing this community before it is too late, for haughtily maintaining her separate status within the ruling class until its doom had become imminent:

> Aber auch die hat einst
> Gegessen vom Brot, das im dunklen Fels
> Gebacken war. In der Unglück bergenden
> Türme Schatten: saß sie gemach, bis
> Was von den Labdakus Häusern tödlich ausging
> Tödlich zurückkam. (BFA 8: 228)

> But she too once ate from the bread that had been baked in the dark cliffs. In the shadow of the towers that sheltered sorrow, she sat comfort-

---

[33]. By expanding a single reference by Sophocles' *Antigone* (*tôn echthrôn kaka*, "evils from our enemies as they coming upon our friends" [Jebb 5, l.10]) to an explicit proclamation, Brecht stresses that Creon acts with brutality against his enemies as well as against Polynices, which undermines any potential legitimacy of his position: "Auf rauhem Ruhplatz / Legtest, Thebe, du das Argosvolk. Stadtlos, grablos / Liegt jetzt im Freien, das deiner spottete. / Und du siehst hin / Wo einst ihre Stadt war / Und du siehst Hunde / Denen glänzet das Angesicht. / Die edelsten Geier fliegen zu ihr; sie schreiten / Von Leichnam zu Leichnam / Und von dem reichlich bereiteten Mahle / Nicht in die Höhe können sie steigen" [BFA 8: 76f.: 128–38] (*On a raw place of rest you, Thebes, laid the people of Argos. Those who mocked you and yours now lie cityless, graveless in the open. And you look to the place where your city once was, and you see dogs with gleaming faces, the noblest vultures fly there; they stride from corpse to corpse and cannot fly back up into the air after that richly prepared feast*).

[34]. See Margaret Setje-Eilers, "*Antigone* in Pre-Wall and Post-Wall German Theatre: Bertolt Brecht's and George Tabori's Power Plays," *Text & Publication* (2007), 173.

ably, until that which left the house of Labdakus in deadliness, returned in deadliness.[35]

In Brecht's view of the tragic landscape, then, an individual's fate is tied to the social relations that structure a community rather than to the will of the gods. This development is already evident in his earliest notes on the adaptation in his work journal, where he writes of his plans to reduce the role of the gods to that of "the local divinity of the people, the god of joy" (*der lokale volksheilige, der freudengott*) (AJ 795, 16. Dec. 1947). The emphasis on provinciality and the *Volk* replaces the distant hegemony of the gods and their influence on the destiny of mortals; Antigone's recognition of her place within the community thus emerges with the discovery that she can no longer isolate herself, that her actions and those of her family bear both personal and public consequences. Indeed, Brecht already saw this social aspect incorporated in Sophocles' *Antigone,* which made it a particularly apt choice for his project of "Durchrationalisierung." A *Berliner Zeitung* review of the Greiz production in 1951 summarizes:

> Brecht says that he chose Sophocles' drama for his adaptation because it is the only tragedy of antiquity that is not completely stifled by the inconceivable doom of a mystical fate. For him it was a matter of showing how social forces—that is, those that can be recognized and mastered by humans—hold sway in the course of the tragedy.[36]

Brecht's displacement of the interplay between gods and mortals in favor of a network of social forces unbound from divine intervention represents less his quibble with Sophocles' (or Hölderlin's) source text than his wholesale rejection of Aristotelian conventions in the framing and staging of tragedy. The move out of the "ideological fog" is simultaneously a break with the force of tragedy as a closed universe in which the audience sympathizes with the hero's inescapable plight and fears for itself as a result.[37] To be more

---

35. In producing a translation of Brecht's adaptation I have consulted Judith Malina's translation from 1984; however, because that translation is fairly transformative, I often resort to my own more literal renderings. See Judith Malina, *Sophocles's Antigone in a version by Bertolt Brecht* (New York: Applause, 1984), 49.

36. *Berliner Zeitung* no. 270, 20 November 1951: "Brecht sagt, dass er das Drama des Sophokles deshalb für seine Bearbeitung gewählt habe, weil es das einzige in der Antike sei, das nicht durch das unbegreifliche Verhängnis eines mystischen Schicksals vollständig erdrückt wird. Ihm aber kam es darauf an, im Gang der Tragödie das Walten gesellschaftlicher, also durch den Menschen erkennbarer und zu beherrschender Kräfte deutlich zu machen."

37. With these modifications to the structure of classical tragedy, Brecht means to mobilize the

precise, then, Brecht's polarizing stance with respect to Aristotle is in fact more directly informed by Lessing's reading of Aristotle than by the *Poetics* themselves, which barely address at all the issue of fate in relation to the gods. Aristotle's discussion of tragic plot is more closely linked to the notion of *philia*, which refers both to family relations and to the social matrix more generally.[38] Understanding tragedy as the collapse of the social order thus ironically places Brecht closer to Aristotle than he would ever have cared to imagine. Nor is it entirely clear, as we will see, that Brecht's erasure of the divine instance (and finally that of kinship) from Hölderlin's text and his consequent shift to a wholly social register is at all successful in disrupting the attraction of empathy (*Einfühlung*).

Fate therefore becomes for Brecht a matter of social rather than divine intervention, culminating in the recognition of the subject's inscription in the community rather than the unsettling exposure to the limits of the self. As a result, the choral passage affirming the monstrosity of every human being in Hölderlin's text—the ineluctable relation to a "nothing" we can only represent as death—is transformed in Brecht's version into a disavowal of excess (*Maßlosigkeit*) as the internal enemy of the self. There is no longer any explicit mention of death at all.

> Überall weiß er Rat
> Ratlos trifft ihn nichts.
> Dies alles ist grenzlos ihm, ist
> Aber ein Maß gesetzt.
> Der nämlich keinen findet, zum eigenen
> Feind wirft er sich auf. (BFA 8: 209)

> In every case he knows what to do; nothing leaves him at wit's end. All of this is limitless to him, but a limit has been set. For he who does not find one becomes his own enemy.

Brecht's Chorus thus comes to a conclusion nearly opposite from that of Hölderlin's: it is the duty of the subject to join the community, thus to reject the solitude that for Hölderlin was essential to tragic experience.

---

transition from an Aristotelian tradition to a "theater of the scientific age." For an interesting account of the development of this "Galilean" theater out of the ruins of the Aristotelian one, see David Roberts, "Brecht and the Idea of a Scientific Theater," in *Brecht aufführung—Brecht performance: Brecht-Jahrbuch 13 (1984)*, ed. John Fuegi et al.: 41–60.

38. For a fascinating discussion of the role of the *philos* in Greek tragedy, see Elizabeth Belfiore, *Murder among Friends: Violation of Philia in Greek Tragedy* (New York: Oxford, 2000).

Nicht den Magen
Kann er sich füllen allein, aber die Mauer
Setzt er ums Eigene, und die Mauer
Niedergerissen muß sie sein! Das Dach
Geöffnet dem Regen! Menschliches
Achtet er für gar nichts. So, ungeheuer
Wird er sich selbst. (BFA 8: 209)

He cannot fill his stomach alone, but he builds a wall around that which is his own, and the wall must be torn down! The roof opened to the rain! He does not value what is human. So he becomes monstrous to himself.

Insofar as monstrosity is linked to the isolation of those who do not value "Menschliches"—do not recognize the relationship of mutual dependency that defines the community—it can no longer be said to characterize each and every subject, as it did so clearly for Hölderlin. This distinction is not at all innocent in its implications for the critical stance Brecht means to inspire in his audience. According to the definition set forth by Brecht's Chorus, only Creon is "ungeheuer"—and we knew that from the start.[39] Rather than bringing it to acknowledge the pervasiveness of monstrosity among all subjects, Brecht permits his audience to distance itself from that monstrosity, to call it by name: *Creon*. Or, as the messenger in Brecht's text calls him, *mein Führer*.

Thus it is far too limited to understand Brecht's *Antigone* text merely as an historical document that condemns Nazi ideology by drawing crude parallels between Creon's Thebes and the Third Reich. A charitable reading would perhaps maintain that the disavowal of monstrosity implicit in Brecht's alterations to the source texts mirrors the epic-theatrical divide between spectator and stage, allowing the audience to reflect critically on Creon's actions and recognize the brutality behind them. However, there may also be more troubling consequences—consequences that, despite the intricacy of the *Modell*, remain out of the dramatist's control. Though Brecht's *Spielweise* explicitly and actively seeks to deny the possibility of identification with any of the figures onstage, there is within the text an

---

39. Creon's barbarism and violence are evident not only in his speech but in the stage directions as well, where he often threatens or disparages his subjects; for example, after hearing the message that Polynices's body has been buried, he "stands up, approaches the watchman threateningly . . . and, standing behind his bodyguard, tests the sword blade with his thumb" (*steht auf, geht drohend auf den Wächter zu, . . . und prüft, hinter dem Leibwächter stehend, die Schwertschneide beziehungsvoll mit dem Daume*n [AB 87]).

implicit temptation to identify with Antigone, duly noted by the interlocutor in the *Modell* and not fully acknowledged in the director's response. Insofar as this temptation accompanies the unmistakable message *not* to identify with Creon, it clearly places audiences on the side of social justice, effectively protecting them from the exposure of any potential culpability of their own.[40] In the scene in which Antigone is brought to Creon as a prisoner, she wears a high, wide board on her back (making her into, in Brecht's words, a "center of unrest" [*Unruhezentrum*] on the stage), and at this point a question arises in the remarks with respect to an audience's possible sympathy.

> QUESTION: Surely this is finally the place where the whole audience can just sympathize with Antigone, for it will feel what she feels and share her arguments?
> ANSWER: It is more important that Antigone feels what the whole audience feels and shares its arguments. It is a considerable temptation for the actress playing Antigone to seek the audience's sympathy in her exchange with Creon. In succumbing to this temptation, however, she would cloud the audience's view into the beginnings of discord in the ruling class, to which Antigone belongs, and endanger the speculations and emotions that this view can provide. (BFA 25: 106)[41]

The "Antwort" does not answer the question at all. The question concerns staging—how Brecht and Neher present Antigone in a crucial scene—and not, as the response seems to indicate, how an actress chooses to portray her. In fact, the stage directions in the *Modell* do make her suffering explicit and visible to the audience: "During the guard's report Antigone staggers under the weight of the board" (BFA 25:102). As the photographs likewise make evident, sympathy is almost inescapable. And where there is sympathy with one in this encounter, there is easy condemnation of the other.

---

40. Brecht's Creon only alters his judgment of Polynices and Antigone when it is clear that the elders are turning against him; he agrees to release Antigone only to secure the support he needs to defend Thebes against attack by Argos. Thus he remains unworthy of sympathy even when he receives the message that Hämon is dead: "*Frage:* Soll Kreon im Unglück die Sympathie des Publikums haben? *Antwort:* Nein" (*Question: Should Creon in his misfortune have the sympathy of the public? Answer: No*).

41. "*Frage:* Hier ist doch endlich der Ort, wo das breite Publikum einfach mit Antigone sympathisieren kann, denn es wird fühlen wie sie und wird ihre Argumente teilen?
Antwort: Wichtiger ist, daß Antigone fühlt wie das breite Publikum und seine Argumente teilt. Es ist eine beträchtliche Versuchung für die Darstellerin der Antigone, im Wortwechsel mit Kreon lediglich auf die Sympathie des Publikums auszugehen. Dieser Versuchung erliegend, würde sie jedoch den Blick des Publikums in die beginnenden Zerwürfnisse der Herrschenden, zu denen Antigone zählt, trüben und Spekulationen und Emotionen, welche dieser Blick gewähren kann, gefährden."

This transformation of the play's antagonists and the stabilization of their conflict continue in many of Brecht's modifications to Hölderlin's text. In casting Antigone's resistance as more political than personal, more in the name of the community at large than for the sake of the brother she cannot replace, he renders impotent the painfully unique relationship between brother and sister on which Hölderlin's translation relied, leaving it simply as one part of a general family dynamic. Not only does he omit Antigone's claim that she would not have defied the state for anyone except her brother—not for a husband, not for a child—but he also mitigates the potentially incestuous desire that forged their bond; while Hölderlin presents Antigone's desire for death clearly as a desire to lie beside Polynices ("Lieb werd' ich bei dem Lieben liegen," dearly I shall lie by the dear one), Brecht modifies the phrase to include her entire family, even suggesting a return to the mother's breast: "Stilled, I will lie with the still ones" (*Gestillt werd ich liegen mit den Stillen* [BFA 8: 202]).

This subtle dilution of the personal in favor of the communal emerges directly from Brecht's rejection of the Greek gods, for Hölderlin's Antigone relies on a sense of the gods that has more to do with personal conviction (as she says of her act, *her* Zeus did not tell her to do it) than with religious convention, and her understanding of the role of fate is formed entirely within the framework of kinship relations. It is this layer of the text that Brecht, in expunging all divine names from the text, ultimately removes as well; Brecht's Antigone might as well have no family any longer, for she acts not in its name but in spite of the wall of privilege it has built around her.

As a consequence, Brecht's Antigone is notable not only for her customary resolve but also for a sheer banality, coded in the play as an essential humanity. Her behavior retains no trace of the defiant solitude that had characterized her for Sophocles and Hölderlin. Whereas Hölderlin's translation often presents an intensification of the Greek lines, Brecht's transformation reverses that tendency on numerous counts. Ismene, for one, no longer deems her sister's determination to be incomprehensible or excessive; Hölderlin's twofold declaration of excess, "It is senseless to do what is excessive" (*Überflüssiges zu thun, ist sinnlos* [FA 16: 271]), becomes the tamer "It is unwise to do what is futile" (*Vergebliches zu tun, ist unweis* [BFA 8: 202]). Meanwhile, Antigone's desire to suffer the powerful and violent ("Laß mich aber und meinen irren Rat / das Gewaltige [*to deinon*] leiden" [FA 16: 273]) is transformed into a retributive gesture, trained toward the restoration of honor where it has been disturbed:

Laß aber mich das Mind'ste tun und

Meines ehren
Wo's mir geschändet. (BFA 8: 203)

But let me at the very least honor my own where I have been disgraced.

There is no mistaking the validity of Antigone's position here, for she no longer stands only for herself. In defending her actions, she now invokes not the enigmatic gods of the underworld but rather a *sensus communis* related to conventional notions of *Menschlichkeit*.

KREON Immer nur die Nase neben dir siehst du, aber des Staats
    Ordnung, die göttliche, siehst du nicht.
ANT. Göttlich mag sie wohl sein, aber ich wollte doch
    Lieber sie menschlich, Kreon, Sohn des Menökeus. (BFA 8: 215)

CREON. You only ever see the nose in front of your face, but the order of
    the state, the divine one, you do not see.
ANT. That order may be divine, but I would rather have it human, Creon,
    son of Menoeceus.

Antigone's disavowal of the divine instance here follows Brecht's stated objectives in the *Arbeitsjournal* at the very start of his engagement with the text: "of all the gods [only] the local divinity, the god of joy remains" (AJ 795: *von den göttern bleibt der lokale volksheilige, der freudengott*). With this almost total removal of the gods from his adaptation—not only from the action of the play but from its very language—Brecht aims to isolate the "highly realistic folk tale" concealed within the "ideological fog" of the Greek. There is no place for the gods any longer now that the *Volk* has reached a point of clarity, a point at which it knows it can rely only on itself.

This self-reliance extends to the understanding of history in the text; whereas the gods were once the record-keepers of the tragic universe, meting out reward and punishment for a family's actions for generations to come, here it is the Chorus who chides Antigone as well as Creon for past missteps against the *Volk*. Yet the substance of their reproach in each case differs on a basic level. While Creon is implicated for his self-isolation in the elders' remark that he becomes "monstrous to himself," Antigone must bear their criticism for her complacency, from which she only awakened when it was in her immediate interest:

Nicht ehe die letzte
Geduld verbraucht war und ausgemessen der letzte

Frevel, nahm des unsehenden Ödipus
Kind vom Aug die altersbrüchige Binde
Um in den Abgrund zu schauen. (BFA 8: 228)

Not until the last bit of patience was exhausted and the last outrage measured did the child of unseeing Oedipus take the blindfold, brittle with age, from her eyes in order to look into the abyss.

Forced by the Chorus to remove her well-worn blindfold, Oedipus' daughter Antigone recognizes the abyss that has defined her family for generations. And in her incapacity to ascertain the importance of standing firm in resistance before it is too late, the Chorus sees the *polis* itself:

So unsehend auch hebt
Thebe die Sohle jetzt, und taumelnd
Schmeckt sie den Trank des Siegs, den viel-
Kräutrigen, der im Finstern gemischt ist
Und schluckt ihn und jauchzt. (BFA 8: 228)

Just as unseeing, Thebes lifts its feet now and giddily it tastes the victory drink, the well-spiced, mixed in the dark, and swallows it and rejoices.

Just as for Sophocles, Hölderlin, and especially Heidegger, Brecht's Chorus remains that part of the *Volk* that can isolate the errors of individuals, in particular of both Creon and Antigone. However, while Creon stands for an inhuman isolation, Antigone takes a step that the elders finally describe in a collective sense; hers is an error shared by the community as such, and therefore it does not isolate her. On the contrary, it permits the *polis* to participate vicariously in her error and subsequent awakening—permits, if not identification in a strict sense, then a positive point of comparison: like Antigone, the community is challenged by the Chorus to peer into the abyss and recognize its own complacency. And as the title of a 1951 GDR review of the Greiz production indicates, the modern audience is sure to follow: "Theben—Chur—Greiz."

Within the logic of Brecht's epic theater, Antigone's act thus represents what Brigid Doherty has described as an imitable gesture, captured in Brecht's hybrid concept of "mitahmen," which he used in conversation with Benjamin in 1931.[42] Neither synonymous with identification (*mitleiden*),

---

42. Brigid Doherty, "Test und *Gestus* in Brecht and Benjamin," MLN 115:3 (2000): 452. Doherty develops the idea of "mitahmen" as a relation in which the spectator's response to a character "will always be mimetic before it can be empathetic"; emphasizing not "one man's innermost likeness

nor entirely comparable to imitation (*nachahmen*), "mitahmen" still invites the spectator's participation in the spectacle in another sense, one more on the level of self-conscious recognition than the emotional investment of classical *Mitleid*. Antigone acts not for the sake of her brother but rather in the name of her community, and the spectator who recognizes this gesture can find a point of resonance in that action.

> FRAGE: Vertritt Hämon das Volk?
> ANTWORT: Nein.
> FRAGE: Vertritt der Chor der Alten das Volk?
> ANTWORT: Nein.
> FRAGE: Welche Stellung einzunehmen soll dann das Publikum veranlaßt werden?
> ANTWORT: Die des Volks, das dem Zerwürfnis der Herrschenden zusieht. (BFA 25: 118)
>
> QUESTION: Does Haemon represent the people?
> ANSWER: No.
> QUESTION: Does the Chorus of elders represent the people?
> ANSWER: No.
> QUESTION: What position should the audience then be induced to take?
> ANSWER: That of the people observing the dissension of the ruling class.

The rejection of a totalizing violence that encompasses the primary substance of Brecht's adaptation thus bears within itself another totalizing form, the establishment of a new community—with the audience—around the exclusive valuation of precisely that rejection. The past incarnations of resistance that Antigone invokes in the gods, in the singular bond between siblings, have lost their relevance, and in their place the tragic heroine appears not as a figure of difference but purely as representative of the *Volk*—thus of an audience that can observe from a distance the dissension and violence that will undermine the ruling class from within. An audience that can safely claim political resistance, therefore, as its own true path.

Where *Modell* stops and text begins, then, the resonance of Brecht's *Antigone* as critical instrument begins to dampen. Perhaps Brecht would argue that it does not matter, that the evolution of performance contains within it the gradual, inevitable ruination of the text per se. However, it does matter,

---

to another, but their interchangeability, a kind of identity the audience will be encouraged to observe critically rather than imitate sympathetically" (453).

for the *Modell* already shows how the dialectics of past and present *can* narrate a history that includes those ruins rather than dispenses with them. On this point, Brecht's *Antigonemodell* truly remains a work in progress, not only by virtue of its expressed claim to a provisional status but also in those moments in which its best intentions might be called into question.

EVEN IF his epic theater is without question a didactic method, Brecht bristled at the notion, newly popularized during the 1940s by proponents of the Stanislawski method, that theater should have a moral basis.[43] That tragedy, and the *Antigone* in particular, had long been understood to confront ethical quandaries relevant to a modern context did not alter his view; as he writes in his work journal, the imposition of a moral message onto art does not constitute an ethical position with respect to art. The only ethical maxim that truly counts is not to lie to the audience.

> What disgusts me most of all about the German Stanislawski book is the pedestrian moral tone (*der hausbacken moralische Ton*) . . . whereas the actor is really only bound to one moral precept: that in presenting human nature he not lie, for instance for the sake of a form of morality. . . . In S. he owes everything imaginable to the "word," or to the "work"; but in reality he owes everything to the audience and, insofar as he ought to have the same concerns, to himself. (AJ 810 [4 Jan. 1948)[44]

The interpreter of a text is in no way obligated to the text *an sich*, then; the ethical dimension of art inheres in its reception. Because, as Brecht writes in the foreword to the *Antigonemodell 1948*, it is impossible to try and summon the "spirit of antiquity" (*Geist der Antike*) in a modern age, adaptation must have a different task: "Even if one should feel obligated to do something for a work such as the Antigone, we could only do so insofar as we let it do something for us" (BFA 25: 75).[45] Any obligation to the ancient text only makes sense when expressed through the text's evolution; preservation merely for its own sake is not preservation at all. On this point

---

43. See Dieter Baldo, *Bertolt Brechts "Antigonemodell 1948": Theaterarbeit nach dem Faschismus* (Cologne: Pahl-Rugenstein, 1987).

44. An interesting counterpoint to Brecht's imperative here is Arendt's view that Brecht himself, who had always spoken the unvarnished truth about the social order, began to "lie" after the second World War, composing and performing work "as if one were standing in the midst of the old, familiar class conflict and as if ethnic persecution were an optical illusion" (Arendt 100).

45. "Selbst wenn man sich verpflichtet fühlte, für ein Werk wie die *Antigone* etwas zu tun, könnten wir das nur so tun, indem wir es etwas für uns tun lassen."

Brecht echoes Benjamin's view of translation as an integral part of a text's history or "afterlife": translation (by an "author"), like performance by an actor, is a means of making a piece of language resonate—in a specific time and place—as truth.

For Brecht, it is in historical moments of crisis that this resonance might most productively occur: "the primary effects seem to be concentrated where primary transitions, decisions, collapses, catastrophes have taken place" (AJ 821 [3 March 1948]). The theater in ruins is the space from which the dramatic stuff of the past can rise, phoenix-like, to new levels of meaning. Its conveyance into the present day depends upon that relationship to catastrophe, insofar as it constantly evokes both the hard lessons of sifting through the rubble and the exhilarating potentiality of transformation: *das Vorher und das Nachher*. The *Antigonemodell* does not only make reference to itself as theatrical device but also "models" a relationship to history that takes shape as its particular form of tragic effect: "main thesis: that a certain kind of learning is the most important pleasure of our age, so that it must assume a significant place in our theater" (AJ 835 [18.8.48]).[46]

What, then, is the audience supposed to glean from *Antigone*? If not the intrinsic value of the "spirit of antiquity" on the one hand, if not the correlations between the themes of Greek tragedy and contemporary politics on the other: what can Antigone give her modern audience? Is there a middle ground between rigid preservation and total transformation? And if there is, how can we conceive of it?

On this point Brecht seems to have benefited from his own hindsight. In his remarks on the Greiz production in 1951, he withdraws from his categorical denial that the play offers any moral standpoint whatsoever. However, the ethical framework he sees in Antigone's act does not permit a modern audience to find solace in her heroism; indeed, the humanity that her act represents now appears as astonishingly callous.

> Die grosse sittliche Tat der Antigone, die sich gegen den Tyrann Kreon auflehnt, besteht darin, dass sie, bewegt durch tiefe Menschlichkeit, nicht zögert, durch offenen Widerstand das eigene Volk in die Gefahr des Besiegtwerdens in einem Raubkrieg zu bringen. (AB 113)

> The great ethical act of Antigone, who rebels against the tyrant Creon, consists in the fact that she, moved by profound humanity, does not hesitate

---

46. "hauptthese: daß ein bestimmtes lernen das wichtigste vergnügen unseres zeitalters ist, so daß es in unserm theater eine große stellung einnehmen muß."

to place her own people, through her open resistance, in danger of being defeated in a predatory war.

Antigone's great ethical gesture, then, is this: she acts as she must, with no regard for her security or for anyone else's. She does not hesitate to take a risk that could destroy her entire community. And for what? No longer only in the name of her brother; that has already become clear. Brecht instead emphasizes that she is "moved by profound humanity" in her decision to act, suggesting that her ethical action is based in a more fundamental sense of *Menschlichkeit* than the substance of society can offer on its own. It is for this reason that Brecht can claim that his adaptation of the play is not "moral" in a conventional sense; the "profound humanity" that inspires Antigone here is not synonymous with the recognition of "human rights" as responsibility to a community of others. It may even run counter to that, insofar as her ethical stance of open resistance leads her to place that community in danger. Conventional morality is suspended, the ethical sacrificed for the sake of a cause that will shake the community to its core. Hers is an essentially irresponsible ethics, then, and yet Brecht insists on its value nonetheless.[47]

The interplay between texts presented in Brecht's *Modell* follows a similar pattern: his practice of adaptation is both responsible and irresponsible, both reverent and impudent with respect to its sources. Its only ethical claim may lie in the willingness, even determination, to sacrifice the status quo—the integrity of the text—for the sake of its audience. As for Antigone herself, responsibility to the past only carries weight when paired with the resolution to change, no matter what the consequences.

Even if Brecht's often fierce defense of the imitative dimension of his *Modell* might undermine this interplay of *Vorher* and *Nachher* in some ways, there is no question that his insistence on accountability to the past in and through change emerges out of a profound dismay—a disillusionment with a post-war German culture in which "'going on' is the parole, we defer and repress" (*es wird verschoben und es wird verdrängt*) (AJ 814 [6. Jan.1948]).

---

47. Kierkegaard's account of Abraham in *Fear and Trembling* offers a similar viewpoint, though obviously tied unlike Brecht's *Antigone* to to the problem of faith. Hent DeVries points out, for example, that Abraham's ordeal shows that in every genuine decision, the ethical has to be sacrificed in the name of an ab-solute duty or obligation. For Kierkegaard, the name of that ab-solute would be "God." "Thus, to say "à Dieu" is to say adieu to the ethical order of universal laws and human rights by responding to a singular responsibility towards an ab-solute other" [33]. Thus I sacrifice the totality of all others; but this does not lessen my responsibility to all the others. Hence I become more guilty as I become more responsible; I remain a hostage in my obligation to those others (de Vries 34). This results in a double bind: "in being responsive and responsible, one must, at the same time, also be irresponsive and irresponsible."

What Hannah Arendt describes as Brecht's deep-seated capacity to sympathize (*mitzuleiden*) and consequent commitment to transforming sympathy (*Mitleid*) into anger (*Zorn*) finds a direct parallel in Antigone's resolution to take action at all costs:

> "The classics," Brecht says, "were the most sympathetic of all men" (and as everyone knows, in Brecht's encoded language the classics are Marx, Engels and Lenin); they distinguish themselves from "unknowing natures" insofar as they "transformed sympathy into anger," because they knew that sympathy is "what one does not deny those to whom one denies help." One can get rid of sympathy if one "does not put oneself in the place of a suffering person in order to suffer, but rather to end his suffering." Thus Brecht arrived at the same conclusion as Machiavelli, whom he scarcely could have known: Whoever wants to take political action must "learn how not to be good."[48]

Brecht's engagement with tragedy thus offers a touchstone for political action not in the name of sympathy (or even of fear for the self, as Lessing might have it) but outrage. Antigone is not a pitiable figure in Brecht's vision—despite the claims to the contrary noted above, for him she is not even a sympathetic figure—and her action strikes the audience not because it evokes the bonds of kinship or the unwritten *dike* of the gods but because it restores authority to the collective where tyranny had reigned. It is surely no coincidence that the Chorus, emboldened by Antigone's apparently reckless deed, turns on Creon when he concedes that the war with Argos has not ended after all.

> Kreon, Sohn des Menökeus
> Immer folgten wir dir. Und Ordnung
> War in der Stadt; und hieltst uns vom Halse
> Unsere Feinde allhier . . . ;
> Und die von Zwietracht leben, die Schreier mit
> Langen Mägen und großen Lungen am Marktplatz
> Redende, weil sie bezahlt sind, oder weil nicht bezahlt,

---

48. "Die Klassiker," sagt Brecht, "waren die mitleidigsten aller Menschen" (und in Brechts verschlüsselnder Sprache sind die Klassiker bekanntlich Marx, Engels und Lenin); sie unterscheiden sich von "unwissenden Naturen" dadurch, daß sie Mitleid sogleich in "Zorn verwandelten," weil sie wußten, daß Mitleid das ist, "was man denen nicht versagt, denen man Hilfe versagt." Man kann also das Mitleid loswerden, wenn man sich "in die Leidenden nicht, um zu leiden, versetzt, sondern um ihre Leiden zu beenden." So kam Brecht zu dem gleichen Schluß wie Machiavelli, den er schwerlich kannte: Wer politisch handeln will, muß "lernen, nicht gut zu sein" (Arendt 93).

Jetzt schreien sie wieder und haben
Mißlichen Stoff auch: hast du denn
Etwa allzu Gewaltiges anbegonnen, Sohn des Menökeus? (BFA 8: 233f.)

Creon, son of Menökeus, we have always followed you. And there was order in the city; and you kept our enemies from our throats. [. . .] And those who live from discord, the rabble-rousers with empty stomachs and strong lungs, speaking at the marketplace because they have been paid, or because they have not been paid, now they cry again and also speak of dangerous things: did you perhaps take on something all too violent, son of Menökeus? (cf. Malina 55f.)

The stage directions for this passage mirror that exchange of authority: "The elders surround Creon. Their tone changes completely, now they speak to him as masters" (BFA 8: 149). By the time a messenger arrives with grave news from the battlefield (the young Theban soldiers, including Creon's older son Megareus, have all been slaughtered in a bloody confrontation, and the Argives are now on their way to Thebes, which can no longer defend itself), Creon is forced to submit to their counsel: "Zum Felsgrund / Eile und löse die Grabschütterin schnell / Antigone löse!" (BFA 8: 156: *To the cliff base / Hurry and quickly release the pourer of grave dust / Release Antigone!*).

While Antigone may model in word and deed a challenge to tyranny in the name of a more basic justice, however, her defiance is no longer the issue by the end of Brecht's play. Indeed, within the framework of the plot it proves not to have had any effect at all; as Brecht's versification of the play (the *Antigone-Legende*) indicates, the elders simply follow their leader into oblivion.

Und elend und furchtsam
unbelehrbar, stolperte er, der viele geführet,
jetzt der stürzenden Stadt zu. Aber die Alten
folgten dem Führer auch jetzt, und jetzt in Verfall und Vernichtung.

And wretched and frightfully unteachable, he who led many now staggered toward the falling city. But the elders still followed the leader, even now into decay and destruction.

Not only Creon is "unteachable," as it turns out. But by depicting the unteachable in its demise, Brecht attempts to open up a space from which to teach. This is what Antigone "can do for us," in his words: the quaking of the rule of law, though stilled by the end of the play, becomes conceivable, while its weary reinscription is exposed as ethically bankrupt. Brecht's reproach that the immediate past "is deferred and repressed" (*wird verschoben und . . . verdrängt*) thus takes on concrete form as the Theban elders follow Creon, one by one, off the stage.

By contrast, Antigone's earlier exit becomes all the more powerful in light of this pathetic exit by Creon and the Chorus:

> Nicht, ich bitt euch, sprecht vom Geschick.
> Das weiß ich. Von dem sprecht
> Der mich hinmacht, schuldlos; dem
> Knüpft ein Geschick! Denkt nämlich nicht
> Ihr seid verschont, ihr Unglückseligen.
> [. . .] Euch beweine ich, Lebende
> Was ihr sehen werdet
> Wenn mein Auge schon voll des Staubs ist! Liebliche Thebe
> Vaterstadt! Und ihr, Dirzäische Quellen
> Um Thebe rings, wo die Wagen
> Hochziehn, o ihr Haine! Wie schnürt's mir den Hals zu
> Was dir geschehen soll! Aus dir sind kommen
> Die Unmenschlichen, da
> Mußt du zu Staub werden. Sagt
> Wer nach Antigone fragt, sie
> Sahen ins Grab wir fliehn. (BFA 8: 127)

I beg you, do not speak of fate. I know that. Speak of him who condemns me in innocence; he has a fate attached to him! Don't think that you've been spared, you unfortunate ones. [. . .] I weep for you, living ones, for what you will see after my eyes are already filled with dust! Lovely Thebes, father city! And you, springs of Dirce encircling Thebes, where the wagons gather, oh you groves! How it chokes me to think of what shall happen to you! The inhuman ones have emerged from your midst, so you must turn to dust. Tell those who ask about Antigone that you saw her flee into the grave.

As Antigone already knows here, the demise of a human being does not result from the gods' imposition of fate but from the actions of other men. And the demise of an entire city will follow. Authority undermines itself when its grasp of power becomes too desperate; Antigone is the only one to recognize that in the end, though the audience is meant to observe it as well. Likewise, where the original held sway over the translation, the *Modell* undermines that authority; the remnants of the past combine with glimpses of the present, and all of it stands as a record only long enough to be changed in the act of imitation as infinite variation. Aestheticized politics tumble into ruins; meanwhile, art gains a political voice in that very same rupture.

CONCLUSION

Re-writing

> Das ist die Lage.
> Geschichte, blutige Koloratur.
> Mehr Atem braucht sie als ein Bote hat.
> Unfertig ist sie in jedem Augenblick.
> Schon scheint vieles besser zu sein. Plötzlich
> brichst du ein auf der Stelle, auf der du stehst.
> Du fängst an zu graben in der Geschichte,
> die nichts entschuldigt, nur erklärt, warum
> es schwer ist, einen Grund zu finden für Schlaf
> und Appetit, ein kurzes Leben lang.[1]

> That is the situation. History, bloody coloratura. It needs more breath than a messenger has. In every moment it is incomplete. Much already seems better. Suddenly you appear, in the place where you stand. You begin to burrow into that history that excuses nothing, only explains why it is so difficult, for an entire brief life, to find reasons for sleep and appetite.

THE STORY has been told now, more than once. Does that mean we have come any closer to it? In his eloquent discussion of the Lutheran Bible's historical significance, Franz Rosenzweig describes the "miraculous" moment in the history of translation in which the foreign work becomes, for better or for worse, a native text, when "the receiving people comes forth of its own desire and in its own utterance to meet the wingbeat of the foreign work."[2] Sophocles' tragedies might be said to have had their miracle in

---

1. Martin Walser, "Prolog," in *Sophokles. Antigone. Übersetzt von Friedrich Hölderlin. Bearbeitet von Martin Walser und Edgar Selge* (Frankfurt: Insel, 1989), 1.

2. Franz Rosenzweig, "Scripture and Luther," in *Martin Buber and Franz Rosenzweig, Scripture*

Hölderlin's translation, in the "sensation" (as Rosenzweig described Luther's translation) of its clash with the German language and the perceived madness of its form. Tragedy had already begun to have its German moment before Hölderlin's texts made their disquieting debut, but his particular approach to the Greeks stands out for its longevity as well as its resistance to systematic resolution. Ultimately Hölderlin's translation has changed the modern tragic landscape not because of its sheer legibility, as was the case with Luther's Bible, but because of its challenges to reading; it compels, continuously and without end, its own revisitation. Indeed, it might be argued that Rosenzweig and his co-translator, Martin Buber—who claimed to have been dismayed precisely at the expressive beauty of Luther's translation, its "smoothed-over conceptual language"[3]—eventually followed a path of translation already laid out by Hölderlin.

As we have already seen in Brecht's adaptation, the ongoing confrontation in the twentieth century with the gaps and incoherencies of these Sophocles translations mimics for some readers the challenge of engaging with an even more incomprehensible history. The struggle with the text figures as a struggle with the past and thus is aligned with a certain approach to history that leaves wounds open. As a result, not just the tale but also its telling amount to "bloody coloratura." "In every moment it is incomplete": we tell that tale to no end, rummaging in its darkest corners for something that would show us how to finish. Yet its meaning—and its conclusion, its burial, as it were—eludes us, for with every shift of light or circumstance we must look upon it differently.

Since Brecht's 1948 production, Hölderlin's Sophocles has remained at the forefront of German classical reproductions: Carl Orff set Hölderlin's *Antigone* to an operatic score for the Salzburger Festspiele in 1949 (Heidegger saw the 1951 production in Munich);[4] a version of *Ödipus Tyrannus*, with adaptation by Heiner Müller, was produced by the Deutsches Theater in East Berlin in 1967; and no less than seven theater companies staged high-profile productions of *Antigone* in the 1960s and 70s.[5] Brecht's *Antigone*,

---

and Translation, trans. Lawrence Rosenwald and Everett Fox (Bloomington: Indiana University Press, 1994), 53.

3. Martin Buber, "On Word Choice in Translating the Bible: *In Memoriam* Franz Rosenzweig," in Buber and Rosenzweig, 73.

4. See Otto Pöggeler, *Schicksal und Geschichte* (Munich: Fink, 2004), 175–76. Pöggeler tells an amusing anecdote about a conversation between Heidegger and Orff: "During the storm of applause after the performance, a little man walked up to Orff on the semi-darkened stage, a man whom he first took to be a stage worker: 'Thank you for reawakening classical tragedy! My name is Heidegger'" (11).

5. Pöggeler discusses the popularity of Sophocles on the German stage from the 1960s to the 1980s, citing 58 productions of Sophocles plays in the 1980s alone, but he does not specify how many

meanwhile, has also been produced and reproduced extensively, both in Germany and in various translations; Judith Malina's Living Theatre alone produced the play over twenty times in sixteen different countries (Malina vii). The incompleteness (*Unfertigkeit*) of these plays, as Walser's prologue indicates, evokes not only the text's chequered past but the inexhaustibility of history itself, the more or less constant encounter of the past with its potential topicality in the present. Such is the status of Hölderlin's *Antigone* (and to a lesser extent, *Oedipus*) in the second half of the twentieth century; Antigone is invoked not merely to call attention to the relationship between past and present but in order to "make history," to render it part of the present while (more or less) maintaining its fundamental estrangement.

In countless more general contexts, Sophocles' *Antigone* has persisted in the twentieth and twenty-first centuries as an exemplary figure of resistance against the modern abuse of political power. As Malina writes in the introduction to her translation of Brecht's *Antigone*, " . . . wherever we played it, it seemed to become the symbol of the struggle of that time and place—in bleeding Ireland, in Franco's Spain, in Poland a month before martial law was declared, clandestinely in Prague—the play is uncannily appropriate to every struggle for freedom, for the personal liberty that Antigone demands for herself" (vii). Irish theater companies, for example, have embraced the Greeks as spiritual compatriots since the early twentieth century and have produced dozens of Greek plays in translation since the 1960s (including, most intriguingly from the standpoint of translation studies, versions in the Irish language).[6] Indeed—in a gesture highly reminiscent of Hölderlin's efforts to let translation amplify dramatic effect—in nations such as Ireland and South Africa, the very act of translation into native tongues (Irish and Afrikaans) lets Greek tragedy resonate with contemporary conflicts and resist dominant hegemonies.[7] Using the classics as specimen piece also often lends enough subtlety to allow political protest to evade censorship; Athol Fugard's 1973 play *The Island,* for example, in which two prisoners on Robben Island attempt to stage *Antigone* as a protest against their imprisonment, managed to earn considerable legitimacy within South Africa while clearly denouncing state oppression (Fugard called *Antigone* "the most powerful political play ever written").[8]

---

of those productions were based on Hölderlin's translations (16).

6. See the anthology *Amid Our Troubles: Irish Versions of Greek Tragedy,* ed. Marianne McDonald and J. Michael Walton (Methuen 2002).

7. See Betine van Zyl Smit, "Multicultural Reception: Greek Drama in South Africa in the Late Twentieth and Early Twenty-first Centuries," in Hardwick and Stray, *A Companion to Classical Receptions* (Wiley-Blackwell, 2011), 373f.

8. Athol Fugard, *Statements* (New York: Theatre Communications Group, 1986). See also Ron

To be sure, some manifestations of this theatrical trend make the leap to classical text (and Antigone in particular) too effortlessly, a tendency that Seamus Heaney criticized in a commentary to his own translation of *Antigone*, which he rechristened *The Burial at Thebes:* "Antigone is poetic drama, but commentary and analysis had turned it into political allegory. . . . I didn't want the production to end up as just another opportunistic commentary on the Iraq adventure, and that is why I changed the title."[9] Insofar as Hölderlin's translations plainly resist this type of transformation, the persistent use and reuse of his *Oedipus* and *Antigone* brings an additional layer of complexity (and an echo of Antigone's stubborn resistance) to this process of "re-writing" the classics. Moreover, the back story of Hölderlin's brilliant yet ill-fated attempts at translation vibrates, at least as subtext, within any new inscription in the German context —indeed, along with the legacies of Benjamin, Brecht, and Heidegger, which likewise belong to the rich *Fortleben* of these texts. Within this context, three appropriations of Hölderlin's translations stand out in particular, both for their engagements with this difficult legacy and their provocative treatments of the texts in contemporary contexts: Heiner Müller's *Ödipus, Tyrann*, which was staged by the director Benno Besson in the above-mentioned Deutsches Theater production (1967);[10] Philippe Lacoue-Labarthe's *Antigone de Sophocle*, produced by Lacoue-Labarthe and Michel Deutsch in Strasbourg in 1977;[11] and Walser's 1989 *Antigone*.[12] Despite the prominence of their respective authors, these adaptations call attention to themselves, like those of Heidegger and Brecht, in their deference to Hölderlin as well as their energetic self-justification. Composing not only in different settings but with different audiences in mind as well, each author argues for the particular timeliness of tragedy in the present day. And not just any tragedy—Hölderlin's tragedy. Meanwhile, the sad conclusion to the poet's own life often functions as an additional layer of both history and drama; though the authors remain fairly reticent on this point in the published texts, there is no question that Hölderlin haunts the stage, underscoring in a different way the contrast between a past that can be recorded and verified and one that constantly threatens to disappear. The task of rewriting the past as mourning play (*Trauer-spiel*) thus echoes

---

Jenkins, "Antigone as a Protest Tactic," *The New York Times*, 30 March 2003: 6.

9. Seamus Heaney, "Search for the Soul of Antigone," *The Guardian*, 2 November 2005.

10. Printed as Heiner Müller, *Sophokles. Ödipus Tyrann. Nach Hölderlin* (Berlin and Weimar: Aufbau, 1969).

11. Philippe Lacoue-Labarthe, *Hölderlin. L'Antigone de Sophocle. Suivi de la Césure du speculatif* (Paris: Christian Bourgois Éditeur, 1978).

12. *Sophokles. Antigone. Übersetzt von Friedrich Hölderlin. Bearbeitet von Martin Walser und E. Selge* (Frankfurt: Insel, 1989).

the special responsibility in the writing of history: a responsibility to preserve the singularity of the past in the face of ideological pressures that threaten with transformation.

In his 1997 article "German Antigone," Hans-Joachim Ruckhäberle gives a fascinating account of *Antigone* productions (most of them using Hölderlin's translation) in the last decades of the twentieth century.[13] In 1977–78 alone, the play was featured in five different theater companies, along with Volker Schlöndorff's nod to Antigone in *Deutschland im Herbst* (Pöggeler 14). In a moment in which West Germany finds itself seized by leftist violence, reeling from the kidnapping and murder of Hanns Martin Schleyer and the subsequent suicides of Andreas Baader, Gudrun Ensslin, and Jan Raspe, *Antigone* becomes "simply too current" (*einfach zu aktuell*), as one of the executives in Schlöndorff's scene describes the film clip he has just seen; in the film, the presentation of "denied burial, rebellious dames" (*verweigerte Beerdigung, aufsässige Weiber*)—in short, a "terrorist play" (*Terrorstück*)—proves uncomfortably destabilizing to the status quo, such that not even various modes of "distancing" can prevent the executives from recommending that the film be shelved.[14]

In general, theater productions of *Antigone* at the time presented the play as an expression of political and social dissent, with Hölderlin playing nearly as prominent a role as Antigone herself. While Lacoue-Labarthe's and Deutsch's version in Strasbourg featured an epilogue in which Hölderlin appears and composes verse, Nel's 1978 Frankfurt production offered the argument that the poet himself experienced the conflicts of the play, the struggle of the individual with the state and the proximity of that struggle to madness. As Ruckhäberle points out, Günter Rambow's posters created for the Frankfurt production illustrate tendencies typical of the recent history of German Antigones: "the longing for the immediate, the primal . . . the attitude of the individual toward the state, state terrorism . . . the critique of the Germans" (Ruckhäberle 489). Paired with several citations from Hölderlin, the image of a burning chair summarizes this stance with its reference to a shattered domesticity: "The piece of furniture that might provide a certain state of sedentariness stands in the wilderness; a piece of civilization burns" (489).

---

13. Ruckhäberle, "German Antigone," in *Documenta X: The Book*, ed. Catherine David and Jean François Chevrier (Ostfildern-Ruit: Cantz, 1997).

14. Rainer Werner Fassbinder, Heinrich Böll, Volker Schlöndorff, Edgar Reitz, Alexander Kluge, *Deutschland im Herbst* (Munich: Filmverlag der Autoren, 1978). See the recent article by Eric Kligerman, "The Antigone-Effect: Reinterring the Dead of *Night and Fog* in the German Autumn," *New German Critique* 38:9 (2011), especially 16–24.

The developments that Ruckhäberle describes thus have a common consequence: Antigone becomes Hölderlin, and both present the terrible price of political and social opposition. The past as mourning play is rewritten to include the author, as tragic heroine and translator meet in their forced subjection to the "terror of normality" (489). The Antigone put on display in a yellow cocktail dress and pushed out onto the dance floor in Nel's Frankfurt production *is* also the poet packaged for mass consumption. To reduce both to a few key representative gestures guarantees popular interest by establishing the potential of both figures to bear contemporary relevance, and yet it also calls attention to a problem, namely, that the process of rewriting inevitably creates new fictions on its path to new "truths." In this respect, post-war productions that align Hölderlin's text with contemporary history do more than, as Ruckhäberle puts it, "transcend borders between presentation and action" (488). Whereas the need to respond provocatively to the problem of state violence prompts a return to Sophocles' and Hölderlin's texts in the 1960s and 70s, for the most part those responses are not concerned with the extent to which that return performs its own violence on the body of text. The possibility of making theater political—of linking presentation with action—is thus undermined from within, as the call to give voice to dissent also amounts to a silencing of the text's inherent resistance to its own actualization.

The next step in this process of bringing the tragedy in line with contemporary history is logical, even predictable, and in some ways even more violent: the Germans become Antigone. Not every adaptation's author takes that step; in fact, some actively avoid it. Brecht, of course, had explicitly rejected this comparison, claiming that "the great figure of resistance in the ancient drama does not represent the German resistance fighters" (BFA 25:74), while Heidegger had alluded to it in his conflation of ancient Greek glory with modern German potentiality. The post-war adaptations of Hölderlin's tragedy, however, face the issue of appropriation from a different perspective, inviting a manner of free association that permits recognition on any number of levels. As Walser asserts in the remarks accompanying his 1989 adaptation, for example, the parallels between Antigone's conscience and the German experience of conscience among the post-war, post-1968 generation guarantee the possibility of such free-form recognition: "Everyone is free to adapt the Antigone example in his own way. One can hear one's own voice in all of those voices that appear here" (15).[15] That recognition of

---

15. "Es ist jedem freigestellt, sich das Antigone-Beispiel auf seine Weise anzueignen. Es kann einer in allen hier vorkommenen Stimmen seine eigene hören."

"voices" implies an identification between the viewer and the play's historical points of reference, whatever they may be. Lacoue-Labarthe's and Deutsch's production, for example, which opened with Antigone and Ismene hiding in an attic, evoked for Sarah Kofman the memory of Anne Frank and thus confirmed the continuing relevance of tragedy for modernity: "And you think that a Greek tragedy translated in this way can concern us once again today" (*Et vous pensez qu'une tragédie grecque ainsi traduite cela peut encore aujourd'hui nous concerner*).[16]

In depicting the process of translation and re-writing as a tenuous balance between maintaining a link to the text's foreignness and inviting parallels to the present, Müller, Lacoue-Labarthe, and Walser contend more or less directly with the legacy of Brecht as well as Hölderlin. This is perhaps as it should be, since the engagement with a text such as Hölderlin's must also take into account its considerable afterlife. But these more recent attempts move forward from Brecht's project insofar as they are punctuated by their need to account for tragedy's significance in the present day, whether through identificatory strategies (as in Walser's or Kofman's remarks above) or a kind of post-Brechtian detachment, as Benno Besson aims to orchestrate with Müller's *Ödipus*. Either way, this is also their major shortcoming.

Authorship unbound: Müller's *Ödipus, Tyrann*

In the German Democratic Republic, Antigone was *persona non grata*. As Horst Domdey notes, the urgency of her task and the determination with which she acts irritate the "Socialist credo of reform" (*reformsozialistisches Credo*) in which the resolution of conflicts depends on the passage of time; there is no possible "futurization" of her conflict, for waiting any longer will result not in profit but in loss.[17] In this respect Antigone represents the "opposite of reform: dissidence. She provokes a *decision*, the break with despotism (*Gegenposition zur Reform—die Dissidenz. Sie provoziert die* Entscheidung, *den Bruch mit der Despotie* [Domdey 288]). Small wonder, then, that the GDR saw no new adaptations of *Antigone* after Brecht's in 1948 and no new productions of Brecht's *Antigone* after 1963 (Domdey 319n.). Nevertheless, in a fascinating analysis, Domdey locates echoes of Antigone throughout Müller's dramatic oeuvre.[18] While Domdey focuses on figures

---

16. Kofman, "L'espace de la césure," in *Critique* 379 (December 1978): 1146.
17. Domdey, *Produktivkraft Tod: Das Drama Heiner Müllers* (Köln, Weimar, Wien: Böhlau, 1998), 288.
18. According to Domdey, Müller engages particularly with Antigone with respect to questions

of personal and political responsibility to the dead and forgotten in original pieces such as *Mauser* and *Zement,* however, as well in the 1983 Medea play *Verkommenes Ufer Medeamaterial Landschaft mit Argonauten,* Müller's *Ödipus* engages differently with *Antigone,* particularly Brecht's *Antigone,* insofar as it appropriates and adapts not only classical subject matter but also the structural rubric of the *Modell.*

Müller is well known for his adaptations of Greek tragedies, of course, from *Philoktet* (1966) to *Medea* (1983). Within this progression, his *Ödipus, Tyrann* might appear to play a fairly insignificant role. The published version appeared in 1969, two years after the stage production and three years after the text was composed. It lies chronologically between two other adaptations, *Philoktet* (1966) and *Der Horatier* (1968–69), and was published just before Müller's return to more concrete socialist themes in *Mauser.* Given its obvious affinities with these "Greek" plays, Hans-Thies Lehmann concludes that the subject matter of this *Ödipus* reflects similarly on the problem of Stalinism, which Müller locates in a fundamental dissonance between theory and practice.[19] And there is no question that this dissonance permeates the play, indeed endows it with its critical thrust by emphasizing, in the figures of Oedipus and Creon, the thirst for power that masks the incommensurability of theoretical "truth" with the experience of reality. In representing the birth of this duality of theory and practice, the play both brings forth the extent to which any claim to communion between the two is shaken at its very ground and points toward the radicalization of that split in a more contemporary context, as Müller asserts in an article accompanying the program notes for the Berlin premiere: "The piece describes its (bloody) birth, its most radical formulation is the atomic mushroom over Hiroshima."[20] In this respect, Müller's rendering casts Oedipus's self-blinding in a new light: it is no longer merely an abdication from the past but also, insofar as it represents a retreat into the realm of pure abstraction, symbolic of the self-satisfied reliance on a theoretical knowledge unconcerned with political responsibility (Schulz 89).[21]

---

of personal and political responsibility towards the dead and forgotten, both post-WWII and in the context of the socialist state.

19. See Lehmann's account of *Ödipus, Tyrann* in *Genia Schulz, Heiner Müller* (Stuttgart: Metzler, 1980), 87.

20. Müller cited in Schulz 87: "Seine (blutige) Geburt beschreibt das Stück, seine radikalste Formulierung ist der Atompilz über Hiroshima)."

21. Müller, cited in Schulz 89: "Die Haltung des Ödipus bei der Selbstblendung . . . ist ein tragischer Entwurf zu der zynischen Replik des Physikers Oppenheimer auf die Frage, ob er an einer Bombe mitarbeiten würde, wirksamer als die H-Bombe, wenn dazu die Möglichkeit gegeben sei: Es wäre technisch süß (technical sweet), sie zu machen. Die Verwerfung dieser Haltung bleibt folgenlos, wenn ihr nicht den Boden entzogen wird."

This is a logically consistent reading, both with respect to this text in particular and within the larger framework of Müller's engagement with classical models. The Oedipus of Müller's *Kommentar* is a figure of brutal self-enclosure in the realm of reflection:

> ... er hat die Zeit überrundet
> In den Zirkel genommen, *ich und kein Ende,* sich selber.
> In den Augenhöhlen begräbt er die Welt.[22]

> ... he overtook time
> Caught in the circle, *I and no end,* himself.
> In his eyesockets he buries the world.[23]

The vocabulary of the *Ödipus* play itself, though it remains notably close to Hölderlin's text, evinces a subtle shift in emphasis from the question of human finitude to a more contemporary critique of the abuse of power; whereas in Hölderlin's translation, the Chorus reports Oedipus's denunciation of Tiresias indirectly to Creon ("People are saying it. In what sort of temper, I don't know" [*Man sagts. Ich weiß es nicht, in welcher Stimmung*]), Müller's Chorus attributes the slur directly to their ruler: "Spoken by the King. No one knows the reason" (Müller 42: *Aus Herrscherwort. Man weiß nicht seinen Grund*). Similarly, the Chorus's concluding remarks present Oedipus not simply as a mortal man exposed to the isolation that describes human beings' distance from the gods and from each other, as in Hölderlin's version, but as a man "who was powerful above all" (Müller 89: *der vor allen mächtig war*).

Müller's recourse to the rubrics of absolute reason and power recall his modifications in *Philoktet,* where the Greek model is altered much more radically to emphasize the tactical *Realpolitik* and moral relativism of Odysseus. However, the provenance and ultimate influence of *Ödipus, Tyrann* are also somewhat more complex. Initially, the adaptation received notably more attention than its immediate predecessor; while *Ödipus* had its première at the Deutsches Theater in Berlin in 1968, *Philoktet,* published in 1965 in *Sinn und Form,* only opened in the GDR for the first time in the mid-1970s and received little attention there (Schulz 71).[24] In a more general vein,

---

22. Heiner Müller, *Kommentar, in Sophokles. Ödipus Tyrann. Nach Hölderlin* (Berlin: Aufbau, 1969), 91.

23. "Oedipus Commentary," in *A Heiner Müller Reader,* ed. and trans. Carl Weber (Baltimore: Johns Hopkins University Press, 2001), 92.

24. *Philoktet* did have a very successful premiere in Munich in 1968. As Schivelbusch notes,

Wolfgang Schivelbusch describes Müller's adaptations of Greek tragedy as a universal "parable form" lacking in "historical and social concretion."[25] These doubts about the relevance of classical material, which are also clearly voiced in the published reactions to *Ödipus, Tyrann,* may reflect more general debates at the time about the importance of cultivating the nation's cultural heritage.[26] On the other hand, *Mauser,* the play that directly follows the publication of *Ödipus, Tyrann,* represents for Schivelbusch the fortunate synthesis of a classically tragic "collision" grounded in socialist history, a worthy successor to Brecht's *Maßnahme* (Schivelbusch 108). Yet to frame *Mauser* in this way also reveals a debt to the practice of adaptation as "reutilization"[27] in the Greek plays, particularly *Ödipus:* only that now Brecht himself is the "Klassiker," with Müller's play presenting, as Schivelbusch puts it, "a more advanced level of historical consciousness on the basis of more advanced historical development and historical knowledge" (Schivelbusch 111).

In this context of debate between a conventional devotion to the literary tradition and more controversial attempts in the 1960s GDR to establish new "Klassiker" such as Brecht, *Ödipus, Tyrann* assumes a far more intriguing status in what has been viewed as Müller's creative development. Insofar as it essentially represents a threefold claim to "classicism" (Sophocles—Hölderlin—Brecht) and at the same time insists upon its recontextualization, *Ödipus, Tyrann* relates to the past as both referent and foil, just as Müller's *Mauser* will later relate to its predecessor, Brecht's *Maßnahme.*[28] What Helen Fehervary describes as the "new historical actuality" of Brecht's drama in *Mauser* thus mirrors the far more complex process of actualization underlying Müller's *Ödipus,* in which not only language and thematics but

---

Müller's "Greek" plays were particularly well received in the West, where their presentation of more universal themes had a wider appeal and Müller was compared to Beckett. Wolfgang Schivelbusch, "Optimistic Tragedies: The Plays of Heiner Müller," trans. Helen Fehervary, *New German Critique* 1:2 (Spring 1974): 106.

25. For Schivelbusch, this emphasis on universal problems accounts for Müller's popularity with western critics.

26. See Jost Hermand, "The 'Good New' and the 'Bad New': Metamorphoses of the Modernism Debate in the GDR since 1956,*" New German Critique* 1:3 (Fall 1974), esp. 87–92.

27. Helen Fehervary introduces this term in her foreword to Schivelbusch's article, which she translated for *New German Review* (Schivelbusch 105).

28. Brecht's *Antigone* was certainly a point of comparisonon critics' and audience members' minds with respect to Müller's text and particularly Besson's 1968 production, as the "Gesprach über 'Ödipus, Tyrann'" makes clear in the published edition (133–134). Brecht's stature in the GDR at this point was unassailable, as David Bathrick has discussed; by the time he was honored in 1968 with a symposium celebrating his seventieth birthday, he had achieved an ironically "classical" status. Within five years, however, that status had been seriously undercut. See Bathrick, "The Dialectics of Legitimation: Brecht in the GDR," *New German Critique* 1:2 (Spring 1974): 90.

also dramatic technique itself (Sophocles' and Brecht's) are appropriated and "reutilized."

While the concept of his adaptation can be situated squarely within the context of Müller's creative development, however—at once consistent with and at odds with the state's view of the relevance of pre-revolutionary material—its execution raised more mundane concerns based within the political present. These concerns make their way into the text's apparatus, which like Brecht's concept of the *Modell* engages the performance and reception of a theater piece with its textual base. Yet the text produced by this mode of appropriation is Brecht's *Modell* turned on its ear: while Brecht maintained a nearly uncanny degree of creative control over the publication and dissemination of the *Antigonemodell*, Müller seems to have ceded his authorial claim entirely, offering no commentary on the text or its production in this published version. Nevertheless, this *Ödipus* is not fatherless, far from it; opinions about how to interpret his fate abound in the published text, which is framed by introductory remarks by Karl-Heinz Müller and a concluding "discussion" (*Gespräch*) between the production's director, Benno Besson, and a group of audience members.

With its multiple authors, the published *Ödipus, Tyrann* appears in theory to present a process of reception and adaptation that takes Brecht's concept of the *Modell* a step further by integrating into the textual apparatus the thoughts of the "common man." The remarks that follow Heiner Müller's rendition of the text are the transcript of a discussion involving "artists, teachers, workers, authors, housewives, state functionaries, engineers, and colleagues" *(bildende Künstler, Lehrer, Arbeiter, Schriftsteller, Hausfrauen, Staatsfunktionäre, Ingenieure und Mitarbeiter)*. This run through the gamut of GDR professions—the butcher, the baker, the candlestick maker—and the use only of single initials to identify each speaker promote anonymity, as if to suggest that anyone may have a hand in the process of re-writing.

At the same time, however, it is clear that the man behind the only identifiable initial, B, ultimately calls the shots. For despite its overtures to communal theatrical practice, the published text does have two "authors" who do not easily relinquish control over text and production: the author of the foreword, Karl-Heinz Müller, and more prominently, Besson (B). In fact, there is no indication within the transcript of the discussion or after it that Besson took any of the group's criticisms to heart. On the contrary, he spends much of the discussion defending his production from what he obviously perceives to be misinterpretation, at times seeming almost incredulous that spectators could have understood the play in this way. For example, when participants in the discussion attempt to describe the play as a tragedy of fate ("Schicksals-Tragödie") with "no spiritual relevance whatsoever to the present" (100), Besson responds in apparent frustration: "Have you seen the production? . . . And you think that in this production the tragedy of fate simply remained intact, that fate is presented in it as inescapable?" (100).[29]

The result of this theatrical tug-of-war—for the discussion after the play is obviously no less staged than the play itself—is more revealing than productive, given its context. Despite the air of indeterminacy and mutability that opens the discussion (like Brecht, Besson describes the production repeatedly as "only an attempt," "a great experiment" (*nur ein Versuch, ein großes Experiment* [Müller 95]), the book in which that discussion appears opens with an interpretation that insists upon itself quite emphatically. Ironically, a central tenet of this interpretation—which is, in effect, a radicalized version of Hölderlin's discussion—is that Oedipus' fate need not be understood as predetermined, that he sets events into motion himself through his excessive will to knowledge. A reading that insists on the indeterminacy of fate thus relies heavily on its own determinacy as a reading. While Oedipus' fate now lies in his own hands, the fate of the spectator—whose autonomy receives lip service but little else—cannot be separated from the dominant interpretation presented in the program, as K, one of the discussants, recognizes: "Everyone who believes he has seen your conception was prejudiced (*vorbestimmt*, literally predetermined) through your comments on *Oedipus*" (Müller 110). Even the word K uses to describe the influence of Besson's interpretation on the spectator, "predetermined" (*vorbestimmt*), suggests a link to Oedipus's helplessness with respect to his own fate.

Nor is that prescribed spectatorial experience meant to be inaccessible to the *reader* of this volume. Early in the introduction, Karl-Heinz Müller describes the parallels between the goals of staging the play and those of presenting it as text:

> The reader should not only concretize his point of view on Sophocles' tragedy, as with the mere reading of text, but rather should also be confronted with foreign points of view. Thus the book aims to communicate something of the process that otherwise takes place in the reception of art in the theater, where author, director, actor, theater technician, spectator—with their various opinions, standpoints, feelings, desires, abilities, means of expression—enter into communication in a production. (Müller 7)[30]

---

29. Haben Sie die Aufführung gesehen? . . . Und Sie finden, dass in dieser Aufführung die Schicksalstragödie weiterhin einfach bestehen blieb, dass in ihr das Schicksal als unausweichlich hingestellt wird?

30. "Der Leser soll nicht nur, wie bei bloßer Textlektüre, seinen Gesichtspunkt zur Tragödie des

Not only the nominal author is responsible for the text's point of view, then; everyone, in effect, is not merely invited but obliged to assume that responsibility. And in being confronted with the contributions of others to the text's development, one also comes to recognize its polyvalent complexity. The engagement with the foreign, always integral to Hölderlin's conception of Greek tragedy within modernity, thus expands as the notion of individual authorship (or individual translation, for that matter) dissolves into multiplicity. That multiplicity—foreign points of view, in the plural—is what the producers of *Ödipus, Tyrann* aim to concretize on the stage.

However, the discussion soon indicates that this mode of presentation only results in the audience's confusion and alienation from the events on stage. Despite the creators' lip service to the notion of collaborative authorship, the participants in the discussion after the play are unified only in their skepticism about the very particular valence of Besson's production. The process of re-writing, stylized in the supposedly productive communication between director and audience, has been preceded and dominated from the start by a contextualized re-*reading*, through which Sophocles' tragedy has attained a more contemporary "function"; the authors' concern is no longer cathartic release, nor the experience of the dialectics of the nation-state developing out of the polis, but rather the unveiling of contradictions inherent in the individual's confrontation with the new classless society:

> With the story of Oedipus, we can gain insight into the process through which the individual constructs himself in and outside of, with and against the new society—which took shape out of the classless and community-conscious tribal society—and about the contradictions in this process. (Müller 10f.)[31]

The introduction goes on to describe the process of re-writing explicitly as a journey of discovery with a recognizable destination, the "discovery of the piece with the actors" (*Entdeckung des Stücks mit den Schauspielern*) and ultimately "the finding of the fable" (*das Finden der Fabel*). Simply put, the

---

Sophokles konkretisieren, sondern sich auch mit fremden Gesichtspunkten konfrontieren. Das Buch will also etwas von dem Vorgang vermitteln, der sonst bei der Kunstrezeption im Theater stattfindet, wenn Autor, Regisseur, Schauspieler, Theatertechniker, Zuschauer mit ihren verschiedenen Ansichten, Standpunkten, Gefühlen, Wünschen, Fähigkeiten, Ausdrucksmitteln bei einer Aufführung eine Kommunikation eingehen."

31. "Mit der Geschichte des Ödipus ist Aufschluß über den Prozeß zu gewinnen, in dem sich der Einzelmensch in und aus der, mit der und gegen die neue Gesellschaft herausbildet, die aus der klassenlosen und gemeinschaftsbewussten Stammesgesellschaft entstand, über die Widersprüche in diesem Prozeß" [10f.].

play now stages the downfall of the individual who abandons the community and thus seals his own fate:

> The great individual, who had once brought good fortune to the community, released himself from the community. Oedipus remains alone with the power of his thought, with a body destroyed of his own accord, at a loss, superfluous (*unnütz*), no one follows him anymore (Müller 16).[32]

Not only at a loss for action but "unnütz," useless, Oedipus exchanges the infrastructure of community for the wilderness of abstraction. For Besson, this is what makes Oedipus a revolutionary figure in his time, an example of the "development of individual consciousness out of the community's consciousness" (*Herausbildung des individuellen Bewußtseins aus dem Stammesbewußtsein* [Müller 124]), whereas GDR society is involved in the reverse movement, in which individuals attempt to conceive of themselves as a social body (*Gesellschaftswesen*). Oedipus insists upon the possibility of crafting his own fate, which renders his position radical; but only an alienated audience can recognize that although he can indeed determine his fate from an individual perspective, he must also take account of the social determination of that fate, how the community affects individual identity.

Besson makes an eloquent argument here, one that is consistent with Karl-Heinz Müller's introductory remarks; however, his discussants still seem skeptical. The tone of the exchange thus remains tense, as both sides reproach one another for drawing anachronistic conclusions ("You are drawing conclusions based on today's way of thinking" (132: *Sie schliessen im heutigen Denkschema*). Yet Besson's final remarks constitute a determined affirmation nevertheless: "Our discussion proves to me, precisely through the protestations that are being made, how correct it is to stage *Ödipus, Tyrann,* and indeed in the way we have produced it: as foreign (154).[33] By emphasizing its distance from the familiar, the play's producers are able to transform the play's alienating effect on its perplexed audience into something productive. In a moment of somewhat elitist condescension, they even suggest that those who approached the discussion "naively" were able to glean the most from it: "those who approached without pre-established views, who let the play work

---

32. "Der große Einzelne, der einst der Gemeinschaft Glück gebracht hatte, löste sich von der Gemeinschaft. Ödipus bleibt mit seiner Denkkraft allein, mit eigenmächtig zerstörtem Körper, ratlos, unnütz, ihm folgt keiner mehr."
33. "Unser Gespräch beweist mir gerade auch durch die Einwände, die gemacht werden, wie richtig es ist, Ödipus, Tyrann aufzuführen, und zwar so, wie wir ihn aufgeführt haben: fremd."

its effect on them and listened (176).³⁴ The organizer "D" thus draws out of the discussion a positive outcome that is meant to apply to the theatrical production itself: the reproduction, after the audience has viewed the play, of a flexibility that combines knowledge (here, the familiarity with classical myth, *Kenntnis der Mythologie*) with openness and the ability to listen.

This obvious dissonance between the prevailing interpretation of the text and its reception reveals a fundamental point of contention in GDR culture, the suspicion of intellectual elitism that hindered the success of most "modernist" art in the 1950s and 60s (Hermand 85–86). The apparatus of this *Oedipus* production falls into a similar category. If the state's goal was to diminish the gulf between "bourgeois" art and the common people, then Besson's attempt to engage in dialogue with workers and peasants of every stripe, though politically intriguing, proves utterly counterproductive. A concluding gesture of "agreeing to disagree" hardly resolves that contradiction, given that the means of production in this case remain in the hands of the play's producers, thus on one side of the argument. While Heiner Müller himself, conspicuously silent at the moment of its publication, appears to have relinquished the play, Besson and company cannot help but claim authority (and perform that claim, both rhetorically and structurally, in their published text). The voices may be many, but the vision remains unmistakably singular.

Walser's *Antigone*

More explicitly than any of the authors we have examined so far, Martin Walser reflects in his 1989 *Antigone* on the problems of writing and rewriting history; in this sense his reading resonates with the central arguments of this book, although it does not correspond to those arguments. The relationship to the past expressed through the perils of translation, which has informed the entire progression from Hölderlin to Heidegger, Brecht, Müller, and others becomes, for Walser, a more specific point of identification between Antigone and the Germans. Simply put, Walser seeks to make

---

34. " . . . der also, der nicht mit bereits festgefahrenen Ansichten an die Sache heranging, der die Sache auf sich wirken liess und zugehört hat." Besson himself exhibits, apparently naively, an elitism disconcertingly tinged with racism when he describes how the actors in the Chorus were unable to make their movements complement their vocalizations until the producers brought in African dancers to demonstrate "wie man tanzen kann" (160). Asserting the difficulty of achieving this dimension of physical "intelligence" in modern "civilization" (160), Besson succeeds in insulting both the East German performers (who were evidently too "civilized" to dance properly) and the "uncivilized" Africans who coached them.

Antigone stand for the post-war struggle in Germany to work through the past, commonly known as "Vergangenheitsbewältigung." The focus of the play as well as her character is, after all, a "burial problem" (*Beerdingungsproblem* [Walser 9]), "because the past has not been cleared up yet" (12); thus Antigone is no historical drama but rather "an example of how to deal with one's own recent history" (12).

Walser's swift transition from Antigone to the collective "we ourselves" serves the argument that, far from requiring "topicalization" (*Aktualisierung*), the conflict of the play in its original context can easily apply to "us": "We do not have to graft our own motives onto Sophocles in order to make him useful to us. Nor must we saddle Hölderlin with topicality in order to make him our contemporary" (11).[35] Distinguishing his adaptation from Brecht's, therefore (and by extension from Müller's as well), Walser instead claims *Antigone* for modernity based on the universality of the play's themes; despite having been written 2400 years ago, he writes, it can still be "our piece" (*unser Stück*).

At the cusp of a stunning historical turning point in 1989, then, Walser places primary emphasis on the "usefulness" of the piece to highlight the correspondence between the problem of burial and a particular set of criteria for historiography, ostensibly inspired by Antigone: "The past must be swept underground, but how? As something incomparably, thus incomprehensibly evil? Or historically determined and explicable, despite all of its unique monstrosity. . . . And already, one would be amidst the buzz of voices and counter-voices (13).[36]

Walser's entire discussion in these remarks focuses on the thematics of Sophocles' play, breaking off only to offer praise for Hölderlin's translation and justification for his adaptation of it. If, however, Walser is concerned with representing our encounter with the past, with our search for a way to be "done" with it, to what extent does this concern extend to his appropriation of Hölderlin's text? He refers often enough, here and elsewhere, to his lifelong devotion to Hölderlin's lyric;[37] yet in this piece he also strives to explain why certain alterations were necessary. Evoking in positively Hölderlinian phrasing the translator's "relentlessly lyrical breadth of expression" (*rücksichtslos lyrischen Ausdrucksweite*), his "'sleepwalkingly' free use

---

35. "Wir müssen Sophokles nicht mit unseren Motiven impfen, um ihn für uns brauchbar zu machen. Wir müssen auch Hölderlin nicht aktuell aufladen, um ihn zum Zeitgenossen zu machen."
36. "Die Vergangenheit muß unter den Boden, aber wie? Als unvergleichlich, also unverständlich böse? Oder trotz aller einmaligen Ungeheuerlichkeit historisch bedingt und erklärbar. . . . Und schon wäre man mitten drin im Geschwirr der Stimmen und Gegenstimmen."
37. Cf. Walser, *Umgang mit Hölderlin*.

of language" (*traumwandlerisch freien Sprachgebrauch*), Walser describes his attempt to dramatize the translation's lyrical dimension: "No general restriction of the elevated tone's frequency, more of an effort to make Hölderlin's elevated tones useful for the purpose of Antigone [*für den Antigonezweck*]" (12).[38]

The reference to the "usefulness" of tone in the service of the "Antigone purpose" (*Antigonezweck*) is, interestingly enough, both consistent with and contradictory to Hölderlin's project; for Hölderlin, as we have seen, tone bears an effect that intensifies and complicates the effects of tragic plot. Walser, however, aims to generate a particular effect through the clarification (and modernization) of Hölderlin's language and syntax. But does this shift to the idea of making tone "useful" as a conveyance of *plot* not simultaneously constitute a "burial" of the text's strangeness, which had essentially defined it? A few glances into Walser's text certainly indicate that this has happened. One of the most striking lines of Hölderlin's translation, for example, Ismene's remark "Was ists, du scheinst ein rothes Wort zu färben?" (*What is it? You seem to color a red word*) becomes "Was ist es? Was bewegt dich so?" (24: *What is it? What agitates you so?*). The Chorus's disconcerting self-assessment "Jetzt aber komme ich eben selber aus dem Geseze" (*Now even I myself am brought outside of the law*) becomes "Jetzt verlier ich auch noch den Kopf" (58: *Now even I am losing my head*), and the striking double valence of seeing Antigone "wandeln" in the same passage (both *to wander* and *to change*) becomes flatter and more concrete: "wenn ich Antigone / seh auf dem Weg / ins alleschweigende Bett" (58: *when I see Antigone on the way into the all-silent bed*).

This reluctance on Walser's part to present the sheer foreignness of the text he is so eager to reference is significant in light of his interest in the problem of historiography, which he describes as the possibility of "clearing up" (*klären*) the past. The formal peculiarities of Hölderlin's text constitute an active rejection of that plea for clarification, a rejection that operates alongside Antigone's own refusal to be "done" with the past. Both Sophocles' text and Hölderlin's translation offer a more complex relation to the ruins of history, letting the past remain open like a wound rather than burying it underground; Antigone's defiance in the name of her brother Polynices is, after all, not simply a burial but a ceremonial gesture meant to preserve his memory. The unending responsibility to the past, despite its irritation, is central to Antigone's resistance of Creon's mandate and to Hölderlin's

---

38. "Keine generelle Frequenzbeschneidung des hohen Tons, eher eine Bemühung, Hölderlins hohe Töne für den Antigonezweck brauchbar zu machen."

method of translating, which always upholds the status of an untranslatable remainder. Re-writing the past for Hölderlin demands the preservation, even the orchestration of the distance which defines our relationship to it. Walser, in claiming simply that *Antigone* has never been "plainer" (*eindeutiger*) than it is today, misappropriates Hölderlin's project in this fundamental sense.

What exactly does Walser find "eindeutig" about the play? The cornerstone of his reading is the question of conscience and its relationship to personal and civic responsibilities. From where does conscience emerge? How is it implemented in public and private contexts? What is its relation to reason (*Vernunft*)—that is, can one follow one's conscience in a direction that is also "unreasonable" (*unvernünftig*), and what would be the implications of that decision? Antigone's act is fundamentally an act of conscience, but it necessitates her becoming guilty; it represents a *Gegenstimme*, an irrational counterpoint to the rationality of the state. She refuses to allow conscience to be proscribed by an outside instance, and in this sense exemplifies the universal struggle against state injustice: "In our intellectual history, Antigone is the first great insurgent against the captivity of conscience (*die erste große Empörerin gegen die Gefangennahme des Gewissens*) (10).

To be sure, this concern for the voice of the individual in counterpoint to the dominance of the state has been central to readings of the *Antigone* for centuries, and is particularly prevalent in recent interpretations, such as Judith Butler's and Martha Nussbaum's, which have focused impressively on the ethical complications posed in both Greek and modern societies by an outlier such as Antigone. The primary problem with Walser's reading, however, is that his emphasis on questions of conscience throughout the remarks invariably ends with the nearly imperceptible shift to "ourselves" (*uns selber*), thus to the more pressing concern with the contemporary articulation of guilt. And that guilt no longer has much to do with Antigone at all. "Is it possible to regulate, to dictate our association with our guilt? Can one association be better than another?" (13).[39] Antigone's striking courage in Sophocles' tragedy emerges not from the recognition of her own guilt; although she does voice that guilt, it is secondary to her resolve to act in spite of the assurance that she will become guilty, at least from the standpoint of the state. How, then, does this relate to the guilt that Germans bear in 1989? The comparison, when we think it through, is problematic. Antigone acknowledges in advance a guilt imposed by a human instance of law while invoking on her own side an unwritten, eternal law associated with the

---

39. "Ist der Umgang mit unserer Schuld reglementierbar, vorschreibbar? Kann ein Umgang besser sein als der andere?"

divine. What does Walser invoke in his discussion of individual conscience and ethical responsibility? In effect, he cannot invoke anything more than a guilt that is undeniable and for which he, and many others, still struggle to find words.

> The public acknowledgment of our guilt has in the meantime led to a competition which is less concerned with guilt itself than with the fact that one is always criticizing another for not expressing our guilt properly. . . . In this way one is already something positive compared with the other. The terrible negative, however, guilt, remains incomprehensible. (14)[40]

As long as words fail, guilt remains at a distance. It is impossible not to find in this statement a frustrated expression of Walser's own experience in taking controversial positions with respect to Germany's troubled history. By equating the difficulty of publicly acknowledging guilt with Antigone's dilemma, Walser places the Germans (and specifically himself) on her side once more. In Walser's defense, however, I read that equation more as a challenge than a self-congratulatory comfort. One should not take Antigone's side because she is "right," or even because she is "innocent," but because she is courageous. Because she risks something. Reminiscent of Brecht's claim that Antigone acts without regard for anyone else, Walser's attempt to provoke his readership places the heroine in the exemplary position of heeding her conscience, which is always "the ownmost thing. Anti-public as such" (*allereigenste Sache. Antiöffentlich schlechthin* [13]).

That this affirmation of risk is conspicuously absent from Walser's approach to Hölderlin's text may not be entirely unavoidable, given that he is constructing the adaptation with a specific audience in mind. Nevertheless, with his version he does describe the approach to the tragic that shaped Hölderlin's interpretation and translation. As Hölderlin did, Walser presents the argument that a tragedy such as *Antigone* does not give us answers but rather raises questions and highlights contradictions. The main difference is that Hölderlin sought to present this sense of contradiction through his translation; Walser, by striving to clarify that problematic thematically and highlight the "usefulness" of the text, manages to dampen the structural impact that constituted Hölderlin's primary contribution.

---

40. "Das öffentliche Bekennen unserer Schuld hat inzwischen zu einem Wettbewerb geführt, in dem weniger von der Schuld die Rede ist als davon, daß immer einer einen anderen kritisiert, weil der unsere Schuld nicht richtig zum Ausdruck gebracht hat. . . . Dadurch ist man selbst schon etwas Positives, verglichen mit dem anderen. Das furchtbar Negative, die Schuld aber, bleibt weiterhin unfaßbar."

A comparison of the final lines of the translation and Walser's adaptation provides a case in point of this simultaneous emphasis and effacement; while Hölderlin's line reads "Um vieles ist das Denken mehr, denn Glükseeligkeit" (*Thinking is about much more than happiness*), Walser's rendering, "Die einzige Glückseligkeit ist doch das Denken" (76, *Thinking is the only happiness*) constitutes a near complete reversal. For Hölderlin, reflection reaches beyond happiness and toward the nothingness of death; for Walser, thought is redeemed as the only legitimate form of happiness. Where Walser's reading and adaptation "settle" in happiness, then, Hölderlin's remains unsettled and unsettling (*unheimlich*), pointing to the subject's status beyond the representable, the translatable, the conceivable.

Lacoue-Labarthe: *L'Antigone de Sophocle*

Of the contemporary adaptations of Hölderlin's Sophocles discussed here, Lacoue-Labarthe's 1978 translation into French, rendered by a scholar of Romanticism and literary theory, is the most philosophically rigorous—and the most successful. Concerned less with literality than with the conveyance of a certain experience of dislocation, Lacoue-Labarthe's project includes, in its published form, both an interlinear translation and a set of remarks. The former may be a nod to Benjamin, who stated in "The Task of the Translator" that the best translation is interlinear, since no translation can be truly literal; the latter is a justly influential essay, *La césure du speculatif,* that converses with both Hölderlin's own remarks and the literary-philosophical thinking of the tragic, a line extending from Aristotle to Schelling to Szondi. Perhaps because it is an attempt to *translate* rather than to adapt Hölderlin's text—thus addressing questions about how closely it hews to the "original"—Lacoue-Labarthe's *Antigone* takes on Hölderlin's *Antigonä* in a manner different from the other appropriations we have seen in the twentieth century; because it is a translation, the author cannot simply change the text to fit a specific purpose but rather must engage in interpretation (not only of Sophocles' plot, but of Hölderlin's mode of translation as well). Lacoue-Labarthe's rendering follows closely from Hölderlin's project, precisely because he arguably thinks more about translation than about the play itself—as Hölderlin did, of course, in confronting Sophocles.[41]

---

41. In the introduction to his essay "La césure du speculatif," Lacoue-Labarthe describes his project in this light: "On n'y trouvera donc pas une 'présentation' d'*Antigone:* ces pages n'ont autre but que d'éclairer brièvement, dans la mésure du possible, le sens du travail théorique mené par Hölderlin sur la tragédie depuis le projet d'*Empédocle* jusqu'à la rédaction des *Remarques* sur la traduction de

Although Lacoue-Labarthe was one of the most prominent interpreters of Hölderlin in France during his lifetime, Hölderlin's poetry in particular has attracted a wide readership and has been translated repeatedly into French.[42] Lacoue-Labarthe's curious decision to translate one of the most difficult translations in the German oeuvre—only Buber and Rosenzweig's Bible translation seems comparable—thus does not emerge from out of the blue. Nevertheless, in his foreword Lacoue-Labarthe points explicitly at the timing of this production: "But what was important was *also* (because it is a matter of some urgency) to *listen* to Hölderlin in France, today, on the stage" (*Mais l'important était aussi (parce qu'il y a bel et bien urgence) de faire entendre Hölderlin, en France, aujourd'hui, sur une scène* [Lacoue-Labarthe 1978, 2]). The historical reference here may, as noted above, be an attempt to evoke the debates surrounding the issue of left-wing radicalism in Germany, debates in which *Antigone* frequently served as a cultural touchstone.

Although his detailed notes to the translation clearly demonstrate his constant attention to small details of Hölderlin's discourse, there is one point at which Lacoue-Labarthe's impressive sensitivity to Hölderlin's text and project becomes especially apparent. Where no one else noticed anything out of the ordinary, Lacoue-Labarthe finds a strange alteration in Hölderlin's text, the condensation of three minor figures in Sophocles' play (the guard who discovers the dust on Polynices' body, the messenger who reports Antigone's act, and the servant who describes the scene in the tomb) into a single "messenger" character. In entrusting to one voice the charge of reporting "that which cannot be represented" (157), Lacoue-Labarthe explains, Hölderlin also compels the representation to expose "the separation . . . between the properly dramatic and the narrative (the scene and its 'outside')" (157: *le partage . . . entre le dramatique proprement dit et le narratif [la scène et son 'dehors']*). The very appearance of this separation guarantees its permanence: "the tragedy never breaks away from narration and does not cease to strive, mournfully, for a 'theatricality' it can never accomplish" (157: *la tragédie ne s'affranchit jamais du récit et ne cesse de s'efforcer, douloureusement, vers uns 'théâtralité' qu'elle ne peut accomplir*). In this sense the messenger is for Lacoue-Labarthe "the pivot of the tragic structure" (157); his appearance and reappearance in Hölderlin's version give him a history and a substance that mark his presence on stage as a caesura and place him in league with the seer Tiresias, whose pronouncements are likewise defined by their narrative quality.

Sophocle" (Lacoue-Labarthe 1978, 185).

42. See Bernhard Böschenstein, "Hölderlin in Frankreich: Seine Gegenwart in Dichtung und Übersetzung," in *Hölderlin-Jahrbuch* 1988/89: 304–320.

That Hölderlin placed this structural and rhetorical disturbance into the heart of a text that constantly tests the disruptive forces of language and syntax is highly significant. Reporting in narrative form "that which cannot be represented" *is* the dramatization of the experience of falling short, of the impossibility of translation itself. Words separate their speaker from the theatrical, set him apart from the mise en scène, making evident that the entire play, at least in Hölderlin's hands, dramatizes the collapse of representation's solid ground—the persistence of remains, unrepresentable and untranslatable, to which the play relates mournfully.

Surely it is in part this separation to which Lacoue-Labarthe refers when he writes in "The Caesura of the Speculative" that *Antigone* is "the most Greek of tragedies," thus not "reconstitutable" in the way that *Oedipus* is (220); however, this very "Greekness," this insistence upon its own difference in our context, is also what makes the tragedy "modern." Sarah Kofman notes the dislocating effects in Lacoue-Labarthe and Deutsch's production, which began to take shape when the audience entered, via a decaying staircase, what looked like the attic of a bombarded house: "you are in an entirely other space than the classical stage, in a place that radically *displaces* 'theater' . . . in the space of the caesura that shatters that of representation—of radical disruption and dislocation" (Kofman 78).[43] The play that ensued was both Greek and modern, evoking in its use of French "three languages, three rhythms, three epochs" (80). If Kofman's account of the staging is reliable (and there is no indication that it is not), then translation once again becomes a crucial dimension of effect here, introducing a gap sufficient to displace the Antigone of Sophocles and let Hölderlin's Antigone emerge, only to emphasize once again *her* distance from a French audience in 1978. Yet in emphasizing that separation, Lacoue-Labarthe evokes at the same time a strange alliance between texts, between spectatorial experiences.

> That which is played out here is the infinite distance that separates Hölderlin from the Greeks and that which distances us from Hölderlin; but in both cases, what is played out in extreme distancing is extreme proximity. (Kofman 81)[44]

---

43. " . . . vous êtes dans un tout autre espace qui celui de la scène classique, dans un lieu qui déplace singulièrement le 'théâtre' . . . dans l'espace de la césure, qui brise celui de la 'représentation,' le trouble et le disloque singulièrement."

44. "Ce qui se joue là, c'est la distance infinie qui sépare Hölderlin des Grecs et celle qui nous éloigne de Hölderlin: mais aussi bien, dans les deux cas, se joue dans l'éloignement extrême, l'extrême proximité."

Kofman captures it well: for Hölderlin and for Lacoue-Labarthe, *Antigone* is "the tragedy of isolation, of the interval, of the in-between; of failure, Hölderlin's and ours" (*la tragédie de l'écart, de l'intervalle, de l'entre-deux; de la défaillance, celle de Hölderlin, la nôtre* [81]). If "we" can learn anything from Hölderlin's Antigone in particular, it is this, that language and representation can only, in the end, show us the blank spaces that gape wherever the stability of law meets its resistance, wherever translation runs up against that which it cannot master. Lacoue-Labarthe lets this strange experience of proximity dominate his rendering of the play, thus deferring more to Hölderlin's method of translating than to the events of the drama. The result is a curiously "Hölderlinian" translation and interpretation, one that refuses to resolve imperfection for the sake of purposeful adaptation.

IN THE FINAL ANALYSIS, it is evident that Hölderlin's approach to tragedy continues to fascinate and confound readers and spectators with an irresistible combination of eloquence and opacity. The unsettling effects of Hölderlin's mode of translation demand further elaboration just as emphatically as the stories they present. By not only preserving the distinctions of the source text—including the fierce contradictions inherent in tragedy—but intensifying the discontinuities that translation *must* produce, he offers the framework for an argument within modern translation theory and practice that would leave such gaps between languages open to interpretation, negotiation, and experimentation. Indeed, this gesture bears a significance that extends beyond the realm of literary studies, as Emily Apter has proposed in *The Translation Zone,* into intersubjective relationships across national, cultural, and linguistic borders:

> Cast as an act of love, and as an act of disruption, translation becomes a means of repositioning the subject in the world and in history; a means of rendering self-knowledge foreign to itself; a way of denaturalizing citizens, taking them out of the comfort zone of national space, daily ritual, and pre-given domestic arrangements.[45]

Apter's inclusion of the experience of history here points up the particular depth and significance of Hölderlin's project and its numerous adaptations in the present day—the considerable "living-on" of an exchange that refuses mere transparency, a somewhat messy history that presupposes its

---

45. Emily Apter, *The Translation Zone* (Princeton University Press, 2006), 6.

own eternal state of incompletion.[46] Indeed, as we have seen, that quality of incompleteness not only motivates adaptation but ultimately becomes enfolded within the dramatic presentation. Hölderlin's legacy, then, is not precisely in the tradition of the "querelles des anciens et modernes," understood as the attempt to situate modernity against a static or idealized notion of antiquity; nor does it suggest that modern discourses ought to translate classical material into current contexts. Rather, his attention to the theoretical problems of translation, always in conjunction with the conflicts presented within the text, allow an ancient text to open up points of contention within modernity itself. Perhaps no other tragedies could be as modern, or as postmodern, for that matter, as Hölderlin's; in the best sense of his own term, they leave room for the "tearing spirit of time," that articulation of the passage of time that cannot finally be calculated, only brought endlessly into contradiction with itself.

---

46. By contrast, Apter points out the new "will to system" inherent in technological approaches to translation, in which "everything (in theory at least) becomes translatable through the medium of digital code" (10). The sheer difficulty of Hölderlin's texts represent a stubborn (and laudable) counterpoint to this idea of translation's "systematicity."

BIBLIOGRAPHY

Primary texts

Aristotle, *Poetics*. Trans. Malcolm Heath. London and New York: Penguin, 1996.
Arnim, Bettina von. *Die Günderode*. Ed. Elisabeth Bronfen. Munich: Matthes & Seitz, 1982.
Benjamin, Walter. *Gesammelte Schriften*. Ed. Rolf Tiedemann and Hermann Schweppenhäuser. Frankfurt: Suhrkamp, 1977.
———. *Illuminations*. Ed. Hannah Arendt. Trans. Harry Zohn. New York: Schocken Books, 1968.
———. *The Origin of German Tragic Drama*. Trans. John Osborne. London and New York: Verso, 1998.
———. *Selected Writings*. Ed. Marcus Bullock and Michael W. Jennings. Cambridge: Harvard University Press, 1996.
Brecht, Bertolt. *Arbeitsjournal 1938–1955*. Berlin and Weimar: Aufbau, 1977.
———. *Aufbau einer Rolle: Laughtons Galilei. Modellbücher des Berliner Ensembles*. Ed. Ruth Berlau. Berlin: Henschelverlag von der deutschen Akademie der Künste, 1962.
———. *Die Antigone des Sophokles. Materialien zur "Antigone."* Ed. Werner Hecht. Frankfurt: Suhrkamp, 1965.
———. *Werke: Große kommentierte Berliner und Frankfurter Ausgabe*. Ed. Werner Hecht et al. Berlin and Weimar: Aufbau, and Frankfurt: Suhrkamp, 1992.
Brecht, Bertolt, and Caspar Neher. *Antigonemodell 1948*. Berlin: Henschelverlag Kunst und Gesellschaft, 1955.
Briefe von und an Hegel. Ed. Johannes Hoffmeister. Hamburg: Felix Meiner, 1952.
Der Briefwechsel zwischen Schiller und Goethe, Erster Band: Briefe der Jahre 1794–1797. Ed. S. Seigel. Munich: C.H. Beck, 1984.
Hegel, G. W. F. *Phänomenologie des Geistes*. Ed. J. Hoffmeister. Hamburg: Felix Meiner, 1952.
———. *Phenomenology of Spirit*. Trans. A. V. Miller. Oxford and New York: Oxford University Press, 1977.

Heidegger, Martin. *Elucidations of Hölderlin's Poetry.* Trans. Keith Hoeller. Amherst, NY: Humanity Books, 2000.
———. *Gesamtausgabe 4: Erläuterungen zu Hölderlins Dichtung.* Frankfurt: Klostermann, 1944.
———. *Hölderlin's Hymn "The Ister."* Trans. William McNeil and Julia Davis. Bloomington: Indiana University Press, 1996.
———. *Gesamtausgabe 53: Hölderlins Hymne "Der Ister."* Frankfurt: Klostermann,
———. *Der Satz vom Grund.* Frankfurt: Klostermann, 1997.
Herder, Johann Gottfried. *Werke in zwei Bänden.* Munich: Hanser, 1953.
———. *Werke.* Munich: Hanser, 1984.
Hölderlin, J. C. F. *Sämtliche Werke (Frankfurter Ausgabe).* Ed. D. E. Sattler. Frankfurt: Roter Stern, 1975–.
———. *Sämtliche Werke (Große Stuttgarter Ausgabe).* Ed. Friedrich Beissner. Stuttgart: Cotta; W. Kohlhammer, 1946.
Hölderlins Sämtliche Werke: historisch-kritische Ausgabe. Ed. Norbert von Hellingrath, Friedrich Seebass und Ludwig Pigenot. Berlin: Propyläen, 1923.
Hölderlin's Sophocles: Oedipus and Antigone. Trans. David Constantine. Highgreen: Bloodaxe Books, 2001.
Kant, Immanuel. *Critique of Pure Reason.* Trans. Norman Kemp Smith. Houndmills: Palgrave, MacMillan, 2003.
———. *Werke.* Ed. Wilhelm Weischedel. Frankfurt: Suhrkamp, 1974.
Lacoue-Labarthe, Philippe. *Hölderlin. L'Antigone de Sophocle. Suivi de la Césure du speculatif.* Paris: Christian Bourgois Éditeur, 1978.
Lessing, Gotthold Ephraim. *Werke und Briefe.* Ed. Wilfried Barner. Frankfurt: Deutscher Klassiker Verlag, 1985.
Müller, Heiner. *Sophokles. Ödipus Tyrann. Nach Hölderlin.* Berlin and Weimar: Aufbau, 1969.
Pound, Ezra, and Rudd Fleming. *Elektra.* Princeton: Princeton University Press, 1987.
Schelling, Friedrich. *Werke.* Ed. Hartmut Buchner, Wilhelm G. Jacobs und Annemarie Pieper. Stuttgart: Frommann-Holzboog, 1982.
Schiller, Friedrich. *Werke und Briefe.* Ed. M. Luserke. Frankfurt: Klassiker, 1996.
Schlegel, Friedrich von. *Kritische Schriften.* Ed. Wolfdietrich Rasch. Munich: Hanser, 1964.
Solger, Karl Wilhelm Ferdinand. *Des Sophokles Tragödien.* Berlin, 1808.
Sophocles. *Ajax, Electra, Oedipus Tyrannus.* Ed. and trans. Hugh Lloyd-Jones. Cambridge, MA: Harvard University Press, 1994.
———. *Antigone.* Ed. Mark Griffith. Cambridge: Cambridge University Press, 1999.
———. *Antigone, The Women of Trachis, Philoctetes, Oedipus at Colonus.* Ed. and trans. Hugh Lloyd-Jones. Cambridge, MA: Harvard University Press, 1994.
———. *The Three Theban Plays.* Trans. Robert Fagles. New York: Penguin, 1982.
The Complete Works of Aristotle. The Revised Oxford Edition. Ed. Jonathan Barnes. Princeton: Princeton University Press, 1984.
Walser, Martin. *Sophokles. Antigone. Übersetzt von Friedrich Hölderlin. Bearbeitet von Martin Walser und Edgar Selge.* Frankfurt: Insel, 1989.
Winckelmann, Johann Jakob. *Sämtliche Werke.* Ed. J. Eiselein. Osnabrück: Otto Zeller, 1965.

Secondary Texts

Adorno, Theodor W. *Noten zur Literatur.* Frankfurt: Suhrkamp, 1965.
———. "Parataxis: Zur späten Lyrik Hölderlins." *Noten zur Literatur III:* 156–209.
Albert, Claudia. "'Dient Kulturarbeit dem Sieg?' Hölderlin-Rezeption von 1933–1945." In *Hölderlin und die Moderne: eine Bestandaufnahme.* Ed. G. Kurz, V. Lawitschka, and J. Wertheimer. Tübingen: Attempto, 1995.
Allemann, Beda. *Hölderlin und Heidegger.* Zürich: Atlantis, 1955.
Apter, Emily. *The Translation Zone.* Princeton: Princeton University Press, 2006.
Arendt, Hannah. *Walter Benjamin, Bertolt Brecht. Zwei Essays.* München: R. Piper, 1971.
Arens, Katherine. "Translators who are not Traitors: Herder's and Lessing's Enlightenment." *Herder Yearbook* 5 (2000): 91–109.
Bachmaier, Helmut. "Theoretische Aporie und tragische Negativität: Zur Genesis der tragischen Reflexion bei Hölderlin." In Bachmaier/Horst/Reisinger 83–145.
———, Thomas Horst and Peter Reisinger. *Hölderlin: Transzendentale Reflexion der Poesie.* Stuttgart: Klett/Cotta, 1979.
Bachmann-Medick, Doris. "Introduction: The Translational Turn." Trans. Kate Sturge. *Translation Studies* 2.1 (2009): 2–16.
Baldo, Dieter. *Bertolt Brechts "Antigonemodell 1948": Theaterarbeit nach dem Faschismus.* Köln: Pahl-Rugenstein, 1987.
Ballengee, Jennifer. *The Wound and the Witness: The Rhetoric of Torture.* New York: SUNY Press, 2009.
Balmer, Josephine. "What comes next? Reconstructing the classics." In Bassnett and Bush 184–95.
Barison, David, and Daniel Ross. *The Ister.* Black Box Sound and Image, 2004.
Barner, Wilfried. "'Durchrationalisierung' des Mythos?: zu Bertolt Brechts 'Antigonemodell 1948.'" *Zeitgenossenschaft: zur deutschsprachigen Literatur im 20. Jahrhundert: Festschrift für Egon Schwarz zum 65. Geburtstag.* Frankfurt A.M. 1987: 191–210.
Bassnett, Susan. *Translation Studies.* New York: Routledge, 2002.
———. "Writing and Translating." In Bassnett and Bush 173–83.
Bassnett, Susan, and Peter R. Bush, eds. *The Translator as Writer.* London: Continuum, 2006.
Bassnett, Susan, and Alejandra Pizarnik. *Exchanging Lives: Poems and Translations.* Leeds: Peepal Tree, 2002.
Bathrick, David. "The Dialectics of Legitimation: Brecht in the GDR." *New German Critique* 1:2 (Spring 1974): 90–103.
Beaufret, Jean. *Hölderlin et Sophocle.* Brionne: Monfort, 1983.
Beissner, Friedrich. *Hölderlins Übersetzungen aus dem Griechischen.* Stuttgart: Metzler, 1933/1961.
Belfiore, Elizabeth S. *Murder among Friends: Violation of Philia in Greek Tragedy.* New York and Oxford: Oxford University Press, 2000.
Benn, M. B. "Hölderlin and the Greek Tradition." *Arion* 6:4 (Winter 1967): 495–516.
Berman, Antoine. *The Experience of the Foreign: Culture and Translation in Romantic Germany.* Trans. S. Heyvaert. Albany: SUNY Press, 1992.
———. "Hölderlin, ou la traduction comme manifestation." In Böschenstein and Le Rider 1987, 129–44.

Bermann, Sandra. "Introduction." In Bermann and Wood 1–10.
Bermann, Sandra, and Michael Wood, eds. *Nation, Language, and the Ethics of Translation*. Princeton: Princeton University Press, 2005.
Bernasconi, Robert, and Simon Critchley, eds. *Re-reading Levinas*. Studies in Continental Thought. Bloomington: Indiana University Press, 1991.
Bernofsky, Susan. "Hölderlin as Translator: The Perils of Interpretation." *Germanic Review* 76:3 (Summer 2001): 215–33.
Binder, Wolfgang. "Kleists und Hölderlins Tragödienverständnis." *Kleist-Jahrbuch* 1981/82. Berlin: Schmidt, 33–49.
Binder, Wolfgang. *Hölderlin und Sophokles. Turmvorträge 1992*. Tübingen: Hölderlin-Gesellschaft, 1992.
Böschenstein, Bernhard. "Hölderlin in Frankreich: Seine Gegenwart in Dichtung und Übersetzung." *Hölderlin-Jahrbuch* 1988/89: 304–20.
Borges, Jorge Luis. "Some Versions of Homer" (1932). Trans. Suzanne Jill Levine. *PMLA* 107:5 (Oct. 1992): 1134–1138.
Bothe, Henning. *"Ein Zeichen sind wir, deutungslos . . ." die Rezeption Hölderlins von ihren Anfängen bis zu Stefan George*. Stuttgart: Metzler, 1992.
Bowie, Andrew. "Non-Identity: The German Romantics, Schelling, and Adorno." In Rajan and Clark 243–60.
Buber, Martin, and Franz Rosenzweig. *Scripture and Translation*. Trans. Lawrence Rosenwald and Everett Fox. Bloomington: Indiana University Press, 1994.
Buber, Martin. "On Word Choice in Translating the Bible." In Buber and Rosenzweig 73–89.
Buden, Boris, and Stefan Nowotny. "*Translation Studies* Forum: Cultural Translation." *Translation Studies* 2:2 (2009): 196–219.
Bunge, Hans, ed. *Fragen Sie mehr über Brecht! Hanns Eisler im Gespräch*. Munich: Rogner & Bernhard, 1970.
Bunge, Hans, ed. *Living for Brecht: The Memoirs of Ruth Berlau*. Trans. Geoffrey Skelton. New York: Fromm International, 1987.
Butler, Judith. *Antigone's Claim*. New York: Columbia University Press, 2000.
Cave, Terence. "Recognition and the Reader." *Comparative Criticism: A Yearbook, Vol. 2*. Ed. E. S. Shaffer. Cambridge: Cambridge University Press, 1980, 49–69.
Chanter, Tina. "Antigone's Dilemma." In *Bernasconi and Critchley* 130–48.
Charlier, Robert. *Heros und Messias: Hölderlins messianische Mythogenese und das jüdische Denken*. Würzburg: Königshausen & Neumann, 1999.
Clark, David L. "'The Necessary Heritage of Darkness': Tropics of Negativity in Schelling, Derrida and de Man." In Rajan and Clark *79-146*.
Comay, Rebecca, and John McCumber, eds. *Endings: Questions of Memory in Hegel and Heidegger*. Evanston: Northwestern University Press, 1999.
Constantine, David. *Early Greek Travellers and the Hellenic Ideal*. Cambridge: Cambridge University Press, 1984.
———. *The Significance of Locality in the Poetry of Friedrich Hölderlin*. Modern Humanities Research Association, 1979.
———. "Translation is good for you." *The Author-Translator in the European Literary Tradition*. Swansea University 30 June 2010. Keynote address.
Cook, Bruce. *Brecht in Exile*. New York: Holt, Rinehart and Winston, 1982.
Corngold, Stanley. "Comparative Literature: The Delay in Translation." In Bermann and Wood 139–45.

———. *Complex Pleasure: Forms of Feeling in German Literature*. Stanford, CA: Stanford University Press, 1998.
———. "Disowning Contingencies in Hölderlin's *Empedocles*," in Fioretos 215–36.
Dallmayr, Fred. *The Other Heidegger*. Ithaca and London: Cornell University Press, 1993.
David, Catherine, and Jean François Chevrier, eds. *Dokumenta X: The Book*. Ostfildern-Ruit: Cantz, 1997.
de Beistegui, Miguel. *Thinking with Heidegger: Displacements*. Bloomington: Indiana University Press, 2003.
De Man, Paul. *The Resistance to Theory*. Minneapolis: University of Minnesota Press, 1986.
de Schutters, Dirk. "The Parergonality of Reading: Heidegger reading Hölderlin." In *Die Aufgabe des Lesers: On the Ethics of Reading*. Ed. L. Verbeeck and B. Philipsen. Leuven: Peeters, 1992 115–33.
Deleuze, Gilles. *Kant's Critical Philosophy: The Doctrine of the Faculties*. Trans. Hugh Tomlinson and Barbara Habberjam. London: Athlone Press, 1984.
den Besten, A. "Ein Auge zuviel vielleicht: Bemerkungen zu einem als apokryph geltenden Hölderlin-Gedicht." In Kimmerle 87–122.
Derrida, Jacques. *Glas*. Trans. J.P. Leavey and Richard Rand. Lincoln: University of Nebraska Press, 1986.
———. "Passages—From Traumatism to Promise." *Points . . . Interviews, 1974–1994*. Ed. Elisabeth Weber, trans. Peggy Kamuf. Stanford University Press, 1995: 372–95.
Deutsche Literaturgeschichte von den Anfängen bis zur Gegenwart. 5th ed. Stuttgart: Metzler, 1994.
de Vries, Hent. "Adieu, à dieu, a-Dieu." In Peperzak 211–20.
Dibble, Gisela. "'Antigone: From Sophocles to Hölderlin and Brecht." In Hartigan 1–11
Doherty, Brigid. "Test and Gestus in Brecht and Benjamin." *MLN* 115.3 (April 2000): 442–81.
Domdey, Horst. *Produktivkraft Tod: Das Drama Heiner Müllers*. Cologne, Weimer, Vienna: Böhlau, 1998.
Eaglestone, Robert. "Levinas, Translation, and Ethics." In Bermann and Wood 127–37.
Euben, J. P., ed. *Greek Tragedy and Political Theory*. Berkeley, Los Angeles: University of California Press, 1986.
Fassbinder, Rainer Werner; Böll, Heinrich; Schlöndorff, Volker; Reitz, Edgar; Kluge, Alexander. *Deutschland im Herbst*. Munich: Filmverlag der Autoren, 1978.
Fenves, Peter. "The Scale of Enthusiasm." In Klein and LaVopa 117–52.
Ferris, David S., ed. *The Cambridge Companion to Walter Benjamin*. Cambridge: Cambridge University Press, 2004.
Fioretos, Aris, ed. *The Solid Letter: Readings of Friedrich Hölderlin*. Stanford: Stanford University Press, 1999.
Fioretos, Aris. "Color Read: Hölderlin and Translation." In Fioretos, *The Solid Letter*, 268–87.
Flashar, Hellmut. "Durchrationalisieren oder Provozieren? Brechts Antigone, Hölderlin und Sophokles." *Das fremde Wort: Studien zur Interdependenz von Texten. Festschrift für Karl Maurer zum 60. Geburtstag*. Amsterdam: B. R. Grüner, 1988, 394–410.
———. "Hölderlins Sophoklesubersetzungen auf der Bühne." In Jamme 291–318.
———. *Inszenierung der Antike: Das griechische Drama auf der Bühne der Neuzeit 1585–1990*. München: C.H. Beck, 1991.
Foley, Helene. *Female Acts in Greek Tragedy*. Princeton: Princeton University Press, 2001.

Forster, Michael N. "Herder's Philosophy of Language, Interpretation, and Translation: Three Fundamental Principles." *The Review of Metaphysics* 56:2 (December 2002): 323–56.
Foti, Véronique. *Heidegger and the Poets: Poeiesis/Sophia/Techné*. Atlantic Highlands, NJ: Humanities Press, 1992.
Fugard, Athol. *Statements*. New York: Theatre Communications Group, 1986.
Fynsk, Christopher. *Heidegger: Thought and Historicity*. Ithaca and London: Cornell University Press, 1986.
———. "Reading the 'Poetics' after the 'Remarks.'" In Fioretos 237–46.
Gasché, Rodolphe. *The Tain of the Mirror: Derrida and the Philosophy of Reflection*. Cambridge: Harvard University Press, 1986.
Gourgouris, Stathis. *Does Literature Think? Literature as Theory for an Antiymthical Era*. Stanford: Stanford University Press, 2003.
Gumbrecht, Hans Ulrich. "Martin Heidegger and his Japanese Interlocutors: About a Limit of Western Metaphysics." *Diacritics* 30:4 (Winter 2000): 83–101.
Hanssen, Beatrice. "'Dichtermut' and 'Blödigkeit:' Two Poems by Hölderlin Interpreted by Walter Benjamin." *MLN* 112:5 (December 1997): 786–816.
———. "Language and Mimesis in Walter Benjamin's Work." In Ferris 54–72.
Hardwick, Lorna and Christopher Stray, eds. *A Companion to Classical Receptions*. Wiley-Blackwell, 2011.
Hartigan, Karelisa V. *Legacy of Thespis: Drama Past and Present*. Lanham, MD: University Press of America, 1984.
Heaney, Seamus. "Search for the Soul of Antigone." *The Guardian*, 2 November 2005.
Hecht, Werner, ed. *Brecht im Gespräch: Diskussionen, Dialoge, Interviews*. Frankfurt: Suhrkamp, 1975.
———, ed. *Brechts Theorie des Theaters*. Frankfurt: Suhrkamp, 1986.
Hellingrath, Friedrich Norbert von. *Hölderlin-Vermächtnis*. Ed. Ludwig von Pigenot. Munich: F. Bruckmann, 1936.
Henrich, Dieter. "Hölderlin über Urteil und Sein. Eine Studie zur Entwicklungsgeschichte des Idealismus." *Hölderlin-Jahrbuch* 1965/66: 73–96.
Hermand, Jost. "The 'Good New' and the 'Bad New': Metamorphoses of the Modernism Debate in the GDR since 1956." *New German Critique* 1:3 (Fall 1974): 73–92.
Hoffmeister, Johannes. *Hölderlins Empedokles*. Ed. R. M. Müller. Bonn: Bouvier, 1963.
Irigaray, Luce. "The Eternal Irony of the Community." Trans. Gillian C. Gill. Rpt. in Mills 45–58.
Jacobs, Carol. "Dusting Antigone." *MLN* 111 (1996): 889–917.
———. *In the Language of Walter Benjamin*. Baltimore: Johns Hopkins, 1999.
———. "The Monstrosity of Translation." *MLN* 90 (1975): 755–66.
Jamme, Christoph, and Otto Pöggeler, eds. *Jenseits des Idealismus: Hölderlins letzte Homburger Jahre (1804–1806)*. Bonn: Bouvier, 1988.
Jenkins, Ron. "Antigone as a Protest Tactic." *The New York Times*, 30 March 2003: 6.
Jennings, Michael W. "Benjamin as a Reader of Hölderlin: The Origins of Benjamin's Theory of Literary Criticism." *The German Quarterly* 56:4 (November 1983): 544–62.
———. *Dialectical Images: Walter Benjamin's Theory of Literary Criticism*. Ithaca and London: Cornell University Press, 1987.
Jusdanis, Gregory. "Farewell to the Classical: Excavations in Modernism." *Modernism/Modernity* 11.1 (2004): 37–53.

Kimmerle, Heinz, ed. *Poesie und Philosophie in einer tragischen Kultur: Texte eines Hölderlin Symposiums mit einem Bildteil.* Würzburg: Königshausen & Neumann, 1995.
Klein, Lawrence E. and LaVopa, Anthony J. *Enthusiasm and Enlightenment in Europe 1650-1850.* San Marino, CA: Huntington Library, 1998.
Kligerman, Eric. "The Antigone-Effect: Reinterring the Dead of *Night and Fog* in the German Autumn." *New German Critique* 38:9 (2011): 9–38.
Koepke, Wulf, ed. *A Companion to the Works of Johann Gottfried Herder.* Rochester, NY: Camden House, 2009.
Kofman, Sarah. "L'espace de la césure." *Critique* 379 (December 1978): 1143-50.
Kommerell, Max. *Geist und Buchstabe der Dichtung. Goethe, Schiller, Kleist, Hölderlin.* Frankfurt a. M.: Klostermann, 1956.
———. *Lessing und Aristoteles: Untersuchung über die Theorie der Tragödie. Frankfurt: Klostermann, 1941 (1957).*
Krell, David Farrell. *The Tragic Absolute: German Idealism and the Languishing of God.* Lincoln: University of Nebraska Press, 2005.
Lacan, Jacques. *Seminar Book VII: The Ethics of Psychoanalysis 1959–1960.* Ed. Jacques-Alain Miller. Trans. Dennis Porter. New York: Norton, 1992.
Lacoue-Labarthe, Philippe. "The Caesura of the Speculative." In Lacoue-Labarthe 1998, 208–35.
———. "Hölderlin and the Greeks." Trans. Judi Olson. In Lacoue-Labarthe 1998, 236–47.
———. "Poetry's Courage." In Fioretos 74–93.
———. *Typography: Mimesis, Philosophy, Politics.* Ed. Christopher Fynsk. Stanford: Stanford University Press, 1998.
Lacoue-Labarthe, Philippe, and Jean-Luc Nancy. *The Literary Absolute: The Theory of Literature in German Romanticism.* Trans. Philip Barnard and Cheryl Lester. Albany: SUNY Press, 1988.
Lefevere, André, ed. and trans. *Translating Literature: The German Tradition from Luther to Rosenzweig.* Assen/Amsterdam: Van Gorcum, 1977.
Loraux, Nicole. *Tragic Ways of Killing a Woman.* Trans. Anthony Forster. Cambridge: Harvard University Press, 1985.
Louth, Charlie. *Hölderlin and the Dynamics of Translation.* Studies in Comparative Literature 2. Oxford: Legenda, 1998.
Mah, Harold. *Enlightenment Phantasies: Cultural Identity in France and Germany, 1765–1914.* Ithaca: Cornell University Press, 2003.
Malina, Judith. *Sophocles's Antigone in a Version by Bertolt Brecht.* New York: Applause, 1984.
Marchand, Suzanne. *Down from Olympus: Archaeology and Philhellenism in Germany, 1750–1970.* Princeton: Princeton University Press, 1996.
McDonald, Marianne and J. Michael Walton, eds. *Amid Our Troubles: Irish Versions of Greek Tragedy.* Methuen 2002.
Meier, Christian. *The Political Art of Greek Tragedy.* Trans. Andrew Webber. Cambridge: Polity Press, 1993.
Mieszkowski, Jan. "Tragedy and the War of the Aesthetic." *Schelling and Romanticism.* Ed. David Ferris. Romantic Circles Praxis Series (June 2000). http://www.rc.umd.edu/praxis/schelling/mieszkowski/mieszkowski.html
Mileur, Jean-Pierre. "The Return of the Romantic." In Rajan and Clark 325–48.

Mills, Patricia Jagentowicz, ed. *Feminist Interpretations of G. W. F. Hegel.* University Park, PA: Penn State University Press, 1996.

———. "Hegel's Antigone." In Mills 59–88.

Nägele, Rainer. "Ancient Sports and Modern Transports: Hölderlin's Tragic Bodies." In Fioretos 247–67.

———. "Benjamin's Ground." In Nägele 1988, 19-38.

———. *Echoes of Translation: Reading Between Texts.* Baltimore and London: Johns Hopkins University Press, 1997.

———. *Theater, Theory, Speculation: Walter Benjamin and the Scenes of Modernity.* Baltimore: Johns Hopkins University Press, 1991.

Nägele, Rainer, ed. *Benjamin's Ground: New Readings of Walter Benjamin.* Detroit: Wayne State University Press, 1988.

Nussbaum, Martha. *The Fragility of Goodness: Luck and Ethics in Greek Tragedy and Philosophy.* Revised edition. Cambridge: Cambridge University Press, 2001.

O'Brien, Joan V. *Guide to Sophocles' Antigone.* Carbondale: Southern Illinois University Press, 1978.

Oudemans, Th. C. W., and A. P. M. H. Lardinois. *Tragic Ambiguity: Anthropology, Philosophy, and Sophocles' Antigone.* Leiden: Brill, 1987.

Pellegrini, Alessandro. *Friedrich Hölderlin: Sein Bild in der Forschung.* Berlin: Walter de Gruyter, 1965.

Peperzak, Adrian, ed. *Ethics as First Philosophy: The Significance of Emmanuel Levinas for Philosophy, Literature, and Religion.* London and New York: Routledge, 1995.

Pfau, Thomas, ed. and trans. *Friedrich Hölderlin: Essays and Letters on Theory.* Albany: SUNY Press, 1988.

———, ed. and trans. *Idealism and the Endgame of Theory: Three Essays by F. W. J. Schelling.* Albany: SUNY Press, 1994.

Pöggeler, Otto. *Schicksal und Geschichte.* Munich: Fink, 2004.

Primavesi, Patrick. "The Performance of Translation: Benjamin and Brecht on the Loss of Small Details." *The Drama Review* 43:4 (1999): 53–59.

Rajan, Tilottama, and David L. Clark, eds. *Intersections: 19th-Century Philosophy and Contemporary Theory.* Albany: SUNY Press, 1995.

Reinhardt, Karl. "Deutsches und Antikes Drama." In *Tradition und Geist* 357–65.

———. "Goethe and Antiquity." In *Tradition und Geist* 274–82.

———. "Hölderlin und Sophokles." In *Tradition und Geist* 381–97.

———. *Sophokles.* Frankfurt: Klostermann, 1947.

———. *Tradition und Geist: Gesammelte Essays zur Dichtung.* Ed. Carl Becker. Göttingen: Vandenhoeck und Ruprecht, 1960.

Roberts, David. "Brecht and the Idea of a Scientific Theatre." *Brecht: aufführung-Brecht: performance. Brecht-Jahrbuch 13, 1984.* Ed. John Fuegi, Gisela Bahr, John Willett, and Carl Weber. Detroit: Wayne State University Press, 1987, 41–62.

Rohde, Erwin. *Psyche: The Cult of Souls and Belief in Immortality among the Greeks.* London: Routledge & Kegan Paul, 1950.

Ronell, Avital. *Stupidity.* University of Illinois Press, 2002.

Ruckhäberle, Hans-Joachim. "German Antigone." In David and Chevrier 48–53.

Rutherford, Jonathan. "The Third Space: Interview with Homi Bhabha." In Rutherford 207–21.

Rutherford, Jonathan, ed. *Identity: Community, Culture, Difference.* London: Lawrence and Wishart, 1990.

Ryan, Lawrence. *Friedrich Hölderlin*. Stuttgart: Metzler, 1962.
Santner, Eric. *Friedrich Hölderlin: Narrative Vigilance and the Poetic Imagination*. New Brunswick and London: Rutgers University Press, 1986.
Sauder, Gerhard. "Herder's Poetic Works, His Translations, and His Views on Poetry." Trans. Wulf Koepke. In Koepke 305–30.
Saussure, Ferdinand de. *Course in General Linguistics*. Trans. Wade Baskin. New York: Philosophical Library, 1959.
Schivelbusch, Wolfgang. "Optimistic Tragedies: The Plays of Heiner Müller." Trans. Helen Fehervary. *New German Critique* 2 (Spring 1974): 104–13.
Schmidt, Dennis. *On Germans and Other Greeks: Tragedy and Ethical Life*. Bloomington: Indiana University Press, 2001.
Schmidt, Dennis. "Ruins and Roses: Hegel and Heidegger on Sacrifice, Mourning, and Memory." In Comay and McCumber 97–113.
Schmitt-Sasse, Jochen. "'Zwischen barbarischen Kriegskultpfählen': Antigonemodell 1948—Bild und Text—Brecht und Neher." *TheaterZeitSchrift* 26:4 (Winter 1988–89): 122–32.
Schulte, Rainer, and John Biguenet, eds. *Theories of Translation: An Anthology of Essays from Dryden to Derrida*. Chicago: University of Chicago Press, 1992.
Segal, Charles. "Greek Tragedy and Society: A Structuralist Perspective." In Euben 43–75.
———. *Oedipus Tyrannus: Tragic Heroism and the Limits of Knowledge*. New York: Oxford University Press, 2001.
———. "Sophocles' Praise of Man and the Conflicts of the Antigone." In *Interpreting Greek Tragedy*. Ed. Charles Segal. Ithaca, NY: Cornell University Press, 1986, 137–61.
———. *Sophocles' Tragic World: Divinity, Nature, Society*. Cambridge and London: Harvard University Press, 1995.
———. *Tragedy and Civilization: An Interpretation of Sophocles*. Cambridge and London: Harvard University Press, 1981.
Schulz, Genia. *Heiner Müller*. Stuttgart: Metzler, 1980.
Setje-Eilers, Margaret. "*Antigone* in Pre-Wall and Post-Wall German Theatre: Bertolt Brecht's and George Tabori's Power Plays." In *Text & Publication* (2007): 169–84.
Shankse, Darien. *Thucydides and the Philosophical Origins of History*. Cambridge: Cambridge University Press, 2006.
Sluga, Hans. "Homelessness and Homecoming: Nietzsche, Heidegger, Hölderlin." In *India and Beyond: Aspects of Literature, Meaning, Ritual and Thought*. Ed. Dick van der Meij. London: Kegan Paul International, 1997, 497–510.
Smit, Betine van Zyl. "Multicultural Reception: Greek Drama in South Africa in the Late Twentieth and Early Twenty-first Centuries." In Hardwick and Stray 373–85.
Sontag, Susan. *Against Interpretation and Other Essays*. New York: Picador, 1966.
———. "The Death of Tragedy." In Sontag 132–39.
Speth, Rudolf. *Wahrheit und Ästhetik: Untersuchungen zum Frühwerk Walter Benjamins*. Würzburg: Königshausen & Neumann, 1991.
Spivak, Gayatri Chakravorty. *Outside in the Teaching Machine*. New York: Routledge, 1993.
———. "The Politics of Translation." In *Outside* 179–200.
Steiner, George. *After Babel: Aspects of Language and Translation*. 3rd ed. Oxford: Oxford University Press, 1998.
———. *Antigones*. New York: Oxford University Press, 1984.
———. *The Death of Tragedy*. New York: Alfred A. Knopf, 1961.

Störig, Hans Joachim, ed. *Das Problem des Übersetzens.* Stuttgart: H. Goverts, 1963.
Szondi, Peter. *An Essay on the Tragic.* Trans. Paul Fleming. Stanford: Stanford University Press, 2002.
———. *Theorie des bürgerlichen Trauerspiels im 18. Jahrhundert: der Kaufmann, der Hausvater und der Hofmeister.* Frankfurt: Suhrkamp, 1973.
———. "Überwindung des Klassizismus: Der Brief an Böhlendorff vom 4. Dezember 1801." *Hölderlin-Studien:* 85–104.
———. *Versuch über das Tragische.* Frankfurt: Insel, 1961.
Taylor, Mark. "Foiling Reflection." *Diacritics* 18:2 (Spring 1988): 54–65.
Tgahrt, Reinhard, ed. *Weltliteratur: Die Lust am Übersetzen im Jahrhundert Goethes. Eine Ausstellung des Deutschen Literaturarchivs im Schiller-Nationalmuseum Marbach am Neckar.* Marbach: Deutsche Schiller-Gesellschaft, 1982.
"Translation Studies Forum: Cultural Translation." *Translation Studies* 2:2 (2009): 196–219.
Turk, Horst. "Das Beispiel Hölderlins." *Hölderlin-Jahrbuch* 1988–89: 248–68.
Übersetzung, Translation, Traduction: An International Encyclopedia of Translation Studies. Ed. Harald Kittlel, Juliane House, Brigitte Schulze. Berlin, New York: W. de Gruyter, 2007.
Venuti, Lawrence. *The Scandals of Translation: Towards an ethics of difference.* London and New York: Routledge, 1998.
———. *The Translator's Invisibility: A History of Translation.* London and New York: Routledge, 1995.
Vernant, Jean-Pierre. "A Beautiful Death and the Disfigured Corpse in Homeric Epic," in Vernant 50–74.
———."Ambiguity and Reversal: On the Enigmatic Structure of Oedipus Rex." In Vernant and Vidal-Naquet 113–40.
———. "The Historical Moment of Tragedy in Greece: Some of the Social and Psychological Conditions." In Vernant and Vidal-Naquet 23–28.
———. "Intimations of the Will in Greek Tragedy. In Vernant and Vidal-Naquet 49–84.
———. "Oedipus without the Complex." In Vernant and Vidal-Naquet 85–111.
———. *Mortals and Immortals: Collected Essays.* Ed. and trans. F. Zeitlin, Princeton University Press 1991.
———. "Tensions and Ambiguities in Greek Tragedy." In Vernant and Vidal-Naquet 29–48.
Vernant, Jean-Pierre, and Pierre Vidal-Naquet, eds. *Myth and Tragedy in Ancient Greece.* Trans. Janet Lloyd. New York: Zone Books, 1988.
Walser, Martin. *Umgang mit Hölderlin: Zwei Reden.* Frankfurt: Insel, 1997.
Warminski, Andrzej. "Monstrous History: Heidegger Reading Hölderlin." *Yale French Studies 77, Reading the Archive: On Texts and Institutions* (1990), 193–209. Rpt. in Fioretos 201–214.
———. *Readings in Interpretation: Hölderlin, Hegel, Heidegger.* Minneapolis: University of Minnesota Press, 1987.
Weber, Carl, ed. and trans. *A Heiner Müller Reader.* Baltimore: Johns Hopkins University Press, 2001.
Weber, Samuel. "A Touch of Translation: On Walter Benjamin's 'Task of the Translator.'" In Bermann and Wood 65–78.
Weineck, Silke-Maria. *The Abyss Above: Philosophy and Poetic Madness in Plato, Hölderlin, and Nietzsche.* Albany, NY: SUNY Press, 2002.

Weisstein, Ulrich. "Imitation, Stylization, and Adaptation: The Language of Brecht's Antigone and Its Relation to Hölderlin's Version of Sophocles." *German Quarterly* 46:4 (November 1973): 581–604.
Wellbery, David. "Benjamin's Theory of the Lyric." In Nägele 1988, 39–60.
Wiese, Benno von. *Die Deutsche Tragödie von Lessing bis Hebbel.* Hamburg: Hoffmann und Kampe, 1948.
Winkler, John J., and Froma Zeitlin, eds. *Nothing to do with Dionysos? Athenian Drama in Its Social Context.* Princeton: Princeton University Press, 1990.
Wöhrmann, Klaus-Rüdiger. *Hölderlins Wille zur Tragödie.* Munich: Fink, 1967.
Wright, Kathleen. "Heidegger's Hölderlin and the Mo(u)rning of History." *Philosophy Today* 37:4 (Winter 1993): 423–35.
Zeitlin, Froma I. *Playing the Other: Gender and Society in Classical Greek Literature.* Chicago: University of Chicago Press, 1996.
———. "Playing the Other: Theater, Theatricality, and the Feminine in Greek Drama." In Winkler and Zeitlin 63–96.
———. "Thebes: Theater of Self and Society in Athenian Drama." In Euben 101–41.

INDEX

Adorno, Theodor W., 167n25
Aeschylus, 2n4, 3, 38; and translation of *Agamemnon*, 28, 40, 41. *See also* Humboldt, Wilhelm von
alienation (*Verfremdung*), and dramatic effect, 6, 197, 205–6, 240–41; and effect of translation, 22, 61; and relation to tragic hero, 50
ambiguity, tragic, 7, 8n15, 26, 91–92, 169
Anouilh, Jean, 195
Antigonä (1804). *See* Hölderlin, Friedrich
Antigone: and conflict with state, 4, 9–10, 87–89, 100, 212, 217, 245; and ethics, 221, 222–23, 245–46; and family relations, 107–108, 171–75; and law (*dike*), 89–90, 95–96, 98–99; and 20th-century German theater, 229–30, 232–34; and GDR politics, 234–35; and identification, 215–16, 219–20, 242–43; and interaction with Chorus, 80–81, 86–87, 94–96, 212–13, 219; and isolation (difference, distinction), 50, 88, 90, 94, 110–12, 116, 120–21; and monstrosity (*deinon, das Ungeheure, das Unheimliche*), 51, 80–81, 86–87, 90–93, 105–106, 108, 136, 163, 167, 174–75, 177–79, 186–87, 215; and the "Oriental," 126; and political resistance, 195, 196–97, 217, 219–20, 223, 230–31, 232, 244; and postwar politics, 195–97, 215–16, 224, 227–28, 233–34, 242–43; and relation to Hölderlin, 136, 232–34, 249–50; and sexual difference, 10, 100, 101n33; and social relations, 116–19, 212–14, 217–20. *See also* tragic hero(ine)
Antigone des Sophokles (1947). *See* Brecht, Bertolt
Apter, Emily, 250, 251n46
Arendt, Hannah, 195, 221n44, 224
Aristotle, 2n3, 7, 8, 31, 31n18, 33, 75–76, 81n61, 101n30, 117n48, 205, 214, 247. *See also* catharsis; Lessing, G. E.
Arnim, Bettina von, 67, 122n1
Aufgabe (task, giving-up), 125; relation to translation, 15–16, 21, 132, 144. *See also* Benjamin, Walter; translation

Balmer, Josephine, 12n23
Barner, Wilfried, 196n7, 205n22
Bassnett, Susan, 13n25, 15
Baudelaire, Charles, 130
Beaufret, Jean, 104n35

Beissner, Friedrich, 43, 53n14, 69n51, 72n53, 199n10
Beistegui, Miguel de, 160n17, 167n24
Benjamin, Walter, 4, 15, 20–21, 23, 56n., 181, 202, 222, 231, 247; and *Blödigkeit* (timidity, stupidity), 136, 141–43; and concept of criticism, 20–21, 56n19, 123–24, 128–29, 131–32; and courage, 136, 138, 141–44; and figure of translator, 142–44; and the "Oriental," 125–30; and task (*Aufgabe*), 125; and *The Task of the Translator,* 130–36; and tragic hero, 138–41; and *Two Poems by Friedrich Hölderlin,* 123–30; and *The Work of Art in the Age of Its Technological Reproducibility,* 194
Berlau, Ruth, 195n14, 198n9, 200n14, 201n15, 202, 208n26
Berliner Ensemble, 202
Berman, Antoine, 3n1, 16n40, 27n7, 32, 39, 40, 51n11
Bermann, Sandra, 18
Bernofsky, Susan, 50, 69n51, 70
Besson, Benno, 231, 234, 237n28, 238–42. *See also* Müller, Heiner; *Ödipus, Tyrann* (1967)
Bildung, 9, 18, 19, 26, 28, 32, 36, 37, 42, 46, 51, 160, 166; and *Bildungstrieb,* 29
Binder, Wolfgang, 101n33, 104n34
Blödigkeit (timidity, stupidity), 136, 141–43. *See also* Benjamin, Walter
Bodmer, Johann Jakob, 12, 14, 25, 32n23, 33
Böhlendorff, Casimir Ulrich, and correspondence with Hölderlin, 66n48, 72–73, 93, 126, 143, 158, 159–60, 180. *See also* Hölderlin, Friedrich
Borges, Jorge Luis, 16
bourgeois tragedy (*bürgerliches Trauerspiel*), 34n30, 129n17, 138n17, 139
Brecht, Bertolt, 4, 12, 22, 23, 190, 231, 233, 234, 237; and *Antigone des Sophokles* (1947), 193, 194–95, 205–221; and Aristotle, 214; and collaboration with Charles Laughton, 199–202, 203, 208; and epic theater, 193, 195–96, 198, 200n14, 204, 205–6, 215, 219; and ethics, 221–23, 225–26; and exile experience, 193, 195n3, 199; and historical awareness, 197–98, 201, 211, 222; and identification, 216–17, 219–20; and imitation, 210; and *Kleines Organon für das Theater,* 198, 204n.; and *Modell,* 193–94, 206–211, 223–24; and National Socialists, 198–99, 215–16; and postwar politics, 192–93, 215–16, 223–24; and process of adaptation, 202–3, 205, 206, 211–13, 214, 217–19, 221–22; and "ruined" theater, 192–93, 208–9; and use of photography, 202, 208. *See also* Antigone; tragic hero(ine)
Breitinger, Johann Jacob, 25
Buber, Martin, 24, 229, 248
Butler, Judith, 4, 10, 101n32, 245

caesura, 67, 77–78, 79, 95, 109, 137–38, 140, 142, 156, 206, 248–49. *See also* Tiresias
Cave, Terence, 33n28
catharsis, 7, 51, 76n59, 81n61, 95, 194n2. *See also* Aristotle; Lessing, G. E.
chorus, role of, 5, 6, 79–81, 86, 94–96, 108n39, 111–12, 168, 171, 175–77, 202–3, 205, 212, 218–19, 236
Constantine, David, 28, 37, 87
contradiction, relation to tragedy, 8, 26–27, 57–60, 69, 91, 167–69, 240, 246, 250–51
Corngold, Stanley, 45, 64n42, 123n5, 124, 125n10, 127, 129n10, 141
courage: and figure of Antigone, 245–46; and figure of poet, 124n7, 125, 128, 136–38, 141–42, 181–82, 188; and figure of translator, 14, 15, 21, 35, 142–43, 145–46. *See also* Benjamin, Walter
Cronin, Michael, 15
Curjel, Hans, 195

INDEX 267

De Man, Paul, 15–16, 60n34, 131n21
Death of Empedocles, The (*Der Tod des Empedokles*). See Hölderlin, Friedrich
deinon (monstrosity, *das Ungeheure, das Unheimliche*), 80, 90–93, 163, 166–71. See also Antigone; Hölderlin, Friedrich; Heidegger, Martin; Oedipus; subjectivity; tragic hero(ine)
Deleuze, Gilles, 55n18, 88n5
Derrida, Jacques, 60n34, 96n19, 100, 101–2
Deutsch, Michel, 231, 232, 234
Deutsches Theater Berlin, 229, 231, 236
DeVries, Hent, 223n47
difference, Greek and modern contexts, 21, 23, 71, 72–74, 75, 98–99, 114–15, 120–21, 152, 159–61, 249; and interpretation, 150; and language, 83n64; preservation of, 14, 16n40, 21, 75, 119–20, 161, 165, 169, 175, 184–85, 187–88, 212; recognition of, 20, 54, 83, 90, 96, 177; and relation to translation, 25, 37, 67, 83, 119–21, 157, 160–61; and subjectivity, 55n18, 60, 94; and tragic effect, 61, 87, 113–14; and untranslatability, 5, 20, 23, 34, 35n35, 119–20, 121, 170–71, 245, 249. See also Antigone; Oedipus; tragic hero(ine)
Dionysus, 7n13, 8, 53n13, 205
Doherty, Brigid, 219–20
Domdey, Horst, 234–35

Eisler, Hanns, 199
Enlightenment, 12, 18, 25–26, 32, 34n30, 41
epic theater, 193, 195–96, 198, 200n14, 204, 205, 215, 219. See also Brecht, Bertolt
ethics: and relation to tragedy, 4, 6, 8–10, 20, 48, 62, 88, 94, 99–102, 120, 197–98, 221–23, 226, 246; and relation to translation, 4, 6, 13, 14–16, 18–22, 45, 50, 52, 94, 120, 145, 154, 185

failure of translation, 12–13, 15–16, 21, 49, 66–67, 144, 250
Fehervary, Helen, 237
female figures, role of, 7–8
Fenves, Peter, 57
Fichte, Johann Gottlieb, 54, 57, 64, 97
foreign (*das Fremde*), significance of, 3, 14, 36, 42–44, 51–52, 93, 129, 130n20, 145, 151, 154, 158–62, 165, 168, 179, 181–82, 184–86, 187–89, 190, 240; and relation to tragic figures, 98–99
foreignness (*die Fremdheit*), effect of, 3, 42–44, 93, 113, 196, 199, 206, 234, 241
Fortleben (living-on, afterlife) of text, 15, 130, 143, 144, 231 See also Benjamin, Walter; translation
Fugard, Athol, 230
Fynsk, Christopher, 76, 81n61

George, Stefan, 115n45, 124, 198
German Idealism, 2, 8–9, 48–50, 54, 56, 59–60, 61, 64n41, 71, 74, 182. See also Kant, Immanuel; Schelling, Friedrich
Germany in Autumn (*Deutschland im Herbst*), 232
Goethe, J. W. von, 1, 9, 11, 12, 13, 18, 20, 25, 30n16, 35, 89, 138, 160, 210; and translation practice, 27, 43–44
Gontard, Susette, 47, 53–54, 86
Gottsched, 30–32, 33, 39, 74, 210
Gourgouris, Stathis, 111n40
Griffith, Mark, 91, 92n15, 104

Haemon, 116–20
Hanssen, Beatrice, 133n28, 140
Heaney, Seamus, 12, 231
Hegel, G. W. F., 97; and *Antigone*, 4, 9–10, 47, 94, 121; and correspondence with Schelling, 58; and *Phenomenology of Spirit*, 99–103
Heidegger, Martin, 4, 18, 21–22, 23, 145,

192, 198, 219, 231, 233; and *deinon* (*das Unheimliche*), 166–71, 174–75, 177–78; *Elucidations of Hölderlin's Poetry* (*Erläuterungen zu Hölderlins Dichtung*), 146–48; *Hölderlins Hymne 'Der Ister,'* 153–87; and homecoming (*Heimkommen, Heimkunft*), 187–90; and hospitality (*Gastlichkeit*), 185–86; and perspective on translation, 148–49, 150–52, 163–65, 167, 169; and poetry of streams, 155–59, 204; and relation to the foreign (*das Fremde*), 181–82; and relation of Germans to Greeks, 159–61, 185; and *Zwiesprache*,151–52, 154, 162–63, 171–73, 175, 178–79, 185–87

Hellingrath, Friedrich Norbert von, 198; and critical edition of Hölderlin's works, 123, 126; and dissertation, 123, 125

Herder, Johann Gottfried, 12, 25, 29–35, 37, 75; and theory of translation, 37–39

Hofmannsthal, Hugo von, 12

Hölderlin, Friedrich, 4; approach to translation, 36–37, 40, 43–44, 45–46, 48–52, 61, 63, 67, 79, 87, 90–93, 102–4, 105–8, 110–12, 117–19; and Aristotle, 75–76; and concept of caesura, 77–78, 95, 109, 137–38, 140, 142, 156, 206; and correspondence with Böhlendorff, 72–73, 93, 126, 158, 159–60, 180; and correspondence with Niethammer, 97–98; and correspondence with Wilmans, 51, 72, 84, 126, 128; *The Death of Empedocles*, 27, 49, 61, 64–67, 70–72, 79, 82, 140–41; and engagement with philosophy, 26, 27, 49, 52, 60–67, 97–99; *Hyperion*, 27; "In lovely blueness" (*In lieblicher Bläue*), 53; and "lawful calculus" (*gesezlicher Kalkul*), 74–75, 95; and madness, 47, 122; and National Socialism, 198–99; and the "Oriental," 52, 73, 126, 128–29, 157; and perspective on antiquity, 27–29, 50, 71–73, 75–76, 80–81,

98–99, 104–5; *Remarks on Antigone* (*Anmerkungen zur Antigonä*), 93–94, 104–5, 108–9, 112–16, 119–20; *Remarks on Oedipus* (*Anmerkungen zum Ödipus*), 67–71, 73–78, 80–81 See also Antigone; Oedipus

Hölderlins Hymne "Der Ister" (1943/44). See Heidegger, Martin

Homer, 73, 91n.; and translation of, 3, 11, 16, 27, 32–33, 34, 37–38, 43. See also Herder, J. G; Voss, J. H.

Humboldt, Wilhelm von, 3, 11, 28, 35, 40; and translation of *Agamemnon*, 3, 11, 40–44

identification (*Einfühlung*), 7, 8, 24, 33–34, 51, 67, 86, 95–96, 117n48, 135, 139, 205, 215–16, 219–220, 234, 242; relation to translation, 27, 37. See also Lessing, G. E.; Brecht, Bertolt; tragic hero(ine)

imitation, of the Greeks, 17, 25–29, 46, 75, 112–13, 203, 209–210, 219–20; and translation, 16, 34, 39, 75, 223. See also Winckelmann, J. J.

Irigaray, Luce, 4, 86n1

Jacobs, Carol, 4, 130n19, 133n29
Jennings, Michael, 124n8, 128n15, 132, 140

Kant, Immanuel, 26, 27, 30, 33, 49, 57, 64, 67n49, 83, 88n5, 140n36, 155; and *Critique of Pure Reason*, 54–56. See also German Idealism; Romanticism

Kierkegaard, Søren, 223n47
Kleist, Heinrich von, 1, 210
Kofman, Sarah, 234, 249–50
Kraus, Karl, 210

Lacan, Jacques, 4, 50n8, 83n64, 86n1, 87n3, 88n5, 89, 100n29, 108

INDEX   269

Lacoue-Labarthe, Philippe, 22; and *L'Antigone de Sophocle*, 231, 232, 234, 247–50; and *The Caesura of the Speculative*, 59, 67, 90, 247n41; and Jean-Luc Nancy, *The Literary Absolute*, 30, 56

Laughton, Charles, collaboration with Brecht, 199–202, 203, 208. *See also* Brecht, Bertolt

law, relation to tragic conflict, 9–10, 19–20, 70, 88–90, 95–96, 98–105, 226, 245. *See also* Hegel, G. W. F.

Lehmann, Hans-Thies, 235

Leibniz, 57

Lessing, Gottfried Emanuel, 8, 9, 25, 30–35, 39, 56–57, 75, 95, 210, 214, 224. *See also* Aristotle; catharsis; identification

Levinas, Emmanuel, 14n30

Louth, Charlie, 11n22, 30n14, 36, 37n40, 39n43, 52

Luther, Martin, 129, 228–29

Malina, Judith, 230

Marchand, Suzanne, 26n4, 28, 42

Miller, A. V., translation of Hegel, 101

Müller, Heiner, 4, 12, 22, 229; and influence of Brecht, 237–38; *Mauser*, 237; *Ödipus, Tyrann* (1967), 231, 234–42; *Philoktet*, 236

Müller, Karl-Heinz, 238, 239–41. *See also* Müller, Heiner; *Ödipus, Tyrann* (1967)

myth, as basis for tragedy, 6–7, 40, 125, 127, 205, 242 *See also* Vernant, J.-P.

Nägele, Rainer, 34n30, 78, 106n38, 112n41, 132n26, 140n36

national identity, development of, 5, 14, 20, 26, 29–30; and relation to translation, 3n7, 20, 26, 30, 32, 51–52, 126, 145

Neher, Caspar, 195, 197, 199, 205, 206, 208, 209, 216

Nel, Christoph, 232, 233

Niethammer, correspondence with Hölderlin, 97–98

Nietzsche, Friedrich, 9, 30n15, 65n43, 122, 165, 205

Novalis (Friedrich Wilhelm von Hardenberg), 29, 37, 39, 51

Nussbaum, Martha, 8, 9, 169n28, 245

Oedipus: and abuse of power, 236–37; and *deinon (das Ungeheure)*, 80–81; and Empedocles, 64, 66–67, 70–71; and excess knowledge, 67–71, 79–80, 90, 103, 157, 239; and guilt, 100–101; and hubris, 71–72, 80; and Idealist interpretation, 57–61; and "In lovely blueness" (*In lieblicher Bläue*), 53–54, 67; and isolation (solitude, difference), 77–78, 108, 240–41; and relation to Stalinism, 235–36; and self-blinding, 62–63, 82, 141, 235; and silence, 142. *See also* tragic hero(ine)

Ödipus, Tyrann (1967). *See* Müller, Heiner

Ödipus Tyrannus (1804). *See* Hölderlin, Friedrich; Oedipus

Orff, Carl, 229

Oudemans, C., and Lardinois, 91

Pfau, Thomas, 54n15, 60n34

philosophy, relation to tragedy, 2n3, 8, 10, 48, 56–61, 247; and translation, 25, 29, 43n50, 131n21. *See also* Hegel, G. W. F; Herder, J. G.; Hölderlin, Friedrich; Schmidt, Dennis

photography, uses of, 22, 193–94, 195, 197, 199, 200n14, 201n15, 202, 205n21, 208, 216. *See also* Berlau, Ruth

Pindar, 53n14, 123, 162, 169

Plato, 50n9, 155, 169

politics, 26, 30, 36; and relation to tragedy, 4, 6–7, 20, 50n9, 145, 193, 195–97, 202, 204, 210, 217, 224,

230–33, 235, 238. *See also* Brecht, Bertolt; Müller, Heiner; Walser, Martin
Pöggeler, Otto, 229n4
Pound, Ezra, 12, 206

Racine, 31, 195
Rambow, Günter, 232
recognition (*anagnorisis*), 33, 117n48
Reinhardt, Karl, 50, 88
Remarks on Antigone (*Anmerkungen zur Antigonä*) (1804). *See* Hölderlin, F.
Remarks on Oedipus (*Anmerkungen zum Ödipus*) (1804). *See* Hölderlin, F.
resistance, 193, 195, 196–97, 217, 219–20, 223, 230–31, 244. *See also* Antigone; politics, relation to tragedy
reversal (*peripateia*), 115–20, 117n48, 183
Romanticism, 5n10, 26n5, 30n16, 49, 51–52, 56, 74, 132n23, 160, 164, 166n22, 247. *See also* Benjamin, W.; Lacoue-Labarthe, P.; Novalis; Schlegel, A. W.
Rosenzweig, Franz, 24n44, 130n20, 139–40, 141, 228–229, 248
Ruckhäberle, Hans-Joachim, 232–33

Sauder, Gerhard, 35n33, 39
Schelling, Friedrich, 2n(3 and 5), 9–10, 30n15, 47–48, 56, 247; and correspondence with Hegel, 56, 58; and *Philosophical Letters on Dogmatism and Criticism* (*Philosophische Briefe über Dogmatismus und Kritizismus*), 57–60, 69
Schiller, Friedrich, 3, 8, 9, 17–18, 25, 76
Schivelbusch, Wolfgang, 237
Schlegel, August Wilhelm, 12, 25, 35, 39, 51; and translation of Shakespeare, 3, 27, 29
Schlegel, Friedrich, 30n16
Schleiermacher, Friedrich, 3, 13–15, 35, 37, 51, 143, 160, 164, 166
Schleyer, Hanns Martin, 232

Schlöndorff, Volker, and *Germany in Autumn* (*Deutschland im Herbst*), 232
Schmidt, Dennis, 8, 30n15, 50n9, 151n5, 174n30
Segal, Charles, 7, 26
Shakespeare, William, 3, 25, 27, 29, 31n18, 32, 39, 195, 200. *See also* Schlegel, A. W.; Wieland, C. M.
Shanske, Darien, 91n12
Sluga, Hans, 168n26, 179
Sontag, Susan, 9
Sophocles, 2n4, 10, 23, 32, 90, 91, 106, 114, 162, 228–29, 229n5; *Antigone*, 86n1, 88, 111n40, 118–19, 145, 151–52, 178, 196n6, 212n33, 213, 217, 230, 243, 245, 248; and *deinon* (monstrosity, *das Ungeheure, das Unheimliche*), 91, 163–64, 166–67, 168, 171; *Oedipus Tyrannos*, 63–64; and translation into German, 11, 35, 38; and use of Chorus, 80–81, 219. *See also* Antigone; Oedipus
spectator, role of, 7–8, 33–34, 67, 72, 117n48, 198, 201, 204–5, 215, 219n42, 220, 238, 239, 249
Spinoza, 57
Spivak, Gayatri Chakravorty, 13, 23n43, 38n41, 46
Stalingrad, battle of, 145, 187–88. *See also* Heidegger, Martin
Steiner, George, 1n1, 3n6, 6n11, 9, 26, 31n18, 40n44, 43n50, 90n7
subjectivity, definitions of, 2, 5, 26, 33, 64n41, 97–98, 135–36; and community, 110–11, 214–15; and courage, 140; and *deinon* (monstrosity, *das Ungeheure*), 80, 87, 108, 119–20; and ethics, 6, 14, 50; and limits of knowledge, 5, 48–49, 54–56, 58, 60–61, 67–72, 93–94; and relation to history, 151, 204; and relation to tragedy, 19–20, 48, 50, 51, 56–59, 90, 94–96, 108–9, 112–13, 116; and relation to translation, 27, 29–30, 40, 41–42, 46, 52, 87, 94, 96, 111, 113–15, 120–21, 250
Syberberg, Hans-Jürgen, 144

Szondi, Peter, 2, 34n30, 56, 56–57n22, 59, 66n48, 115n45, 247

Task of the Translator, The (*Die Aufgabe des Übersetzers*). See Benjamin, Walter
Tiresias, 64, 70, 77–78, 80, 82, 109–10, 138, 142, 156–57, 236, 248
tragic hero(ine), 6–7, 33, 49n4, 58–61, 157, 205, 212, 220, 233; and courage, 141–42; and difference, 94–96, 98–99; and ethics, 100–101, 222–23; and hubris, 64–65, 67–72, 78–82; and identification with translator, 136, 142, 144; and reversal, 117n48; and silence, 138–41; and solitude, 50, 88, 111; and suffering, 54, 61, 67, 73–74, 78–79, 83, 102–3, 107–8, 112–13, 115, 120, 143–44, 174. See also Antigone; Oedipus
translation; and *Aufgabe* (task, giving up), 15; and establishment of national identity, 3n7, 20, 26–28, 30, 32, 51–52, 126, 145; and ethical responsibility, 6, 12–13, 14–15; and *Fortleben* (living-on) of source text, 15, 16, 18, 130, 143, 144, 231; and negotiation with source text, 15, 17–18, 19, 21, 37, 160–61, 164–65, 200–1, 250; and *Über-tragung* (carrying-over), 24, 163; and untranslatability, 5, 20, 23, 34, 35n35, 119–20, 121, 154, 170–71, 245, 249; and violence, 11–13, 17–18, 21–22, 170–71, 175, 198
translator, figure of, 11–12, 21, 28n11, 29, 34–35, 38–39, 41–43, 83, 233; and courage, 14, 15, 21, 35, 136–37, 142–43, 144–45; and invisibility, 12–13, 144; and responsibility, 15, 44, 48, 129, 132–33, 170; and vulnerability, 13–14, 16, 36–37, 135–36, 143. See also Benjamin, W.; Hölderlin, F.; Schleiermacher, F.
Two Poems by Friedrich Hölderlin (*Zwei Gedichte von F.H.*). See Benjamin, Walter

Venuti, Lawrence, 3n7, 12, 14n31
Vergangenheitsbewältigung, 22, 243–44
Vernant, Jean-Pierre, 6, 26, 59n30, 66n46
violence, 6–7, 73, 163, 171, 175, 193, 212, 220, 232–33; of reading, 21, 153–54, 170, 190; of translation, 11–13, 17–18, 21–22, 170–71, 175, 198
Voss, Heinrich, 2, 25; and translation of Homer, 3, 11, 27, 43–44

Walser, Martin, 4, 6, 22, 228, 230, 231, 233, 234, and *Antigone* (1989), 242–47
Warminski, Andrzej, 62, 64, 66n48, 116n47, 163
Weber, Samuel, 4, 16n38, 135n31.
Weigel, Helene, 193, 202, 210
Wellbery, David, 129n18
Wieland, Christoph Martin, 25; and translation of Shakespeare, 27
Wilmans, Friedrich, 49n5, 51, 72, 73, 84, 126, 128
Winckelmann, Johann Jakob, 11, 17, 25–26, 27, 28, 38–39, 56

CLASSICAL MEMORIES/MODERN IDENTITIES
Paul Allen Miller and Richard H. Armstrong, Series Editors

This series consistently explores how the classical world has been variously interpreted, transformed, and appropriated to forge a usable past and a livable present. Books published in this series will detail both the positive and negative aspects of classical reception and will take an expansive view of the topic. Therefore, it will include works that examine the function of translations, adaptations, invocations, and classical scholarship in the formation of personal, cultural, national, sexual, and racial identities. This series's expansive view and theoretial focus thus separate cultural reception from the category of mere *Nachleben*.

Richard Alston and Efrossini Spentzou
  Reflections of Romanity: Discourses of Subjectivity in Imperial Rome

Sean Gurd
  Philology and Its Histories

Paul Allen Miller
  Postmodern Spiritual Practices: The Construction of the Subject and the Reception of Plato in Lacan, Derrida, and Foucault

www.ingramcontent.com/pod-product-compliance
Lightning Source LLC
Chambersburg PA
CBHW020642230426
43665CB00008B/280